LINDBERGH:

THE CRIME

LINDBERGH: THE CRIME

NOEL BEHN

THE ATLANTIC MONTHLY PRESS
NEW YORK

Published simultaneously in Canada
Printed in the United States of America

FIRST EDITION

Library of Congress Cataloging-in-Publication Data

Behn, Noel.
Lindbergh: the crime / Noel Behn.—1st ed.
Includes bibliographical references and index.
ISBN 0-87113-544-2
1. Lindbergh, Charles Augustus, 1930–1932.   2. Hauptmann, Bruno
Richard, 1899–1936.   3. Kidnapping—New Jersey—Hopewell—History.
4. Trials (Kidnapping)—New Jersey—History.   I. Title.
HV6603.L53B44   1994   364.1′54′0974965—dc20   93-24563

Design by Laura Hough

The Atlantic Monthly Press
841 Broadway
New York, NY 10003

FIRST PRINTING

For Bob, whose dare set me to writing.

And for Jay, who took it from there.

ACKNOWLEDGMENTS

The author cannot thank enough or praise too highly the intrepid group of inordinately talented people who helped in collecting data during the nearly eight years required to write this book, starting with, chronologically: Terry George, Patrick Farrelly, Joey Hamill, Dorothy Keller, Gianna Ranaudo, Alison Price Becker, Holly Forsman, and Ian Shearn. In the long, grueling middle stretch, ardent and stunningly keen Diane Reiners took over, with a sterling assist from Christine Tangare.

Siv Svendsen, there alone for the closing eighteen months, glowed bright and brilliant while working on the repeated edits and made sure that the manuscript, at long last, was delivered.

The stalwart reader through it all was Kevin Richardson. Many more people, whose names are not listed, contributed to all aspects of the book, and to them a heartfelt "thank you." I particularly want to extend my appreciation to Governor Hoffman's daughter, Hope Hoffman Nelson, and the late Harry Green. I am also grateful for the cooperation extended me by Lieutenant Thomas De Feo of the New Jersey State Police Museum in West Trenton, New Jersey, and Mark Nonestied of the Harold Hoffman Collection at the East Brunswick Museum, East Brunswick, New Jersey.

The institutions and archives cooperating in this undertaking include the New-York Historical Society, the New York Public Library, the New York Police Department archives and library, the office of the Bronx District Attorney, the New York University archives and library, the John Jay library, the Columbia University library, the Rutgers University library, the Library of Congress, the FBI public archives, and the National Archives. The Freedom of Information Act provided information from the FBI, State Department, Justice Department, and Secret Service.

Other authors and their works were of tremendous value. Who they are and what they wrote will be evident as the reader progresses. I thank them all.

This book ultimately reflects the wisdom of its editor, Anton Mueller. He convinced the author to make for whiter and more perilous waters whenever possible; navigate at the chanciest.

The memory of Mary Lea Johnson looms large. Some eight years back, it was she and her husband, Marty Richards, along with Sam Crothers who brought Bill Pelletreau's black box to Owen Laster, my agent.

CONTENTS

CONTENTS

CONTENTS

The important thing is to start; to lay a plan, and then follow it step by step no matter how small or large each one by itself may seem.

CHARLES A. LINDBERGH, *The Spirit of St. Louis*

1

MOTH TO
FLAME

- - -

CELEBRATED CRIME, STEEPED IN THE WARP OF PASSING DECADES, CAN BECOME
more fiction than fact. Small matter that the illicit act went unsolved or
was duly prosecuted and punished; partisans emerge to champion lore
regarding its commission. This is the stuff from which legends are
spawned, not to mention culture and entertainment. Fresh data need not
be unearthed to set theorists of a certain offense—say, the John F.
Kennedy assassination—at the throats of countertheorists.

I, for one, become shamelessly intrigued by the discovery of new information concerning almost any classic American case, which is what occurred on a sunny April morning in 1986. The material contained in a
black wooden box that was resting on my literary agent's table dealt
with the most infamous perpetration in this country's history: the 1932
kidnapping-killing of twenty-month-old Charles Lindbergh, Jr. One
document in particular, I was assured, named the true slayer of the
child—and it was not the person who had been convicted of the crime
and died in the electric chair.

The black box measured two and a half feet by two feet by one and a half feet and had been discovered hidden away between two rafters in the attic of a house on Belgrove Drive, Kearny, New Jersey. The owners of the residence took the find to their lawyer, who brought it to the executor of the estate of the home's previous owner, Doris A. Pelletreau. Doris had died on October 6, 1976. Her husband, Jesse William Pelletreau, had passed away on December 3, 1958, and there was no doubt that the contents of the black box belonged to him. What to do with the material was solved when an independent television-commercial maker learned of its existence. She teamed with a pair of prestigious play and movie producers. The documents were purchased—and now rested on my agent's desk, where I had my first look at them.

Bill Pelletreau, I soon learned, was a private investigator who had been called into the Lindbergh kidnapping case in late 1934 by the attorney for a thirty-five-year-old illegal German alien named Bruno Richard Hauptmann. Hauptmann, a carpenter living with his wife and baby son in the Bronx, was being held at the Bronx County jail, charged with extorting ransom money from Lindbergh. At the time Pelletreau joined the case, New Jersey officials were trying to have Hauptmann extradited so they could try him for the murder and kidnapping of the child, crimes the German avidly denied committing.

The kidnapping had occurred some two and a half years earlier, on March 1, 1932, at the rural Lindbergh estate near tiny Hopewell, New Jersey. A series of twelve written messages demanding ransom were received before money was paid. A thirteenth message, which said where the child could be found, alive and healthy, proved a lie. The missing infant's corpse was discovered in a shallow grave within earshot of the family home. It was estimated he had been dead since the night of his disappearance.

The first marked bill from the ransom appeared two days after the payment was made. Ransom currency continued to surface, mainly in the New York City area, for two and a half years, until September of 1934, when Hauptmann was picked up for passing a ten-dollar note. Another small-denomination bill from the ransom was found on his person; several more were recovered at his home. They were gold-certificate currency that had been taken out of circulation over a year earlier. Hauptmann confessed to having horded gold notes and spending several with full knowledge that to do so was illegal—a minor and common offense in America.

Bruno Richard Hauptmann not only lived near the Bronx cemetery where one moonless night back in 1932 a Lindbergh intermediary had paid fifty thousand dollars in ransom to a supposed member of the kidnapping gang named John, but the German carpenter also resembled artists' sketches of John. However, there had been no reliable eyewitness who could place Hauptmann or anyone else near the Lindbergh home at the time of the kidnapping. The German also had a group of friends and associates who claimed he was with them in New York City, over sixty miles away from the abduction scene, that fateful evening.[1] After subjecting Hauptmann to a "foolproof" test, the police department's handwriting experts were certain the immigrant carpenter had not authored the thirteen ransom messages received by Lindbergh and his designees.

The New York Police Department was in favor of releasing Hauptmann; the New Jersey State Police, which had jurisdiction if the kidnapping-murder ever went to trial, wanted him held longer. Law officers, dismantling Hauptmann's garage, discovered another fourteen thousand dollars in ransom loot. The gaunt, lanky carpenter shifted his story. Now he claimed the money had been left by a friend who had returned to Germany and since died—left in a shoe box that Hauptmann had stored on an upper shelf in a kitchen closet and forgotten. A recent rainstorm caused a ceiling leak that inundated the closet. Not until taking down and opening the wet shoe box had Hauptmann discovered what it contained—fourteen thousand dollars. Because the dear departed friend owed Hauptmann approximately seven thousand dollars, Bruno appropriated that amount for himself and left the rest for the dead man's relatives. To safe-keep the money, he devised a series of hiding places in the garage. The dead friend's name was Isador Fisch. No one bought what became known as the Fisch story.

After being held incommunicado for thirty-six hours and with still nothing to link him to the actual kidnapping-murder, Dick Hauptmann, as he preferred to be called, was finally arrested—for the crime of extortion—and remanded to the Bronx County jail at the Bronx County Courthouse. A relative of his German-born wife, Anna, contacted a Brooklyn lawyer, James M. Fawcett, who agreed to defend him.[2] Though the Bronx grand jury indicted Hauptmann for extorting ransom money from Charles A. Lindbergh, Fawcett realized the real legal battle would occur over New Jersey's well-publicized intent to extradite Hauptmann and try him for the murder of Charles Lindbergh, Jr., in the county where the death had allegedly occurred.

Private detective Bill Pelletreau was one of several handwriting specialists engaged by Fawcett to prove that Hauptmann had not written the ransom messages. As the defense attorney suspected would happen, the Bronx DA bowed to New Jersey's request for an extradition hearing at the Bronx courthouse. Fawcett was ready, or at least thought so. He had records and witnesses to prove that Hauptmann had been at work as a carpenter in New York City the day of the kidnapping; he had other witnesses to establish Bruno was with them in the Bronx that night. The employment records disappeared along with the employment witnesses. Alibi witnesses for the night either couldn't be found or informed the defense lawyer they were afraid to testify. The presentation by New Jersey's fiery attorney general was dramatic and persuasive. So was Charles A. Lindbergh's presence in the courtroom. Bill Pelletreau never testified as to his handwriting findings. Hauptmann was extradited to New Jersey in October of 1934 to await prosecution for the kidnapping and murder of Charles Lindbergh, Jr. James M. Fawcett was replaced as his lawyer. Pelletreau was also let go.

The trial of the century began January 2, 1935. The proceedings took thirty-two days and ended on Wednesday, February 13, with the jury finding Hauptmann guilty of murdering Charles Lindbergh, Jr. The judge sentenced him to die in the electric chair. A round of appeals began that would last more than a year.

Back in April of 1933, President Franklin Delano Roosevelt, as part of his policy to remove the depression-racked United States from its monetary gold standard, proscribed the private ownership of gold bullion, gold coins, and gold-certificate currency. Since a majority of bills in the ransom payment were gold certificates, the list of their serial numbers was reissued to banks and businesses. On May 1, 1933, more than a year before Hauptmann would be apprehended, the final day for the turn-in, $2,980 in ransom-loot notes was exchanged for legal currency at the New York City branch of the Federal Reserve Bank. The teller handling the transaction could not recall who had deposited the listed bills but believed it was a man. The signature on the deposit slip was J. J. Faulkner; the address he wrote in, 537 West 149th Street, New York. No one by that name could be found on West 149th Street, or anywhere else. The $2,980 deposit and photographs of Faulkner's signature made world headlines. One year and five months later, with Hauptmann in custody and awaiting extradition to New Jersey to stand trial for the kidnapping-murder, experts who had sworn under oath that Bruno was the author of the ransom messages also conceded that the J. J. Faulkner signature had not been written by him. William Pelletreau went further. He found that key letters, especially the *k*'s, in the Faulkner signature and ransom messages were identical and that none, in his opinion, had been written by Hauptmann.

Pelletreau had discussed his findings with Erastus Mead Hudson, a New York doctor and fingerprint expert who had been a prominent defense witness at Hauptmann's New Jersey murder trial. Dr. Hudson had found some five hundred fingerprints on the kidnapping ladder, none of them Hauptmann's, after the New Jersey State Police had failed to produce even one latent print. Offended that his testimony had been so thoroughly disregarded, and feeling that the prosecution had publicly tried to discredit him, Dr. Hudson readily volunteered to assist in the secret reinvestigation of the case undertaken by New Jersey's young bombastic governor, Harold G. Hoffman. At Hudson's suggestion, Governor Hoffman invited Pelletreau in for a chat. It was now November of 1935, and Bruno Hauptmann was running out of legal appeals. Impressed by Pelletreau's presentation, which showed that someone other than Hauptmann had written both the ransom notes and the J. J. Faulkner signature, the governor recruited the Jersey City private eye as one of his covert fact finders. Not long after, the balloon burst.

Americans believed in Charles Lindbergh. He was their supreme hero and remained so through the darkest years of the ongoing Great Depression. The death of his son was a national tragedy and disgrace. Hauptmann the German had been proved guilty and sentenced to die by a legal system that the public trusted as much as it did Lindbergh or the flag. Justice had been pronounced, and the nation wanted it served—wanted Hauptmann dead and the matter over with. Then word leaked out that Governor Hoffman had not only reopened the Lindbergh investigation but had secretly gone to the state prison in the middle of the night and interviewed Hauptmann in his death row cell. The resulting furor was instantaneous, international, and unanimous in its condemnation of the governor's actions. When the Lindberghs suddenly fled America and took up exile in England, pointing a silent finger at Harold Hoffman, a movement was mounted for the governor's impeachment. Hoffman, in the course of a year, went from being one of the country's most popular young politicians to being the second most hated man in the land—second only to Bruno Richard Hauptmann.

One of Pelletreau's first assignments for the governor-under-siege came in mid-December of 1935. Dr. Hudson had received a letter from J. J. Faulkner, saying that Bruno Hauptmann was innocent. After analyzing the writing, Pelletreau was certain it was composed by the same hand that had left the signature on the bank deposit and penned the ransom notes. On January 1, 1936, the governor himself received a letter from J. J. Faulkner—in the same handwriting as the Hudson letter, the bank-deposit slip, and the ransom notes, according to Pelletreau. Governor Hoffman allowed the press to reproduce the message. In two pages of scrawling text, J. J. Faulkner stated that Bruno Hauptmann was completely innocent, that his only crime was being a victim of his own greed. The embattled governor told reporters that he placed great importance on the Faulkner letter—and for good reason. He thought he knew the identity of Faulkner. William Pelletreau began to home in on the "true" author of the ransom notes—and killer of the Lindbergh baby, based on the material in the box.

On January 11, 1936, the same day New Jersey's court of pardons refused to commute Hauptmann's death sentence to life imprisonment and confirmed January 17 as the date of his electrocution, two New York City prison inmates were telling the governor's investigators about a man they were sure had committed the crime. Five days later Pelletreau heard the story for himself. The prime informant was Wally Stroh, a perpetual petty crook who related that back in 1931, while serving time in New York's Hart's Island jail, he befriended a fellow inmate named Jacob Nosovitsky, also known as the Doc, or Doctor. According to Stroh, Nosovitsky was a certified physician who had been a famous international spy—famous enough to have the *New York American* print weekly installments of his life story. Stroh claimed Nosovitsky had gone to Mexico to perform an espionage mission for Lindbergh's father-in-law, who was a partner of the great financier J. P. Morgan, Jr. Nosovitsky had delivered what he said he would, but the Morgan people refused to make their final payment to him—a payment of fifty thousand dollars. When Nosovitsky pressed them for his money, they had him arrested on a morals charge of taking an underage girl across state lines. This prompted him to marry the girl so she couldn't testify against him— thereby committing bigamy, the crime for which he served time on Hart's Island. Doc Nosovitsky swore to seek revenge on Lindbergh's father-in-law.[3]

After their release from jail, Nosovitsky invited Stroh to participate in a sure-bet kidnapping of a famous person's baby. Stroh declined but recalled that Nosovitsky had told him that "babies can't identify you."[4]

The Doc also boasted of having devised a method of dissolving human bones in an acid solution and flushing them down the toilet. Just prior to the Lindbergh kidnapping, Stroh received a card from Nosovitsky, postmarked Cleveland, in which the international spy said everything was fine. That was the last Stroh heard from Doc.

Pelletreau's black box provided extensive samples of Nosovitsky's handwriting as well as copies of all thirteen ransom notes, the Faulkner bank receipt, and the Faulkner letters to Dr. Hudson and Governor Hoffman. Blowups of the *k*'s indicate they were the same in every document. So were other key letters. The physical description of Nosovitsky fit those published on John. Pelletreau and several other of the governor's investigators were convinced that Nosovitsky was John, the killer of the Lindbergh baby. But where was he?

A deal was offered Hauptmann for life in prison rather than death if he would name an accomplice. He refused. In a move that prompted worldwide public and media denunciation, Governor Hoffman granted Bruno a thirty-day reprieve. Pelletreau and other investigators went all out to track down Nosovitsky. The international spy was nowhere to be found. The thirty days ran out. On death row Bruno Richard Hauptmann was made ready for execution. A last-minute confession by another man delayed the process for a day. At 8:41 P.M., Friday, April 3, 1936, Hauptmann left his cell and walked the few steps into the adjoining room, where he was strapped into the electric chair. The current was turned on at 8:44 P.M. Three minutes later the voltage was cut off. As the fifty-seven guests who were crammed into the tiny chamber could see, Hauptmann was dead.

Pelletreau continued in his efforts to convince officials that the wrong man had been executed. He went as far as to get an arrest warrant for Nosovitsky. What came of these efforts was not included among the documents he left behind.

— — —

Several days were required to read through the black box information and get back to the owners of the material, who asked if I thought Pelletreau's revelations were true, and if so, was I willing to write a book on them. I replied there was no way of judging the validity of the information until I knew more about the Lindbergh case. An interim agreement was reached in which the owners agreed to underwrite the research by which I could better estimate the accuracy of Pelletreau's documents and assertion that Nosovitsky, not Hauptmann, stole and murdered Charles Lindbergh, Jr.

I read three books on the kidnapping. The first, *Kidnap,* had come out in 1961 and was written by George Waller, who found fault with the New Jersey State Police participation in the investigation and parts of the trial but had no doubts that Bruno Hauptmann was guilty. The second book, *The Airman and the Carpenter,* was written in 1985 by the award-winning BBC investigative journalist Ludovic Kennedy. Kennedy also faulted the state police and made a persuasive argument for Hauptmann's being totally innocent. Nosovitsky was not mentioned in either book. *Scapegoat,* written by newsman Anthony Scaduto in 1976, maintained that Hauptmann was framed by the New Jersey State Police, and he provided the confession of the man he considered the true kidnapper-murderer: Paul Wendel. Again no reference was made to Nosovitsky. I did cursory checks of local New York newspapers. Nosovitsky appeared, but not in any way that directly linked him to the crime—not yet, at least.

It was now July of 1986, and the more I learned about the crime, investigation, and trial, the less sense any of them made to me. In part this was due to the monumental documentation regarding the case. Before the year was out, I had my answer. The black box contained material Pelletreau had collected for an article he sold to *True Detective* magazine, in which he names the mysterious Mr. X—Nosovitsky—as the kidnapper-killer. Nothing in the article, as had been true with the black box documents, could corroborate that Nosovitsky was the culprit. Pelletreau's claims were unsubstantiated speculation. But I knew this. Information had already been discovered by me that showed Nosovitsky was in the Midwest at the time of the kidnapping.

The notion of writing a book on Nosovitsky as the kidnapper-killer self-destructed. But the lure of the Lindbergh case persisted. I knew I had gone through only a fraction of the existing material on the matter. Then, too, additional avenues of data were now open that had not been available to the investigators of yesterday. The Freedom of Information Act would produce over two thousand never-seen-before pages of data on Nosovitsky alone.

Of the many lingering bits of information I had picked up during the protracted research into the case were two theories regarding the ransom messages. The first held that the person who wrote the first note also wrote the next twelve. The second theory was that two people were involved. One had written the original note, found in the baby's nursery;

the next twelve messages were penned by a different person, forgeries done in the style of the first message.

Months after the project was laid aside, inquiries made earlier continued to be answered—and I grew ever more confident that Nosovitsky had written the J. J. Faulkner letters and signed the bank receipt. When it came to the ransom notes, I differed with Pelletreau. He accused Nosovitsky of writing all thirteen messages. I came to believe that Nosovitsky had written only the last twelve; his motive: simple extortion. The question that loomed largest for me was: Who had written the first one, the original message that Lindbergh found in the nursery after discovering that the baby was missing from his crib?

As fetching as the answer to this might prove, I had steadfastly turned my back on the project. No more Lindbergh—and no more funds for research. Not that I didn't continue to speculate on aspects of the case. I had become convinced, for example, that Hauptmann's trial was a raucous travesty, that with few exceptions prosecution witnesses had either distorted the truth or committed flat-out perjury, that the state police had tampered with physical evidence and, in many cases, suppressed vital information. But enough. No more Lindbergh!

Eight months elapsed, and I was explaining my decision for abandoning the Lindbergh project to a young television journalist by the name of John Miller. Miller pondered for a time before saying, "I heard something about the kidnapping not long ago." Then with a snap of his fingers and a thumb hitched toward Westchester County, he recalled, "From up in Westchester, by this woman who's an artist for NBC News." The next day I was at NBC, chatting with Libby Dengrove, who related that she and her husband knew the lawyer for Governor Harold Hoffman. His name was Harry Green, and he was still alive, living somewhere in L.A. As I listened to what Green had told the Dengroves, nagging questions about the case were answered, and a new overview began to form. If Harry Green was right, Hauptmann was innocent of the crime—and I knew the identity of the child's killer. So had Lindbergh. The death seems to have occurred three days earlier than reported, and no kidnapping was involved.

The allegation left no doubt as to who had purposely altered the truth and perpetrated the cover-up: Charles Lindbergh. But was he masterful enough to have done so? Had I, like everyone else, been sent looking in the wrong direction by the Lone Eagle?

- - -

I flew to California. At first ninety-three-year-old Harry Green refused to see me. Finally he did but declined to be taped while recounting in far greater detail the story the Dengroves had told me. I took Harry and his eighty-six-year-old girlfriend to lunch the next day at the Beverly Hills Hotel. Present to witness the old lawyer's statements was Irene Webb, my literary agent, from the Los Angeles office of the William Morris Agency. Walking ninety-three-year-old Harry through the Beverly Hills lobby was a wondrous sight. He relished every moment of it. What he had to say, haltingly, added an amazing new dimension to the Lindbergh case while also explaining why Governor Harold Hoffman became involved. If Harry was a liar, he was the most satisfying one I've come across. The book project was revived. And here we are, seven years later.

No smoking gun will be offered regarding the Lindbergh case. The account to be presented constitutes a personal, ergo biased, portrait of a criminal happening and its time. The path to be followed is often intricate and contradictory, but with the reader's indulgence the author hopes to illustrate how his conclusion was reached. Central to the saga is Charles Lindbergh himself, who I suspect may have acted as the coconspirator in a possibly humane ruse gone awry.

I believe it possible that Charles Lindbergh, Jr., was not kidnapped on the night his father led us to believe.

I think it likely that there never was a kidnapping.

I do believe the child was killed—murdered or accidentally killed three days before his father announced to the world the tot was missing.

I believe the culprit was most likely a member of the Lindberghs' immediate family circle—which means an innocent man was executed.

Ultimately, this becomes a story of how it was possible for one man, in fact or hypothetically, to delude a nation, the circumstances that allowed it to happen—and the fate of the solitary person who tried to challenge him, Harold Hoffman.

Book One

LINDBERGH

The Home Front

Prelude

———

THE SECTION THAT FOLLOWS PRESENTS THE HOME FRONT PHASE OF THE INFA-
mous kidnapping: the actions that occurred within the Lindbergh estate.
Evidence introduced and reevaluated here will corroborate the author's
subsequent speculations and conclusions. Since the combined archives
regarding the Lindbergh crime are enormous and the case for this book's
premise relatively meager, close attention to detail will be appreciated.

The supposition of the book, as well as of each section, is simple
enough: If there is a possibility that the official explanation of what happened during the official investigation of the child's disappearance and
the Hauptmann trial are flawed, and if Charles Lindbergh may have
committed some stripe of deception, how does this play out in the events
under examination?

——— ———

Few people had estimated their fame better, and used it more efficiently,
than thirty-year-old Charles Augustus Lindbergh. From the moment his

celebrity exploded on the world—May 21, 1927, after flying the Atlantic Ocean—he instinctively understood the potential powers bequeathed an idol of his stature. By the evening of March 1, 1932, he had honed the possibilities into an awesome reality. As much as any man of his time, Lindbergh was a masterful self-promoter who knew that less is more, that aloofness makes the public's heart grow fonder. He was too insensitive to be insecure, too observant not to be humble and charismatic when it served his ends. Limited in formal education, awkward and squeaky in conversation—but with an amazing gift for the written word—he managed to impress many of the personages of his day and bend them to his will. Regionally bigoted, he was able to hold his more radical beliefs in check, without premeditation, thereby sustaining the public's adoration of him. An unmitigated egoist, it never occurred to him that he could be wrong. There was no malice involved, mind you. If Lindy said it, Lindy knew it had to be. That was the way of the Eagle.

Charles Lindbergh trusted no one but his wife, and perhaps his mother and his wife's parents. Obsessed with what he considered a perpetual invasion of his privacy, he was forever concocting plots to outwit the unwanted. In and of itself, there was a joy to besting adversaries, real or imagined, a challenge that stirred the blood, let the white knight mount his great steed and do battle. The media was his supreme hobgoblin, the snorting dragon who had quested him from the moment of his apotheosis. Their battles had been ceaseless. Bitter experience, at long last, had taught him how to keep the beast in check on important matters—or so he thought.

Now, on March 1, 1932, his son was gone, a fact that the fourth estate would communicate with its own zealous gusto. If Lindbergh wanted to deceive the world press, he was better qualified to do so than nearly any man on earth. But did he deceive? If his intent was bending the truth and protecting the guilty party, he must manipulate the media into believing the events as he presented them—send the hounds packing off in the wrong direction. Despite his awesome public relations skills, was this possible?

If a subterfuge had indeed been devised, had it taken more time than expected? It was already Tuesday, and Lindbergh was still at the house he and Anne were building near Hopewell. The family had never been here on a Tuesday before. Because construction was incomplete, they only spent the weekends—*always* arrived on Saturday morning with the baby, *always* departed Monday morning. There was no secret that Lindbergh was a creature of habit, an automaton when it came to maintaining patterns he had set.

Tuesday or not, had a plan of action been put at the ready? Was false evidence in place and the three-person staff rehearsed? Were they to make it appear that a kidnapping had taken place when it hadn't?

Would it work? Could the world be made to look in the wrong direction? Gaze off into the future rather than glance back at the fateful Saturday of February 27?

Lindbergh gave the go-ahead.

2

WHAT THE POLICE WERE

TOLD

THE TELEPHONE COMPANY IN HOPEWELL OCCUPIED A SINGLE ROOM OVER THE post office, across the street from the tracks of the Reading Railroad. Hopewell's population was barely nine hundred, and after sundown there was so little activity that the night switchboard operator was provided with a couch on which she could sleep. At approximately 10:20 P.M., Tuesday, March 1, 1932, she was awakened by a call from one of the few phones in the region not sharing a party line and the only one with an unlisted number, HOpewell 303. On the wire was Ollie Whateley, the butler-chauffeur for the town's most prominent citizen, Charles Augustus Lindbergh. Whateley asked to be put through to the police. The operator plugged him in and rang. Constable Charles W. Williamson picked up. Whateley, an Englishman, spoke in a calm voice, "Colonel Lindbergh's son has been stolen. Will you please come at once."

This, more likely than not, was the launching of a conspiracy to obscure details of the disappearance of twenty-month-old Charles Lindbergh, Jr.

It was a cold, dark, wind-wrapped night, and the roads being traveled by Constable Williamson, who had picked up his chief, Harry H. Wolfe, were narrow, unlighted, and partially unpaved. The Lindbergh estate was isolated and new—360 wooded acres at the base of the forbidding Sourland Mountain, along the Werstville-to-Hopewell road, with a house that had recently been constructed and was not completely furnished and with grounds that were only partially cleared and still being landscaped. Even so, everyone in the area knew the exact location. It had become a major tourist attraction, overshadowing a spot on the nearby Delaware River where George Washington had made his historic crossing. Charles A. Lindbergh was not only New Jersey's foremost celebrity, but he was, quite literally, the most famous man in the world.

Though less than four miles from tiny Hopewell, which is in Mercer County, the Lindbergh estate stretched across both Mercer and Hunterdon counties. The house itself was in a corner of East Amwell Township, Hunterdon County, thereby giving the jurisdiction to investigate the missing-child complaint to the New Jersey State Police. Since the state police had not been notified, it was Hopewell PD's Chief Wolfe and his constable who were the first to arrive. As they turned off the road to Werstville and started up the estate's curving half-mile-long cinder drive, they met Ollie Whateley, who was motoring to Hopewell to purchase a flashlight. The policemen had a flashlight. Ollie returned with them to the home at the top of a rise called Sorrel Hill—a two-and-half-story-high French-manor-style house that was constructed of whitewashed fieldstone and whose windows, though fitted with outside shutters, did not all have curtains or shades. Charles Lindbergh was standing in the doorway, holding a Springfield rifle and wearing an open leather flying jacket. The time was approximately 10:35 P.M.

Lindbergh took charge—as would be his wont throughout the investigation. Using Chief Wolfe's flashlight, he brought the two Hopewell police officers around to the side of the house where the nursery was. Portions of the ground were so muddy that the daytime workers had put down wooden planks, which Lindbergh and the policemen now used. Approximately seventy-five feet from the house they came across a section of a wooden ladder. Close by and still attached to each other were two more ladder sections. On the ground not far away lay a dowel pin and a chisel. A search of the soft earth beneath one of the two second-floor nursery windows revealed a pair of imprints that could have been made by the base of the ladder. Seen leading off in a southwest direction were fresh footprints that appeared to have been made by a man. They retrieved the double section of ladder. Its legs fit into the mud imprints under the nursery window.

Lindbergh escorted Wolfe and Williamson into the house and up to the nursery, where he granted them a brief inspection. They were shown the empty crib and an open window—the window below which, in the mud, were the two ladder holes. Lindbergh directed their attention to an envelope that rested on the sill. It was left by the kidnappers, he told them—even though the envelope was sealed and contained no writing on the front or back.

Downstairs the two officers were allowed short conversations with the other four people who had been in the residence throughout the evening: the missing infant's mother, twenty-six-year-old Anne Morrow Lindbergh; the baby's English nursemaid, Bessie ("Betty") Mowat Gow, twenty-seven; Aloysius ("Ollie") Whateley, forty-seven; and Whateley's forty-seven-year-old wife, Elsie Mary, who was also English and was employed as the family cook. Elsie Mary was crying. It appeared to Williamson that Mrs. Lindbergh was very nervous and restless; Whateley, nervous and depressed; Colonel Lindbergh, collected; and Gow, "the coolest of the lot."[1] With two exceptions, these truncated interviews of the staff and his wife by the Hopewell officers were the only ones permitted by Lindbergh for the next ten days.

Chief Wolfe asked if Lindbergh suspected anyone of taking the baby. The answer was in the negative. Harboring no doubts that the missing child had been stolen, the chief suggested the state police be notified.

If Charles Lindbergh was playing a game of deception, his initial ploy had convinced the two-man constabulary of Hopewell that a kidnapping had occurred. The next hurdle was the New Jersey State Police, who were more sophisticated than the Hopewell duo. Since the state police also had the legal jurisdiction to investigate the matter, their validation of Lindbergh's claim would make kidnapping the crime of record.

The phone call received at the New Jersey State Police training school at Wilburtha, near Trenton, was from Colonel Lindbergh himself.[2] He reported that his son, Charles Augustus Lindbergh, Jr., had been kidnapped from his nursery between 7:30 P.M. and 10:00 P.M. The training school telephoned the information to a state-police post at Lambertville, the station nearest the Lindbergh home, and then called the trooper barracks at Morristown, where a Teletype alarm was issued for New Jersey,

New York, and Pennsylvania. The Lambertville station left phone messages for its troopers on patrol to call in immediately. Corporal Joseph A. Wolf responded and was ordered to the scene.

Lindbergh was ready and waiting when Corporal Wolf reached the estate at 10:55 P.M.—and found that the two local Hopewell policemen had a twenty-minute head start on him. Lindbergh repeated for the corporal, and for the record, that his twenty-month-old son, Charles Jr., had been taken from his crib and carried away by an unknown person. Betty Gow had placed the infant in the crib for the night at 7:30 P.M. She checked the bed again at 10:00 P.M., discovered he was gone, and notified Lindbergh, who went to the nursery and saw that the right window in the east wall was unlocked and that the right half of the outside shutter was open. On the windowsill of the nursery rested a sealed envelope, which Lindbergh believed had been left by the person or persons who had carried off his child. He told the state policeman that he had not touched the letter or disturbed anything else in the room, and he related what he had found on the ground outside the nursery window and beyond—ladder segments and fresh footprints.

Trooper Wolf posed the same question Chief Wolfe had asked earlier: Did Colonel Lindbergh have any suspicions who committed the crime? Lindy again answered that he did not. The trooper asked if he could recall any incident, such as strange noises or actions of the family dog, that might give an indication of when the kidnapping had occurred. Again Lindbergh answered no. Corporal Wolf phoned the Lambertville station, confirming that the child was gone, and asked one of the men there to make sure that headquarters and the state-police boss, Colonel H. Norman Schwarzkopf, had been notified. Then he followed Lindbergh up to the nursery.

The room measured twelve feet by fourteen feet and was covered by a drab-colored rug. Directly in the center of the floor were a low table and two children's chairs. The door through which they had entered was in the middle of the north wall. To the right of it was a bureau, on top of which were toilet articles. The wall above the bureau supported three small shelves for toys. To the left of the door stood a small wooden table bearing a white tray containing antiseptics, powders, and other pharmaceuticals. In the middle of the south wall was a French-style window that opened in from the center. Directly beneath the window was a built-in chest that extended out into the room. On top of the chest were a toy dog and a number of children's picture books. A toy ark rested on the floor to the left of the chest. One end of the west wall contained a door that led into a bathroom; the other end, a door opening into a clothes closet. Set between the doors was a four-poster wooden baby's crib. Alongside the foot of the crib, which was flush with the wall, was a cream-colored portable baby's toilet chair. At the other end was a sun-lamp. The head of the bed and the lamp were cut off from the rest of the nursery by a pink and green screen with pictures of farmyard animals on it. Across the room, in the center of the east wall, was a fireplace, on whose mantel were three toy birds. A three-wheeled Kidicar was on the floor to the right, and to the left were a small chair and a reflector-type electric heater. On each side of the fireplace was a regular up-and-down-sliding window. The catches on the window to the left and on the outside shutters were securely fastened. It was the window to the right of the fireplace that Lindbergh seemed certain the kidnapper had used.

The window was closed but not locked. The right side of its shutter was also closed; the left lay open. On the sill was the unopened envelope. Under the window was a small wooden chest with a black leather suit-case resting on top. Lying on the suitcase was part of the roof that be-longed to the toy ark. State Trooper Wolf took note of a small, muddy mark directly on the suitcase and a second muddy mark on the hard-wood floor. He saw that the blankets on the crib were still pinned to the sheets at the top to prevent them from slipping off, and he was told that the stolen child was wearing a Dr. Denton sleeping suit.

At 11:25 P.M. four more state policemen reached the Lindbergh estate. Troopers Cain and Sullivan were from the Lambertville station, and Cor-poral Wolf dispatched one of them to the main gate to give directions to arriving fellow officers. He also would claim that he detailed the second officer to protect the crime-scene area in the immediate vicinity of the house from being disturbed or destroyed. The other pair of officers had come from the state-police training school, and one of them, Trooper Lewis J. Bornmann, went to the nursery with Lindbergh, where he cor-roborated the evidence of the undisturbed crib, the suitcase with a smudge of "yellow" mud, and another smudge of mud on the floor "about in the center of the room."[3] Bornmann was still there at mid-night, finishing a sketch of the room, when the state police identification expert from the Morristown barracks, Frank A. Kelly, arrived and began dusting for fingerprints.

Lindbergh conferred with Major Charles A. Schoeffel and Lieutenant Arthur T. ("Buster") Keaten of the state police, who were brought to the nursery by Corporal Wolf. Trooper Kelly had used a nail file to slit open the envelope on the windowsill and was now examining its contents for fingerprints. None were found on the envelope or on the message inside, or anywhere else in the nursery. (Later he would dust the sections of ladder, and again no prints would be detected.)

Lindbergh's restraint regarding the unopened letter had been Jobian, if not slightly bizarre, considering he was positive it contained a communication from the kidnappers—information that unquestionably dealt with the fate of his son. Now that it had been processed, he shared. Rather than reading it himself, as might be expected of the father of a stolen child, Lindbergh had Major Schoeffel read the text aloud. Corporal Wolf claimed he was not present for this. Unlike Wolf, Williamson stated he had not only been in the room but had also been obliged to raise his hand and take the vow of silence Lindbergh asked for regarding the message, a claim the state troopers would alternately ignore and refute.

Lindbergh, accompanied by Lieutenant Keaten, Detective William F. Horn (who would later become Lieutenant Keaten's principal assistant on the case), Corporal Wolf, and another trooper, toured the neighboring houses to learn if the occupants had heard or seen anything suspicious earlier in the evening. They returned at 4:30 A.M. By then other troopers had followed the footprints from the ladder sections to an old road on the property called Featherbed Lane, where they seemed to stop alongside impressions from automobile tires.

What Corporal Wolf either didn't notice or failed to mention in a later report was that perhaps as many as two hundred newspeople and untold numbers of official and unofficial sightseers were meandering unchecked about the grounds, sometimes surging from one discovery point to another, and destroying vital evidence.

Sunrise allowed the searchers their first view of the surrounding terrain. The back of the Lindbergh house faced south and looked down on open fields that were dotted with small clumps of trees and bushes. The vista was much the same on the east, or nursery, side of the building, where the fields stretched to the Hopewell-Werstville road. Close to the house on the eastern side, and running parallel with the Hopewell-Werstville road, was Featherbed Lane. The front of the house faced north. Before it lay a circular driveway. On the western side of the driveway was a spacious, multicar garage. For approximately ninety feet the ground in front of the house and on the nursery side had been leveled and covered with fresh dirt, which was wet and often muddy. Beyond the clearings to the north and northwest rose the heavily wooded Sourland Mountain.

With the breaking of dawn, Corporal Wolf joined four other troopers in a search of the woods, where nothing of relevance was discovered. From there he went to write his summary, which would be the official record of the event. It was now March 2, but he backdated the report to read March 1. Much of what he recorded paralleled what Constable Charlie Williamson had already told reporters. Due to this and to an ongoing antagonism between the press corps and the New Jersey State Police, accusations would be made that because they had failed to follow basic police procedures the night of March 1, and therefore botched the early aspects of the investigation, the troopers, trying to cover up and appear efficient, had appropriated as their own what had actually been done by the two Hopewell policemen.

Wolf's four-page Major Initial Report used a standard departmental form that began with him listing the disappearance as a kidnapping. The corporal described the victim, Charles Augustus Lindbergh, Jr., as white, twenty months and ten days old, twenty-nine inches tall, weighing twenty-seven to thirty pounds, and with a light complexion, dark blue eyes, and blond, curly hair. The report stated that "at this time" no one has been accused of the kidnapping and that no suspects exist. Wolf, who claimed not to have seen the contents of the envelope, had filled in the paragraph titled "Probable Motives" with "Avarice, kidnapped the child for payment." In preparing the "List of Witnesses" Mrs. Anne Lindbergh is spelled "Mrs. Anna Lindbergh," and Mr. and Mrs. Whateley are called "Whitley." Under "Complete List of Evidence" he entered the ladder, the chisel, and "one plain letter envelop containing a note left on the window sill of the nursery by the kidnapers" but made no mention of the dowel.

Though Wolf's typewritten report had not given specifics regarding the footprints, his attached handwritten notes stated, "2 sets of fresh foot prints leaving off in a s.e. direction (i.e., from beneath the nursery)." Most of the prints were obliterated by the unrestrained crowd; however, one very clear impression survived. No photograph had been taken or ruler used, but by rough measurement it was twelve to twelve and a half inches long and four to four and a quarter inches in width. This did not appear in the report or notes, but the notes revealed what Trooper Nuncio De Gaetano had seen: "SOCK MARKS from foot of ladder to where ladder lay."

The "Description of Methods Employed" in the Wolf report stated:

> It is obvious that the kidnapers arrived in a car which was parked some distance from the house either in the

vicinity of the Lindbergh's private lane or a rough road known as Featherbed Lane which runs parallel to the Lindbergh lane about ¼ mile south. Then they proceeded on foot to their object and assembled a three section extension ladder which was placed against the east side of the house. Apparently one person climbed the ladder and entered the nursery on the second floor, took the child from its crib, leaving in the same manner and carrying the victim back to the waiting automobile [and] escaped to an established hiding place. It is obvious that this crime had been carefully planned and the layout [and] routine of the Lindbergh home studied.[4]

It would soon be discovered that the lower section of the ladder had a shattered riser and a broken rung—and Lindbergh would later recall hearing a "cracking" sound outside the house around 9:30 P.M. But to all intents and purposes, Corporal Joseph A. Wolf's initial report contained most of what would be known and believed for two and a half years regarding the disappearance of Charles A. Lindbergh, Jr.

An important physical element that had not been mentioned by Wolf were the thumb guards on the baby's sleeping apparel. Something else Wolf, the state police, or Charles Lindbergh overlooked was Hopewell's Constable Williamson, who was already recalling for reporters that Lindbergh—though claiming that the lack of a flashlight had kept him from examining the ground below the nursery until the policemen arrived—had led the way on their trek and seemed to know where everything was; that Lindbergh had discovered the ladder holes and footprints; that Lindbergh had found the ladder sections; that Lindbergh had been the first to spot the dowel and chisel.

If a ransom note was the key to Lindbergh's strategy for getting the world to look in the wrong direction, it had begun to work. The envelope had been opened and the text examined and accepted by authorities. The twelve-line message had been written in pencil in an exaggerated, uneven script on a single piece of paper. It read:

> Dear Sir!
> Have 50,000 $ redy 25,000 $ in
> 20 $ bills 15,000 $ in 10 $ bills and
> 10000 $ in 5 $ bills. After 2–4 days
> we will inform you were to deliver
> the Mony.

> We warn you for making
> anyding public or for notify the Police
> the child is in gute care.
> Indication for all letters are
> signature
> and three holds.[5]

Three perforated holes in the lower right-hand corner of the page ran across a "signature" of a solid circle of red inside two larger, interlacing circles.

— — —

If Lindbergh, for all his posturing of secrecy and confidentiality, desired to let the press and public know what the text said, he did it in a unique fashion—by simultaneously denying and confirming that the ransom note had been found.

3

CROWDED IDOLS

- - -

ON LEARNING OF THE KIDNAPPING EARLIER IN THE EVENING, A STAND-UP CO-median in a Chicago speakeasy suggested that President Herbert Hoover took the Lindbergh baby because he needed the ransom money to keep the White House from being repossessed. Other Americans would soon be accusing the president of the crime, not out of an attempt at black humor but from the frustration and enmity incurred by the severest economic crisis in the country's history. America was in the grip of the Great Depression, and unemployment, which had been at 1.5 million before the stock market crash of 1929, shot up to 4 million in 1930, and by the time of the kidnapping in 1932 was heading for 13 million, nearly one third of the nation's work force. The name Hoover, once synonymous with hope and humanitarianism, had become an obscenity for much of the country. A rash of ramshackle shantytowns slapped together by swelling armies of the disfranchised were called Hoovervilles; empty pockets turned inside out were Hoover flags; horse- or mule-drawn flivvers were Hoover carts; newspapers with which the legions of new poor covered themselves at night were Hoover blankets; freight cars being illegally ridden by hobos and a quarter of a million nomadic youngsters were the Hoover express. Hoover hogs were the rabbits farmers caught for food; Hoover steaks, the rodents many were forced to eat in the cities; Hooverberries, the apples being peddled on the streets. Not that long before, Herbert Clark Hoover had been the second most respected and trusted man in the land. The first was Charles Augustus Lindbergh.

In 1919, a New York City hotel owner by the name of Raymond Orteig offered a twenty-five-thousand-dollar prize to anyone who could fly "an aeroplane" nonstop between New York and the shores of France. Orteig, an aviation buff, had been inspired by two historic flights made that same year, both of which had crossed the Atlantic Ocean. The earlier had been achieved by the NC-4, a U.S. Navy seaplane piloted by Lieutenant Commander A. C. Reed. Despite the fact that he had touched down at the Portuguese Azores and in Spain before reaching England, Reed was the first man ever to have flown the Atlantic. His accomplishment was overshadowed when a pair of British aviators, Captain John Alcock and Lieutenant Arthur Whitten Brown, flew nonstop from Rope Walk Field at St. Johns, Newfoundland, to Clifden, Ireland, in a Vickers-Vimy biplane. The battered aircraft gave testament to the difficult weather they had encountered. (Alcock had been born in America; nevertheless, he was knighted, along with Brown, for the feat.) Still in 1919, the dirigible R-34 also ran into bad weather during its transatlantic crossing, from East Fortune Airdrome, Scotland, and had to put out an SOS before touching down at Mineola, New York.

The highly publicized Alcock-Brown flight had been inspired by a fifty-thousand-dollar cash award posted by the London *Daily Mail*. Raymond Orteig, the owner of New York City's Brevoort and Lafayette hotels, was concerned that U.S. achievements in aviation were being overshadowed. After conferring with the National Aeronautic Association of America, he put up his own twenty-five-thousand-dollar prize for a direct New York–to–France flight, a challenge many experts criticized as being next to impossible with the equipment and technology at hand. The term of the offer, which was five years, expired without a single taker. Orteig reinstated the prize in 1925. It went unclaimed for another year and a half. By now flying was the international rage, and three different dirigibles had carried a total of sixty-eight people over the Atlantic. The year before, a pair of round-the-world U.S. Army planes made the crossing by way of Iceland, Greenland, and Newfoundland. Even in May of 1927, as twenty-five-year-old Charles Lindbergh and his Ryan monoplane, *The Spirit of St. Louis,* reached Long Island, New York, the takeoff point for his contemplated twenty-five-thousand-dollar flight to Paris, he again was not the first.

Lindbergh, whose nickname was Slim, had read about the Orteig prize in an aviation-magazine article that recounted the failure of Paul-René Fonck, the great French World War I ace, to make the trip and win the money. Fonck's overloaded tri-engine plane had crashed on takeoff from Long Island's Roosevelt Field, killing two of his four-man crew. Fascinated by the prospect of flying nonstop over the Atlantic to Europe and believing that a streamlined monoplane using the new, powerful 220-horsepower J-5 Whirlwind engine manufactured by the Wright Aeronautical Corporation had the best chance of success, Lindbergh persuaded a group of aviation-oriented businessmen in St. Louis to finance such an undertaking. A contract to build the plane—Whirlwind engine included—in sixty days went to the Ryan Airlines Corporation of San Diego for $10,508. Before the work was completed, four other aircraft had entered the Orteig contest. Two were multi-engined and two single engined. During a test flight one of the multi-engined planes crashed in a swamp, killing the crew. The other was damaged and its crew injured when it nosed over on a landing. One of the single-engine craft suffered a minor accident as well as being beset with legal problems. The second took off from France, crossed the Atlantic coast of Europe, and disappeared. Construction of *The Spirit of St. Louis* was completed on schedule. Lindbergh conducted the test flights in California and then flew to St. Louis for the official dedication ceremonies, but the trip was cut short when he learned that two of the damaged aircraft were now repaired and ready to take off in quest of the Orteig prize.

On May 12, 1927, Slim Lindbergh flew *The Spirit of St. Louis* to Curtiss Field, Long Island, in record time to find that a new predicament confronted him, one he would spend a lifetime grappling with: the media. A dozen or more newspaper reporters, photographers, and motion picture cameramen ran out into the area where he planned to land. Lindbergh touched down a safe distance away but was soon besieged by the press. Knowing that publicity for the flight would draw attention to aviation, as well as increase his own influence and earning prospects— among other likelihoods, his backers hoped to establish airline service between St. Louis, New York, and Europe—he granted interviews and allowed endless photographs. At first he enjoyed seeing his name and picture on the front pages of great newspapers, but it didn't take long for him to be dismayed by the exaggeration and exploitation in many of the articles. Contacts with the press became increasingly unpalatable for him. He felt that interviews and photographs attempted to perplex and abase life, particularly those printed in the tabloid papers. His pet peeve was what he considered to be a "trick" technique used with pictures. He was infuriated by the first composite photograph in which he appeared. His mother had come to New York to see him off. While they did pose together for photographers, he refused to assume the lachrymose postures often asked for. The next day he was stunned by newspaper photographs showing them in exactly those positions. "I thought it cheaply sentimental and thoroughly dishonest on the part of the papers," Lindbergh explained. "At New York I began to realize how much irresponsibility and license can lurk behind the shining mask called 'freedom of the press.' "[1]

Lindbergh had a more serious difficulty to tend to at Curtiss Field: He wasn't eligible to go after the twenty-five-thousand-dollar purse, the money with which he had hoped to pay back his investors. A contest rule required that sixty days must elapse between the Orteig Prize Committee's acceptance of entry papers and the contestant's takeoff for the flight. Lindbergh didn't have that much time. At neighboring Roosevelt Field two eligible planes were waiting for the overcast to lift so they could leave for France: a single-engine Bellanca named *Columbia,* which was piloted by Clarence Chamberlin and Lloyd Bertaud, and *America,* a trimotor Fokker like the one Paul-René Fonck had crashed in on this very airfield the year before. The *America* and its crew were led by the world-famous North Pole explorer Lieutenant Commander Richard Byrd, who had already made a historic flight over the top of the world. Though Byrd claimed he was not an official entrant, Orteig had personally invited him to participate, and the media treated him as a competitor.

Lindbergh telephoned his backers in St. Louis and explained that if he was to be the first to Paris, he would have to forfeit the prize money. He was told to hell with the money and to leave when he was ready. Weather was still a problem; so was the weight that the extra gasoline needed for the crossing had added to his plane. Though Lindy had never tried to take off with a full load of fuel, he knew to do so required a lengthier runway than Curtiss Field provided. Accepting an invitation from Commander Byrd, he had *The Spirit of St. Louis* towed next door, to the longer airstrip at Roosevelt Field reserved for the *America.*

If Charles Lindbergh was not yet destiny's child as he made final preparations in the predawn drizzle at Roosevelt Field on May 20, 1927, he was certainly the media's. The young aviator was greatly responsible for an escalating international interest in, if not a fervor over, the impending flights. News folk were taken by his pink-cheeked good looks and his stern, boyish daring in attempting a thirty-six-hundred-mile solo flight across the forbidding ocean without a radio, sextant, or front window. His silver-winged plane was designed in such a way that an oversize fuel tank in the nose section of the fuselage had precluded the cockpit from having a forward windshield. The only means the young pilot had of seeing straight ahead was through a periscope fixed in the roof or by hanging out the door window. His only guidance system would be the stars and a folding map. A few sandwiches and a canteen of water were to sustain him. Learning that friends had dubbed Lindbergh Lucky because he had escaped death by parachuting from troubled aircraft on more than one occasion and that other of his aerial antics had earned him appellations such as the Flying Fool, the national media were already calling him Lucky Lindy and the Flying Fool. As dawn broke at Roosevelt Field, he had gone without sleep for twenty-three hours—thanks in part to a noisy poker game in a room near his sleeping quarters—and would have no time to rest before embarking on what could be a day and a half aloft. The reporters on hand to see which of the three competing planes would leave first were clearly rooting for the rangy, six-foot-two, blue-eyed, tousled-haired, handsome former barnstorming airmail and military-reserve pilot whose father had been a congressman from Minnesota. At 7:52 A.M. Lindbergh did what his more conservative competitors dared not and took off in the overcast, barely clearing the telephone wires at the far end of the field.

Radiophones and the transatlantic cable buzzed with word that he was en route. Newspapers around the world gave the story front-page attention and kept apace of his progress throughout the day. When he was spotted passing over St. John's, Newfoundland, at 7:15 P.M., it seemed that every country on earth received instant word. At New York City's Yankee Stadium, where Joseph Paul Cukoschay, a Lithuanian-born boxer known professionally as Jack Sharkey, knocked out fellow heavyweight contender Jimmy Maloney in the fifth round, the largest cheer of the evening came when an updated report on Lindbergh's flight was conveyed over the public-address system. At the request of the announcer, the crowd of fifty thousand rose and offered a silent prayer for the young aviator's safety, then noisily returned to the fisticuffs at hand.

The greatest excitement seemed to be in France. Besides the fact that

Lindbergh would be landing there, in the minds of the French he had named his aircraft not for a Missouri city but after the man that city's name commemorated, one of their nation's most venerated saints, King Louis IX, who died in 1270 during the Eighth Crusade of medical, not battle-related, causes. As in other cities, towns, and villages around the globe, bulletin boards sprung up on which the latest flight reports could be read. The government announced that, weather permitting, they would test out a new system of powerful lights that could lead *The Spirit of St. Louis* from the coast of France right into Paris.

Thirty-three hours and twenty-nine minutes after leaving Roosevelt Field, and having traveled at an average speed of 107½ miles per hour, Lindbergh made a night landing at Paris's Le Bourget Air Field, where a roaring crowd of twenty-five thousand well-wishers broke through police lines, rushed the plane, and hoisted him onto their shoulders. "Well, I did it," were the first words from his lips. Then they bore him off to a celebration like none ever seen before, and possibly since.

In an age of ballyhoo and instant fame, Charles Augustus Lindbergh instantly became the most monumentally heralded idol of his era, an honor with which he was amazingly and eloquently well prepared to deal, even though he would profess that he was not. Circling the Eiffel Tower on his way to Belgium, he had already received France's Legion of Honor. Lindy dropped a farewell message on the Place de la Concorde that read, "Good-bye, dear Paris. Ten thousand thanks for your kindness to me." Landing in Brussels, he told King Albert, "I have heard much of the famous soldier-king of the Belgians."[2] There was not always time or a need to speak. When he tried to land at England's Croydon Aerodrome, a crowd of one hundred thousand broke through the police barricades and swarmed across the field, forcing Lindbergh back into the sky. On a second pass he touched down only to take off again as the surging thousands blocked his path. The field was cleared, and his third attempt was successful, but before he could climb out of the plane, the adoring mob was on him, leaving the official welcoming committee isolated in the distance.

President Calvin Coolidge sent the U.S. Navy cruiser *Memphis* to bring him from England directly to Washington, D.C., where three U.S. mail trucks, displaying large signs that read THE PEOPLE OF THE UNITED STATES BY AIR MAIL CONGRATULATE LINDY, presented him with five hundred thousand letters of felicitations. The Western Union Telegraph Company and the Postal Telegraph-Cable Company, who had been advertising any of twenty different welcoming messages for thirty-six cents, delivered seventy-five thousand telegrams to the returning hero. A crowd of 150,000 shouted itself hoarse as he was driven up the capital's Pennsylvania Avenue to where President Coolidge and another crowd of 150,000 was waiting. The president pinned the Distinguished Flying Cross to Lindbergh's lapel and commissioned him—he had started his flight to Paris as a major in the National Guard Reserve—a colonel in the Officers Reserve Corps. He spent the night at the temporary White House and in the morning set off for New York City.

Twelve thousand New York City policemen carrying no clubs linked arms, used their hands, or charged on horseback, trying to keep a roaring crowd of four million delirious New Yorkers from enveloping the ticker tape parade along narrow lower Broadway. When Lindbergh reached City Hall, Mayor James J. Walker presented him with the Medal of Valor. A quarter of a million spectators were on hand in Central Park to watch New York's governor, Alfred Emanuel Smith, bestow upon the Lone Eagle the state Medal of Honor. Manhattan's Wall Street matched the ardor of the rest of the city. Not only did it provide a good portion of the ticker tape used in Lucky Lindy's parade—according to the New York City Street Cleaning Department, 1,800 tons of paper, compared with 155 tons after the armistice celebration in 1918—but trading in airplane stocks was brisk, continuing the rally that had started with shares in Wright Aeronautical Corporation, the manufacturer of the engine that powered *The Spirit of St. Louis.* Wright's stock jumped from twenty-nine and three quarters to thirty-four and three-eighths when the plane was only halfway to Paris. Not to be outdone by Wall Street, the city's Tin Pan Alley already had available in sheet music twenty-five songs honoring Lindbergh, and before the year was out that number would be multiplied by a hundred.

Though Lindbergh hadn't qualified to compete in the New York–to–Paris contest, Raymond Orteig awarded Lindy the twenty-five-thousand-dollar prize. Lindbergh was inundated with business offers, including fifty thousand dollars to endorse a brand of cigarettes, half a million dollars and 10 percent of the gross to star in a motion picture, and an estimated four hundred thousand if he would appear on the vaudeville circuit. He turned almost all of them down, thereby adding to his image the virtues of being both principled and not purchasable. He did choose to write a book on his flight. Its title, *We,* referred to Lindbergh and his airplane, *The Spirit of St. Louis.* Not to buy a copy was un-American.

For the United States' boom-time Roaring Twenties, the attractive twenty-five-year-old was precisely the right man at the right moment. It was a hoopla era of yellow journalism obsessed with bigness, glamour, and daring, and he was the biggest and most glamorous and most daring. More headlines and front-page space were given to him than to any American hero before, and newsstand sales soared. The flapper set, high-rolling market speculators, and gangsters each honored him in their own inimitable styles—the Lindy Hop became the national dance rage; speak-easies and bootleggers sold drinks and entire brands of illicit booze with such names as Lone Eagle, American Eagle, and Charlie Boy; Lindbergh-style flying breaches became a hot item for fashionable tailors; the Chicago mobster Hymie ("Loud Mouth") Levine, alleged inventor of the one-way ride, bought a hundred pairs of Lindy flying caps and goggles and passed them out among his friends. Building model airplanes, already a fad among the young, became a favorite pastime of prison inmates who could be trusted with knives or razor blades.

The bulk of the country, disillusioned by the press's lurid exploitation of scandal, crime, and immorality, viewed Lindbergh as the reformation of traditional American values, not the least of which were chivalry, patriotism, self-dedication, and nobility of intention. He appeared on the cover of *Time* magazine as its very first Man of the Year, with the sub-caption HE DEFEATED FAME. In the magazine's text, under the title of "Heroes," his habits were listed as "smokes not; drinks not. Does not gamble. Eats a thoroughgoing breakfast. Prefers a light luncheon and dinner when permitted. Avoids rich dishes. Likes sweets." *Time*'s consulting calligrapher stated that Lindbergh's handwriting revealed "superiority, intellectualism, cerebration, idealism, even mysticism." The "Characteristics" of *Time*'s Man of the Year for 1927 were "modesty, taciturnity, diffidence (women make him blush), singleness of purpose, courage, occasional curtness, phlegm."[3] The nation's Prohibitionists, or "drys," took him as their nominal leader. The second greatest hero in America that year was a baseball player and infamous tippler nicknamed the Sultan of Swat—Babe Ruth, who had hit a record-breaking sixty home runs.

The wet-dry issue was essentially all that separated the two presidential candidates during the 1928 election, which pitted the pro-Prohibition Republican party's Herbert Hoover against the anti-Prohibition Democratic party's Alfred E. Smith. Both men advocated supply-side economics, a policy that the departing New Era Republican administration of President Calvin Coolidge had presided over for three years of unparalleled prosperity. Prosperity was the root issue of the election, a continuation of Republican-led affluence under the steady hand of Herbert Clark Hoover, whose campaign slogan was "a chicken in every pot, a car in every garage." The economy did look stronger than ever, as attested to by Henry Ford's having manufactured his fifteen millionth Model T automobile several months before. Hoover beat Smith by a landslide six million votes. Not long after, the stock market crashed, panic reigned, and the prosperity unraveled.

In his 1776 treatise, *Inquiry into the Nature and Causes of the Wealth of Nations,* the Scottish economist Adam Smith postulated that under certain conditions the production of goods creates its own demand and marketplace. A hundred fifty-three years later, on the eve of the Great Depression, this view of supply creating its own demand was a hallowed tenet for most of America's business community. Economists would never agree on what caused the devastating financial collapse, but by 1929 America's productivity had increased at a far more rapid pace than wages. Another imbalance was the distribution of earning power. Seventy-one percent of America's families had an income under twenty-five hundred dollars, while the 24,000 richest families enjoyed incomes in excess of one hundred thousand dollars, including 513 families that reported incomes above one million dollars. Distribution of wealth was even more extreme. Some 2.3 percent of the families accounted for two thirds of all American savings, while 21.5 million families had no savings at all. The rich, during the six years of Coolidge-Hoover New Era prosperity, had become richer at a far faster rate than the poor had become less poor.

Herbert Hoover had moved into the White House with the reputation of being a gruff humanitarian and miracle-performing manager. A dedicated Quaker, Hoover had lost both his parents before reaching his teens and worked his way up from near poverty to become an internationally famous geologist-engineer-metallurgist-financier who was widely quoted as having said that if a man "has not made a million dollars by the time he is forty, he is not worth much." Hoover was worth four million and known as the Great Engineer when America entered World War I, and he took charge of the Commission for Relief in Belgium, which subsequently fed more than nine million people. He moved on to become America's wartime food administrator and, later, the director general of the American Relief Administration, whose postwar

European efforts were credited with saving upward of one hundred million lives.[4] To "Hooverize" in those days meant to economize for a noble purpose. In many European towns, streets were named in his honor.

President Herbert Hoover, renowned for being a wise and often infallible manager, at first seemed stunned by the onslaught of the Great Depression; then he tried to initiate many measures that would later be attributed to his successor, Franklin Delano Roosevelt. As the crisis worsened, he became blind to the fact that help was required for millions of his fellow citizens; he grew rigid in his resolve to do nothing. Complicating matters was Hoover's dichotomous personality. He was both shy and publicity hungry, private and egocentric, incisive and stubborn. Failure was anathema to him, and when the counterdepression actions he initiated did not work, he first refused to admit they had failed and later became withdrawn. Worst of all was the national perception of his personality. He was an aloof and reserved man, characteristics his campaign publicity staff had successfully sold to the voters as scientific detachment and administrative efficiency. Now, with public suffering and desperation reaching unimaginable proportions, his cool demeanor was viewed as fiendish indifference by millions of his countrymen. Some politicians and political writers feared that anarchy was near.

The Democrats, whose national convention was approaching, scrambled to find the right candidate with which to claim the White House. As the pressure mounted on all sides, Hoover took to locking himself in his office in times of extreme stress. The group he tried to shut himself off from the most, and whom he had grown to detest, was the very one he had done so much to court in his early political career: the media. They were demons attempting to blame the entire depression on him and had to be avoided at all costs. The irony was that Herbert Hoover had been the first candidate ever to employ a press agent during a presidential campaign.

- - -

Charles Lindbergh's popularity and prestige did nothing but rise. His desire to help develop aviation resulted in his taking *The Spirit of St. Louis* on a highly publicized three-month flying tour of the United States in 1927, which was underwritten by the Daniel Guggenheim Foundation for the Promotion of Aeronautics. In an even more widely reported incident at the end of 1927, he was flying the plane to Mexico on a goodwill mission when he temporarily got lost, and the world skipped a heartbeat.

The next year he joined Transcontinental Air Transport, a passenger airline, as a technical director.

Lindy's displeasure with the press often rivaled that of Herbert Hoover, particularly when it came to his private life. Fame, he believed, was a handicap except when it was used to generate enthusiasm in a grand cause. His cause was aviation. He had become its greatest promoter, and toward this end he could be cooperative and genuinely congenial with the fourth estate. Those reporters he seemed to favor were from conservative publications that sustained his American-hero image and that he could usually manipulate. But even they were victims of an elaborate deception he worked out after the announcement of his engagement to Anne Spencer Morrow, the daughter of millionaire Dwight W. Morrow, the U.S. ambassador to Mexico and a former partner of J. P. Morgan, Jr.

The subterfuge at Next Day Hill, the Morrow estate in Englewood, New Jersey, was Lindbergh at his illusive best. Few impending royal or state weddings received the attention afforded that of Lindbergh and his twenty-three-year-old fiancée. Reporters and cameramen camped outside the gates of Next Day Hill, where the ceremony was to be held on an unspecified date in the future. Comings and goings were closely watched to determine if the big event was about to take place. Lindy, wishing to have privacy on his honeymoon, was correct in assuming that newsmen expected he and his bride would fly to wherever it was they were going after the ceremony. His favorite aircraft, a two-seater Curtis Falcon with a six-hundred-horsepower engine, was at Roosevelt Field, and the day before the wedding he called there with orders to have the plane serviced and ready for flight at 8:00 the next morning.[5] A host of media people hurried to the field and joined those already watching the hangar in which the fully prepared Curtis Falcon was waiting. A second strategy was directed at the press people beyond the gates of Next Day Hill. Lindy would later fess up and claim that on May 27, 1929, he and Anne drove out of the Morrow estate several times, wearing the same outfits. As friends arrived later in the day for a small reception being given in honor of Lindy's mother, who had come east for the wedding, nobody expected anything but the announced party. To the surprise of the guests and most of the servants, the marriage ceremony was performed, with Anne wearing a simple white chiffon wedding dress and Charles in a plain blue business suit. The cake, which had been smuggled in, was sliced. When Lindy and Anne drove through the gates on their usual afternoon spin, he was still wearing the business suit, and she had changed back into the dress reporters had seen earlier in the day. Anne waved to them, and they waved back, thinking no more of it. The car drove down the hill and turned the usual corner toward the ferry. A little farther on it pulled into a back street, where a friend was waiting with Lindy's Franklin. When Dwight Morrow, at 6:45 P.M., told the press that the reception had actually been the wedding, the young couple was safely aboard a secret honeymoon yacht.

In a scramble to locate the newlyweds, reporters tried to bribe members of the Morrow household staff, as well as offering the public rewards for information on their whereabouts. When they were spotted by airplane aboard the boat ten days later, a public controversy broke out as to Lindbergh's right to privacy. An editorial in one tabloid said that a grade-A celebrity like Lindy did not have any. The *New York World* replied that a grade-A celebrity had every right to lead his own life. The *New Republic* pointed out that whatever the merits of the argument, Lindy owed his fame and fortune to the press and that some reporters didn't enjoy having to cover him any more than he liked them being there. Another disagreement was over just how the young couple had tricked the media at the Englewood estate. Several writers contended that the Lindberghs had eluded them by wearing disguises and that Anne's dress had nothing to do with the matter.[6]

Despite polemics, Lindy and Anne remained the world's most publicized couple, and aviation had a great deal to do with it. His name had become synonymous with flying and the aircraft industry, and much of what was happening there wasn't good. Several attempts to duplicate his Atlantic crossing had ended fatally, as had countless other flights throughout the world. Flying was hazardous, a fact that added to its appeal and romance. Whatever the crash or casualty, Lindbergh's advocacy of aviation helped maintain the public's confidence in progress in the sky. So did new flying records between here and there that someone or other always seemed to be establishing. Not that Lindy didn't add a paragraph or two to his own legend aloft. On Easter Sunday of 1930, flying from Los Angeles to New York in a new Lockheed Sirius airplane, and with Anne as his navigator, he broke the transcontinental speed record.

Word that Anne was pregnant resulted in the media again massing outside the Morrow estate in Englewood, where the delivery was to occur. Reporters—generally more aggressive than when the Lindberghs had been married—attempted to enter the house disguised as servants and again tried to bribe staff members for information.

– – –

It was a chancy world that the Lindbergh baby would be entering. Japan was waging war on China, and many diplomats were urging America to intercede. The Great Depression was worldwide, and while Britain, which had gone off the gold standard and reorganized its empire into a commonwealth, remained the predominant world force, America had replaced Germany as the second greatest power. Germany, with only half the population of the United States, had nearly a million more unemployed, a crisis of which an Austrian-born rabble-rouser living in Bavaria made the most by extolling his philosophy of fascism. Adolf Hitler's National Socialist (Nazi) party numbered in the millions, and his paramilitary brown-shirted Storm Troopers were creating havoc in the streets they did not already control. The *New York Times*'s year-end list of top world leaders would include Hitler and Hoover along with the premier of France, Pierre Laval; Soviet Russia's Joseph Stalin; Britain's prime minister, James Ramsay MacDonald; and a man who was causing Mr. MacDonald a great deal of grief and whom the British authorities would soon slap into jail again, India's sixty-two-year-old Mahatma Gandhi.

Many a Republican power broker doubted that Herbert Hoover was up to coping with the other international heads of state, let alone with his own domestic problem. One particularly potent group of GOP pols was even suggesting that a far better candidate for the coming presidential election would be Dwight W. Morrow, the maternal grandfather of the highly anticipated Lindbergh baby.

4

THE EAGLET

WHEN CHARLES AUGUSTUS JR. ARRIVED ON JUNE 22, 1930—HIS MOTHER'S twenty-fourth birthday as well—radio programs were interrupted to spread the news, and a song composed for the event aired within the hour. President Hoover and world leaders sent congratulations, as did tens of thousands of ordinary people. So many gifts were received that the family could no longer fit them into the room assigned them. The press dubbed baby Charles the Eaglet, and the entire nation of France "adopted" him as its own. The demand for photographs was enormous. Lindbergh provided them only to journalists he deemed friendly, which prompted one blackballed editor to offer a bounty of five thousand dollars for a picture of the baby.

Dwight Morrow, the Eaglet's grandfather, was also making news. An often-mentioned presidential candidate by anti-Hoover Republicans, Morrow had entered the New Jersey senatorial race. The fifty-seven-year-old former ambassador, who advocated repeal of the Eighteenth Amendment, won the GOP primary by three hundred thousand votes, the statewide election by two hundred thousand, and took office in December of 1930. By then Lindy and Anne lived in a rented farmhouse outside of Princeton, New Jersey, but had purchased a 360-acre tract of land they spotted from the air. It was on the southern slope of the nearby Sourland Mountain, and construction of their house was under way.

— — —

In a *Saturday Evening Post* magazine article that appeared in early summer of 1931, Lindbergh disclosed that even though his fan mail was down to a hundred letters a day, he and Anne had recently taken to wearing disguises, since it was the only way they could go out in public without attracting a crowd.[1] Another revelation was that the Lone Eagle often referred to his son and heir as It. An attempt was made by the story's author to answer charges of Lindy's being a mean-spirited practical joker who had intentionally splattered mud on fans watching him taxi his plane along a runway and, in another moment of mischief, had intentionally put a passenger-filled plane he was piloting into a nosedive. The magazine attributed to Lindbergh an "inflexible policy" of dealing only with the conservative metropolitan press and of having made a "clean break" with his old nemesis, the exploitive newspapers that continued to infringe on his personal life even though he would issue them an occasional press release. The story left no doubt that the new home they were building near the remote Sourland Mountain would provide him and his family with the privacy he had so long sought and so well deserved.

In February of 1931, pretty Bessie ("Betty") Mowat Gow came to work at the Lindberghs' home near Princeton. A highly recommended nursemaid for the baby, Betty joined a household staff that consisted of herself and two other servants: Ollie Whateley, the family butler-chauffeur, and his wife, Elsie, who was the Lindberghs' cook. The Whateleys were English; Betty Gow, Scottish. With the onset of summer and the Lindberghs preparing to embark on an extended flying expedition, Betty and the baby went to the Morrow vacation home at North Haven, Maine. Whether in New England or Princeton or at his grandmother's estate in Englewood, it was an isolated existence for the Eaglet. The Lindberghs and the Morrows were different: richer, more famous and sought after, more adored and hated. For every letter of adulation the Lone Eagle or his family received, there seemed to be another containing threats and expletives.

Charles and Anne Lindbergh were back in the news. It was the end of July 1931, and with a Lockheed Sirius floatplane checked out and supplied, they began an epic air flight over the top of the world. The journey was to be an unscientific assessment of the commercial aviation possibilities of what was being called the Great Circle Route to China via Canada, Alaska, and Japan. Anne, by now a licensed pilot, acted as the radio operator. Because the Sirius had pontoons rather than wheels, they could land only on water. The Lindberghs flew from North Haven, Maine, to Ottawa, Canada, and later landed at Moose Factory, Ontario. Then they followed the northwestern shore of Hudson Bay to Churchill, Manitoba. The next night they reached Baker Lake in Canada, a place so far north the sun never set and they had no problem spotting a welcoming committee of Eskimos, a Northwest Territories mounted policeman, and several Caucasian trappers. The visage of Anne in the eternal twilight fascinated two small Eskimo boys, who had never seen a white woman before. The following day's eleven-and-a-half-hour flight to Aklavik, Canada, was the longest leg of the journey to date. Three days after that, flying over the fog-choked Alaskan coastline of the Arctic Ocean, they lost radio contact with Point Barrow, the northernmost stop on their travels. They were too far from Aklavik to turn back, and they couldn't see to land. The Lindberghs continued blindly on by instrument. The Barrow radio finally beamed gratuitous word that the weather was lifting. They set down safely on a Point Barrow lagoon.

Eighteen days later the Lindberghs landed in Nemuro, on Japan's island of Hokkaido. By September 17, they were in Osaka, Japan. Two .days after that they landed on Lotus Lake, in Nanking, China. The country was being ravaged by disastrous floods. Told that their aircraft was the only one in the country with sufficient range, Charles and Anne spent the balance of the month making survey flights over the inundated terrain for the Chinese government and shuttling doctors and medical supplies to isolated areas. They took off and landed on the Yangtze River. On each return the Sirius was hoisted onto the British aircraft carrier *Hermes* for the night. While being lowered back into the river one morning, with Charles and Anne inside, the plane was spun around by the rapid currents and capsized. The Lindberghs swam to safety and were given doses of castor oil to protect against the Yangtze's contamination.[2] The plane was lifted onto the aircraft carrier badly in need of repair.

News that U.S. Senator Dwight Morrow, Anne's father, had died on October 5, after only ten months in office, ended any chance that America's First Couple would continue their journey. They returned home on the state-of-the-art transportation of the period, a ship.

Over the summer the Eaglet's nursemaid, Betty Gow, found herself a beau. He was a twenty-five-year-old Norwegian seaman by the name of Finn Henrik Johnsen, better known as Henry ("Red") Johnsen. They met when Thomas W. Lamont's yacht, *Reynard*, on which Red worked, was berthed at North Haven. In mid-October, Betty and the Eaglet moved from North Haven to the Morrow estate in Englewood. With the *Reynard* in dry dock and not expected back in service until March of 1932, Red was soon a regular visitor to Englewood, where he took a room at a local boardinghouse. When he wasn't in Englewood, he stayed with his brother in West Hartford, Connecticut.

On October 23, fresh from the Orient, the Lindberghs reached Englewood and were reunited with their baby son. Two days later, Sunday, October 25, accompanied by Mrs. Morrow and Anne's older sister, Elisabeth, they visited the new estate near Hopewell. Work was still under way, and since there were no beds in the newly constructed house atop Sorrel Hill, they returned to Englewood the same day. The next Saturday, October 31, Anne, her mother, Elisabeth, and the baby spent their first night at Sorrel Hill. Betty Gow was not along, and the women tended to the child with help from Elsie Whateley. Elsie and her husband, Ollie, had moved from the Lindberghs' Princeton house three days earlier and were now in permanent residence at the new estate's servants' quarters.

The Lindberghs had a suite of rooms at the Morrow estate, Next Day Hill, but with their child under the watchful eyes of Betty Gow and Anne's mother, Anne was able to work on a book about their trip to Asia, which when published would be titled *North to the Orient*. She was also active on behalf of Chinese flood relief. Charles spent time in New York City, where he had an office in the law firm of his attorney and close friend, Henry Breckinridge.

For Charles Jr. life provided an unexpected trauma. Anne's older sister, Elisabeth, who was still unmarried, had founded a Montessori-type preschool in Englewood that Mrs. Morrow seemed determined that her grandson attend. Named the Little School, it catered to children between two and five years of age. Anne was not keen on the idea and protested that her son was too young to enroll. Anne's resistance may have also been rooted in her ongoing competition with Elisabeth, who was vivacious, charming, and beautiful and who, prior to Anne's marriage to Lindbergh, had been romantically linked in the newspapers to the Lone

Eagle. Family pressure and assurances from the school staff that Charles Jr. would receive special care made her capitulate. His first morning there he got punched in the back by a fellow classmate. Charlie did what any well-protected, unworldly sixteen-month-old could be expected to do: He sat right down and cried. The Eaglet continued on at the Little School, being chauffeured back and forth to the Morrow estate, often in the company of Aunt Elisabeth.[3]

During November and the early part of December, the Eaglet's weekends were usually spent at Sorrel Hill with his parents. Very often the Lindberghs brought him from Englewood themselves. On other occasions he was driven there by one of Mrs. Morrow's chauffeurs. After missing three weeks in December, the Lindberghs and their baby returned to Sorrel Hill for New Year's Eve. With them was Lindy's mother. Anne, Charles, and Charles Jr. were back the weekends of January 16, 23, 30, and February 6. Because Anne and the baby came down with a cold, the weekend visits of February 13 and 20 were canceled.

— — —

Charles Lindbergh's bent for order and routine was reflected in the trips to Sorrel Hill. The family always arrived on Saturday morning and never stayed overnight beyond Sunday. Monday mornings usually saw Lindy drive to his office in New York City while Ollie Whateley chauffeured Anne and the baby back to Englewood. This changed drastically the weekend before leap year day, February 27, 1932. So did Lindbergh's meticulous record of never missing an appointment. Manhattan newspapers carried word that the coming Tuesday, March 1, New York University would be celebrating its one hundredth anniversary with a gala dinner for eighteen hundred guests. Lindbergh was to be a guest of honor, and he confirmed the date before the weekend began.

For what was to happen next, history, to date, has relied solely upon the word of Charles and Anne Lindbergh and their staff.

Weekend before Leap Year Day 1932

According to Anne Morrow Lindbergh,[4] on Saturday afternoon, February 27, she and the baby were driven from Englewood to Sorrel Hill by Charles Henry Ellerson, one of Mrs. Morrow's two chauffeurs. Since Betty Gow had weekends off, they were accompanied by Miss Root, also of the Morrow household staff. They arrived at the Hopewell estate at approximately 5:30 P.M. Anne, Miss Root, and Elsie Whateley fed, undressed, and washed the baby and had him in his crib by 7:30 P.M. About the same time, Lindbergh arrived from New York by car with the couple's weekend guests, Henry and Aida Breckinridge. Anne checked on the baby at 10:00 P.M. He was sneezing, and she held him for a time. An hour later, accompanied by her husband, Anne checked on the child and put some medication in his nose.

On waking the next morning, Sunday, February 28, the baby was attended to by Elsie Whateley. After breakfast he seemed fretful. Anne put him back to bed and stayed with him in his room most of the day. After treating him for his cold, she tucked him in for the night. Anne joined her husband and her guests for supper. Following the meal, she and Lindy drove the Breckinridges and Miss Root to the Princeton Junction railroad station. The Lindberghs returned home at approximately 9:00 P.M. Anne called her sister Elisabeth at Englewood and told her of the child's cold. At 10:00 P.M. she gave the baby nose drops and other medication. Then the nursery lights were turned off and the shutters closed, but a French window was left open.

On Monday morning, February 29, leap year day, Lindbergh drove off to New York City. Finding that the baby "was quite miserable with his cold," Anne, rather than motoring to Englewood after lunch, called her mother's estate and informed Betty Gow that she intended to stay on at Sorrel Hill so her son could remain in his room.[5] Except for two short walks, Anne was with the ailing Eaglet throughout the afternoon and early evening. He was medicated and tucked in for the night at 7:00 P.M. Three hours later Lindbergh called to say he was spending the night in New York City. Learning that Anne was unsure as to when she and the Eaglet would return to Englewood, he said he would join them wherever they were the next evening. Anne and Elsie again medicated the baby. The cold had moved down to his chest, which Anne now rubbed. She slept with the connecting door open between her bedroom's bathroom and the nursery. It was the first time ever that a family member had stayed overnight on a Monday.

When by midmorning Tuesday, March 1, the Eaglet's cold was still relatively thick, Anne had Ollie Whateley ring up Betty Gow at Englewood. Once on the line with Gow, Anne instructed the young Scotswoman to come to Sorrel Hill and help with the baby.

Gow had been to the Hopewell estate on three previous occasions. Twice, while the house was under construction, she had been driven there by her boyfriend, Red Johnsen. These were Sunday sightseeing excursions, and on one of them the Whateleys gave the young couple a tour of the home. Betty's only working assignment at the new estate had come on New Year's Day 1932. Again she had been driven there by Johnsen, who dropped her off. On March 1, it was Mrs. Morrow's second chauffeur, Henry Ellerson, who drove her to Hopewell. Before leaving, Betty called Henry ("Red") Johnsen, at his boardinghouse. She had a date with him for that night, which now had to be canceled. Henry wasn't in. Betty left word with his landlady, Mrs. Sherman, for him to call her at Sorrel Hill.

Betty Gow arrived at the Lindbergh estate at 2:00 P.M., had a quick bite of lunch, then went upstairs, took the baby out of his crib, and dressed him. His cold had improved, and Betty minded him as he played in the nursery. Anne and Elsie Whateley joined her around 4:30 P.M. Later, at Anne's suggestion, Betty and Elsie brought the baby downstairs to the living room. It was about 5:00 P.M., and Anne was having tea. Anne took the child while Betty and Elsie went to the servants' sitting room, off the kitchen, and had their own tea with Ollie Whateley. They were back in the kitchen when the baby ran in, babbled "hello Elsie" at Elsie, and began to race around the table. Betty caught him, took his hand, and led him upstairs to the nursery. She read to him until about 6:00 P.M., left for two minutes to go downstairs and fetch some cereal, and fed him his dinner. Anne came in and helped Betty ready the little boy for bed. They took off his clothes, put drops in his nose, rubbed his chest and gave him a physic. The two women decided to replace the flannel bandage he was wearing with a flannel nightshirt. Anne brought in scissors and thread and played with her son while Betty cut and sewed together a garment. Wearing the newly fashioned flannel shirt over his Dr. Denton sleeping suit, he was put into his crib. Anne and Betty now moved to the windows and locked the shutters. A shutter at the back of the room was warped and wouldn't completely close. When Anne departed, Betty went to the French window fronted by the warped shutter and pulled it halfway open. She then put out the light, closed both doors to the nursery, and left. The time was approximately 7:30 P.M. She washed some of the baby's clothes in the baby's bathroom and looked in on him again.[6] He was fast asleep and breathing comfortably. She took two large safety pins and fastened the covers over him to the mattress. It was now about 7:50 P.M. Betty turned off the light in the bathroom as well as in her own room, which was across the hall from the nursery; then she went down into the cellar to hang up the clothes she had washed. According to subsequent statements by the Lindberghs and their staff, Betty was the last one to see the child alive.

Anne was at her desk in the living room when Betty entered to say that the baby had fallen asleep quickly and was breathing easily. Because Lindbergh had called at around 7:00 P.M. to say that he would be a little late, Ollie Whateley decided that the staff should eat before his return. Ollie snacked first; then Betty joined Elsie for supper in the sitting room. The weather outside was nasty, and the wind had begun to howl. Even so, Anne, who was still at her desk, thought she heard the sound of car wheels on a gravel driveway. It was about 8:15 P.M., but no one arrived. Ten to fifteen minutes later the sound of an auto horn was clearly heard in the sitting room. Knowing that Colonel Lindbergh had arrived home, Elsie Whateley went to the kitchen and helped Ollie in preparing dinner. Anne heard the horn as well and also the sound of her husband's approaching car.

Lindbergh parked in the garage, entered the house through the back door, passed the sitting room, and crossed the kitchen. Anne accompanied him as he went upstairs to wash his hands. Their bathroom connected to the nursery, but they did not look in on their son. At 8:35 P.M. they were served supper in the dining room. Ollie took the phone call that came in at approximately 8:45 P.M. It was Red Johnsen wanting to speak with Betty. She came into the kitchen and got on the line. Red said he was sorry he had missed her at Englewood and that he would have liked to have seen her before she left. He also told her he was going to West Hartford. Betty returned to the sitting room and turned on the radio. Whether or not the family dog, Wahgoosh, who usually slept outside the nursery door, was with her would become a point of contention.

Charles and Anne finished dinner shortly after 9:00 P.M. and retired to the living room, where logs were burning in the fireplace. They sat talking on the sofa. Charles heard a noise, which he attributed to something dropping in the kitchen, such as a wooden orange crate. In the dining room the Whateleys cleaned away the dishes without any mishaps. After spending some five minutes in the living room, the Lindberghs went upstairs to their bedroom. They chatted for ten to fifteen minutes; then Lindy took a bath. Having finished washing the dishes, the Whateleys went to the sitting room, where Betty was reading a book and listening to the radio. His day's chores done, Ollie sat down to peruse the newspapers. Elsie took Betty up to their bedroom to inspect a newly purchased dress. After bathing, Lindbergh dressed and went downstairs to the library to read. Upstairs, Anne drew a bath for herself. Discovering that she had run out of tooth powder, she went into the baby's bathroom and, without turning on the light, appropriated the needed powder. Returning to her own bathroom, Anne brushed her teeth and then summoned Elsie, whom she asked to prepare some hot lemonade. Elsie went downstairs to do as she was bade. Anne took her bath. It was approximately 10:00 P.M.—time for Betty Gow to check on the baby.

Betty used the kitchen staircase to reach the second floor; then she followed the hall past a pair of facing guest bedrooms, the Lindberghs' master bedroom, and on into the baby's bathroom at the end of the passageway. There was a chill in the air, so she turned on a heater. She entered the unlighted nursery. It was also too cold for her liking. Betty closed the window and activated the heater. She headed for the crib, from which no sound of breathing could be heard. She reached down to pick up the baby—and felt around inside. The blankets were still pinned to the mattress, and the pillow was in place. But the child was gone.

Anne had finished her bath and was in the master bedroom when Gow entered. Not wishing to alarm her mistress, Betty asked if by any chance Anne had taken the baby or if Colonel Lindbergh might have him. Anne thought it possible that the child was with his father, who was downstairs.

Anne, in a letter to her mother-in-law, would say that her first reaction was that her prankster husband was playing another of his infamous and often not-too-funny practical jokes on her.[7] Betty Gow also thought it might be a trick. She ran downstairs into the library and asked the master of Sorrel Hill, "Colonel Lindbergh, do you have the baby? Please don't fool me."[8]

"No, of course not," he answered. "Isn't he in his crib?"

"You must have the baby," she told him, "he's gone."[9]

Lindbergh ran upstairs with Gow at his heels. Anne was coming out of the nursery as her husband rushed in. He went to the empty crib, then hurried into the master bedroom and took a Springfield rifle from the closet. He was back in the nursery along with Anne. Whether they saw the envelope resting near the window on this or on their previous visit remains confused, but Lindbergh had no doubt what had happened and told his wife, "Anne, they've stolen our baby."[10] Anne hastened back to her own room and, she later related, without thinking what she was doing, threw open the window and leaned out. She thought she heard what sounded like a cry in the general direction of the woodpile. Elsie thought it was a cat or possibly the wind.

The underground telephone line to Sorrel Hill was encased in metal tubing. Even so, Lindbergh reacted as if the wire may have been cut.[11] He strode from the nursery to the top of the stairs and shouted down to Ollie Whateley to see if the phone was working. When Whateley reported that it was, Lindbergh ordered him to call the Hopewell sheriff. By now Anne was dressed and, along with Gow and Elsie, began a desperate search for the baby. They started with the nursery closets and continued on through the house. Lindbergh, Springfield rifle in hand, went out on the private drive leading to the house. It was too dark to see. Whateley started up the car and trained the lights along the roadside as Lindbergh searched. The process was cumbersome. Lindbergh ordered him to drive into town and buy a flashlight so they could explore the area more thoroughly. Ollie was nearing the front gate when a car carrying Chief Wolfe and Constable Williamson entered the grounds. He turned around and escorted them up to the house atop Sorrel Hill.

And so the record read for sixty years. Little or nothing was challenged. Authorities established the brief period between 8:30 P.M. and 9:00 P.M., when a "crash" was heard, as the probable time when the kidnapping was perpetrated, without giving much thought to what a narrow time frame this allowed the criminals to steal the child. Also ignored or downplayed was the fact that the Lindberghs and their child never stayed at Sorrel Hill past Monday morning. This negated theories that the crime was long and meticulously planned. The fact that it happened on a Tuesday, when even the Lindberghs hadn't expected to be there, pointed to a crime of opportunity—and immense luck.

Another event to which investigators and the media would pay little or no attention was taking place some sixty miles away, at the Waldorf-Astoria Hotel, in New York City: New York University's All Alumni Centennial Dinner. Eighteen hundred guests, including scores of prestigious names, graced the 111 tables and thirty theater-style boxes. Considering that it was the worst year of the Great Depression, the gala offered a dignified but not garish menu of grapefruit with Maraschino cherries, cream soup St.-Germain with toasted croutons, celery, olives, a choice of *escalope* of bass in lobster sauce with parsley potatoes or breast of roasted chicken with new green peas in butter, salad with California angel dressing, coffee, and a dessert of frozen log *écossaise*. Songs were to be provided by the Chapel Choir of the New York University Glee Club. The seating list placed nineteen men on the dais, seven of whom would speak and two of whom were guests of honor. One of the guests of honor never appeared: Colonel Charles A. Lindbergh.

Organizers of the centennial celebration had given up a frenzied quest to locate Lindbergh, and the dinner proceeded without him. The main obstacle to locating Lindy was that his phone number at Hopewell was unlisted. Henry Breckinridge had been reached in New York and said he'd do what he could to find his missing friend and client. If Henry did phone Hopewell, no mention of this seems to be have been made by Anne or the staff to the arriving Lindbergh, not according to their sworn statements in court or to state-police investigators. Anne says nothing of it in her published writings. If the Lone Eagle prided himself on anything, it was that he never forgot an appointment. Lindy would never acknowledge that he had overlooked the speaking engagement at the Waldorf.

Nearly two years later the FBI Summary Report would claim Lindbergh sent a telegram of apology to the NYU banquet that very night. The bureau was not the prime investigator of the crime, did not have direct access to Lindbergh, and had not officially questioned him. A search of the entire bureau file on the crime, from which the summary was extracted—some 140 volumes of three hundred pages each plus appendixes—produced no agent's report or other verification that such a telegram was sent, nor was any mention made of the NYU dinner or if Breckinridge was a go-between. It appears only in the 407-page summary.[12]

Henry Breckinridge would maintain that Lindbergh had been misinformed about the date of the New York University dinner. The organizers of the tribute could probably have proved otherwise, but no one cared.

Other, more spectacular, events were occupying the police and the media.

5

OLD ENEMIES AND
FRIENDS

DURING THE LATE EVENING OF MARCH 1 AND THE EARLY MORNING OF March 2, 1932, as radios crackled with accounts of a kidnapping, the press corps descended on Charles Lindbergh as it never had before, and all the old friends and enemies were to be counted.

If indeed Lindbergh had a master plan to alter the truth, as I suspect was possible, it would have had to rely on the media's spreading the gospel of the kidnapping according to his dictates and no one else's. Once he had accomplished this, it would be necessary to cut himself and his family off from them as best he could. Only in this way would the fourth estate ride off in search of the nonexistent kidnappers, focus the public's and the law enforcement's interest on the future rather than have them looking back and perhaps becoming suspicious as to what actually occurred the previous Saturday. Skill and a great deal of luck accounted for the ease with which this strategy was implemented.

The earliest newspeople to reach Sorrel Hill were local reporters and stringers; then came the vanguard of national and international journalists. Lindbergh invited a select group of writers into his living room for a press conference he would personally conduct. They were, by and large, tried and true believers who defended his image as the Lone Eagle and tended to write what he wanted. A second group would be invited in the next day.

While Ollie Whateley provided coffee and sandwiches, Lindbergh told the journalists of his son's disappearance, explained that he needed their cooperation in disseminating photographs and descriptions of the child to the public on the chance that someone would spot the Eaglet, as well as in persuading the kidnappers not to harm him. He revealed that the infant had a cold and was being fed a special formula, which he wanted printed and broadcast in hope that it would be followed by the kidnappers. Lindy even allowed for a brief period of questions but would not accede to reporters' requests to talk to his wife or members of the household staff. In this first encounter with the press, Lindbergh made at least one slipup that nobody caught at the time. The missing child had recently had his baby locks shorn. The photographs Lindbergh passed out to reporters were not of his blond, short-haired son but of a long, curly-haired pretonsorial Eaglet.

Lindy's prime contradiction involved what was in all probability his most effective ploy. While he vehemently denied to the group of reporters that a ransom note existed, he privately confirmed for several individual sources, including the *New York Times,* that it had been found. Despite his continued disavowal, headlines would soon be proclaiming that such a message had been left by the kidnappers—which was pivotal to Lindbergh's scenario.

The roads leading to Hopewell and the estate were already jammed with media people—four hundred would be counted in the first twelve hours. The Associated Press had dispatched four carloads, and the United Press, three cars. William Randolph Hearst, Jr., was personally directing the activities of the ten men and one woman he had ordered to the scene. Hearst's International News Service, which had its entire staff en route, would soon convert a pair of rented ambulances into mobile darkrooms so pictures of the kidnapping site could be printed on the spot and rushed back to town. Those newsmen who had already arrived wandered the grounds at will, as did random sightseers and state and county officials with no part in the investigation. One correspondent likened it to the circus coming to town and all the neighbors rushing over to get first looks. Radio host Long John Nebel recalled, "Down on the road the cars were bumper to bumper waiting to get in or parked there bumper to bumper. They [the New Jersey State Police] were overwhelmed. So was everyone else. There were hundreds of us walking around that place in a stupor, maybe even a thousand, if you count the folks in the woods. There were people walking all over the woods." In the process two vital pieces of evidence were disturbed: Footprints in the ground outside the nursery were destroyed, and ladder segments were picked up and examined by curious officials and journalists.

After his need for reporters was fulfilled by the living room press conference, Charles Lindbergh's tolerance of the marauding media came to an end. While leading a search of the grounds, he told a group of writers who approached him, "I hope you boys will excuse me, but I would rather the state police answer your questions. I'm sure you understand how I feel."[1] Major Charles A. Schoeffel, the deputy to the state-police superintendent, Colonel H. Norman Schwarzkopf, was the designated trooper liaison with the press at the estate.

A car carrying a newswoman and several of her fellow New York City reporters reached Hopewell about 1:00 A.M. They worked for the Hearst newspaper chain and discovered that Gebhart's Hotel and refreshment parlor in the center of the little town had opened to accommodate the influx of journalists. After getting a cup of coffee and directions, they joined the caravan of vehicles heading out for the Lindbergh estate. As they grew near, the hilly, wooded terrain was illuminated by flares being dropped from unseen airplanes. There was no trouble driving onto the grounds and walking up to the house in which every room was lighted, but they were kept from going in by state troopers wearing wide-brimmed hats, smart blue jackets, and dark motorcycle breeches. Looking through the living room windows, they saw Anne Morrow Lindbergh pacing and talking with the household staff. She was nervous but dry eyed. They returned to their car and started cruising around the grounds to see what could be found. On a steep, muddy lane they encountered another car. It stopped, and Lindbergh, hatless and wearing his familiar leather flying jacket, got out and walked up to them. On learning they were reporters, he said familiarly, "Boys, I rely on you to stay off my estate and not annoy me. For my part I promise to give you a good break."

As they watched him walk away, one reporter commented, "Hell, that was what you call nonchalant."

"The Lindberghs are like that," a fellow scribe explained. "They never show any emotion."

"Still, God Almighty, that man's baby has been stolen—dead, maybe—in the hands of some nut or fiend," said the only woman reporter in the group.[2] Her name was Laura Vitray, and she knew that writing about Lindbergh's nonchalance was pointless. Composure doesn't make good copy; grief does.

Hostility between state policemen and the press became evident when the troopers regrouped and began clearing newspeople off the estate. Their methods often were not gentle, and even when they were, the media folk did not always cooperate. Well before dawn the removal was complete. Except for a few pet journalists, who were escorted up to Lindy's home on the hill for special briefings, the press had access to nothing but a small holding area at the far end of the estate, where they had been told announcements would be made. The nearest telephone was on a five-party line in a farmhouse a mile up the road. Official statements and press releases were slow in coming. Reporters racing up to the farmhouse and waiting in a long line to make a call were not cheered at the sight of workmen laying telephone and telegraph lines to the Lindbergh garage, where a communications center was expected to be operative by morning. When complete, the lines would link the estate with Princeton, less than twenty miles away.

The Lindbergh news blackout extended far beyond Sorrel Hill. City editors intent on getting stories from Lindbergh-Morrow relatives ran into an impenetrable iron curtain, even though Lindy would later attest he had not yet informed his mother, Evangeline, or in-laws of the tragedy. Efforts to talk with the baby's grandparents, Mrs. Elizabeth Morrow, in Englewood, and Mrs. Lindbergh in Grosse Pointe, Michigan, were intercepted by spokesmen. The missing infant's uncle and aunt, Dwight Morrow, Jr., and Constance Morrow, refused comment. A second aunt, Elisabeth Morrow, could not be located. No one connected with the Morrow household was available to the press.

The main source of information remained the front gate to the Lindbergh property, where troopers allowed journalists to overhear them when they chatted with one another. Many of the eavesdropping correspondents began to suspect they were being intentionally misled or lied to. Others realized a news blackout was being imposed. Most reporters, in a fierce competition for any bit of information on what was already the crime story of the century, kept their grumbling to themselves, but several didn't. Animosity between the state-police press liaison at Lindy's estate, Major Schoeffel—Laura Vitray likened him to Napoléon—and several writers fell just short of combat. The media, which had never been overly fond of the trooper boss, Colonel H. Norman Schwarzkopf, found him to be as uncooperative as ever.

If Major Schoeffel and the imperious Schwarzkopf were playing the role of bad cops with the media in the wake of the kidnapping, then tall, suave Henry Breckinridge, Lindbergh's friend and lawyer, was the good cop. Breckinridge, like Schwarzkopf, had reached the estate early in the morning of March 2, and Henry had taken an immediate interest in the reporters. Whether by design or chance, he became a popular visitor with the news folk waiting at the front gate. In Laura Vitray's estimation, he showed an evident desire to keep reporters happy. "We always looked at Breckinridge as one who had our interests at heart. He seemed to keep in mind that what keeps a story on the front page is something happening."[3]

When Vitray had passed through Hopewell at 1:00 A.M. the morning of March 2, it had been a sleepy little backwater town with nothing open but the hotel. When she returned from the Lindbergh estate many hours later, Hopewell had been transformed into a Forty-second Street that overflowed with motion picture news crews, newspaper reporters, photographers, radio reporters and technicians, motorcycle police, and sightseers. Gebhart's Hotel, opposite the railroad tracks, was the hub of the activity. Vitray's paper had taken an office there, and sitting in the hotel's dinette, reporters were able to compare notes.

Despite the news blackout, journalists had acquired quite a bit of information that first night and early morning: A ransom message had definitely been left; the Lindberghs only used the Hopewell house on weekends; mud was left on the floor of the nursery between the crib and an open window; ladder marks were found outside in the mud below the window to the nursery; impressions—not shoe or footprints—were also found outside in the mud, which led investigators to conclude that the kidnappers had worn socks or moccasins; a second set of footprints joined the first set near the edge of the woods; all the impressions had been destroyed because of the state police's failure to control the crowd and preserve the area; a ladder had been discovered sixty feet away from the house. It was also reported that Anne was six months pregnant with her second child.

One of the first official press releases distributed to reporters had contained a copy of the special diet that Anne Lindbergh wrote out in hopes that the kidnappers who read it would be merciful enough to feed it to her sick baby. In a letter to her mother-in-law the next day, Anne would reveal that even though the papers were saying the baby was sick, he wasn't—that the infant was just over a cold and had been dressed extra-warmly that night. Was it true that the infant was not ailing, which meant the story of the illness had been concocted, or was it simply a daughter's attempt to try to pacify an already-distraught grandmother? The letter also answered a question the press was yet to learn of and raise: why the family dog, Wahgoosh, who usually slept outside the door to the nursery, hadn't barked during the kidnapping. Anne explained in the letter to the baby's paternal grandmother that Wahgoosh was in the opposite wing of the house that night and couldn't have heard anything through the howling winds from such a distance.[4]

Laura Vitray didn't have access to Anne's correspondence, but she did have a copy of the diet, which was already appearing on front pages around the country:

> One quart of milk during the day.
> Three tablespoons of cooked cereal morning and night.
> Two tablespoons of cooked vegetables once a day.
> One yolk of egg daily.
> One baked potato or rice once a day.
> Two tablespoons of stewed fruit daily.
> Half cup of orange juice on waking.
> Half a cup of prune juice after the afternoon nap.
> 14 drops of a medicine called Viosterol during the day.

Vitray wondered if a simpler diet wouldn't have been more practical and more to the baby's interest. "Or did the Lindberghs believe," she wrote, "that their child was being cared for by persons of intellect with whom their complicated instructions for feeding would register?"[5]

Even though Lindbergh had moved the news corps off his property, there seemed to be more media people in the area than ever. They had rented every available house, farm, room, barn, or plot of land in the vicinity of the estate. Portable photo labs and improvised city desks rushed thousands of photographs and ten of thousands of printed words to a flotilla of dispatch cars and motorcycle messengers waiting to express the material by chartered airplanes or race it directly to New York City, Philadelphia, Baltimore, and Washington, D.C. This wasn't what the Lone Eagle had in mind.

On the afternoon of March 2, in a ground-floor bedroom of the Sorrel Hill house, Lindbergh again allowed himself to be interviewed by a small, select delegation of newsmen he considered as friendly and trustworthy as people of that profession could be. His face appeared tense, and his eyes were heavy lidded. He was nervous and shifted his weight from one foot to another.[6] Speaking off the record, he would neither affirm nor deny the report that a fifty-thousand-dollar ransom had been demanded by the kidnappers. He pretended not to hear other pointed queries and asked his visitors to be kind enough not to ask him embarrassing questions. He then surprised the delegation by abruptly proposing that the media not only withdraw from around the estate but also from Hopewell. The reason he offered for this was that "the local telephone exchange has been swamped with calls, impairing the function of the officials who are seeking the return of the child. As a substitute it has been arranged with Captain J. J. Lamb of the state police and Governor A. Harry Moore for a trooper to be stationed at the office of the Governor's secretary in Trenton from where all other information will be given out."[7]

When the group consented, Lindy "smiled with pleasure" and, with a wave of the hand, dismissed them. State troopers were summoned to "speed the parting pressmen to the state road half a mile east."[8] Some of the delegates lingered at the front gate; others rushed to the telegraph office in Hopewell. Regardless of the agreement by the delegation, Hopewell was where most of the media would remain, in force. It was the first major rebuff of a Lindbergh dictate since the kidnapping was announced, but it didn't affect the ultimate game plan all that much. Henry Breckinridge, Lindbergh's confidant and aide-de-camp, went right on providing newsmen with information at the front gate of Sorrel Hill—information he and the Lone Eagle wanted disseminated.

When Vitray and her peers compared notes on what they had seen and been told, the New Jersey State Police were not spoken of kindly. The bad blood between troopers, who in the main were from small towns or rural areas, and the predominantly big-city journalists had gotten worse. The power to deny the media access to the Lindbergh estate and to critical news lay with the troopers, and they had often used this advantage without tact. The power the media possessed was in their pens, many of which were depicting the state police as being a quasi-military force with little experience in crime detection, as attested to by their inability to find a single fingerprint in the nursery or on the ladder sections or preserve the footprints. Older scribes couldn't resist mentioning the state-police involvement in perhaps the greatest debacle of modern-day crime fighting, the investigation of the still-unsolved Hall-Mills murders ten years before in New Brunswick, New Jersey.

A particularly fetching target for the more acrimonious reporters was the thirty-seven-year-old superintendent of the trooper organization, Colonel H. Norman Schwarzkopf, a ramrod-stiff crew cut fellow with a blond Charlie Chaplinesque mustache who was a West Point graduate and World War I veteran. Schwarzie, as he was known, had once worked as a floorwalker at Bamberger's Department Store, a fact writers were gleefully making the most of. Their main attack was on his ineptness at directing the investigation.

Schwarzkopf wasn't in charge of the investigation. Lindbergh and Henry Breckinridge were. To a degree, so was a man named Donovan.

6

COLONELS

THREE MEN WHO WOULD ASSIST LINDBERGH WITH IMPLEMENTING THE STRAT-
egy regarding the public and press reached Sorrel Hill during the late
evening and early morning of March 1 and 2. Like Lindbergh they each
held the rank of colonel. The most important of the trio was forty-six-
year-old Henry S. Breckinridge, a friend of the Morrow family who had
become Lindy's lawyer and one of his closest friends and confidants.

Henry was the dashing stripe of fellow that reporters cottoned to, a
third-generation Kentuckian whose father was a major general in the
army and whose forebears boasted Thomas Jefferson's attorney general,
many a Confederate hero, and a pre–Civil War vice-president of the
United States. Born in Chicago, Henry had graduated from Princeton
University and the Harvard Law School. In 1913, at the age of twenty-
seven, he became assistant secretary of war under President Woodrow
Wilson and later resigned in protest over Wilson's refusal to enlarge the
army. During World War I he served as an army intelligence officer and
received honors for combat in the Meuse-Argonne offensive. Henry left

the military with the rank of lieutenant colonel, moved his law practice to New York City, became a member of the United States Olympic fencing team that competed in the 1920 Olympics at Antwerp, and captained the Olympic team that went to the 1928 Amsterdam games.

Henry Breckinridge had a way with words and ladies, which made him popular on the social and speaking-engagement circuit and in newspaper columns. His first marriage broke up in 1920, and it took another five years before he found an ideal mate in the wealthy New York City socialite Aida de Acosta, the ex-wife of Oren Root, who was the president of several railroad companies and the nephew of former senator Elihu Root. Both Henry and Aida were gregarious, social, and industrious. Her passion was philanthropic and charitable causes, and over the previous few years she had served as an executive for the American Child Health Association. Politically she leaned toward the Republicans. Henry was a staunch and active conservative Democrat who reveled in factional debates and had gained the reputation of being "an antagonist with words as sharp as a meat-axe." In the presence of the press, he was sweetness and tact, and reporters respected him.

Henry harbored political ambitions, and he understood the importance of good public relations. So did Aida, whose position at the Child Health Association was director of publicity and promotion. When they were married, on August 5, 1927, two years after having issued a joint statement saying they didn't intend to wed, Henry and Aida Breckinridge became one of the first modern media couples. She was forty-three, he forty-one, which gave gossips of that day a little more to cluck about. Three months later Henry crossed party lines and voted for the Republican candidate for president, Herbert Hoover, because of his admiration for the Great Engineer's performance as secretary of commerce under President Warren G. Harding. In 1929, President Hoover appointed Aida assistant director in charge of public relations to the White House Conference on Child Health and Protection

Following the celebrated 1927 New York–to–Paris flight, Henry Breckinridge became Charles Lindbergh's lawyer. They were soon close friends, and in the case of Lindy's marriage to Anne, Henry helped orchestrate the plan that kept the wedding and beginning of the honeymoon a secret from the press. After the ceremony at the Morrow home, when the bride and groom drove past the reporters who camped outside the gate without rousing suspicions, then descended the hill, rounded a corner, and vanished, it was Henry who helped with the vanishing. The newlyweds turned into a back street, where Henry was waiting for them with Lindy's Franklin. Now in 1932, if Lindbergh was planning yet another hoax, Henry Breckinridge would still be his prime ally.

In the early hours of March 2, 1932, Henry again came to the aid of the Lindberghs, this time bringing his wife. The Breckinridges, who had spent that weekend at Sorrel Hill, returned and took charge of an area with which they had done so well in the past: public relations. Aida manned the solitary phone in the Lindbergh house, screened calls, and became a spokesperson for Anne. Henry acted as Lindy's chief of staff and, among other things, handled the press.

There is a likelihood that Henry never left Sorrel Hill over that weekend of February 27, as he and Aida claimed. They had been the Lindberghs weekend guests who ostensibly went back to New York on Sunday night. It is just as possible that Henry arrived on Saturday to help advise Lindbergh over the death of the Eaglet that same day. A lingering question remains regarding Henry's conversation with the Waldorf-Astoria banquet sponsors trying to locate Lindbergh on March 1. With eighteen hundred guests waiting for dinner, many of them close friends of both Lindy and Henry, why didn't Breckinridge just give them the unlisted number at Sorrel Hill? Could it be that the Lindbergh scenario was about to begin?

Another colonel was to make an appearance at Sorrel Hill, a hero who in military circles was nearly as well known as Sergeant Alvin York: William J. Donovan.

Colonel William Joseph Donovan had limited time. A Republican, he was planning to run in New York State's upcoming gubernatorial election, particularly if the incumbent governor, Franklin Delano Roosevelt, became the Democrats' presidential candidate. Whether or not Donovan actually went to Sorrel Hill is debatable, but no less an authority than the BBC's Ludovic Kennedy places him at the Lindbergh estate early in the morning of March 2.[1]

A winner of the Congressional Medal of Honor and personal friend of such New York gangster overlords as Owney Madden, Bill Donovan had served as a special assistant attorney general of the United States. If he didn't personally possess the expertise to advise Lindbergh and Breckinridge in the fine points of staging a bogus kidnapping, he knew who did, assuming he was asked.

Born in Buffalo, New York, to working-class second-generation Irish-Catholic parents, Will grew up in the First Ward, a rough-and-tumble waterfront section of the city known as the Irish Quarter. Endowed with awesome aggressiveness, natural good looks, a fetching personality and wonderful singing voice, and an innate sense of how the social system operated, he worked his way up through parochial schools, and in 1903, to better his chances of being admitted to a top-flight law school, transferred to Columbia University, where he dropped Will in favor of Bill and won an award for public speaking. His prowess as quarterback on the Lions football team led to him being dubbed Wild Bill.

Upon receiving his law degree, Donovan returned to Buffalo and was taken on by a small legal firm, where his ability to speed-read amazed co-workers. In 1911, he opened his own office with the scion of one of Buffalo's leading families. Less than a year later they merged their practice with the town's most prestigious law firm. A strong oarsman, Bill switched from the Celtic Rowing Club, where his father had once rowed, to the aristocratic Buffalo Canoe Club, for which he became captain of the crew as he had been with the Celtics. In 1912, he helped recruit Canoe Club members and other patrician young men for an elite National Guard cavalry unit called Troop One. Bill, who had never been on a horse in his life, was voted the unit's first captain. He embraced the GOP, the preferred party of the privileged class, and gave many rousing political speeches. His long-time flirtation with acting stood him in good stead when he became a member of the Studio Club, where well-to-do Buffalonians put on amateur theatricals for charity. It was here that he met Ruth Rumsey, whose late father had been the city's first and wealthiest citizen—and leading Presbyterian. Their wedding took place on July 15, 1914, in the Rumsey mansion and was performed by the Donovan family priest. Bill was thirty-one.

By 1916, no finer National Guard cavalry unit existed than that of the elite young riders of Troop One under the command of Galloping Bill Donovan. They were ordered to the Mexican border for combat with the marauding forces of Pancho Villa. Pancho never appeared. When Troop One was not allowed to participate as a unit in World War I, Bill accepted command of a battalion known as the Fighting Sixty-ninth. Major Donovan led the Sixty-ninth in some the fiercest battles of World War I, was wounded three times, and became one of two American fighting men to win his country's three highest miliary honors: the Congressional Medal of Honor, the Distinguished Service Cross, and the Distinguished Service Medal, not to mention France's Legion of Honor and Croix de Guerre and Italy's Croci di Guerre.

Following the war Donovan returned to Buffalo and the practice of law. During 1920, his firm landed a major client, J. P. Morgan, one of whose partners was Dwight Morrow. In 1922, Bill was appointed U.S. district attorney for the Western District of New York and energetically set about enforcing the Volsted Act, even though he wasn't a Prohibitionist. That same year he accepted the Republican nomination for lieutenant governor of New York and was soundly defeated. Between 1925 and 1929, Donovan served as assistant attorney general of the United States and gained a reputation as being a tough, trust-busting prosecutor. One of the earliest enemies he made in Washington was J. Edgar Hoover, who in 1924 was insisting on being named director of the Justice Department's Bureau of Investigation.[2] Bill was against it. Their mutual dislike would last a lifetime. He was far friendlier with another Hoover: Herbert.

Bill Donovan was one of the few New York Republicans to support Herbert Hoover, and during the campaign he became a top adviser to the candidate. After the election he expected to be named attorney general despite the fact that the Ku Klux Klan and other anti-Catholic factions were lobbying against him. When he was passed over in favor of the solicitor general of the United States, William D. Mitchell, a Democrat who had also supported Hoover, Bill made no secret of his bitterness, turned down the president-elect's offer to become either governor general of the Philippines or secretary of war, and returned to private life.

He transferred his family and his law practice to New York City, where Donovan's expertise with antitrust cases helped make his already-prestigious law firm into one of the most successful and influential in the country. So did his political connections. By the night of March 1, 1932, as he was preparing to run for the governorship of New York, it was his criminal-law experience that counted. Even though he could not participate that actively or openly, he could entrust a bulk of the details regarding the child's disappearance to a young lawyer in his office who was friendly with the Lindberghs, Robert A. Thayer. Thayer, married to a society debutante and a regular on the café-society scene, was friendly with a good many underworld characters. He would remain a regular on the case. But if there was any one person with the ability to concoct a strategy that fit Lindbergh and Breckinridge's needs, it was Donovan.

Either at their own insistence or that of President Hoover, two old adversaries of Bill Donovan would soon be contacting the Lindbergh estate and offering their services: the attorney general of the United States, William D. Mitchell, and the head of the U.S. Bureau of Investigation, J. Edgar Hoover. Their being kept out of the investigation would be attributed to the superintendent of the New Jersey State Police: Colonel H. Norman Schwarzkopf.

H. Norman Schwarzkopf arrived at the Lindbergh estate toward midnight on March 1. The grounds around the main house had not been sealed off, and reporters and sightseers roamed the area at will, destroying essential evidence. Though this was identical to what had occurred ten years before in the Hall-Mills murders and was a failing for which the state police had shared severe criticism, Schwarzkopf initially did nothing to preserve the scene outside the Lindbergh house. He also rejected suggestions that bloodhounds be set on the trail of the kidnappers, by saying the animals were not available. Contradicted by a neighbor who claimed that several hundred of the dogs could have been rounded up and put into action, Schwarzie shifted explanations and said he had been told that bloodhounds were not effective when the ground was wet. This would come back to plague him, as would his adamancy at conducting a thorough inspection of the estate and surrounding terrain. He turned down the offer made by a Lindbergh family friend, Dr. John Grier Hibben, who was the president of Princeton University, to have his students mount a massive foot-by-foot search of the entire countryside. When Schwarzkopf did take direct action in those early hours, such as clearing the estate of media people and unauthorized visitors, it seemed to come at the behest of Lindbergh and his advisers.

Herbert Norman Schwarzkopf marched in the shadow of great men, and he was comfortable there. The first great man, in his estimation, was his father. Herbert was born in Newark, New Jersey, on August 28, 1895, the only child of second-generation German Americans. Disliking the nickname Bertie, he took an early lead from the disciplinarian father he both admired and adored, J. George Schwarzkopf, a jewelry designer, and dropped Herbert in favor of its initial. H. Norman graduated from Newark's Barringer High School and in June of 1913 entered the U.S. Military Academy at West Point. Schwarzie, or "the genial German gink," as he was known by his brother cadets, offset average grades with ferocious athletic overachievement and music.[3] Built somewhat like a beer keg, he played football, basketball, handball, and polo; he swam, boxed, was a sharpshooter, managed the handball team, and sang in the choir for three years. Schwarzie's ravenous appetite at the football-training table became legendary among his peers. Fourteen days after the United States officially went to war with Germany, he graduated from West Point with the ranking of 88 in a class of 136.

Lieutenant Schwarzkopf's cavalry regiment was converted into an artillery unit and sent to France as part of the American Expeditionary Force's recently created Third Division. He was put in command of D Battery, which joined the division at the Marne River in June of 1918. On July 15, the Boche attacked. Their shelling smashed the Allied artillery, and the French retreated. The Americans held and fought back the German onslaught. Lieutenant Schwarzkopf had survived his first ordeal by fire. He spent fifty more days of sporadic fighting at the front before being felled by mustard gas. His combat days over, he convalesced and entered the land of his ancestors, Germany, with the Army of Occupation. He spoke German and was made provost marshal of an agricultural area, where he also functioned as mayor and civil judge. Following a two-year absence, he returned to America a career officer.

Lieutenant Schwarzkopf's idol was General John J. ("Black Jack") Pershing, commander of the AEF, who had demanded the near superhuman from his men, remained aloof, and didn't care a hoot what anyone said about him as long as the job got done, qualities Schwarzie would attempt to emulate most of his life. Once stateside, he reported to the Seventh Cavalry at Fort Bliss, Texas, and was appointed assistant provost marshal for the El Paso district. His promotion to captain was followed by orders to lead a border-patrol unit that was on the lookout for Pancho Villa. Before he could assume command, his father fell ill.

On July 15, 1920, Captain H. Norman Schwarzkopf, the professional soldier (whose son one day would lead the coalition forces in Operation Desert Storm), resigned his commission and went home to New Jersey to care for his disabled parent. Among the civilian jobs he took was floorwalker at a local department store. One of the old friends he came in contact with had been a fellow officer in France, Captain Irving Edwards, whose father, Edward I. Edwards, was governor of New Jersey. The governor was searching for someone to organize and run the newly legislated state-police force. Irving Edwards urged Schwarzie to send in his application. H. Norman complied.

Most towns and rural villages in New Jersey, whether they had a constable or not, relied on the county detective in matters of serious crime. The state's larger municipalities and emerging industrial centers had their own police departments, which usually didn't need assistance from the county. As the automobile began to erode their protective cloak of distance, communities in the hinterlands demanded more extensive services. Some legislators thought the best way to achieve this was by creating a statewide police agency. The county detectives, who felt they were providing adequate protection, opposed the idea. They had powerful allies on both the right and the left. Conservative legislators perceived such a police force as an intrusion on home rule. Pro-labor politicians viewed it as another antiworker weapon in a state already noted for its union-busting tactics.

In 1921, after seven years of bitter and often divisive haggling, the New Jersey legislature voted on the bill introduced by Clarence E. Case, the senator from Somerset County, to create a state police. Party politics prevailed with the pro-police antilabor Republicans outpolling the antipolice pro-labor Democrats. Governor Edwards, a Democrat, vetoed the bill, only to be overridden by the state senate and assembly. On March 29, the creation of a state-sponsored police force was recorded as law.

Jersey City's power broker Democrat mayor, Frank Hague, who had initially opposed a state police—among other objections, he viewed it as a threat to his control over the existing urban police departments—now actively sought to place one of his underlings in charge of the newly enacted organization. Governor Edwards, a maverick who was beholden to Hague, surprised the Jersey City boss and most everyone else by picking an unknown former army officer to be superintendent, H. Norman Schwarzkopf, whose main qualifications for the job seemed to have been that he was nonpolitical and a friend of the governor's son.

Mediawise the new superintendent was an utter novice. Those papers that had endorsed the state-police bill tended to support his appointment and early progress. Many of those who fought the bill, predictably, were critical. It was with the individual reporters that Schwarzie had a hard time. He was described as a "cold fish,"[4] and a perception persisted of the superintendent's being a minor martinet without a sense of humor. Discrepancies regarding his past, the mother's milk of muckraking journalism, were found. According to military records, he was born in 1885 and was therefore thirty-six years old when he assumed the position. Certain papers were printing he was twenty-nine or even twenty-five. That the state's new anticrime czar had been a floorwalker became a standard gibe. His most ardent antagonist was Jersey City's *Jersey City Journal,* which had supported Frank Hague's choice for the post of state-police superintendent. A favorite rumor by detractors held that Schwarzie tended to fib not only about his age but about his height as well.

H. Norman Schwarzkopf organized and trained his initial group of state-police recruits in a thoroughly military fashion, thereby giving rise to criticism that he was creating a militia rather than a law-enforcement agency. He had little knowledge of civilian police procedures and crime and displayed small interest in the subject. Most everything about the newly created organization was military. Schwarzkopf's four aides-de-camp were former army officers, and the first state-police academy was comprised of army tents set up at the National Guard summer training ground at Sea Girt. Though they came from all walks of life, most of the trainees had seen military service. A portion of the men were drilled in the riding and care of horses. Others were prepared for operating motorcycles and automobiles.

Of the 116 recruits who started the first training camp, 66 graduated as troopers, and 15 were assigned other duties. Schwarzkopf designed a tailored, military-type uniform for his organization: tan boots, olive riding breeches, leather belt, and a dark blue fitted blouse with a roll collar. Officers sported a version of the Sam Browne belt that forced them to "brace" like a West Point cadet. The mounted troopers were issued U.S. Cavalry–style campaign hats. The motorcycle police and all other personnel wore stiff crown caps, which were designed to make them tuck in their chins and hold their heads erect. The three points of the triangular badge and shoulder patch on the uniform emphasized the motto of the new police force, "Honor—Duty—Fidelity," a paraphrase of the motto of West Point.

Superintendent Schwarzkopf was an absolute commander whose word was gospel. His General Order 1 set forth the mission of the trooper in the field: to prevent crime, to pursue and apprehend violators, to execute any lawful warrant or order of arrest, to give first aid to the injured, to act as warden in the protection of fish and game, to have the powers of motor vehicle inspectors, to be subject to the call of the governor, and to preserve law and order throughout the state.

On December 5, 1921, the first New Jersey State Police motorcycle unit mounted Harley-Davidsons and roared out on duty, generally in the central and northern parts of the state, where the roads were paved. The horseback troopers were assigned to the remote farms and villages in the southern portion of New Jersey, where dirt thoroughfares abounded. After six months of patrolling, the troopers had tallied 767 arrests for motor vehicle violations, including speeding, driving without a license, and drunken driving. The majority of their 431 criminal-violation arrests were for drunk and disorderly conduct and petty larceny and burglary. By the end of the year, Prohibition had reached New Jersey, and on Christmas Eve 1921 the state police raided their first still and seized two hundred gallons of hooch.[5]

As 1922 progressed, Schwarzkopf's police proved no match for New Jersey's rampaging bootleggers. Neither did anyone else, with the possible exception of Ellis Parker, Sr., a county detective with a national reputation for crime fighting and whose exploits had an uncanny knack of finding their way into newsprint. Schwarzie himself coveted publicity but was extremely sensitive to criticism. Troopers were instructed by Schwarzkopf to cut out and send in only those articles that depicted the superintendent and the state police in a positive light.[6] There weren't all that many, not in the larger city newspapers, anyway. When H. Norman did make contact with reporters, he was still awkward and often inept. Thanks in part to Ellis Parker, who had opposed the formation of the state police and who was a past master at chatting up news folk, the general impression prevailed that troopers were glorified traffic cops with no ability to conduct a criminal investigation. This image wasn't helped when in October of 1922, Governor Edwards ordered the state police to solve New Jersey's, and the nation's, most sensational and most publicized crime, the Hall-Mills murders. The troopers had only a minimal hand in the Hall-Mills investigations and trial, but they were to be stigmatized by the same accusations of inefficiency, stupidity, and incompetence that were leveled against those in charge of the monumentally bungled case.

Schwarzkopf had created no Scotland Yard, bragged of no first-rank detectives, and had no need of them until the evening of March 1, when the Lindbergh baby was reported missing.[7] If he and his men were beyond their element in having the jurisdictional responsibility to investigate what instantly became the most notorious crime of modern times, Schwarzkopf never let it be seen by reporters, from whom he tried to distance himself. From what the press could observe, he was perfectly content to let someone else deal with them, and he appeared peacock proud to be in the company of Lindbergh and his prestigious advisers, Henry Breckinridge and Congressional Medal of Honor–winner William J. Donovan.

7

SLEIGHT OF HAND

SORREL HILL HAD BECOME A BUSTLING COMMAND POST RULED ENTIRELY BY
Charles Lindbergh. The garage now included twenty police operators
manning the phones and Teletypes installed in an improvised communications center to which special cables from nearby Princeton were being
laid. Stringent secrecy was the order of the day. Lindbergh's rationale for
extreme security measures, echoed by Breckinridge, was his firmly stated
resolve to have a free, unfettered hand in dealing with the kidnappers,
with no interference by police or investigatory agencies of any ilk. In one
respect this proved effective. Even though they were being told there was
no ransom note, most everyone beyond Lindy's inner circle, including
law-enforcement organizations and the media, believed a message had
been left and anticipated the kidnappers' next move. They kept their
attention on the future meeting with the kidnappers and ignored the
past, particularly the specious past, which reporters and policemen rou-
tinely examine when it comes to crimes such as a kidnapping. There

would be one or two minor items in the New York papers about Lindbergh's missing the Waldorf-Astoria banquet the night before, March 1, and local scribblings that Anne's sister Elisabeth had not been seen for several days, but this was lost under a tidal wave of breaking stories on the child's abduction and the efforts to find him. The specious past, had anyone bothered to search in depth, might have provided answers to crucial questions to come.

By the afternoon of March 2, Lindbergh, who had gone without sleep, appeared not the least bit weary and seemed to oversee and direct every detail in the effort to recover the missing child. All personnel, police or civilian, answered to Lindy. Nothing could be done without his approval. He expected no one to disobey an order he had issued. But his dictates, like his determination to deal directly with the kidnappers, were subject to contradictions and inconsistencies.

Lindbergh and Breckinridge included Schwarzkopf in some but not all of their strategy meetings. This had more to do with the superintendent's keeping the police in check and out of the way than it did with policy decisions. One of Lindbergh's announced procedural objectives for making contact with the kidnappers was to do nothing to scare them off, and if the police had to sit on their hands, so be it. Schwarzkopf obliged by limiting the activities of his own troopers and the sprinkling of experienced men he had brought in from the Newark and Jersey City police departments. He performed an even greater service to the secrecy so cherished by Lindbergh in excluding almost every other investigatory organization—including New Jersey's county detectives, the New York City Police Department, and J. Edgar Hoover's Bureau of Investigation—from anything other than support roles, if that. This was as much a result of Schwarzkopf's xenophobia and thirst for control as it was to please Lindbergh. Schwarzkopf perceived his troopers to be more forceful and in control than they were. His animosity toward Hoover was particularly strong, and he was on the record, unofficially, for saying that he wouldn't mind taking over the bureau. When Governor Moore attempted to channel all volunteering outside law-enforcement agencies into a massive support system for the troopers, Schwarzie readily cooperated and rarely used any of the waiting manpower.

Lindbergh and his fellow planners were afforded even more privacy when Schwarzkopf moved the state-police manhunt headquarters from Sorrel Hill to Trenton while leaving troopers to man the communication nerve center in Lindy's garage. The change of headquarters also split news personnel between Trenton and the town of Hopewell.

One of the most debilitating restrictions Lindy imposed on Schwarz-kopf's investigators was his refusal to let them interview Anne Lindbergh and the family staff. The two Hopewell policemen and the troopers' Corporal Wolf had managed to ask a few cursory questions the night before, but there was far more that the police wanted to know.

While investigators accepted Lindbergh's explanation that the baby's cold was the reason the family was still at the estate on a Tuesday night—which, as we have seen, is partially contradicted by Anne Lindbergh's private correspondence—the predominant suspicion of those officers privy to the information had to do with what other person or persons also knew the infant was there. Since Lindy, Anne, and the Eaglet had never before remained at Sorrel Hill beyond Monday morning, how could the kidnappers have anticipated they would be there a day and a half later? The answer for many a state trooper and the handful of local police officers allowed to assist them was that it had been an inside job—that a member of the household staff had tipped off the abductors. Lindbergh dismissed such suggestions out of hand. He vouched for the integrity of his employees. The ban on talking to them remained—a prohibition that included the twenty-four-member household staff at his mother-in-law's estate in Englewood.

Lieutenant Arthur T. ("Buster") Keaten of the New Jersey State Police disobeyed Lindbergh's edict and engaged Betty Gow in casual conversation. She let it drop that her boyfriend, Finn Henrik ("Red") Johnsen, not only knew she was at Hopewell on Tuesday helping with the sick baby but had called her there at approximately 8:45 P.M.[1] When Betty explained the circumstances for having to cancel their date, Red told her he would drive to West Hartford, Connecticut, and spend the evening at his brother's home.

Lieutenant Keaten now had an answer for how the kidnappers learned the baby was still at the estate on Tuesday night—and the state police had their first prime suspect in the crime. An alert went out for Red Johnsen. Rumors spread among reporters that indeed it was an "inside job."

Confronted with this new information, Lindbergh let troopers talk further with Gow, which they did at length on March 3. That same day they were able to interview Ollie Whateley about Betty's arrival and activities at Hopewell on March 1. It would be another week before the police would be allowed to obtain statements from Anne Lindbergh and Elsie Whateley.

While continuing to insist that no ransom note had been left, Lindbergh agreed to a public action that was generally associated with the receipt of word from a kidnapper: He announced the appointment of "go-betweens" to deal with the felons holding his son. The use of go-betweens—intermediaries acceptable to both parties—was a common practice for families of snatch victims. The two men selected to fill this role for the Lindberghs were Douglas G. Thompson, a former mayor of Englewood, and the late Dwight Morrow's secretary, Arthur Springer. The press gave this announcement maximum coverage, thereby ensuring the kidnappers would know.

But if Lindbergh's professed intention was to demonstrate to the kidnappers that he was cooperating fully, following their written instructions to the word, why risk offering them something they hadn't requested: go-betweens? All the ransom note had demanded was fifty thousand dollars and that he not contact the police.

Another violation of the ransom-message instructions, and one that received far less notoriety in the press than the naming of go-betweens, was Lindbergh's employment of several other men. The night before, Lindy had hired a local mountaineer, who was a former sheriff, to track the footsteps found on the grounds.

But then why had he refused to let H. Norman Schwarzkopf employ bloodhounds at approximately the same time? Lindbergh refused to accept any questions on the subject, just as he declined comment when he refused the offer of his friend the president of Princeton to provide a foot-by-foot search of the estate and nearby terrain by his student body.

While Lindbergh recruited the mountaineer, Henry Breckinridge brought in his own investigators, a pair of private eyes, William E. Galvin and John Fogarty. Even before this, Robert Thayer, the young attorney in William J. Donovan's New York law office, as well as a family friend of the Lindberghs', had very definite ideas on who should be contacted.

As Lindbergh's highly publicized vigil for word from the kidnappers to make contact continued, Schwarzkopf, good on his word not to interfere, kept his men busy in other areas. Cars throughout the state were being stopped and examined in the hope that the baby might be inside. The same was being done in adjoining New York, Pennsylvania, and Delaware. Troopers manning the garage communication center were exchanging information with law-enforcement agencies conducting a nine-state manhunt that included an estimated one hundred thousand law-enforcement officers. Call-in tips were being received by the hundreds. Beyond this, impromptu searches, which Lindbergh and Breckinridge very well may not have anticipated, had sprung up across the country. It was already the largest manhunt in American history, and it was accelerating.

Henry Breckinridge held press conferences every evening at eleven. For newswoman Laura Vitray it seemed that his main concern was making sure the Lindbergh story stayed on the front page. His information seemed always to be accurate. Vitray recalls that whenever he gave a bulletin out at the front gate of Sorrel Hill, the reporters did a swift marathon to the farmhouse up the road with the five-party telephone. "To the thinner belongs the spoils," she says, "and they usually held the line long enough for their paper to go to press."[2]

Thursday, March 3, began with widespread radio appeals to the kidnappers to start negotiations with the go-betweens and with pledges of secrecy by the Lindberghs. The lead newspaper stories dealt with a bogus ransom postcard received from Boston, a spreading land-sea-air search as "abduction stirs whole nation," President Herbert Hoover's putting all federal agents on the search, New York City's entire nineteen-thousand-man police force being ordered out on "Lindbergh duty," the parents of the baby waiting for a direct proposal from "daring abductors whose window sill note warned them not to call police," speculation that the kidnappers might ask that the ransom be dropped by plane, the number of stolen cars being traced, Mrs. Lindbergh being quoted as having said she believed the kidnap gang had watched their home for weeks, looking for a chance to steal the baby (even though she would not be officially interviewed by the police for seven more days), false "clews" by the score being traced in the kidnapping hunt, cars across the country being watched for blond, blue-eyed boy babies, the number of cars being stopped and searched, pressure on the U.S. House of Representatives to enact a federal antikidnapping bill, various profiles on who the abductor might be, the number of phone-in tips being received, and London's perception that the United States was ruled by gangsters. The lead photograph in one paper was of the three-section ladder; that in another was of the baby and his pet dog, Wahgoosh.

The front-page news for March 4 told of the search in Detroit and Chicago for an old-time kidnapper and his girlfriend and of the search by the New Jersey State Police for the boyfriend of Betty Gow, the missing baby's nurse. The headline in the *New York Post* let it be known that LINDBERGH GETS WORD FROM KIDNAPPERS. It was not true, but the *Post* had adopted a policy of identifying the source of such information, as the opening paragraph of the story attests: "Hopewell NJ, March 4—Lieutenant Walter J. Coughlin of the New Jersey State troopers informed newspaper men at Trenton this morning that Colonel Charles A. Lindbergh received a message 'from the kidnappers' of his infant son."

— — —

Three-hundred-pound Paul T. ("Pop") Gebhart could hardly find time to be interviewed and wasn't sure he should be, considering the tragedy that had happened up the hill at Colonel Lindbergh's place. But dodging reporters wasn't all that easy when everywhere you turned there were more reporters. An erstwhile plumber, forty-eight-year-old Pop was the proprietor of Hopewell's leading hostelry and luncheonette, Gebhart's Hotel. "Ain't never seen anything like it," he said, referring to the horde of media people who had descended on a town of less than a thousand inhabitants. Gebhart's establishment was in the center of Hopewell and usually closed at 9:00 P.M., but since the night of the kidnapping it had been open around the clock. "Despite the fact that we got seventeen rooms and ain't had a lot of trouble filling 'em before with railroad and Western Union men, I ain't never seen a business like this before."

With a telephone that didn't stop ringing and waitresses who hadn't slept since the fateful night, Gebhart estimated the overflow crowd of reporters, photographers, sound men, and everyone else "professionally interested" in the crime had resulted in a thousand people clamoring for "hamburgers with" and "hotdogs without." Gebhart went on to say, "All of us around here pity the Colonel, wish him success in his efforts to find his boy."

One reporter credited Pop with having made the famous sandwiches that Lindy ate during his flight to Paris in 1927, but Pop didn't want to comment on this other than to say he wasn't any hero. "I never had such business as now, but I'm sorry it had to come the way it did." Then Pop went off and joined Ma in an overheated kitchen, where "hundreds of dishes were being prepared for men more than fed up with the weary journey up to the Lindbergh establishment."[3]

The most interviewed person in Hopewell was Constable Charles W. Williamson, the first man to be called by the Lindbergh household and told of the kidnapping, among the first to reach the estate, and the only one to admit to reporters he was present when the ransom note was read. Since one of his chores for the Hopewell PD was directing traffic in front of Pop Gebhart's hotel, Charlie was very accessible to newspeople. The more he was interviewed, the more he tended to expand his role in the investigation, at the expense of his chief and the state police. Williamson's account of having seen footprints that led from outside the nursery to the ladder sections and on to the lane was a nagging reminder that the scene had not been properly protected, that every footprint except one had been obliterated, and that no mold was made of that solitary surviving bit of evidence.

Laura Vitray interviewed Williamson and subsequently referred to him as Chief Williamson. Her paper had taken an office at Gebhart's Hotel, and she had talked to most anyone else she could find around Hopewell. Vitray was harsh about the state troopers' indifference to many tips she considered to be promising. Though she was partial to Henry Breckinridge and usually believed what he had to say, Vitray was confused by a press release he had distributed and was appearing on front pages in the form the reporters had received it: a letter from the Lindberghs to the kidnappers:

> Mrs. Lindbergh and I desire to make a personal contact
> with the kidnappers of our child.

Our only interest is in his immediate and safe return and we feel certain that the kidnappers will realize that this interest is strong enough to justify promises that we may make in connection with his return.

We urge those who have the child to select any representative that they desire to meet a representative of ours who will be suitable to them at any time and at any place that they may designate.

If this is accepted, we promise that we will keep whatever arrangements that may be made by their representative and ours strictly confidential, and we further pledge ourselves that we will not try to injure in any way those connected with the return of the child.

Charles A. Lindbergh's signature appeared in the lower right-hand corner, directly above the signature of Anne Lindbergh.

What gave Laura Vitray pause was that the Lindberghs again seemed to be treating the kidnappers as if they were people of intellect. What is their perception of a criminal? she asked. Who do they think they are in today's age?[4]

She may have been on to something.

— — —

On March 2 of 1932, Colonel Schwarzkopf wasted no time in acceding to Lindbergh's request that the state troopers step aside so that Lindy and his advisers could deal directly with the kidnappers of his infant son or do anything else required to ensure the safe return of his baby. This was not an unusual demand or concession with kidnappings for ransom that involved rich and prominent people in America. That the superintendent agreed so rapidly might have been due in part to his regard for the Lone Eagle.

The reins of the investigation lay more firmly than ever in the hands of Lindbergh and Breckinridge, and controlling the press was still among their top priorities.

— — —

H. Norman was not a man who comprehended or practiced grand deceit. In the steaming political climate of New Jersey, he might have been better off if he did. He had created the state police and managed to keep the organization free of politics. But he and his men had suffered at the hands of local power brokers—and at the hands of the press, whom he never quite understood. Stoic, rigid, and vain, Schwarzkopf was a military man who knew how to give orders and obey them. His association with Lindbergh and Breckinridge was to serve them far better than himself.

8

NOBLE GANGSTERS

WHETHER THEY LOVED THE LINDBERGHS, AS MILLIONS DID, OR DISLIKED them, as a surprisingly large number seemed to, Americans were fascinated by every aspect of the child's disappearance, including the house on Sorrel Hill. At a time when only 65 percent of the nation was electrified—in rural areas like Hopewell, only 10 percent of the homes had electricity—the interior of the Lindbergh home was a peek into the scientific and industrial promise of the country, a preview of what most citizens would eventually possess.

When it came to consumer goods, the Lindberghs were among the one out of every five citizens who owned a car. They and fifteen million other families, or approximately 30 percent of the country's households, had telephones. Over a million refrigerators had been manufactured the previous year and half a million washing machines—and according to what articles you read, the Lindberghs had one or the other or both. Electric ranges were just becoming popular, and twelve million families already owned radios—and it was not unusual for a manufacturer and, particularly, salesmen to aver that their product was the one used by Charles and Anne, who steadfastly declined to make product endorsements.

The Lindberghs, their calamity, and what they had and had not were the nation's diversion, a fleeting respite from the all-oppressive Great Depression. America the first week of March 1932—and 1932 would prove to be the worst year of the depression—was a country with one foot firmly rooted in twentieth-century production-line technology and the other mired in the agrarian past. The population stood at 122.7 million, and the average life expectancy was sixty-one years. Unemployment had jumped from four million to eight million, which meant that one out of every fifteen Americans was out of work. Spending power was drastically reduced, and so was manufacturing. Some 28,300 businesses had failed in the last year, suicides and chow lines established new records, and bank closings reached a peak of 507 in one month.

Business shutdowns and layoffs had popularized the five-day work week and created a new dilemma: what to do with the newly imposed leisure. Despite hard times and tight money, Americans chose to spend on entertainment. Half their amusement dollars went for vacation travel, where a two-month worldwide steamship voyage could be had for under one thousand dollars—20 percent down and a year to pay the balance. One of the period's rages was miniature golf, on which $125 million was spent in 1931 alone. Marathon dancing, with its cash rewards to the winners, became a national addiction, as did flagpole and tree sitting and backgammon. The very rich were cautious, if not embarrassed by their resplendent life-style, and so continued to give up their large country estates and move to the city, where they replaced lavish balls with dining out at select restaurants and bistros, thereby creating what was being called café society.

The Lindberghs, who had the means to fly where and when they liked, shared two major pastimes popular with their fellow Americans and the balance of the depression-racked Western world: taking a spin in a motorcar and going to the movies. Moviegoing in America was an attractive diversion, especially when it occurred in one of the more luxurious theaters, massive and ornate palaces that made it all the easier to escape for several hours from the realities of the depression-time world outside, particularly if the main attractions were a musical or a comedy. Europe, too, was constructing movie palaces. The recreation that remained uniquely American was frequenting a speakeasy—something the Lindberghs were not on record as having done.

This is not to say Charles Lindbergh didn't betray more than a passing interest in the mobsters who ran the speakeasies, as well as in criminals in general. By the onset of the kidnapping, not only did they hold a fascination for Lindy, but in many instances he came to trust and rely on them more than on law-enforcement agencies. Assuming my supposition is correct, this might have been expected. If his master plan were to work, criminals would have to participate.

Prohibition had evolved a new economic and social curiosity: the rich, influential, and often-glamorized gangster. Americans, with their inveterate reverence for the frontiersman-type hero, had begun to confuse those hearty, self-reliant loners like Daniel Boone who ventured beyond the territorial bounds of their society with sociopathic loners who stood against their society—crooks. Lurid criminal reportage that the twenty-four-newspaper empire of William Randolph Hearst helped perfect was the inspiration for a subdivision of Hollywood's bustling motion picture industry known as the B movie.[1]

While D. W. Griffith was making his first talkie and Greta Garbo was also speaking for the first time, on the set of *Anna Christie,* the studio back lots were cranking out B crime movies with titles like *Up the River* and *Outside the Law.* Often the gangster runs a speakeasy and rubs shoulders with glamorous society girls, a case of art copying life. Crime never paid on the silver screen, or at least the gangster was always punished for his illicit activities, usually by being shot to death or electrocuted. But audiences were developing a genuine affection for the mobsters and racketeers, particularly when the roles were cast with actors such as Jimmy Cagney, Edward G. Robinson, Humphrey Bogart, and Spencer Tracy, all of whom spent their early Hollywood days portraying quite a few bad guys. Before the kidnapping two of the four gained stardom playing gangsters in a pair of milestone productions: Edward G. Robinson was Little Caesar; Jimmy Cagney, the Public Enemy. One of Broadway's most respected dramatic actors, Paul Muni, had agreed to go before the cameras in the coming months as the lead in a motion picture entitled *Scarface: The Shame of a Nation,* a fictionalized version of the rise and fall of America's most notorious, and often most admired, badman, Al Capone, who was currently in jail. Capone, directly and indirectly, would soon try to impose himself on the Lindbergh investigation. So would other criminals, several of whom were personal friends of people close to Lindy. By March 3, word was out that Al disapproved of the kidnapping—a condemnation not to be taken lightly in underworld circles.

- - -

Two real-life gangsters who had recently fared better with the legal system than Big Al Capone, but worse with the competition, were well versed in ransom kidnapping and its consequences: Jack ("Legs") Diamond and Vincent ("Mad Dog") Coll, né Collins. Eight days before Christmas of 1931, the Rensselaer County Court in Troy, New York, found Legs innocent of kidnapping a rival bootlegger and his assistant. Three days after Christmas in New York City, twenty-three-year-old Mad Dog was acquitted of killing five-year-old Michael Vengali, who had been caught in a cross of machine gun fire.

Coll managed to stay alive almost another six weeks before he was tommy-gunned to death on February 7, 1931, while telephoning from a West Twenty-third Street, New York City, outdoor booth. Legs didn't even last twelve hours. Following his trial in Troy, he returned to Albany and an acquittal party in his honor at Freddy Young's speakeasy on Broadway, across from the railroad station. He drank heavily, then ducked out of Young's, dropped in on Marian ("Kiki") Roberts, his girlfriend, and later took a taxi to his ten-dollar-a-week Dove Street boardinghouse.[2] Legs was so drunk the cab driver had to help him to his room and pour him into bed. Around 4:50 A.M. three or four men entered the room and killed him with three bullets in the head. It was widely suspected that Brooklyn beer lord Salvatore Spitale had arranged for the rub out and may have been one of the hit men.

Coll's execution was generally attributed to his blood feud with Dutch Schultz, but the author William Kennedy believes it was most likely ordered by New York City's most powerful mobster, Owen ("Owney") Madden, in retaliation for the Mad Dog's kidnapping earlier that year of Madden's partner, Big Frenchy Demange, a snatch in which Legs Diamond acted as the go-between.[3] Madden had paid the ransom negotiated by Diamond, and Big Frenchy was released. It was widely held that Legs not only masterminded the entire caper but that he used a chunk of the ransom money to pay the lawyers in his Rensselaer County trial for kidnapping.

Whatever the true facts, Madden and Spitale would soon find their way to Sorrel Hill and meet with Charles Lindbergh.

Racketeers kidnapping other racketeers had been commonplace in Chicago and several other large cities as the bootlegging-spawned mobs fought for territory and supremacy in the halcyon days of Prohibition. By 1930, gangs had formed in the Midwest that specialized in kidnapping wealthy members of communities for ransom. Extortionists got into the act even earlier, as had been the case in April of 1929, when fifteen-year-old Milton Academy student Constance Morrow, Anne's younger sister, received a letter that threatened her with mutilation and death if fifty thousand dollars was not left at a location to be designated later.

By the beginning of 1932, the kidnapping for ransom of rich and well-to-do people had accelerated to the point where two groups of prominent citizens, one from St. Louis and the other from Chicago, had joined forces and were testifying before the U.S. House of Representatives Judiciary Committee in support of their proposed Cochran bill, which called for making the crime a federal offense punishable by death. They presented statistics showing that 279 persons had been kidnapped in twenty-eight states during the previous year. The Associated Press had already set the 1931 figure of reported kidnappings at 208 but estimated that unreported incidents were probably ten times that number. Others appearing before the committee tended to agree that the majority of perpetrations were not reported and that most likely several thousand kidnappings had been committed during the year.[4]

By March of 1932, an escalating fear within the nation's business community seems to have come true: that with the possible demise of Prohibition no further away than the November elections, more mobsters than ever would turn to kidnapping for ransom as their alternate source of revenue. And why not? The crime was easy to perpetrate and get away with because the families of most victims preferred paying the money without contacting authorities and also because there were few standardized laws concerning it. There were no federal statutes regarding kidnapping and little likelihood the Cochran bill or some other legislation would be passed. With no national law or agency to combat the crime—the FBI was still the BI, the Bureau of Investigation, which was without the authority and wherewithal to investigate anything much besides white slavery—the pursuit and prosecution of kidnappers fell to the individual states. Punishment in seven states included the death penalty. Life imprisonment was the maximum sentence in sixteen other states. In the remaining twenty-five states prison terms varied from one to seven years (in Colorado) to ten to ninety years (in New Mexico). While all forty-eight states had kidnapping legislation, laws specifically recognizing kidnapping for ransom existed in only twenty-five of them.

A region highly conducive to the perpetration of a successful kidnapping for ransom was the four-state area of Connecticut, New York, New Jersey, and Pennsylvania. No greater concentration of wealth existed anywhere else in the country, including fortunes such as that of the late Dwight W. Morrow, whose estate had been publicized to be worth twenty million dollars, and that of his son-in-law, Colonel Charles A. Lindbergh, an estimated two million dollars. Cooperation between interstate law-enforcement agencies was minimal. New York City alone was one of the nation's largest repositories of criminals and criminal-support systems, including expert forgers who could concoct untraceable ransom messages; money changers who would swap hot ransom bills for unmarked, usable currency; and in the case of apprehension, the finest criminal lawyers in the land. Hostility existed between the NYPD and most every other police agency.

Pennsylvania's penalty for kidnapping was a thousand-dollar fine and a fifteen-year maximum prison term; Connecticut's, imprisonment for not more than thirty years; New York's, imprisonment for not less than ten years nor more than fifty years. New Jersey's punishment had included the death penalty; then in 1928 it was amended to thirty years to life imprisonment. New Jersey did have a felony murder statute, however, which mandated that if during the commission of a felony a victim was accidentally killed, the perpetrator could be tried and executed for murder.

─ ─ ─

"If you ever have friends who are involved in a kidnapping case," Morris ("Mickey") Rosner had once told attorney Robert Thayer of William Donovan's New York City law office, "get in touch with me because I know how to handle this type of case."[5] On March 2, Thayer reminded Rosner of this and asked if there was anything he could do regarding the Lindbergh snatch. A convicted felon, Rosner was currently out on bail for grand larceny in connection with the sale of fraudulent stocks. A previous conviction and jail sentence for an obstruction-of-justice violation had been reversed. Rosner, who boasted friendships with such well-known gangsters as Waxy Gordon, Legs Diamond, and Owney Madden, had supposedly done undercover work for the Department of Justice and was vouched for by two U.S. senators. Mickey very much wanted to be involved in the Lindbergh kidnapping, and it was characteristic of him to upgrade his own importance rather than credit Thayer with seeking him out. He would claim it was Congresswoman Ruth Pratt who had contacted her good friend, and Thayer's boss, Bill Donovan in his behalf and said, "You must put Morris Rosner on that case."[6]

Thirty-one-year-old Harvard-educated Bob Thayer was Ruth Pratt's son-in-law. His wife, like her congresswoman mother, was an heiress to the Standard Oil fortune. The Thayers, who counted Charles and Anne Lindbergh among their friends, were a popular part of New York City's café-society set, which had helped turn the illegal speakeasies and gambling joints around town into a booming business.

Thayer had represented Mickey Rosner in the past, and the two men had stayed in touch. Rosner, a nervous bantam-cock braggart and self-promoting contact man, had the reputation of being "a rather clever individual" who "had never double-crossed either the underworld or overworld."[7] What better way to discover which crook or gang had the missing baby than through Morris Rosner's criminal contacts? Bill Donovan, a man known to appreciate a good drink and understand big-time racketeering, voiced no objection to Rosner's being brought in. When mob kingpin Owney Madden, with whom Donovan had once shared a liquor locker, heard about the idea, he was dumbstruck, but by then it would be too late.[8]

Bob Thayer caught up with Rosner on March 2 at the East Thirty-fifth Street court, where Mickey was suing his sister to collect on a five-hundred-dollar note she had given him. Thayer got the judge to expedite the proceedings, then asked Rosner to do what he could about the Lindbergh kidnapping. An hour later Mickey called the lawyer and said he had received very important information, the nature of which he could not discuss but insisted Thayer relay the message to Lindbergh himself. Donovan told Thayer to do nothing unless Rosner was more explicit.[9]

At approximately 4:00 P.M., after having phoned every half hour, Rosner came to see Thayer and related that a very well known man in the underworld with a record of kidnapping had disappeared just before the Eaglet was taken. He said that the underworld was convinced this man had something to do with the crime. According to Rosner, the underworld, if authorized by the Lindbergh family, would do everything it could to recover the child. He also claimed he was a great personal friend of the chief of Unione Sicilione, who could have his entire organization out looking for the kidnappers and gathering information. Donovan relayed what had transpired to Henry Breckinridge, who was willing to hear out Rosner.

Breckinridge and one of his private investigators, Captain William E. Galvin, met with Rosner at Thayer's New York City home later that same day. The man the underworld suspected of knowing about the crime was Abie Wagner, a snatch artist and machine gun specialist. To locate Wagner or others with information, Rosner said he would have to send emissaries to various gang leaders throughout the country, including Owney Madden, Waxy Gordon, and Salvatore Spitale in New York, the Purple gang in Detroit, Bobo Hoff in Philadelphia, and the successor to Al Capone in Chicago. He would require ten emissaries in all, and each would have to be paid $250.

While Rosner waited upstairs for a decision on his proposal, Thayer told Breckinridge and Galvin that neither he nor Bill Donovan could recommend paying the money because they didn't fully trust Rosner. Breckinridge replied that since he and Lindbergh were absolutely in the dark as to who took the baby, the current strategy was to get all the help possible from any quarter, to go to any length to obtain information.

Rosner was given twenty-five hundred dollars in cash and told to initiate his plan. He stipulated two provisos, which were agreed to by Breckinridge: that he not be followed or interfered with by the police and that the Lindbergh family should insist the U.S. Secret Service be kept away because the underworld feared them. Rosner went to the phone and called several numbers. It wasn't long before two men arrived and were shown to another room in the Thayer house. Rosner peeled off approximately five hundred dollars from the bankroll and put part of the cash in one trouser pocket and the balance in the other; then he joined the two visitors, whom he hadn't bothered to introduce or identify. The men departed with Rosner telling Thayer that the pair was going directly to Chicago. Thayer would later learn that one of the two men worked for Salvatore Spitale, the Brooklyn beer-lord questioned in regard to the Legs Diamond murder, and that Rosner had only given him twenty dollars to go see his boss.[10]

That same evening at Sorrel Hill, Morris Rosner was introduced to Charles Lindbergh. His visit, like Thayer's contacting him, was kept secret from Colonel H. Norman Schwarzkopf and his New Jersey State Police. After talking with Lindbergh and members of the household staff, Rosner asked to see, and was shown, the ransom note. Three versions exist as to what occurred next. One report holds that Rosner was given a photostatic copy of the note; another, that a tracing, not a Photostat, was made; the third, that he took the actual note with him back to New York City, where he had copies made. In any event, early on March 3, copies of the ransom note, or possibly the original, began being shown around New York City's underworld in hopes that the style would be recognized and the writer revealed. There, at the bottom of the message, for all to see, was the "secret signature" of interlacing circles and perforations. The criminals to whom Rosner displayed the message included expert forgers and extortionists—who were not above copying a kidnapper's ransom note and extorting the money for themselves.

On the premise that the Lindbergh scenario had allowed for two possibilities regarding the nonexistent kidnappers, the first, and most likely, was that no one would respond to the ransom letter that had been left in the nursery, that after an extended manhunt the state police would give up the search for the missing child and the matter would be forgotten without anyone's being affected by the conspiracy to cover up what had really happened to the child.

The second possibility in the scenario, a long shot and the most desired for pivotal action, was now actually happening: The underworld had been viewing the note and the secret symbol. The question was, What extortionist, if any, would take the bait—copy the message's style and try to claim the ransom as his own? If this did occur, then the manhunt could turn into a long and arduous struggle to catch up with the extortionist, thereby further isolating and obscuring the actual killer.

9

GO-BETWEENS

WITH A NATIONAL EPIDEMIC OF KIDNAPPINGS PLAGUING THE LAND, LIND-bergh and his Sorrel Hill advisers appeared aware of two specific rules by which the snatch gangs played: Ransom messages from the kidnappers were usually answered in newspaper ads, and go-betweens were often selected to deal with the release of the victim. The ransom note found in the nursery March 1 mentioned nothing about the use of go-betweens. Even so, on March 2, Lindbergh, who was still denying that a ransom note was left, named Douglas G. Thompson and Arthur Springer to be his negotiators with the kidnappers, an act that implied a ransom communication had indeed been received. By midafternoon of the following day, Mickey Rosner's attempt to usurp Thompson and Springer ran into a major stumbling block: Owney Madden, one of the most powerful mobsters in New York. Suspecting that Rosner was in league with federal agents, Madden was reluctant to cooperate in Mickey's proposed plan. A panicky Rosner wasn't to be denied.

At 11:00 P.M. that night, March 3, Rosner had attorney Robert

Thayer drive him to Broadway and Forty-seventh Street. Getting out of the car, he told Thayer to wait, warning that if he didn't return within an hour, it meant he was in serious trouble and that help should be sought. He had not mentioned Madden by name but left little doubt that was who he was about to see. Rosner entered a building, came out within the hour highly agitated, and asked to talk to Colonel Donovan. Donovan was in Albany, so Thayer arranged for them to confer with Henry Breckinridge. The three men rendezvoused at a Princeton, New Jersey, luncheonette at 4:00 A.M., March 4. Rosner, who still had not identified Madden, told Breckinridge that he had just met with someone who had definite information concerning the kidnapping and that this person had imposed two conditions for cooperating with them: The Lindberghs must exonerate the kidnappers upon the safe return of the child, and Rosner must be given a clear, untapped phone wire from the Lindbergh home so that this person could be reached without fear of federal or local police interference.

They proceeded on to Sorrel Hill and entered into a long conference with Lindbergh and Schwarzkopf, who for the first time learned of the Rosner connection. Schwarzkopf and Lindy went along with the terms being imposed by Rosner.[1] William Galvin drafted a soon-to-be-issued statement by the Lindberghs that exonerated the kidnappers—and when it appeared in print, it prompted New Jersey's attorney general to serve notice that neither Lindbergh nor the state police had the power to grant immunity.

The Lindbergh house was now both a command post and dormitory. The Breckinridges had moved into one of the bedrooms, and Henry's private investigators, Fogarty and Galvin, occupied another. At night many of the large rooms downstairs were fitted out with cots and bedrolls for the detectives and policemen who worked there on kidnapping business during the day. Rosner was given his own room and provided with a clear telephone line—a line the Bureau of Investigation would later claim had been tapped by the state police. During the day and through the night of March 4, Rosner stationed himself at the phone. Every now and then he would dial a number and say, "This is X. Have you any news for me?" No one seemed to.[2]

Over a thousand letters and cards were contained in the Saturday morning, March 5, mail that was delivered to the estate. Sorting through it with the trooper assigned to the task, Lindbergh himself picked out an envelope that had been sent at 9:00 P.M. the evening before from a post office station near Borough Hall, Brooklyn, New York. He opened it.

The pencil-written message seemed to be in the same hand as the one left in the nursery by the kidnappers. Unlike the previous note, which had been a single-sheet communication, the text of this message required two full pages. Lindbergh, as he had done with the ransom note found in the nursery March 1, had someone else read the text aloud, in this case the officer in charge of the mail.

> Dear Sir,
> We have warned you note to make
> anything public also notify the police
> now you have take consequences—
> means we will have to hold the baby until everything
> is quiet. We can note make any appointments
> just now. We know very well what it
> means to us. It is realy necessary to
> make a world affair out of this, or to
> get your back as soon as possible
> to settle those affair in a quick way
> will be better for both such. Dont be
> afraid about the baby—
> keeping care of us day and night.
> We also feed him
> according to diet

The right-hand lower corner of the page had the same "signature" as the previous message: three perforated holes across a solid circle of red inside two larger, interlacing circles. The second page contained this message:

> We are interested to send him back in
> gut heal. And ransom was made aus for 50000 $
> but now we have to take another person to it and
> probably have to keep the baby for a longer time as we
> expected. So the amount will be 70000
> 20000 in 50$ bills 25000 $ in 20 $ bill 15000 $
> in 10$ bills and 10000 in 5$ bills Don't mark
> any bills or take them from one serial nomer.
> We will form you latter were to deliver the
> money. But we will note do so until the
> Police is out of cace and the pappers are quite.

The kidnaping we prepared in years so we
are prepared for everyding.[3]

Lindbergh brought the message to Galvin, who was looking it over
when Rosner came in. According to Thayer, Rosner, on reading the text
for himself, "turned very white and was trembling all over."[4] Rosner
took the letter with him and was driven by state troopers to see Henry
Breckinridge in New York City. Breckinridge and Rosner returned to
Sorrel Hill around midnight, bringing with them Salvatore Spitale, Irving
Bitz, and Mr. Bartow (most likely Frank D. Bartow, a Morgan and Company partner), a representative of J. P. Morgan and Company, which had
volunteered to arrange for the ransom money.

A former dance-hall bouncer who had muscled his way to power in the
underworld during the booming Prohibition days, Salvatore ("Salvy")
Spitale was a mob boss who controlled a good portion of Brooklyn's
illicit beer trade, owned restaurants, and lived in an expensive Manhattan apartment on Central Park West. Salvy was credited with having
brought his old pal Jack ("Legs") Diamond into the rackets and with
later having Legs executed, a murder he might have seen to personally.
Spitale's police record showed numerous arrests and no convictions.
Irving Bitz's importance in criminal circles was that he was Spitale's
cohort.

At Sorrel Hill late that night of March 5, and on through the early
hours of the morning, Bartow, Thayer, Breckinridge, and Charles Lindbergh conferred with gangsters Spitale, Bitz, and Rosner. When the meeting ended, Douglas G. Thompson and Arthur Springer had been
downgraded as Lindbergh's official go-betweens. The morning papers of
Sunday, March 6, carried a statement explaining the change:

> If the kidnappers of our child are unwilling to deal directly,
> we fully authorize "Salvy" Spitale and Irving Bitz to act as
> our go-betweens. We will also follow any other method
> suggested by the kidnapper that we can be sure will bring
> the return of our child.
>
> Charles A. Lindbergh
> Anne Lindbergh

One reason why Rosner had urged Lindbergh and Breckinridge to use Spitale and Bitz was that they headed a large gang of Italians and Jews who could immediately be put to work combing the underworld. During their visit to the estate, Salvy and Bitz had been introduced to Anne Lindbergh, who wrote her mother-in-law that she had met two "underworld kings" who she was convinced would be helpful—two men who had shown more sincerity in their sympathy than a lot of the politicians who'd been to the house.[5]

Reading that two local hoodlums had been named Lindy's representatives, New York City's police commissioner, Edward P. Mulrooney, was outraged. So were civic and religious leaders and newspaper editors across the land.[6] A rash of criticism was directed at Colonel H. Norman Schwarzkopf for having allowed Lindbergh to consort with gangsters.

Owney Madden wasn't happy either. During the night-long conference with Spitale, Bitz, and Rosner at the Lindbergh house, Madden had called and talked with Mickey while Thayer listened in. Told that Spitale and Bitz were there, Madden had expressed his anger and said they couldn't do any good in recovering the baby. Madden further predicted that Lindbergh would hear from the kidnappers again on Tuesday, and before hanging up, he instructed Rosner to call him every hour. When Rosner learned that Thayer had repeated Madden's prediction to Lindbergh, Breckinridge, Galvin, and Fogarty, he became incensed. He denied that Madden had said anything of the sort and accused Thayer of not understanding how to interpret the meaning of Madden's language. While Spitale and Bitz established their manhunt headquarters in a Forty-first Street, New York City, speakeasy, Rosner and Thayer manned the secure phone at the Lindbergh house through the night and into the next day, with no results.[7]

During the afternoon of March 6, some twelve hours after the meeting with Spitale and Bitz took place, a telegram had come to the Lindbergh estate and was shown to Rosner. It read

Communicate with me at once regarding your boy's whereabouts—for further particulars telephone HArlem 7-1147

Rev. Berritella

Rosner called the number and asked the person who answered to come immediately to Hopewell. Around 2:00 P.M. a message was received from Rev. Berritella, who was in nearby Princeton. Rosner and Breckinridge went to interview him and found that he was accompanied by Mary Cirrito, a medium. The party proceeded to a room in the Princeton Inn, where Berritella conducted a seance in which the medium Mary stated the child was in a house four and half miles northwest of the Lindbergh estate. When asked if any message had been received from the kidnappers, Breckinridge replied in the negative. The medium then said that Breckinridge should not remain in Hopewell but should be at his office in New York City every morning at 9:00 A.M.

Henry Breckinridge did not heed the advice and was not present when at 1:00 P.M. on Tuesday, March 8, a letter addressed to him was delivered to his office at 25 Broadway, New York City. Inside was a sealed envelope and an unsigned note from the kidnappers that asked that the envelope be given to Lindbergh. An office associate brought it to Princeton Junction, where Breckinridge and Rosner were waiting. The country had already expressed its disapproval of the use of two gangsters, Spitale and Bitz, as go-betweens. Now the kidnappers had their say:

> Dear sir: Did you receive ouer letter from March
> 4. we sent the mail in one off the letter—near
> Boro Hall, Brooklyn. We know Police interfer with
> your privatmail. How can we come to any
> arrangements this way. in the future we will send
> out letter to Mr. Breckinridge at 25 Broadway. We
> believe police captured two letter and let not
> forwarded to you. We will not accept any go-
> between from your sent. We will arrang theas
> latter. There is no worry about the boy. He is
> very well and will be feed according to the diet.
> Best dank for information about it. We are
> interested to send your boy back in gut health.
>   It is neccisery to make a world-affair out of
> it, or to get your boy back as soon as possible.
> Why did you ignore ouer letter which we left in
> the room the baby would be back long ago. You
> would not get any result from the Polise becauce
> out kinaping was pland for a year allredy. But we
> were afraid the boy would not be strong enough.
>   Ouer ransam was made out for 50000 but now we
> have to put another to it as propperly have to

hold the baby longer as we expected so it will by
70000$ 20000 in 50$ bills 25000 in 20$ bills
15000$ in 10$ and 10000 in 5$ bills. We warn you
against not to mark any bills or take them from
one ser. No. We will inform you latter how to
deliver the money but not before the polise is out
of this cace and the pappers are quite.[8]

The accompanying note to Breckinridge also contained orders that an item be placed in the *New York American,* confirming that the ransom message had been received. After consulting with Lindbergh, Breckinridge and Rosner drove to New York, where Rosner placed the following ad in the *American:*

> Letter received at new address. Will follow your instructions. I also received letter mailed to me March 4th and was ready since then. Please hurry on account of mother. Address me to the address you mentioned in your letter. Father.

That evening Owney Madden arrived at Sorrel Hill and met with Lindbergh, Breckinridge, and John Fogarty. After Madden left, there was consensus that he probably did know something about the kidnapping but that he had been vague about what it was.[9]

Thayer was having growing doubts about Rosner, whom he never fully trusted. Earlier that day Rosner had confided in Thayer that he had received word that the kidnappers had a collaborator inside the Lindbergh household. As a result, Rosner had waited until Breckinridge was away from Sorrel Hill, then searched the room being shared by Fogarty and Galvin, and discovered evidence that they were the guilty parties. Just what the evidence was remained hazy. Thayer took to remaining in proximity to Rosner, who tried everything he could to shake the young lawyer.

Thayer expressed his distrust of Rosner to Lindbergh and Breckinridge. Lindy and Henry felt Rosner should stay. Secretly they had already approved a third person, paying money to yet another self-professed go-between.

On March 2, the same day Morris Rosner wangled his way into the kidnapping in New York City, tall, portly, balding, and double-chinned fifty-three-year-old Gaston B. Means was doing the same thing in Washington, D.C. Means had prevailed on two friends of Lindbergh's. The first to whom he spoke was Colonel M. Robert Guggenheim. On March 4, while Guggenheim waited to hear back, Gaston shifted directions and met with the other friend of the Lindbergh family, Mrs. Evalyn Walsh McLean. He hinted that he had already made contact with the kidnappers and suggested that she ask her friend, who was Lindbergh's cousin, Captain Emory S. Land of the U.S. Navy, to join them.

The daughter of a Colorado mining mogul and the estranged wife of the owner of the *Washington Post,* Edward Beale McLean, Evalyn lived in a grand style, was one of the capital's most opulent hostesses, and counted among her many priceless possessions the cursed forty-four-and-a-quarter carat midnight-blue Hope diamond. Kidnapping had been a phobia with Mrs. McLean since the 1909 birth of her son, Vinson, whom the papers had termed the Hundred Million Dollar Baby. She so feared Vinson's being stolen that the child was under constant guard. One day he was playing near the estate's fence when a delivery truck arrived. As the gates were opened to let it in, eight-year-old Vinson dashed through. His guards gave chase. The child ran out onto the street and into traffic. He was struck by a car and killed.

- - -

Gaston Bullock Means was born on a plantation at Blackwelder's Spring, near Concord, North Carolina, in 1879. The highly esteemed Means family had been large landowners in the area for generations. His great-grandfather had been governor of North Carolina. Gaston's father, Colonel William G. Means, was a lawyer and former mayor of Concord. An uncle had been Concord's chief of police. After graduating from the University of North Carolina, he disregarded the family tradition of working the land and running for office and entered professional life as an extremely adept towel salesman for Cannon Mills.

In 1910, Gaston went to work for the William J. Burns Detective Agency as a private investigator. He was still with the company in 1912 when two events occurred in quick succession: He was sued for breach of promise, and he fell from the upper berth of a railroad Pullman car. Gaston sued the Pullman Company, claiming among other things that the chain from which the berth was suspended had broken. It was discovered that the chain had been partially filed, but when no evidence could be developed to prove that Gaston did the filing, Pullman settled. Rumors that the injuries he sustained in the spill from the berth had altered his personality might have contributed to the breach of promise suit against him being dropped.

By 1917, Means was the business manager for Mrs. Maude King, the widow of a millionaire Chicago lumber baron who had left most of his fortune to an old man's home bearing his name. While visiting Means in North Carolina in August of that year, she was mysteriously killed in a field not far from his home. At first Gaston claimed Maude had committed suicide. Later he contended that the two of them were on a moonlight target party and he had gone for a drink of spring water, leaving the gun in the crotch of a tree. In his absence Mrs. King recovered the gun and accidentally shot herself. The questions of how she could have fired a bullet into the back of her own head and why there were no powder burns on her seemed to be of no relevance when he was tried for her murder in his hometown. The local jury acquitted him, and Means promptly sued the prosecutor for a million dollars on the contention that the murder trial had been an attempt to prevent the probate of Maude's recently discovered but rightful will, of which he was entitled to a fourth. At a probate hearing Means was accused of presenting the court with a forged will and with already having bilked the late Mrs. King out of four hundred thousand dollars. When his veracity was challenged, Gaston stunned the court with a claim that during World War I he had been a spy for Germany but quit when the United States entered the conflict. The judge called Means's testimony a fabrication and the will a fraud and tossed the case out of court.

In 1921, Gaston Means was made a special agent of the U.S. Bureau of Investigation by his old detective-days boss, William J. Burns, who had been brought in by Attorney General Harry Daugherty to head the BI. Two years later Means was suspended by Daugherty after being indicted for accepting sixty-five thousand dollars from a manufacturer of glass coffins, as well as for violating the Prohibition laws by obtaining the illegal release of two hundred thousand dollars worth of liquor from government warehouses. Daugherty dropped him for good when the cases went to court. The trial was interrupted so Means could testify before the Senate committee looking into the Teapot Dome scandal, which involved Daugherty and other government officials. Gaston kept the senators "fascinated" with his revelations, not the least of which were his exploits as a German spy and as a confidential investigator for

Mexico, Great Britain, and many private individuals. The committee decided that his testimony was "a tissue of lies." He was indicted for forgery but never prosecuted. Gaston would later claim he had been hired to do investigative work on the Teapot Dome scandal by the owner of the *Washington Post,* which was how he came to know Mrs. Evalyn Walsh McLean. Found guilty and convicted in the glass-coffin scam and for releasing liquor from a federal warehouse, Means spent most of his two-year prison term at the federal penitentiary in Atlanta. After his release in 1928, he took the pauper's oath and collaborated on a book entitled *The Strange Death of President Harding,* in which he depicted himself as the champion of right and the nemesis of Daugherty. His coauthor, Mrs. Mary Thacker, later repudiated both the book and Means.

Evalyn Walsh McLean met with Gaston Means on the evening of March 4 at her lavish Georgetown house, Friendship.

> "I've come to realize that honesty is the best policy," he told her. "I've made mistakes, bad mistakes. I've served jail sentences for them. But I want to do more. I want to do something to wipe out my past record so that I can hold up my head again and look my fellow citizens squarely in the eye.
> "I know the head of the kidnap gang. With your help, I can have the baby back to his mother inside two weeks."[10]

Means explained that while in a New York City speakeasy several weeks before, he'd run across a fellow inmate from the Atlanta Penitentiary, who asked him to come in on a "big kidnapping." Gaston refused to participate. But since the disappearance of the Lindbergh baby, he had checked around and become certain the former inmate and his associates were the actual kidnappers. Means was confident he could contact them and deal for the child, but he didn't want to do so without a go-ahead from someone close to Lindbergh, such as Mrs. McLean. Mrs. McLean encouraged him to find out if these men indeed were the kidnappers. The next day, March 5, he reported back to her, saying he had communicated with the inmate and his gang and that not only did they have the baby but they were willing to return him for a fifty-thousand-dollar ransom in unmarked money, the amount being reported in most of the newspapers.

Means wanted Mrs. McLean to get Lindbergh's permission to work on the case privately. He also asked her to find a Catholic priest who could assist them, since the kidnappers preferred to turn the child over to a priest when the appropriate time arrived. Means stressed secrecy and suggested that their communications to one another be partially coded. She, for example, would be known as Number Eleven; the leader of the kidnapping gang, Number Nineteen.

Mrs. McLean and Captain Land conferred. What Means had said sounded plausible to them. Mrs. McLean knew just the priest for the job, Reverend J. Francis Hurney, pastor of the Church of the Immaculate Conception. She decided to pay the ransom herself, pending Father Hurney's decision. He met with Means on March 5 and felt that Gaston's representations were so. He told Mrs. McLean he would be glad to participate but suggested that she should obtain Colonel Lindbergh's permission. Captain Land volunteered to go to Hopewell, where he presented his cousin with the proposition. Lindbergh and Breckinridge approved but wanted it understood that if the baby was recovered by this plan, they would reimburse the ransom money to Mrs. McLean.

On March 6, with many papers saying that Lindbergh was willing to pay a one-hundred-thousand-dollar reward, Means informed Mrs. McLean that the kidnappers had doubled their original demand of fifty thousand dollars in unmarked bills. On March 7, with Morris Rosner and Robert Thayer manning the safe phone at the Lindbergh's Hopewell estate and with a fellow inmate of Al Capone's telling federal authorities that Big Al had planned the kidnapping so he could cut a deal and get out of jail, Gaston B. Means went to Mrs. McLean's home, and in the presence of Father Hurney he was given one hundred thousand dollars in unmarked bills to pass on to the kidnappers.

The evening of March 9 at Sorrel Hill, Robert Thayer took a phone call from New York City. On the line was a man who identified himself as John F. Condon.[11] The Lindbergh case would never be the same.

10

JAFSIE

AROUND MIDNIGHT AT SORREL HILL, ROBERT THAYER WAS CALLED TO THE
phone. On the line was a man who claimed that he had an important
communication for Colonel Lindbergh, that he was under instructions to
give it to nobody else. Thayer explained he was in charge of telephone
messages for the colonel. The man then identified himself as John F.
Condon, rattled off his degrees and honors and the fact that he held the
title of professor. He also disclosed that he had received an envelope that
day that contained two letters, one directed to himself and the other one
sealed and addressed to Colonel Lindbergh. Over the phone he read the
letter addressed to himself:

> Dear Sir: If you are willing to act as go-between in
> Lindbergh case pleace follow stricly instructions.
> Handel incloced letter *personaly* to Mr. Lindbergh. It
> will explain everything. Don't tell anyone about it. As

soon we found the Press or Police is notifyed
everything are cansell and it will be a further delay.
    After ytou gett the mony from Mr. Lindbergh put these
3 words in the New York American

MONEY IS REDY

Affter notise we will give you further instruction.
Don't be affrait we are not out fore your 1000$ keep
it. Only act strickly. Be at home every night between
6–12 by this time you will hear from us.

Written in two lines on the enclosed envelope was

Dear Sir: Please handle incloced letter to Colonel
    Lindbergh.
It is in Mr. Lindbergh interest not to notify police.[1]

Robert Thayer instructed Condon to open the second letter and read
what it said.

Dear Sir, Mr Condon may act as go-between. You may
givve him the 70,000$ make one packet. the size will
bee about

At this juncture Condon told Thayer that the message contained the
drawing of a box in which the money was to be delivered. The dimensions printed alongside were "seven by six by fifteen."

we have notifyt you allredy in what kind of bills. We
warn you not to set any trapp in any way. If you or
someone els will notify the Police ther will be a
further delay. affter we have the mony in hand we will
tell you where the find your boy. You may have a
airplane redy it is about 150 mil awy. But befor
telling you the adr. a delay of 8 houers will be
between.[2]

Thayer asked if there was anything else on the page. Condon described the symbol of interlacing circles and perforations that had sig-
natured the previous ransom messages. Condon was requested to bring

the letters to Sorrel Hill as soon as possible and not mention to anyone what had happened.

John F. Condon offered a slightly different version of the event. He would contend that during the phone call to the estate he demanded to talk directly to Lindbergh, and a third voice, which sounded tired, came on the line and said it was Lindbergh speaking. After hearing the text of the second message, according to Condon, the following exchange took place:

> "Is that all?" asked the Colonel. He seemed suddenly without interest.
>
> "There were two intersecting—"
>
> I could literally feel the tension of his voice as he shot staccato repetitions of the words back at me. *"Circles? Intersecting?"*
>
> "I would call them secant circles, if I might be permitted . . ."
>
> Again the staccato rush of words. "Yes, yes, I understand."
>
> "There are three dots or holes across the horizontal diameter of the intersecting circles. The circles are tinted—one red, one blue. Now that I have explained the contents, Colonel, is this letter I have important?"
>
> "It is very important, Professor Condon. I shall come at once. Where are you?"
>
> "Suppose I come to you, Colonel. You have anguish enough and you are needed at home. I can come to Hopewell immediately."
>
> "Very well. It is kind of you. You will come at once?"
>
> "At once," I promised.[3]

Thayer denied that the colonel spoke to Condon over the telephone. Almost all documentation, save for statements by Condon, bears him out.

Several hours later at the Lindbergh estate, it was Henry Breckinridge who picked up the phone. Condon was on the other end, calling from Princeton to say he was en route. He made no mention that he had lost the way three times.

Breckinridge was waiting at the gate of Sorrel Hill when a car drove up and he first cast his eyes on the six-foot-tall, two-hundred-pound gray-maned and mustached John F. Condon, a physical-fitness buff with a ruddy complexion who looked younger than his seventy-two years.[4] To Breckinridge's surprise, the old professor was accompanied by two friends he had not bothered mentioning on the phone, Max Rosenhain, the owner and operator of a restaurant Condon frequented, and clothing salesman P. Milton Gaglio. Henry rode on their running board up to the house and, according to Condon, didn't identify himself until they entered.

Condon introduced Rosenhain and Gaglio. Rosenhain, in a nervous, essayed humor, said, "We are a committee. A Wop, an Israelite, and a Harp."

It was approximately 3:00 A.M., and Condon alone was taken up to a bedroom by Breckinridge, who pardoned himself and left. The most expansive account of the event, as it always would be, was John F. Condon's:

> I sat down on the bed. I heard him telling Colonel Lindbergh I had arrived. A moment later he [Breckinridge] came back into the room accompanied by a tall, slender, clear-eyed young chap dressed in brown trousers and a short jacket. I recognized the famous aviator immediately, and arose.
>
> "Good evening, Colonel Lindbergh."
>
> He crossed the room and shook my hand cordially. "It was kind of you to come out here. I hope I have not caused you too much trouble, Professor Condon."
>
> "No trouble, whatever," I assured him. "I want you to know, now, Colonel, that my only purpose is to serve you. I am completely at your disposal. I mean that, sincerely."
>
> I took the letter from my pocket and handed it to him as he thanked me. We sat down—the three of us—on the bed. The two colonels studied intently for many minutes the enclosures.
>
> "This letter is genuine," Colonel Lindbergh said. "The interlocking circles are the symbol agreed upon by the kidnapper. They match perfectly the symbol on the original note."
>
> "May I ask you some questions about yourself, Professor Condon?" inquired Colonel Breckinridge.
>
> "Anything you wish."

"Where do you teach?"

"I am Professor of Education at Fordham and Principal of Public School Number Twelve in the Bronx."

"Have you been teaching long?"

"For fifty years." I smiled. "I'm rather proud of the fact that in that time I lost only nineteen hours."

"An excellent record, indeed. And your birthplace?"

"The most beautiful borough in the world. The Bronx. I've lived there all my life."

Colonel Breckinridge nodded. "In itself an excellent recommendation. Any other interests besides teaching?"

"Athletics of all kinds, music, children and—I hope I do not seem immodest—helping others."

"Not at all. You have a family, of course?"

"A wife and three splendid children."

He turned to Colonel Lindbergh. "Professor Condon has my vote. He's earnest, frank. The letter he bears is genuine and suggests him as intermediary. I think we should arrange to give him the fifty thousand dollars asked for in the original note and see if he cannot obtain your child."

"I don't like that arrangement," I interposed. "After all, I am a stranger to you. I would much prefer that you first verify my standing."

"I am sure," Colonel Lindbergh said, "that you will be able to assist us. You'll stay here tonight, of course?"[5]

Hyperbole to the side, this was essentially the extent of the questioning of Dr. John F. Condon by Lindbergh and Breckinridge. Henry would later admit having grave reservations about the garrulous teacher from the Bronx, but he seems to have kept them to himself.

There was no place for Rosenhain or Gaglio to sleep in the crowded Sorrel Hill house. After exchanging handshakes with Lindbergh and swearing to say nothing of the night's happenings, they drove back to New York.

Condon claimed to have returned upstairs with the colonel and relates this:

"If I might," I told him, "I would like to meet Mrs. Lindbergh."

We went into her room. I saw her, a tiny, child-like, pretty creature, sitting on the edge of her bed. She was dressed in a simple frock of some sort. In a few months she again would be a mother, but at the moment it was obvious that her thoughts were with her first-born.

"This is Professor Condon," Colonel Lindbergh said. I remember that she stretched out her arms toward me instinctively in the age-old appeal of motherhood. "Will you help me get back my baby?"

"I shall do everything in my power to bring him back to you."

As I came closer to her, I saw the gleam of tears in her soft, dark eyes. I was thankful, at that moment, for the gray hairs of my seventy-two years; for the lifetime spent in learning the ways of the young. I smiled at her, shook a thick, reproving forefinger at her. With mock bruskness, I threatened Anne Lindbergh. "If one of those tears drops, I shall go off the case immediately."

Her arms rose. The fingers of her hands sought her eyes. She brushed away the tears. When her hands went away from her face again, she was smiling, sweetly, bravely. "You see, Doctor, I am not crying."

"That is better," I said. "That is much, much better."

When we were in the corridor outside her room once more, Colonel Lindbergh turned to me. His face was grave, his voice hushed, as he paid me the finest compliment I have ever received. "Doctor Condon, you made my wife smile tonight for the first time since our baby was taken."[6]

It is plausible to believe that Anne may have smiled prior to the arrival at the house of Dr. Condon. In a letter to her mother-in-law dated March 10, she does not mention having met the loquacious educator in the early morning hours of that day, but she says that there was progress and that she felt happier.[7]

Lindbergh led Condon to the south end of the house and opened a door, explaining that this was the only unoccupied room, the nursery. Lindbergh brought in an armful of army blankets, which he made into a bedroll for the old gent, then left. Once under the blankets at the foot of that empty crib, Condon relates this dialogue:

Often, when I am alone and my heart is full, I speak aloud to myself. In the darkness, now, my own voice spoke quietly:

"Condon?"

"Yes?"

"Don't you need help?"

"What's that?"

"Don't you need help?"

"Yes."

I got out from beneath the warm blankets. I put my hands around the rung of the missing "Lone Eaglet's" crib. On my knees, I prayed:

"Oh Great Jehovah, assist me in the work which I am about to carry on in Thy honor and that of the most glorious Blessed Virgin Mary, Mother of the Son of God, whose anguish, too, was great, as her divine Son suffered crucifixion. Divine Mother assist me in my cause."

Solemnly, hands clasped, my eyes deep in that empty crib, I took my oath:

"By Thy grace and that it may redound to Thy credit and that of Thy immortal Son, I swear that I shall dedicate my best efforts and, if necessary, the remaining days of my life, to helping these unfortunate parents."

I finished with a fervent petition.

"Let me do this one great thing as the crowning act of my life. Let me successfully accomplish my mission to the credit of Thy Holy Name and that of Thy Divine Son. Amen!"[8]

In the morning John F. Condon had an "American breakfast of orange juice, bacon, eggs, toast and coffee."[9] At the table with him were the Lindberghs, Henry Breckinridge, the young police officer whose voice had been the first he had heard on the phone the night before, and Anne's mother, Mrs. Dwight Morrow. Except for Mrs. Morrow's questions to Condon, which related to the kidnapping, the conversation was on general topics, including an avid discussion between Breckinridge and Condon concerning football.

Lindbergh was called away from the table and soon had Condon and Breckinridge join him in his upstairs bedroom. He said he believed Condon was in contact with the people who had taken his son—Condon claimed he never heard Lindbergh use the word *kidnap* or *kidnapper*—and he would arrange for fifty thousand dollars to be placed at his disposal immediately, and in a day or so he would have the additional twenty thousand being asked for. He handed a note to Condon dated

March 10, 1932, signed by him and his wife, which read, "We hereby authorize Dr. John F. Condon to act as go-between for us."[10]

Lindbergh assigned Breckinridge the task of inserting the money-is-ready notice in the *New York American*. Breckinridge felt it was imperative that they find a pseudonym with which to sign the ad, a code name the kidnappers could use to identify all future communications. It didn't take long for Condon to come up with an acronym from his own initials, J.F.C.: Jafsie.

Returning downstairs, Condon met trooper boss H. Norman Schwarzkopf and Bob Coar of the Jersey City Police Department. He was also introduced to Morris Rosner but not by his own name. Rosner, who was still staying at the house and had returned late the night before, was told Condon was Dr. Stico and little else.[11]

John Francis Condon loved Jesus Christ, Uncle Sam, and "The Star-Spangled Banner" best and, next to them, the Bronx, New York. "America is the finest country in the world," he was fond of remarking, "the Bronx the most beautiful borough in it."[12] Lindbergh and Breckinridge got a sense of these sentiments early on. Had they inquired further, they would have discovered that many people who knew Condon found him to be eccentric, if not a flat out "nut," sentimental, sycophantic, histrionic, patronizing, pseudo-humble, and "anxious to see himself and be seen by others in the best possible light."[13] However, Lindy and his lawyer displayed little interest in checking the background of the aging educator, who favored old-fashioned, dark winter suits and a black derby hat even during the hottest months of summer.

Condon had graduated from the College of the City of New York in 1884, took his M.A. at Fordham University, and taught in New York City schools for forty-six years, for twenty-five of which he served as a school principal. After retiring, he lectured at Fordham on pedagogy, acted as a part-time swimming instructor, and lectured frequently on a multitude of subjects at schools and organizations throughout the city. He resided with his wife, Myra, in a satisfactory two-story house at 2974 Decatur Avenue in the Bronx. Their two sons were lawyers, and their daughter had been a teacher until her recent marriage to a young architect.

One of Condon's favorite pastimes was writing poems and occasional articles for a local daily paper, the *Home News for the Bronx and Man-*

hattan, which was better known as the *Bronx Home News,* since the majority of its hundred thousand readers came from that borough. He had become friendly with the editor and was a regular contributor who often used pen names such as P. A. Triot, J. U. Stice, L. O. Nestar, and L. O. Nehand.

John F. Condon made it mellifluously clear that for him the kidnappers of the baby of the greatest hero in the world, Charles A. Lindbergh, had disgraced the flag and defiled the national honor. According to Condon, at a family dinner on Sunday, March 6, he had been greatly agitated by the day's news: Charles and Anne Lindbergh had appointed Spitale and Bitz, a pair of common criminals, to act as their intermediaries. He commiserated with a newspaper editorial that expressed a sense of outrage at Lindy's action and handed the article to his daughter, telling the family that, by golly, Uncle Sam would restore the baby. Condon claimed that as he went on about the crime's being a humiliation that everyone was taking too lightly, his daughter interrupted: "Dad, you're not going to get mixed up in the Lindbergh case?" He began to say it was the duty of every citizen, but she interrupted him again, and his sons joined her to say, among other things, that the Lindberghs had all the investigators they needed. "You won't get mixed up in this, dear?" his daughter pleaded. "Promise?" His only reply was an unintelligible grunt.[14]

Condon claimed that late the following night, March 7, dining with his cronies at Max Rosenhain's restaurant in the Bronx and discussing the crime, he took umbrage at a remark that the Lindbergh kidnapping probably couldn't have happened anywhere but in the United States. He went home, brought out the purple ink he made himself, and in an "elegant, Spencerian hand" wrote the editor of the *Bronx Home News:*[15]

> I offer all I can scrape together so a loving mother may again have her child and Colonel Lindbergh may know that the American people are grateful for the honor bestowed upon them by his pluck and daring.
>
> Let the kidnappers know that no testimony of mine, or information coming from me, will be used against them. I offer $1000.00 which I've saved from my salary (all my life's savings), in addition to the suggested $50,000. I am ready, at my own expense, to go anywhere, also to give the kidnappers the extra money and never utter their names to anyone.

If this is not agreeable, then I ask the kidnappers to get any Catholic priest, with the knowledge that every priest must hold inviolate any statement which may be made by the kidnappers.

The letter and a story incorporating much of the text received prominent positions in the *Bronx Home News* edition of Tuesday, March 8. The piece was captioned DR. JOHN F. CONDON OFFERS TO ADD ONE THOUSAND DOLLARS OF HIS SAVINGS TO RANSOM LINDBERGH CHILD.

The text provided Condon's address, a line or two of biography on him, and a reminder that if he were to act as go-between, "he would be responsible to no person for information which he might obtain from the abductors."

Returning home at 10:00 P.M. the next evening, March 9, Condon went through the day's mail and opened an envelope whose large block letters spelled out his name and address. This was the message that prompted his phone call and first visit to Hopewell.

Henry Breckinridge and Jafsie Condon left Hopewell at 2:00 P.M. March 10 for their ultrasecret mission of placing an ad for the kidnappers in a New York City paper. According to Condon, they drove directly to his home in the Bronx, where in the living room awaiting them was a newspaper man. Condon relates this account:

> I saw Colonel Breckinridge's look of dismay as I introduced him to Gregory F. Coleman of The Home News. Coleman, too, noticed the expression and hurried to reassure him.
>
> "I've already conferred with Mr. Goodman and Mr. O'Flaherty, the editor and the publisher. They agree that this is one of the biggest stories of all time and that we have an obligation to our readers. But they feel that a still more sacred obligation is to see Colonel Lindbergh's child safely returned. You may be sure than anything that is revealed to me will be held in strictest confidence. We shall publish nothing that will in any way endanger your negotiations and the child's return."
>
> Colonel Breckinridge thanked Coleman and I introduced

the Colonel to Al Reich who, learning from Rosenhain of my visit to Hopewell, had come to the house to reassure members of my family lest they be alarmed by my overnight absence.[16]

It seems more likely that they went directly to Breckinridge's office at 25 Broadway, where he dispatched his secretary to put the notice in the classified section of the *New York American,* and then he drove Condon home to the Bronx. The ad had been placed too late for the March 10 edition of the paper.

The next morning, March 11, the following notice appeared not only in the *New York American,* as the kidnappers' message had said, but in the *Bronx Home News* as well, which was not in the abductors' instructions:

I accept. Money is ready. Jafsie.

Around noon on March 11, the Condons' phone began to ring. Jafsie was away. His wife, Myra, went into the front hall and picked up.

"Is Doctor Condon there?" asked a man with a guttural, accented voice.

Myra Condon replied that her husband was giving a lecture and would be home between six and seven.

"Tell the Doctor to stay at home," the man said. "I will call him again about seven o'clock."[17]

Book Two

EXPANSION

Prelude

— — —

ASSUMING LINDBERGH WORKED A DECEPTION, IT HAD TAKEN DEEP ROOT. PO-
lice and officials did not question that a kidnapping had occurred. The
press and public certainly believed the crime had been perpetrated. Better
yet, Lindbergh was in total charge of the manhunt, had literally been
handed the reins of control by the reverent Schwarzkopf, who at Lindy's
bidding barred all major police organizations from the investigation.
Sorrel Hill was the seat of Lindbergh's power, and here he ruled supreme. But the tentacles of the search were moving beyond the estate,
moving into areas where his authority, though respected, was no longer
manifest.

The ransom message left in the nursery was the device by which Lindbergh hoped to set the pack running in the wrong direction, and he had
played an astute game of denial and confirmation to make its existence
an issue. The naming of the initial go-betweens, Springer and Thompson,
was a further ploy to mislead. The hounds had taken the bait, were
poised and pointed the wrong way, yelping and sniffing in place.

It may be that Lindbergh's ideal scenario would have had no forger trying to claim the ransom money. Then the public interest in the make-believe crime would have abated slowly but completely, without the discovery of any suspect. That wasn't to be. The ransom message had been shown around the New York underworld, perhaps to lure an extortionist and little more. And extortionists came. So did wanted and unwanted middlemen and persons who may have firmly believed they were in touch with the actual kidnappers.

Suddenly Lindbergh had three balls in the air regarding go-betweens. There was Morris Rosner, Spitale, Bitz, and their underworld cohorts. Mrs. Evalyn Walsh McLean had given Gaston Means a hundred thousand dollars, and she eagerly expected delivery of the stolen child. Jafsie Condon was the latest and the most troubling. The hand-written messages he presented to Lindbergh and Breckinridge masterfully approximated the original they had concocted. This would probably take the investigation beyond the gates of Sorrel Hill, and more likely than not, a ransom would have to be paid to the clever extortionist. The most troubling aspect became John F. Condon. Was the florid rhetorician part of an extortion plot, or wasn't he? One thing was for certain: If ever there was a loose cannon, Jafsie was it. Breckinridge seems to have had his doubts about dealing with Condon; Lindbergh apparently didn't. Waiting in the wings and yet to be heard from was another wannabe go-between: John Hughes Curtis.

Lindy and Breckinridge, whatever their misgivings, now had to play out their hands as if a kidnapper existed—and the baby was still alive.

11

JUGGLING

LINDBERGH, THE CALM, METHODICAL CONTROL FREAK WITH A PILOT'S COOL, attempted to keep abreast of everything that was going on with the manhunt, and this could not be done. He was usually accessible to those who resided or worked at Sorrel Hill, but talking to him could be chancy. One moment he might be chatty and warm; the next he could become distant and aloof or outright curt and might, if approached, spin on his heels and stride gruffly off. As the celebrated Lone Eagle, a persona he seemed to display most often, he was an awesome and seemingly omniscient presence. He was also Slim Lindbergh, the notorious practical joker. Though his behavior was generally sober and responsible, he managed to catch several people off guard with a prank. In general conversation he was usually brief, pleasant, and restrained. A good night's sleep left him buoyant for a time. He was focused and intent when receiving reports, but in the course of long descriptions he might drift or smile when there was not a thing to smile about. Talking with Henry Breckinridge or other old friends, he might ramble on. When issuing orders, Lindy was terse, sure, and monosyllabic. What prompted him to give an order varied. Sometimes it came as a result of long deliberation. Just as often it was a random proclamation that even took Henry Breckinridge by surprise. He tried never to lose his temper but occasionally did. Often when he was about to fly off the handle, Henry Breckinridge would step in, but Henry couldn't always be there. To disobey a command was one way of sending Lindy into a state, as was the case when the troopers tampered with his secure line of communication. One fact was observable to those around him: Lindbergh showed no outward signs of grief or loss or revenge in regard to his missing son. None of the Morrows did, not publicly. The job on hand for Lindy was to get the child back. He didn't betray the least bit emotionally as he went about it—as long as it was done his way.

Lindbergh's own telephone wire at Sorrel Hill, which had been encased in an underground metal tube at the time the estate was built, was the one on which he conducted his private dealings regarding the kidnapping. Schwarzkopf had been ordered not to let his men pick up the phone or monitor the conversations. Denied the right to hear what was being said on this instrument, the state police assigned a trooper to the telephone-company office in Hopewell and had him listen in on the forbidden calls from the main switchboard. Learning of it, Lindbergh was infuriated; he drove to Hopewell and barged in on the eavesdropping trooper at the switchboard. "Don't plug it in—not even halfway," warned the drawn and finger-pointing master of Sorrel Hill. "Heed what I am saying!" The young officer gave assurances it wouldn't happen again.[1]

Back at the estate Lindbergh walked into his den and found Captain John J. Lamb of the Jersey State Police speaking on the selfsame private phone the young trooper had been monitoring. Lindy shouted, "What are you doing on the telephone?" Lamb explained that it rang, and he had answered. "I want it understood very clearly and now," Lindbergh said, "that neither you nor any other policeman is to touch that phone for any reason. You are here through my courtesy, and I ask you not to interfere with my business."[2]

⁓ ⁓ ⁓

At 11:00 A.M. on Saturday, March 5, H. Norman Schwarzkopf had to address the hundreds of local New Jersey, out-of-state, and federal investigators that Governor Moore invited to a Lindbergh-kidnapping coordinating conference in Trenton.[3] Included at the gathering were J. Edgar

Hoover and the man responsible for putting Al Capone behind bars, Elmer Irey, chief of the IRS Law Enforcement Division. Schwarzkopf briefed the gathering on the crime and progress to date and opened the session to a heated debate over the handling of the case so far and the paths that should be followed in the immediate future.

Officials attending the conference wanted to be part of the manhunt, particularly the New Jersey County Detectives and Hoover's Bureau of Investigation—which was exactly what Lindbergh did not want. The Lone Eagle, via Schwarzkopf, prevailed. The heavy in the matter, the one who was scorned and took a public battering for excluding every other organization from the state-police chase, was H. Norman. In the eyes of most media people, Lindbergh was credible—he could do no wrong.

The Bureau of Investigation was to become a major nuisance for Schwarzkopf. Despite being excluded from the inquiry, J. Edgar Hoover would have his special agents find out what they could about the crime—without state-police approval and, often, without their knowledge. The same was true for New Jersey's young, aggressive commissioner of Motor Vehicles, Harold G. Hoffman. Hoffman's department had its own detective corps, which was unleashed to find the kidnappers. What was worse for the troopers, the man Hoffman brought in to head his inquiry was the one person who had continually embarrassed and out-shone the state police and Schwarzkopf in the past and who was receiving as much publicity as they were now: the outspoken seventy-year-old chief of detectives of Burlington County, considered by many to be the greatest detective in the world: Ellis Parker, Sr.

The press proved a far more critical and growing problem for Schwarzkopf. So did Charles Lindbergh.

- - -

To the media people exiled at nearby Hopewell and Trenton, the Lindbergh house atop Sorrel Hill had become an unapproachable Xanadu, and Lindy himself, Kubla Khan in a leather flying jacket. Troopers guarded every approach to the foothill acres and patrolled the outer perimeters, shooing off, if not temporarily detaining, the occasional interloper. Official visitors, many driving the back roads to avoid being detected and many being chauffeured in limousines, entered and left the estate under the far-off gaze of reporters watching from whatever vantage points they could find. The Lindberghs, after all, were America's couple. They had spent weekends fishing with the likes of President

Hoover—Herbert's flustered wife referred to them as the Lingrins—and they counted among their intimates Ford, Edison, Guggenheim, and Will Rogers. The visitors coming to see them in the days after the kidnapping often could be identified by sharp-eyed journalists; when they couldn't, the delicious guessing game of who they might be often ended up in print. Investigators and staff inside the estate usually had no better idea of who was coming and going.

Within the gates of Sorrel Hill, Charles Lindbergh held supreme sway over a household that had taken on the trappings of a baronial castle under siege. Those about him formed the court. Henry Breckinridge was his all-powerful chancellor. H. Norman Schwarzkopf headed the palace guard. Anne's lady-in-waiting was Aida Breckinridge. Affairs of state were usually conducted in the first-floor community rooms, which still doubled as staff dormitories at night. The family quarters on the second floor were normally sacrosanct, but Anne, her mother, and Aida could be displaced if a room was needed for an urgent conference. The pervasive atmosphere, according to Anne, was bedlam. The telephone never stopped ringing. Hundreds of men "stamped" in and out. And Wahgoosh, the family dog, who had not barked the night of the kidnapping, now never stopped barking.[4]

Adding to Schwarzkopf's frustration at being omitted from much of the planning was the presence of Jimmy Finn. At the very time the state police were trying to limit the participation of outside law-enforcement agencies in the investigation, at the liege of Lindbergh, Detective Finn of the New York Police Department was admitted to the Sorrel Hill inner circle, where he had access to the two colonels. During Lindy's triumphant postflight welcome to Manhattan in 1927, Finn had commanded the elite group of cops who served as the Lone Eagle's private bodyguard. The two men had remained friendly, and in the wake of the kidnapping Lindbergh had asked that Finn come to Sorrel Hill while simultaneously keeping the New York Police Department out of the investigation. Finn was consulted about some aspects of the Lindbergh strategy to recover the child, but like most other advisers, he was kept in the dark about the others.

In the second week of March, Lindbergh and Breckinridge allowed Elmer Irey, head of the IRS Law Enforcement Division, to join their inner circle.[5] This could have been as much for show as for practicality. Irey's job would be to advise on the ransom payment, when and if negotiations reached that point, as seemed possible in the case of go-between Jafsie Condon. Lindbergh would soon make it clear that he was not going to permit marked ransom bills to be given to the kidnappers. Without marked currency the law had no way of capturing the extortionists should they escape from the transfer location unseen.

Lindbergh's ability to interfere with routine police procedures was nowhere more blatant than with the interviewing of himself, Anne, and their staff in the wake of the disappearance. A crucial function of an investigation of this nature is to interview witnesses as close to the time of perpetration as possible. Lindbergh had refused to let official questioning of himself, Anne, and Mrs. Whateley be done for ten days. The same would have applied to Betty Gow and Ollie Whateley if the police hadn't learned that the pretty Scotswoman had received a call from her boyfriend, Red Johnsen. When finally obtained, the statements from the Lindberghs and their staff were all essentially the same and added nothing of value.

A certain black humor emerged as the clandestine and compartmentalized operations at Sorrel Hill inspired courtiers to vie with one another for dominance and survival. Morris Rosner's interception of phone calls and his failure to relay many of the messages to Lindbergh and Breckinridge had been symptomatic of this. Another example was the digging down to, and attempted tapping of, Lindbergh's buried phone line by Jersey troopers after he had forbidden them to monitor his calls at the switchboard in Hopewell.[6]

For the state policemen charged with obeying his edicts, Lindbergh's decisions were often discrepant and mortifying. Schwarzkopf had been impressed by the results of the newly developed lie detector machines and suggested that the household staff at Hopewell be tested by one. Lindbergh, a believer in science and technology, refused. One of his reasons for this was that the system was still unproved. When a thirty-five-year-old New York City doctor named Erastus Mead Hudson volunteered to provide an innovative process for finding fingerprints, trooper brass could be forgiven for dragging their feet: Hudson's technique—exposing latent fingerprints by applying a solution of silver nitrate—was no better validated than lie detector testing. But Lindbergh approved.

Dr. Hudson's arrival at Sorrel Hill posed a credibility problem for the trooper organization. Their expert, Corporal Frank A. Kelly, had not found a single fingerprint in the entire nursery, on the outside of the house, on the ladder, or anywhere else. What if Hudson did? The answer came on Sunday morning, March 13, when the doctor went to the nursery and sprayed the baby's toys with a silver nitrate mist. After the toys were exposed to sunlight, hundreds of red-brown stains emerged, of which thirteen were identifiable latent fingerprints believed to belong to the missing child. Before the stains faded, they were photographed by a special camera. The next day the ladder sections, which had been soaked in silver nitrate and put out in the sun, produced five hundred stains. He would later find more prints. Two hundred six of them were complete latent prints, and of these, eight were clear enough to be of help. Seven of the eight could not be identified. The eighth belonged to Lieutenant Lewis J. Bornmann of the Jersey State Police, who had taken charge of the ladder the night the baby was reported missing.

What was disquietingly missing from Hudson's findings were latent prints of Charles Lindbergh, Sr., who had admitted going from the empty crib to the window the night of March 1 and placing his hands flat against the wall as he looked out in search of his son and the abductors. Nor did Hudson find any prints belonging to Betty Gow in the nursery. One of his early conclusions was that someone had gone to the trouble to erase relevant prints. Certain members of the state police downplayed the Hudson fingerprint method as untested.

The Lindbergh-Breckinridge approach to the press remained as paradoxical as that with the state police. Lindy not only insisted on the news blackout that had driven the media off the estate and dramatically reduced the number of printable stories, but upon suspecting that someone inside the Sorrel Hill nerve center was leaking information to a major news organization, he adopted the role of spy master: He dispatched a young police officer to infiltrate the reporters hanging around Gebhart's Hotel in Hopewell.[7]

Laura Vitray again witnessed Henry Breckinridge playing good guy to Lindbergh's bad guy. When the *New York Sun,* whose headlines had been dominated by the crime, dropped it as the lead news piece, Breckinridge sought out one of the paper's reporters. "I notice that the *Sun* is beginning to play this story down," he said to the journalist. "Use your influence, if you can, to have them keep it on page one. You boys down there are doing splendid work. The situation is just as we want it to be. With Schwarzkopf snapping at you and everybody apparently knocking the press around, which creates the right public impression, you are still running plenty of good cock-and-bull stories that are doing a lot of good. Thanks!"[8] Colonel Henry's reason for wanting good cock-and-bull stories in print: to keep pressure on the kidnappers to deal with Lindbergh.[9]

The one area where Lindbergh and Breckinridge did not impose their views and rules, and where they were profusely tolerant of the most outrageous and debilitating actions—often at the price of secrecy and projected future dealings with the kidnappers—was with the go-betweens.

Lindy and Henry were having more than their share of headaches from news stories being leaked by Morris ("Mickey") Rosner. Why they ignored Thayer's recommendation to get rid of Rosner is puzzling. Their alternative action—an attempt to isolate the acerbic little underworld character from the rest of the household—was both tepid and flagellatory. Discovering that he had not been told of Owney Madden's visit to the estate, Mickey tried to bolster his position vis-à-vis the investigation by a private public relations campaign in the press, one result of which was the March 10, *New York Daily News* report that Madden had been brought in on the case by Rosner. The *New York Mirror* revealed that it had been Al Capone who ordained that Spitale and Bitz—Madden had opposed recruiting them—should be the underworld go-betweens for Lindbergh.

The greatest slight of all for Mickey was learning that he had not been told that a fourth ransom note had been received by Condon.[10] Rosner confronted Lindy and Henry with the assertion that he had been in contact with the kidnappers through a different set of newspaper ads from those he placed for Breckinridge and that the kidnappers were furious he had been bypassed and not shown the fourth ransom message. How had the kidnappers found out he was being bypassed? Rosner contended that Breckinridge had sent his secretary to the *New York American* to place an answer to the fourth ransom note and that the *American* refused to publish it unless the identity of the person inserting it was revealed; as a result of this, Henry had been forced to call a contact at the paper and acknowledge the ad was his. The secretary returned with the text but had to sign a receipt before it was accepted. Rosner maintained that once Breckinridge acknowledged being the person who inserted the ad, the kidnappers found out and were so angry they postponed negotiations indefinitely and threatened to kill the child. Rosner claimed he had worked assiduously to convince the kidnappers to continue negotiating. He believed they would. He also believed the infant would be delivered within the next twenty-four hours or so.

When Lindbergh and Breckinridge still did not confide in him, Rosner went to Thayer with his story, adding that the two colonels were astonished that he knew about the fourth ransom note, and as a result they were now convinced he must be the one who was in communication with the kidnappers. Nevertheless, Rosner said he believed they were attempting to get the child back without his knowledge. He also told Thayer that the fourth note had come through a Dr. Stacey, who was connected with Fordham University. Mickey asked the young lawyer to provide him with the doctor's true name and address.[11]

Jafsie Condon got home shortly after 6:00 P.M. on March 11. Henry Breckinridge arrived a little later. Condon's wife, Myra, told them of a noon call from a man with an accent who said he would telephone back at 7:00 P.M. Al Reich, a former boxer and Condon's closest chum, also showed up at the house, waited with Breckinridge, the Condons, and their daughter, also named Myra, for the kidnappers to make contact. Seven P.M. came and went without incident. The phone rang. Condon lifted the receiver and said, "Who is it, please?" Only he would be privy to the conversation which, according to him, went as follows.

An accented, guttural voice of a man asked, "Did you get my letter with the *sing-nature?*"

Condon said he had.

"I saw your ad in the *New York American.*"

"Yes. Where are you calling from?"

"Westchester Square. Doctor Condon, do you write sometimes pieces for the papers?"

"Yes, I sometimes write articles for the papers."

Condon claimed that after a pause the man spoke in a dimmer voice, which seemed directed away from the phone, as if he had turned his head from the mouthpiece as he repeated, *"He say sometimes he writes pieces for the paper."*

Condon "realized with sudden shock" that the man was talking with a companion.

"Stay in every night this week." The guttural voice was loud again. "Stay at home from six to twelve. You will receive a note with instruction. Ect accordingly or all will be off."

"I shall stay in," Condon promised.

Condon reported to have heard a second voice on the other end saying, *"Statti citto!"* He knew it was Italian and meant "shut up."

"All right," said the guttural voice that was talking to Condon. "You will hear from us."[12]

The voice had an accent, either Scandinavian or German, as best Condon could tell. All the ransom messages to date had phrasing and spelling that indicated they may have been written by a German or a Scandinavian.

For law-enforcement officials—and historians—there would be something far more important regarding Condon's account of the phone call. The old professor maintained he distinctly heard a second voice say "shut up" in Italian. This meant that at least two people were involved, giving further credence to the "kidnap gang" theory.

Henry Breckinridge, who probably knew as well as Lindbergh that the baby had not been stolen, now declared he was satisfied that Jafsie was in touch with the actual kidnappers. A pair of immediate tasks loomed. The first, to assemble the ransom money, would be handled by the Morgan bank. The second was that a box must be found or built in which the money could be delivered to the kidnappers, one that met the specifications in the letter the extortionists had Condon take to Lindbergh. Condon had just the item in his attic, an 1820 ballot box constructed of five different woods and fitted out with a brass lock and brass bindings—a distinctive container that, if found again after carrying money to the extortionists, might bare valuable evidence, such as fingerprints. Henry Breckinridge approved the use of the box. It was also agreed that Condon should find a cabinetmaker who could alter the box to fit the specifications.

On March 12, the Jafsie ads were repeated in the *New York American* and the *Bronx Home News*.[13] By early evening Condon, his wife and daughter, Al Reich, and Henry Breckinridge had gathered downstairs at the Condon home to await word. Condon informed Breckinridge that the altered box would be ready within four days, at a cost of three dollars for labor and materials. Jafsie's son-in-law, free of charge, would submit a blueprint from which the craftsman could work. Milton Gaglio and Max Rosenhain joined the group waiting at the Condon home.

At 8:30 the doorbell rang. Condon opened the front door. Standing before him was a cab driver. Parked at the curb was a taxi. "Dr. Condon?"

Condon nodded, "I am Doctor Condon."[14]

The driver held out a white envelope, on which were written Condon's name and address in the large, crude lettering seen in the previous ransom messages.

Condon had the driver wait in the parlor as he took the envelope into the living room. Breckinridge was at his side when it was opened. The message was in the familiar hand of all previous communications. The symbol of interlocking circles was identical to the others. The text read as follows:

> Mr. Condon
> We trust you but we will note come in your Hause it is to dnager. even you can note know if Police or secret service is watching you
> follow this insruction. Take a car and drive to the last supway station from Jerome Ave, here 100 feet from last station on the left seide is a empty frankifurther stand with a big open porch around. you will find a notise in senter of the porch underneath a stone. this notise will tell you were to find uss/
> Act accordingly
> After ¾ a houer be on the place. bring money with you.[15]

They didn't have the money yet. Jafsie wasn't concerned. This was an opportunity to meet the kidnappers and show them that he was anxious to work with them. Condon didn't drive. Since Breckinridge and Reich both had cars, it might have been expected that Henry would insist on taking Condon to the rendezvous on the off chance he could get a glimpse of the kidnappers. After all, it was the money of his client that was at stake—and the child of his closest friend. Henry also had more than his share of doubt regarding the veracity, and also the mental balance, of Condon. But Henry didn't make the crucial trip with Condon. Instead, Henry agreed to let Al Reich drive the old pedant.

Condon, Breckinridge, Reich, Rosenhain, and Gaglio confronted the slightly startled cabby waiting in the parlor. He said his name was Joseph Perrone and that earlier in the evening he had been hailed at Gun Hill Road and Knox Place by a man who wore a brown topcoat or overcoat and a brown felt hat that hid much of his face. The man tried to get into the backseat. Finding that the door was locked, he came up to the driver's window, which was partially open, and asked if Perrone knew where 2974 Decatur Avenue was. Perrone said he did, and the man handed him the envelope, gave him a dollar bill, told him to deliver the envelope, then walked to the rear of the cab and seemed to be jotting down the cab's license plate number. Before Perrone drove away, Milton Gaglio was able to check the identification number on the shield he wore on his chest against the identification card inside the taxi itself.

Henry Breckinridge accompanied Condon and Reich down the steps. Before they left in Reich's Ford coupe for the rendezvous, he gave them his blessings and shook their hands.

It was a cold, blustery night with little traffic as they drove to Jerome Avenue and followed it north to the last subway station. Approximately one hundred feet farther, on the opposite side of the street, was a deserted frankfurter stand. Making a U-turn, Al Reich pulled in beside it. Condon, who already had the door open, wasted little time in getting out and climbing onto the stand's dilapidated porch. A large rock rested in the center of the sagging wood floor. Beneath the rock was another long, white envelope. Condon moved under the streetlight near the car, slit open the envelope, withdrew the page, and read loud enough for Reich to hear:

> Cross the street and follow the fence from the cemetery
> direction 233rd street.
> I will meet you there.[16]

They drove along empty, fence-fronted Jerome Avenue for nearly a mile before stopping fifty feet short of 233rd Street. In the darkness on one side of them stretched the shadowy expanses of Van Cortlandt Park. Behind a nine-foot-high iron fence on the other side was Woodlawn Cemetery. Slightly beyond where they were parked was one of the cemetery's main entrances, a triangular plaza of three locked heavy iron gates.

"When they shoot you tonight," Reich quipped, "they won't have to take you far to bury you."[17] Then he asked to come along and protect Condon in case the kidnapper tried something. If he did try something they could nab him. His requests were refused.

Seventy-two-year-old John F. Condon got out of the car, walked up the desolate street to the looming iron gates, and waited in the darkness before them. Sensing that he might be watched, he took out the message, read it again, returned it to his pocket, strolled back and forth in front of the gates. Time passed. He returned to the car, got in, discussed with Al what could have gone wrong. Al spotted a man coming toward them from 233rd Street and alerted Condon, who got out and started for the stranger. Passing Condon without any sign of recognition, the man continued on his way.

Condon returned to the cemetery entrance. It was cold, and he was standing slightly turned away from the gates. Something moving caught his eye—a cloth of some sort. He glanced over and saw an arm protruding from the vertical bars of the iron fence and waving a handkerchief. Barely visible on the other side of the gate was the dim figure of a man.

"I see you," Condon called. As he approached the gate, the man retreated several feet, stopped, and held the handkerchief up before his face. He had on a dark overcoat and a pulled-down soft felt hat. Silhouetted in the darkness behind him were barren trees and tombstones.

"Did you gotted my note?" the man asked with a guttural accent.

Condon was certain it was the same voice that had called him at home the night before. "I got it."

"You gotted the money with you?"

"I could not bring the money until I saw the baby or—"

The sound of a cracking twig was heard. A guard approached from farther inside the cemetery.

"There is a cop," the man cried. He jammed the handkerchief into his overcoat pocket, clambered up the eight-foot-high gate, vaulted over the top, landed on both feet in front of Condon, and thrust a hand into his pocket as if to grasp a gun. "Did you call the cops?" Condon, who couldn't make out the face in the darkness, swore he hadn't. A guard appeared inside the gate, shouting what was going on. The man bolted across the street and into Van Cortlandt Park. Condon yelled at the guard not to worry. Then the seventy-two-year-old former trophy-winning distance runner followed after the fleeing man in the overcoat and soft felt hat, calling, "Hey, come back here. Don't be so cowardly."

The man ran into a little clump of trees near a shack in Van Cortlandt Park. Condon caught up with him there. The man's head was bowed forward, and his left hand had drawn the lapels of his coat together over his chin and the lower part of his face. The right hand was thrust ominously into a pocket. He allowed Condon to grip him by the elbow and lead him to a nearby bench and obeyed the order to sit while the elderly pedant made sure the coast was clear.

"Hey," said Condon, who was sitting beside him on the bench now, "you mustn't do anything like that again. You are my guest."

"It's too dangerous," the man explained. "Might be twenty years or burn. Would I burn if the baby is dead?"

"What is the use of this, what is the meaning? Why should we be here carrying on negotiations, if the baby is dead?"

"The baby is not dead. The baby is better than it was. We give more for him to eat than we heard in the paper from Mrs. Lindbergh. Tell the Colonel not to worry, the baby is all right."

To determine if he was talking to the right man, Condon took out the safety pins he had removed from the crib of the Lindbergh baby the night he stayed at Hopewell. "Have you ever seen these before?"

"Yes. Those pins fastened the blanket to the mattress in the baby's crib. Near the top, near the pillow."

Convinced that he was talking to at least one of the kidnappers, Condon said, "You know my name. Please tell me yours."

"John."

"My name is John, too. Where are you from, John?"

"Up farder than Boston."

"What do you do, John?"

"I am a sailor."

"*Bist du Deutsch?*" Condon asked in German. John seemed not to understand. "Are you German?"

"No, I am Scandinavian."

"You don't look like the kind of man that would be involved in a kidnapping. Is your mother alive, John?"

"Yes."

"What would she say if she knew you were mixed up in a thing like this?"

"She wouldn't like it. She would cry." He coughed once, sharply, into the lapels of his coat.

"Your coat is too thin for this time of year. Take my coat. I have another at home."

"No," said John.

"Come with me then, and I will get you something for your cough." When John only shrugged, Condon said, "You have nothing to be afraid of. We're alone. I have been square all my life and I am square with you now. You have nothing to fear." Condon suddenly barked out an order. "Take down that coat."

John hesitated. "Well—"

"Well, nothing. Take down that coat!"

John brought his right hand out of his pocket. He was not holding a gun. Condon let loose the left elbow. With his left hand John put down the collar of the coat, but his right hand shot back into the pocket as if reaching for a weapon, and he turned his head away and looked down. In that instant Condon was able to see that John's mouth was small, his eyes deep set above high cheekbones. In the semidarkness his complexion appeared sallow. Condon estimated him to be about thirty-five years old.

Condon had John by the left arm again. "Give me a chance. I promised Colonel and Mrs. Lindbergh that I would help them get their baby back. I am not here to harm or trap you. Where is the baby?"

"Tell Colonel Lindbergh the baby is on a boad." John was suddenly talkative and explained that the boat was six hours away and that the child was being cared for by two "womens." The boat was marked by removable white cloths on its mast. He went on to say that the kidnapping gang was composed of six members. The number-one man, the boss, worked for the government and in private life was a very high official. "Number Two knows you well," John told Condon. "He says we can drust you."

"Then why doesn't Number Two come to see me?"

"He's afraid. He might be caught from you."

"What are you getting out of this, John?"

John explained that out of the seventy-thousand-dollar ransom, Number One was to receive twenty thousand dollars; he and two other "mens" and the two nurses were each to have ten thousand dollars.

"You made a bargain with Colonel Lindbergh to return his baby for fifty thousand dollars. You should stick to your word."

"Colonel Lindbergh talked to the police." John explained that the protracted negotiations were not only incurring additional expense but imperiling the gang.

"It seems to me, John, that you are doing the most dangerous work in the case."

"I know it."

"You are getting only ten thousand dollars. I don't think you are getting what you ought to get."

"I know. I'm sorry I got mixed up—"

"Look, John," Condon said. "Leave them. Come with me to my house. I will get you my one thousand dollars. Then I will take you to Jersey to see if I cannot get the money for you from Colonel Lindbergh. That way you can be on the side of the law." He went on to say that he knew lawyers who could represent John. "Take me to the baby. I promise you that I shall act as a hostage until every cent of the money is paid." John seemed not to understand the word *hostage*.

"I shall be with the baby until the money is in your hands."

"No," said John. "They would schmack me oud. They vould drill me."

"Leave them. Don't you see? Sooner or later you will be caught."

"Oh, no. We have planned this case for a year already."

"Come, now, John. You can't expect us to pay the money without seeing the baby and knowing that he is alive and the right baby." Condon tapped his coat pocket. "I have some of the baby's toys with me. And I know some words the baby can speak. I will be able to tell whether it is the right baby. And I shall remain with the baby until every cent of the money is paid."

"No, the leader vould drill the both of us. He vould be mad if he knows I said so much and stayed so long."

"Don't go yet. We have to make arrangements. I want to return the baby personally. But I would gladly give up that privilege if you wish to handle things without me—just so the baby is returned to its parents. Transfer it to any priest, John. He will keep your name secret. He will not report you to the police. He will see to it that it is returned safely to its parents."

"I go now," John said. "I have stayed too long already. Number One will be mad. I should have gottit the money."

"All right. Get your men together in a decent way and have the work done on a cash-and-delivery basis. You are sure the baby is all right?"

"The baby is better than it was. It is happy and well. Number One told me I should tell you the baby is well. So put an ad in the *Home News* Sunday, like this, to show Number One that I gave you the message, 'Baby is alive and well.' And put this in too, 'Money is ready,' to show my friends I saw you and you will pay the money."

The papers had been filled with stories on Henry ("Red") Johnsen, who was being held as a possible suspect in the kidnapping. He was the boyfriend of the missing baby's nursemaid, Betty Gow. Condon now asked if Johnsen and Gow were implicated.

John reacted emotionally for the first time in their conversation. "Red Johnsen is innocent. He must be freed. The girl too! Red Johnsen had nuitting to do wid it. It was worth my life to come here, and now it seems you don't druts me. Don't you believe that we are the ones who gottit the baby—that we are the ones who should gottit the money? Now I go. I will sent by ten o'clock Monday morning a token."

"The sleeping suit from the baby."

The two men were standing, and Condon told John, "I will put the ad in the *Home News* tomorrow."[18]

They shook hands and parted—with Condon not knowing if John was Scandinavian or German. There was something else Condon did not know, because he had not been shown the previous ransom messages received by Lindbergh and Breckinridge or told what they contained. In the letter sent to Breckinridge, the extortionist had made a claim John also revealed to Condon in the cemetery: The crime had been planned for a year.

On the twelfth of March, as Prohibition indictments against Spitale and Bitz made the newspapers, the commissioner of the New York Police Department, Edward Mulrooney, let reporters know that Lindbergh's "personal secretary," Morris Rosner, had once been indicted on three counts of land fraud. If, as reported, Lindbergh and Breckinridge were infuriated by the commissioner's statement, which Henry took to be malicious, they couldn't have found much solace on learning of Rosner's latest ploy: He implied to reporters that he, Spitale, and Bitz were merging forces with the greatest mobster of them all, Al Capone.

In 1930, "Scarface" Al Capone was the most powerful and compelling gangster in the world. A strutting cock who gloried in the spotlight, his net worth was estimated at twenty-four million dollars, and he was earning another one million a month. In October of 1931, no one was more surprised than Big Al when a federal court in Chicago found him guilty of income tax evasion and sentenced him to eleven years in prison.

At the time the Lindbergh baby was reported stolen on March 1, Al had been in jail four months, pending his appeal of the eleven-year sentence. Word of his anger at the child's being kidnapped was in several March 2 newspapers. Reports over the subsequent few days had him offering to help find the infant. The Wednesday, March 9, *New York Mirror,* which said Al had ordered Spitale and Bitz into the case, also stated that Capone was said to have underwritten any and all expenses incurred by the two underworld emissaries, including payment to the kidnappers of any ransom moneys they expected to recover. According to the article, Capone's involvement in the case was mentioned to Lindbergh as early as Saturday, March 5, by a delegation of Chicago police officers attending the manhunt conference in Trenton called by Governor Moore. The *New York American* of March 11 announced that Capone had been interviewed by Arthur Brisbane, editorial director of the Hearst papers, to whom he said that he would do anything in his power to get the baby back and that no one was more capable of achieving this than he. Al, however, pointed out that there was little he could accomplish while sitting in a jail cell. If he were at liberty for a time, he was certain he could get results and was willing to post a two-hundred-thousand-dollar bond to guarantee he would return to incarceration after his release. The *New York Daily News* echoed Capone's comments the next day. The paper also reported that an airplane was standing by at Newark Airport to take Max Silverman, a New York bondsman, to Chicago with more than two hundred thousand dollars in bonds to secure Big Al's release. U.S. Attorney General Mitchell said that no such request for Capone's release had been received by the Justice Department.

The same morning that the *New York Daily News* article appeared, Rosner, Spitale, and Bitz met with Lindbergh and Breckinridge to argue the merits of enlisting Capone's help in recovering the child. They didn't claim that Al had the infant or knew his whereabouts, but they were confident that with his manpower and connections, Capone would soon have the baby back home. What's more, Al would pay the ransom. All that was needed was to secure a temporary release from jail for him, something Rosner and his associates were sure Lindbergh and Breckinridge could arrange with ease. And what did Big Al expect in return for his services? Only a small favor, such as a pardon or commutation of his sentence or parole. Lindbergh and Breckinridge said no to the plan, making it one of the few times they had rejected what appeared to be a promising contact with the kidnappers.[19]

Rebuffed by the two colonels, Rosner, Spitale, and Bitz went to Thayer, who doubted that anything could be done to secure Al's temporary release or meet his other conditions. Rosner explained that getting Spitale and Bitz to approach Capone was his "ace in the hole" should the kidnappers refuse to negotiate as a result of the mistake caused by Breckinridge's failure to take him into his confidence regarding the fourth ransom note. Also pressured by Spitale and Bitz, Thayer said he would look into what could be done for Capone but gave no guarantees.

Just who was leaking information to the press about Spitale, Bitz, and Capone remained moot, but someone had been, and the papers that day also published a statement by H. Norman Schwarzkopf in response to a question about the mobsters:

> The Police have not issued any request for the assistance of any of the characters mentioned. In the honest desire, however, to accomplish the return of the baby they will

welcome information of any kind leading to its recovery regardless of the source.

The identity of all people disclosing information leading to the recovery of the baby, whether the information be valuable or not, will be treated with confidence. This confidence is guaranteed in this circular and we will adhere strictly to it.[20]

At 6:00 P.M. Thayer, who was manning the phone at the Lindbergh house, received a call from the United Press informing him that Rosner had made a statement to the Associated Press saying he had definite knowledge that the baby was safe and well and that he would be returned to his parents in a few days. The UP reporter had assured Thayer that the AP reporter who ran the story was reliable. Confronted by Thayer, Rosner explained that the AP reporter had gained admission to his apartment under false pretenses and at the conclusion of the conversation had asked, "Do you think the baby is still alive." Rosner claimed he was shocked by the question and answered, "Of course. We have always hoped that the baby was alive and well."[21]

Early the next morning, Sunday, March 13, under intensive questioning by Thayer, Rosner admitted that to date Owney Madden, Spitale, and Bitz had not been able to locate the child but that they might yet succeed. Called into a conference later in the day with Lindbergh and Thayer, Rosner repeated in substance what he had told Thayer earlier but denied that he ever said that Madden, Spitale, and Bitz had failed in the effort to find the Eaglet. Rosner's new position was that even though Madden, Spitale, and Bitz had never admitted in so many words that they had made contact with the kidnappers, they might very well be in touch with them and for whatever their reasons they were not yet letting anyone know.

At the onset of his involvement in the case, Rosner had told Breckinridge that if an organized gang had the child, the underworld would produce it, and no ransom would be paid. He had also said that if the child wasn't held by the underworld, this, too, would be found out, thereby narrowing the possibilities of where he might be. Lindbergh and Breckinridge now agreed with Thayer's conclusion that, one, the gangs had failed to recover the infant and, two, Rosner, by dropping a word here and a word there, was giving the impression they were in contact with the kidnappers, which would facilitate his and his associates' taking credit even if the Eaglet were returned through other channels than the underworld.[22]

A Thursday, March 17, story in the *New York Mirror* stated that Morris Rosner, "man of super mystery" in the shadowy group that included Spitale and Bitz, was definitely informed at Hopewell by a spokesman for Lindbergh that he could consider his official relationship with the search for the baby at an end. Despite what the article said, Morris would find a way to stick around.

- - -

Between March 7 and March 17, Mrs. Evalyn Walsh McLean had waited at either her house in Washington or her country home, Far View, in Bradly Hills, Maryland, expecting the baby to be brought to her. Gaston B. Means offered various excuses for the delays, including that the kidnappers were having a difficult time getting through the heavy police ring drawn around the baby. To avoid the police-encirclement problem, Mrs. McLean suggested the delivery be made to her summer home in Aiken, South Carolina. Means agreed. On March 18, he requested an additional four thousand dollars for expenses. Mrs. McLean provided the money. Two days later she and her retinue of servants set off for South Carolina to await delivery of the baby.[23]

- - -

On returning home from his March 12 cemetery meeting with John, Jafsie Condon had told Henry Breckinridge that when his request to see the infant was denied, he had demanded assurances that John and his gang had the Eaglet, and John had volunteered to send them the child's sleeping suit. He further reported to Breckinridge that John's gang, wanting to be sure they were dealing with the authentic Dr. Condon, had given Jafsie the wording of a message he was to place in the papers.[24]

Reporters going over the personal ads in the *New York American* on Monday, March 14, came across the same notice that had appeared in the *Bronx Home News* the day before:

Money is ready. No cops. No secret service no press. I come alone like the last time. Please call Jafsie.

On Wednesday, March 16, the post office delivered a soft package to John F. Condon's home. Breckinridge denied Jafsie's request that they wait for Lindbergh to arrive and carefully undid the brown-paper wrapping. Inside was a neatly folded one-piece sleeping suit. The bundle also contained a long message that was written in a familiar hand on the front and back of a piece of paper and bore the signature of interlocking circles and perforations:

Dear Sir: Ouer man faill to collect the mony.
There a no more confidential conference after we
meeting from March 12. Those arrangemts to
hazardous for us. We will not allow ouer man to
confer in a way like befor. circumstance will not
allow us to make transfare like you wish. It is
impossibly for us. wy shuld we move the baby and
face danger. to take another person to the place
is entirely out of question. It seems you are
afraid if we are the right party and if the boy is
allright. Well you have ouer signature. It is
always the same as the first one specialy them 3
holes.

Now we will send you the sleepingsuit from the
baby it means 3 $ extra expenses because we have
to pay another one. please tell Mrs. Lindbergh not
to worry the baby is well. we only have to give
him more food as the diet says.
    You are willing to pay the 70000 note 50000 $
without seeing the baby first or note. let us know
about this in the New York-American. We can't do
it other ways because don't like to give ouer
safty plase or to move the baby. If you are
willing to accept this deal put these in paper.
    I accept mony is redy
    ouer program is:
After 8 houers we have the mony received we will
notify you where to find the baby. If there is any
trapp, you will be
    responsible what
    will follows.[25]

Wearing a disguise, Lindbergh left his estate and slipped past reporters. He reached Condon's house in the Bronx at 1:30 A.M., Thursday, March 17, and examined the garment at great length before pronouncing, "This is my son's sleeping suit. I wonder why they went to the trouble of having it cleaned."

"What?" asked Breckinridge.

"The sleeping suit, it has been cleaned before being sent here. I wonder why?"[26]

When Breckinridge and Condon offered no answer, Lindbergh said, "We must pay the ransom as soon as possible. There should be no delays. After all, this man has kept his word with us throughout. And he knows that we've kept our word. I will not permit any schemes to trap him. He wants the money. And if he gets it, I see no reason why he won't keep his end of the bargain and return my boy."

Jafsie was still of the opinion that the baby should be seen before money changed hands and that mention of this be made in their response. Lindbergh dismissed the old man's suggestion saying, "We're going to play by their rules. Run the ad they want."

The March 17 notice in the *New York American* read as follows:

> I accept. Money is ready. John, your package is delivered and is O.K. Direct me. Jafsie

The kidnappers had specified only that the ad be placed in the *American*. Thanks to Jafsie Condon, it also ran in the *Bronx Home News*, as had been the case with all the previous messages.

12

OPEN SECRETS

DESPITE OFFICIAL DENIALS, REPORTERS KNEW A RANSOM NOTE HAD BEEN
found the night of the kidnapping. Many of them correctly reasoned that
Lindy might follow the established practice used by kidnappers and relatives of a stolen victim and negotiate for the return of the baby via personal ads in the daily newspapers. They were unaware of who Condon
was, let alone that he had come to Sorrel Hill in the dead of night and left
the next day with Henry Breckinridge, but reading the March 11 edition
of the *New York American,* sharp-eyed newsmen came across an ad that
said, "I accept. Money is ready. Jafsie." From then on, Jafsie watching
became a prime pastime for the press.

If reporters covering the crime hadn't noticed that the Jafsie ads were
also running in the *Bronx Home News,* the paper's readership did. Calls
and letters had been received inquiring as to the notices. Fearing that
Condon's secret role in the negotiations might be compromised, the editor of the *Home News* publicly denied that the Jafsie messages had anything to do with the Lindbergh case. This didn't prevent a New York

City daily from sending a young writer to Condon's door on the evening of March 17, as the old professor and Breckinridge were waiting for Lindbergh to arrive and examine the sleepwear. Condon's wife fibbed in telling the reporter that her husband wasn't home. The newsman, ostensibly doing a follow-up story, asked what kind of response, if any, had occurred as the result of Condon's public offer to add a thousand dollars to the reward and act as intermediary. Mrs. Condon replied that other than a few crank letters, nothing much had come of it. The young reporter left.

Whereas Lindbergh and Breckinridge had reached Condon's home undetected and no one yet linked the chatty old man to the Jafsie notices, the press was closing in. Either on a hunch or as the result of a tip, the banner story on the front page of the *New York Mirror* for that same Thursday, March 17, was that the J. P. Morgan and Company bank had made available to the Lindberghs $250,000 with which to buy back their child. The report was partially correct. In the afternoon the Morgan bank sent one fifth of that amount, fifty thousand dollars, in currency to the Fordham branch of the Corn Exchange Bank, where it was placed in a special vault to which Condon had twenty-four-hour-a-day access.

The next morning, Friday, March 18, Condon awoke to find the young journalist among a horde of reporters waiting outside on the sidewalk. Donning a disguise, and with the assistance of Al Reich, Jafsie sneaked out of the house and gave a scheduled lecture. When he returned home, the inquiring newsmen were gone.

On Monday, March 21, Condon received a letter in the same distorted handwriting as that of the previous ransom messages and bearing the identical signature of perforations interlocking circles:

> Dear Sir: You and Mr. Lindbergh know ouer Program.
> If you don't accept den we will wait until you
> agree with ouer deal. we know you have to come to
> us anyway But why should Mrs. and Mr. Lindbergh
> suffer longer as necessary we will note
> communicate with your or Mr. Lindbergh until you
> write so in the paper.
>   we will tell you again; this kidnapping cace
> whas prepared for a year already so the Police
> won't have any luck to find us or the child. You
> only puch everything farther out did you that
> little package

to Mr. Lindbergh? It contains
the sleepingsuit for the baby.
the baby is well.

On the backside of the paper was this:

Mr. Lindbergh only wasting time with his search.[1]

It appeared that John had not seen the last ads. Breckinridge agreed that a new notice should be placed but differed with Condon, who continued to insist they must see the baby before paying the ransom. Lindbergh had ordained that they comply with every term laid down by the kidnappers, including not seeing the stolen infant prior to delivery. Even though this was how Breckinridge meant the matter to rest, this is the item Condon put in the March 22 editions of the *Home News* and the *New York American:*

> Thanks. That little package you sent me was immediately delivered and accepted as real article. See my position. Over fifty years in business and can I pay without seeing the goods? Common sense makes me trust you. Please understand my position. Jafsie

That same day at Sorrel Hill, Lindbergh greeted John Hughes Curtis, the Reverend Mr. H. Dobson-Peacock, and Admiral Guy Burrage. He had extended the invitation after receiving a letter from Burrage imparting that the kidnappers had instructed "Sam" to have Curtis organize a group of Norfolk, Virginia, citizens into a negotiating committee for the return of the stolen child.

Burrage had been in command of the U.S. warship that brought Lindbergh back to America after his historic flight to France, and the two men had remained friendly. Burrage had been recruited by the highly respected H. Dobson-Peacock, rector of the largest church in Norfolk. Dobson-Peacock was convinced that the tale told him by the owner of one of the largest shipbuilding yards in the South, John Hughes Curtis, was true: that the kidnapping gang had designated a man named Sam as their go-between, and Sam had asked the forty-three-year-old Curtis, whom he had met several years back, to help him get in touch with Lindbergh. Dobson-Peacock and Burrage had not met Sam—and never would. Even so, Curtis convinced them that Sam, a former rumrunner with many aliases, was the true go-between.

Once in their presence, Lindbergh apologized for not having responded sooner and pointed out that so much mail was being received that even a letter from the White House had been mislaid and not answered for ten days.[2] Curtis, a six-foot-two, two-hundred-pound Knute Rockne look alike, attempted to recount his conversations with Sam, only to be interrupted by numerous summonses that repeatedly took Lindbergh from the room.

According to Curtis, Sam told him that though the kidnappers were growing impatient, they had hired a special nurse, who was following the diet in the newspapers, and the baby was in good health. The nurse had also bought new clothes for the Eaglet. The baby was being held on a boat that might possibly be concealed along the shoreline of Chesapeake Bay, or it might be waiting beyond the territorial waters of the United States. Four days earlier Sam had made a concrete proposal by which Colonel Lindbergh could display his good faith to the kidnappers: Deposit twenty-five thousand dollars in a Norfolk bank under the names of Curtis, Dobson-Peacock, and Burrage.[3]

Lindbergh appeared unimpressed by the Curtis story and avoided stating how much ransom money he intended to pay. Burrage guessed the amount was fifty thousand, as the papers were speculating.

"I cannot agree on any sum until I have positive proof I am dealing with the right people," Lindbergh said. "They must show me they are not impostors. If they really have my child, they can easily prove it by describing certain characteristics which have not been made public." The Lone Eagle expressed his appreciation of the three Norfolk men's desire to help recover the infant, warning, "But I have to tell you, I think this Sam is deceiving you. I don't know what his game is, but I think he's a phony. I can't tell you how I know this, but I'm certain it's true."[4] Ostensibly, Lindbergh is here alluding to his inside information concerning Jafsie. But if he really believed Jafsie was in touch with the true kidnappers—which he gave every indication of believing—why would he keep the door open to this lead? But that's what he did. Adding to the legacy of contradictions that had marked his handling of the case to date, Lindbergh let it be known that if Sam could provide proof he was speaking for the kidnappers, he would negotiate with him.

On Thursday, March 24, word circulated that three Norfolk men, John Hughes Curtis, Admiral Burrage, and Rev. Dobson-Peacock, were not only in touch with the kidnappers but were preparing to pay the ransom. The news corps arrived, and Dobson-Peacock submitted to an afternoon interview, in which he confirmed that they had met with Lindbergh at Hopewell. He also substantiated their claim that they were in touch with the kidnappers, who had promised to return the baby prior to demanding the ransom payment. The next day, March 25, headline stories across the nation proclaimed that John Hughes Curtis was about to give the kidnappers fifty thousand dollars for the return of the baby, who was on a boat.

At Lindbergh's bidding, Schwarzkopf—several tabloids were printing that the trooper boss was on the outs with the Lone Eagle—informed the press, "The three citizens of Norfolk who visited Colonel Lindbergh gave him information which, on being investigated, was found to have no special significance."[5] John Hughes Curtis's reply, carried on the country's front pages, regretted the publicity he was causing and let Schwarzkopf know that no sooner had he returned from seeing Colonel Lindbergh at Sorrel Hill than Sam called him from Philadelphia with assurances that he represented the crooks who had the child. The Reverend Dobson-Peacock's statements to the press not only contended that he, Curtis, and Admiral Burrage had Lindbergh's authority to negotiate for the child's return but twitted Schwarzkopf by saying, "That man Shootskoff, or what ever his name is, has tried to hinder us from the outset."[6]

The trooper superintendent faced a problem more serious than criticism. He had run out of money with which to investigate the crime. The New Jersey State Police Emergency Fund consisted of only five thousand dollars. The investigation so far had cost ten times that amount. Several days earlier, as the public spat between himself, Curtis, and Dobson-Peacock filled the papers, he petitioned the State Finance Committee for more funds, promising to cut back on all nonessential expenditures regarding the case.[7]

As Morris Rosner had been irate about Dr. Condon's coming to the Lindbergh estate without his knowledge, Condon himself, still undiscovered by reporters, demanded to know what all the stories about John Hughes Curtis were. Breckinridge admitted that Curtis and associates had visited Sorrel Hill but assured Condon that he and Lindbergh had discounted the trio's story, that they remained committed to the old teacher's John as the man who would get the baby back, not Curtis's widely reported Sam.

Keeping Curtis in check was another matter. He informed Dobson-Peacock and Admiral Burrage that he would be meeting Sam on Sunday, March 27, in a New York City cafeteria.

That same Sunday, Condon, who had waited vainly for word from the kidnappers, ran another ad in the *Bronx Home News*:

> Money is ready. Furnish simple code for us to use in paper. Jafsie.

A single-page letter written in a familiar hand and bearing the three-circle, three-perforation signature arrived at Condon's home on Tuesday, March 29:

> dear Sir: It is note necessary to furnish any
> code. You and Mr. Lindbergh know ouer Program very
> well. We will keep the child in ouer same plase
> until we have the money in hand, but if the deal
> is note closed until the 8 of April we will ask
> for 30000 more. Also note 70000–100000.
> How can Mr. Lindbergh follow so many false clues
> he knows we are the right party ouer signature is
> still the same as in the ransom note. But if Mr.
> Lindbergh likes to fool around for another month,
> we can help it.
> Once he has come to us anyway but if he keeps on
> waiting we will double ouer amount. There is
> absolute no fear aboud the child it is well.[8]

Breckinridge was at Condon's house when the letter arrived. Lindbergh, costumed in a hunting cap and dark glasses, joined them past midnight.[9] After reading the text, he instructed Breckinridge to place a newspaper ad in which John's terms were accepted. Condon continued to press for their seeing the baby before turning over the money and volunteered to be a hostage. Again he was overruled. The ad appeared in both the *New York American* and the *Bronx Home News* that Tuesday afternoon of March 31:

> I hereby accept. Money is ready. Jafsie.

On April Fools' Day, Condon received a letter that had been mailed from the nearby Fordham Station branch of the post office. Inside was another envelope and the following instructions:

> Dear Sir, please handel inclosed letter to Col.
> Lindbergh. It is in Mr. Lindbergh interest not to
> notify police.[10]

It was not until now that Lindbergh chose to inform H. Norman Schwarzkopf of the plan to have Condon pay John the ransom. H. Norman, whose organization had no mandate to operate outside the state of New Jersey, wanted his men to go to New York and tail Jafsie to the meeting, then follow John, and pick him up after the baby was returned. Lindbergh would have none of it. He forbade Schwarzkopf to follow anyone and ordered him to stay out of the picture.

The author could find no record of Schwarzkopf's reaction to the curt and often humiliating commands of Charles Lindbergh. Whatever frustrations he and his men felt were often vented on others but never on the Lone Eagle.

Lindbergh arrived at Condon's home around noon. The letter in the envelope addressed to him had the familiar handwriting and the circle-perforation signature.

> Dear Sir: have the money ready by Saturday
> evening, we will inform you where and how to
> deliver it. have the money in one bundle we want
> you to put it in a sertain place. Ther is no fear
> that somebody els will take it, we watch
> everything closely. Blease tell us know if you are
> agree and ready for action Saturday evening—if
> yes put in paper
>   "Yes everything O.K."
> It is a very simple delivery but we find out very
> sun if there is any trapp. After 8 houers you gett
> the Adr: from the boy. on the place
> you find two
> ladies. the are
> innocence.

On the other side of the page was this:

If it is too late we put in the New York American
for Saturday morning. Put it in New York Journal.[11]

An ad prepared for the next day's editions of the *New York Journal*
and the *Bronx Home News* stated the following:

Yes. Everything O.K. Jafsie

Charles Lindbergh had refused all offers of financial assistance, including that from his millionaire mother-in-law, and had insisted on putting up the money himself. Lindy was a well-to-do man on paper, but
converting this into seventy thousand dollars in hard cash during the
worst year of the Great Depression required him to sell off a good portion of his stock market holdings at one fifth their value.[12]

— — —

A potent indication that Lindbergh might have known there was no real
kidnapping was his staunch refusal to have the ransom bills marked.
Once the money was paid, the extortionists would be free to go their own
way and couldn't mistakenly be charged with a kidnapping they hadn't
committed. It was hoped the whole matter of the child's disappearance
would be forgotten all the quicker. The ransom letters had demanded
unmarked bills, and Lindy let it be known firmly that he intended to
comply; he would do nothing else to upset the criminals. The first fifty
thousand dollars the Morgan bank had already sent to the Fordham
branch of the Corn Exchange Bank was in bills that were not marked.

Detective Jimmy Finn of the NYPD disapproved. So did Elmer Irey,
the U.S. Treasury Department's chief law-enforcement agent. Irey had
come to Sorrel Hill with IRS intelligence agents Frank J. Wilson, Pat
O'Rourke, and Arthur B. Madden to advise Lindbergh on methodolo-
gies for making a ransom payment.[13] Lindbergh contended he did not
want to scare off the kidnappers. The lawmen argued that should a ransom be delivered and the child not returned per the agreement, the currency was one of the few ways of tracking down the criminals. Physically
marking the bills was not necessary, but a record of the serial numbers
must be kept. Irey was insistent that U.S. gold certificates, which were
easier to spot, be included among the currency. The intractable Lindbergh finally acceded. The fifty thousand dollars in the special vault of

the Fordham branch of the Corn Exchange Bank was returned to the Morgan Company.

On Friday, April 1, IRS agents and fourteen Morgan bank clerks took eight hours to assemble and record the serial numbers of seventy thousand dollars in used currency according to the denominations specified by John.[14] No two bills had sequential numbers, and a majority of the ten- and twenty-dollar notes were U.S. gold certificates. The money was divided into two bundles, the larger of which contained fifty thousand dollars and the smaller, twenty thousand dollars. The bundles were tied together with string. Within each bundle, packets of bills were held together by paper-currency bands from the Morgan bank and arranged in neat stacks. Samples of the string as well as the paper-currency bands were set aside for later identification.

On that same April Fools' afternoon, while the ransom money was being prepared in New York City, Elsie Whateley, the Lindbergh family cook, and Betty Gow, the nursemaid, discovered a shiny object while walking up to the house atop Sorrel Hill: one of the two metal thumb guards the baby was wearing the night it disappeared. The string that had tied the guard to the infant's wrist was still attached. The women had been chatting with one of the state policemen on duty at the main gate and on their return to the house spotted the metal restrainer along a section of gravel driveway that they had traveled almost every day since the infant's disappearance. Since most law-enforcement agents stationed at the house had also passed this same tract every day for a full month, questions arose as to why they, too, had not noticed the thumb guard. One answer was that until recently it hadn't been there.

While the "Yes. Everything O.K. Jafsie" ads ran in the April 2 editions of the *Journal,* the *New York Daily News* reported that the wife of John Hughes Curtis was off on secret kidnapping business and Curtis himself was waiting to hear from Sam. Curtis phoned Sorrel Hill, wanting to speak with Lindbergh, and ended up on the line with Rosner, whom he told that he was with an emissary from the kidnappers. The emissary had a letter for Lindbergh and only Lindbergh. Mickey rose to the occasion and finally got through to Lindy, who with Breckinridge, John Condon, and Al Reich were at Jafsie's home in the Bronx, awaiting the imminent and prearranged word from the kidnappers. Lindbergh's message for Curtis was that the emissary and the message he bore would have to wait.[15]

Early in the day of April 2, Lindbergh had used Al Reich's Ford to pick up the two packages of ransom money and drive the money to Condon's house, where he remained, intent on chauffeuring Jafsie to the rendezvous, hopefully that very night. Lindy would later explain that having reasoned that the old man was the only one who could identify John, and therefore might be at risk once the money was transferred, he was armed with a small handgun. Nobody had anticipated the volume required for seventy thousand dollars in five-, ten-, and twenty-dollar bills. Only with great difficulty was one of the two bundles of currency, the larger package, containing fifty thousand dollars, wedged into the wooden container that had been requested by the kidnappers.

It seems probable that Charles Lindbergh invoked one final safeguard to ensure that the extortionists not be captured: He insisted that no policemen be in the area of Dr. Condon's home and that he and Jafsie not be followed should they have to leave the house. With that large an expanse off limits to the police and a no-follow rule in effect, the culprit had a virtual passport to freedom. Lindbergh's order was easily complied with by H. Norman Schwarzkopf, who hadn't been invited to New York and was being told next to nothing about what was happening. The commissioner of the New York Police Department, Edward P. Mulrooney, whose men had the jurisdiction and obligation to apprehend a kidnapper or extortionist, acceded to Lindbergh's wishes. Mulrooney's order for the night of April 2 dictated that the area above 125th Street and the Harlem River was off limits to New York's finest. Adherence to the Lindbergh proscription meant that the kidnappers could not be followed once the ransom was paid them. It would also result in the police, most of whom were unaware of what was about to take place, not making arrangements to examine the scene of the money transfer immediately after the fact. The Lindbergh-Breckinridge cloak of secrecy was now complete—but it had already been penetrated. A third law-enforcement agency, J. Edgar Hoover's Bureau of Investigation, which had received no official notification of the ban, was in the forbidden territory and keeping Condon's house on Decatur Avenue under surveillance from a room across the street.

Not only had the BI been shut out of the kidnapping investigation by

H. Norman Schwarzkopf since the inception of the crime, but an offer conveyed by two of its special agents to assist in finding the missing child had been personally rebuffed by Lindbergh himself, whom the operatives listed in one of their reports as being uncooperative. So total was the bureau's isolation from the case that its personnel still weren't certain if a ransom message had been found in the nursery the night the child disappeared. But the organization did have a potential informant.

The BI's most promising contact with anyone close to the inner machinations of Sorrel Hill had been an aviator friend of Lindbergh's by the name of Thomas Lanphier. The BI man in the process of gaining Lanphier's confidence and aid was E. J. Connelley. On March 23, Lanphier had arranged for Connelley to visit Sorrel Hill. Lindbergh volunteered no more information than before, but while giving Lanphier and Connelley a ride back to New York, Cal (the acronym the BI would later use in reference to the Lone Eagle) let it be known that he was meeting with Breckinridge and two officers from the Special Intelligence Unit of the Internal Revenue Service, Frank Wilson and Arthur Madden. Lanphier subsequently informed Connelley that Lindbergh distrusted Wilson and Madden—who were advising him on procedures by which the ransom money could be made easier to trace—and that he had avoided giving them information about the kidnapping.[16]

Five days later, March 28, acting on what Connelley alleged was a significant lead, Lanphier contacted Henry Breckinridge, who was spending most of his time at Condon's home, awaiting word from the kidnappers. A meeting was arranged away from the Decatur Avenue house. The special agent's information proved to be of small relevance, but in the course of their two-hour conversation the "very cagey" Breckinridge opened up enough for Connelley to learn that Lindbergh had definitely heard from the kidnappers, that a go-between had already rendezvoused with the gang in a graveyard, that the kidnappers had agreed to return the baby two hours after the ransom was paid.[17] Another thing he said was that the kidnapper appeared to be German or Germanic.

At the close of March, Connelley found out from Lanphier that the original ransom demand of fifty thousand dollars had been increased to seventy thousand dollars. Far more important was Lanphier's disclosure that the Lindbergh representative who had met the kidnappers in the cemetery was a Dr. John Condon of 2974 Decatur Avenue in the Bronx. Condon was attached to Fordham University and had used his initials, J.F.C., to place the Jafsie ads in the *New York American* and the *New York Journal*.

Connelley initiated an immediate background investigation of Condon at Fordham and discovered that a lawyer from Breckinridge's office had beaten the BI to the information. Connelley also placed mail coverage on 2974 Decatur Avenue—and spotted the April 1 letter to Condon that contained a sealed message for Lindbergh. One special agent would later contend that the crude writing on the outer envelope left him with the impression that the author might have been German. Lanphier, fearing that danger was imminent, pressed Connelley to initiate protective action. A special agent by the name of Lackey took up surveillance in a room opposite Condon's house. Two backup special agents, who were ready to move on a telephone command, went into a room a block away.

— — —

At 7:45 P.M. Saturday evening, April 2, the night the ransom message had told Lindbergh to be ready for action—and with BI agents waiting across the street and up the block—a taxicab pulled up in front of Jafsie Condon's house. The driver got out and brought a letter up to the front door.

13

PAYOFF

AT 7:45 P.M. Saturday, April 2, the bell at 2974 Decatur Avenue rang. John F. Condon's daughter, Myra, opened the front door to a taxi driver. He was thin, dark, young, and definitely not the same cabby who had delivered the March 12 message, which had sent Condon and Al Reich to Woodlawn Cemetery, where Jafsie met with John. The driver handed an envelope to Myra, went to his cab, and drove off. Myra brought it inside, where Lindbergh, Breckinridge, Condon, and Reich were waiting. The handwriting Lindy read was familiar:

> Dear Sir: Take a car and follow tremont Ave. to the
> east until you reach the number 3225 tremont ave.
>   It is a nursery
>   Bergen
>   Greenhauses florist
> Ther is a table standing outside right on the door.

> You find letter undernead the table covert with a
> stone, read and follow instruction.

Then came the interlacing signature of three circles and three tiny perforations and more of the message:

> Don't speak to anyone on the way. If there is a radio
> alarm for policecar, we warn you we have same
> equipment. have the money in one bundle
> we give you ¾ houer to reach the place.[1]

Special Agent Lackey, in a stakeout across the street, failed to observe
Charles Lindbergh and John F. Condon as they exited 2974 Decatur
Avenue, carrying a wooden box containing fifty thousand dollars' ransom as well as a package in which another twenty thousand dollars was
wrapped. Nor did he notice them get into Al Reich's Ford coupe—a car
John might have seen when he met with Condon at Woodlawn Cemetery—and leave.

Lindbergh drove; Condon was beside him. Heading in the direction of
Long Island Sound, they arrived at 3225 East Tremont Avenue, a dark,
closed floral shop and greenhouse bearing the name J. A. Bergen. Condon walked up to a table outside the establishment. On the table was a
stone. Beneath the stone was an envelope, which he brought back to the
car. Under the dash lights, he and Lindbergh read the instructions:

> cross the street and walk to the next corner and
> follow whittemore Ave to the soud
> take the money with you. come alone
> and walk
> I will meet you.[2]

Lindbergh wanted to accompany Jafsie. The old man, who had so
often ignored instructions contained in ransom communications, resisted
on the grounds that the messages of this day stipulated that only he
should meet with John. Lindbergh remained at the car.

Condon dealt more liberally with other dictates of the current ransom
notes. Instead of bringing along the money as the unknown author
stated, he left it with Lindbergh before crossing the street and starting
along Tremont Avenue. The previous point of rendezvous had been a
graveyard, Woodlawn Cemetery, and so, it turned out, was this. The

section of Tremont Avenue he was walking along ran beside St. Raymond's Cemetery, a swampland reclaimed in 1877 and long favored by the families of Bronx-Irish politicians but whose most notorious denizen was the recently interred twenty-three-year-old Vincent ("Mad Dog") Coll.

Lindbergh watched from the Ford coupe as Condon, rather than obey the message's final instruction and turn onto Whittemore Avenue, an ominous dirt road leading in among gravestones, behind which a whole kidnapping gang could hide, continued on along Tremont Avenue, gazing beyond the tombstones nearest him. He stopped at the main gate of the cemetery, looked about for a moment or so, then walked back to the Whittemore Avenue intersection, from which he yelled to Lindbergh in the car, "I guess there's no one here. We'd better go back."[3]

From inside the cemetery a voice called out what would prove to be the most fateful words of the entire event, "Hey Doctor, over here."[4] Jafsie heard it. So did Lindbergh, who was sitting a distance away in the car.

Condon disappeared into St. Raymond's Cemetery. Lindbergh could not see or hear him. Some ten or twelve minutes later Jafsie returned to the car, bearing good news indeed. Two previous ransom messages had warned that information as to the child's whereabouts wouldn't be forthcoming until eight hours after the ransom had been paid. Now Condon told Lindbergh that not only had he just talked to John in the graveyard but that John had gone to fetch a "receipt," a note saying just where the baby was. Jafsie also contended that John had agreed to accept fifty thousand dollars as ransom, rather than seventy thousand dollars.

Lindbergh handed Condon the wooden box containing the fifty thousand dollars, which the aged pedant carried into the graveyard. After a brief interlude he returned to the car without the box. Condon gave Lindbergh an envelope and relayed "what had happened and what had been said."[5]

"John said you are not to open it for six hours. He said the baby is all right. They need six hours to escape. The child, according to Condon, was on a boat called the *Nelly*."[6]

In an action that a preponderance of investigators and newsmen would find incredible, Lindbergh put the unopened envelope into his pocket and drove off. Why not read it on the spot? Because, as it would later be explained, Lindy was honoring his end of the bargain with the kidnappers.

Less than a mile from the cemetery, Condon had them stop at a house he owned. Once on the porch, Jafsie provided Lindbergh with a rationale for reading the message without further delay: "You didn't promise the kidnappers anything. I made the promise."[7]

Lindbergh opened the envelope. The note was written in a hand similar to all the other ransom communications.

> the boy is on Boad Nelly
> it is a small Boad 28 feet
> long, two person are on the
> Boad, the are innosent.
> you will find the Boad between
> Horseneck Beach and gay Head
> near Elizabeth Island[8]

Special Agent Lackey saw Charles Lindbergh and John F. Condon return to Condon's home and would subsequently report that they were in possession of two black bags. He would also say that when they came out again, they were with Henry Breckinridge. By all other accounts, Al Reich was also with them.[9]

The four men left in Lindbergh's car and drove to Mrs. Morrow's townhouse, at 7 East Seventy-second Street, Manhattan, where other members of the inner circle were waiting. While Condon spoke with T-men Irey and Wilson about John, Lindbergh, Breckinridge, and other advisers began making preparations. The plan that evolved through the night and in the early hours of April 3 had the U.S. Navy and Coast Guard supporting an effort in which Lindbergh would use an amphibious navy plane to land at the *Nelly* and retrieve the child, then fly with him to the Aviation Country Club in Hicksville, Long Island.[10]

At dawn Condon was along as Lindbergh, Breckinridge, and Irey boarded a huge Sikorsky aircraft outside Bridgeport, Connecticut. Al Reich, left behind on the ground, drove Lindbergh's car to the Hicksville country club to await their arrival with the Eaglet.[11]

— — —

Though the atmosphere in the cabin of the airborne Sikorsky was charged with optimism, the singular voice heard above the reverberating clamor of the engines was that of Jafsie Condon reciting *Hamlet*.[12] With Lindbergh at the controls for much of the morning's search above Martha's Vineyard, off Cape Cod, and the adjoining Elizabeth Islands, many of the sweeps were flown only a few feet above the surface of the ocean. After six hours in the air, no boat that fit John's description of the *Nelly* had been spotted, nor was the craft seen by a navy warship and the half dozen Coast Guard boats that had joined the search armada.

Landing in Buzzards Bay, Massachusetts, and debarking for lunch at the Cuttyhunk Hotel on Cuttyhunk Island, Lindbergh and his party were confronted by a group of reporters who had been tipped off to his flight over the area. Breckinridge did what he could to cut off their questions and protect his party behind a wall of no comments. Never having seen or heard of Condon, the journalists presumed he was John Hughes Curtis, and ergo, for the wrong reason they correctly surmised that Lindbergh was looking for the ship on which his son was allegedly being kept.

The afternoon search from the Sikorsky and by navy and Coast Guard ships failed to locate the *Nelly*. At day's end Lindbergh landed the large seaplane at the prearranged spot on Long Island, where Al Reich was waiting with his car. Lindy drove Reich, Condon, Breckinridge, and Irey back to New York City in silence. When he finally did speak, it was to tell Condon that they'd been double-crossed by the kidnappers.[13]

Pulling up to a subway stop, Lindbergh asked, "Well, Doctor, what's the bill for your services?"[14] Jafsie would later write that he was insulted by the offer and that he marveled at Lindbergh's naïveté in believing the kidnappers could be trusted, even though it was Condon himself who had strenuously implied that John was telling him the truth and could be dealt with.

— — —

In the wake of Special Agent Lackey's reports for the night of April 2, the BI realized that a ransom had been paid not by John Hughes Curtis, as the papers were implying was about to occur, but by a man whose identity Charles Lindbergh and Henry Breckinridge had gone to untoward lengths trying to keep secret, John F. ("Jafsie") Condon. For J. Edgar Hoover and his men it was a profound breakthrough and particularly sweet revenge for having been excluded from the case until now. With Treasury Department people already on the scene and with the ransom payment occurring on NYPD turf, those agencies would be active in tracking down the men who got the money, but BI operatives appeared confident that they also had a firm foot in the manhunt door.

BI operatives wasted no time in speaking to Condon and learning of his nocturnal meeting with John in St. Raymond's. One of the things he revealed was that John, to come and meet him that night, had scaled a low fence at the cemetery. Jumping to the ground on the other side, John's foot sunk into the soft earth. On Monday morning, April 4, with Lindbergh back in the air searching for the *Nelly* and the previous "Yes. Everything O.K. Jafsie" ad running again in the *New York American*, BI Special Agent Thomas H. Sisk accompanied Condon and his son-in-law, Ralph Hacker, in a probe for the footprint John may have left when leaping over the wall. They found it on top of a grave.[15] Hacker and Sisk made a plaster of Paris cast of the impression.

The joint Lindbergh–Navy–Coast Guard air-and-sea hunt for the *Nelly* that same April 4 was being well covered by reporters. The Lone Eagle, who was flying alone, had switched to a Lockheed-Vega monoplane and brought along a small suitcase and his son's favorite blanket. The combined search was no more productive than that of the previous day. Lindbergh landed at New Jersey's Teterboro Airport and drove back to Sorrel Hill, where it was later reported that he spoke by phone to Henry Breckinridge, who was at Condon's home. Breckinridge, with Jafsie overhearing, told the Lone Eagle it was premature to assume they had been betrayed by John and the gang. He expressed confidence that the baby was well.[16] Patience and a firm belief that the kidnappers would make contact became the strategy for the specious future. Condon thought it might help to rouse John through a series of ads in the *Bronx Home News*. Breckinridge agreed. The first one ran on Tuesday, April 5:

> What is wrong? Have you crossed me? Please, better directions. Jafsie.

Jafsie received no word that day or the next. On April 7, headlines announced that John Hughes Curtis claimed to have met with the kidnapping gang. Gaston Means was continuing to tell the same thing to Mrs. Evalyn Walsh McLean.

It's conceivable that Charles Lindbergh's ostensible preoccupation with locating the *Nelly* after leaving St. Raymond's Cemetery the night of April 2 provided an understandable explanation as to why more care wasn't taken not to bend, fold, or excessively touch the final message from John, thereby preserving whatever latent fingerprints the kidnappers may have left. Dr. Erastus Mead Hudson's silver nitrate technique of print detection offered both a possible method of identifying the kidnapping gang and a way of making sure the baby was still alive. Early on in the investigation, Hudson recovered latent prints from toys in the nursery believed to have been those of the missing child. During the protracted communications between Condon and the mythical kidnappers, Lindbergh could have asked that fingerprints of the Eaglet be provided to establish that the gang actually had his son. This was not done. Nor had there been any methodical attempt to preserve latent prints on the messages received by Lindbergh, Breckinridge, and later, Condon.

As the Lone Eagle took to the air and began his search for the *Nelly*, the primary means that investigators had of tracking down John and the gang was through the ransom money. If Lindbergh had had his way, this, too, would have been denied the police.

The risk involved in circulating the list of serial numbers for the currency was evident to any law-enforcement agency: Should news of what had been done get out, the kidnappers might feel betrayed and recover the child before Lindbergh could reach him on the ship. And news did get out. The U.S. Treasury Department prepared a fifty-seven-page list of serial numbers for the ransom loot, which it began to distribute on April 6. To ensure that the media, and ergo the kidnappers, not know, the booklets were distributed to banking institutions without saying the money was related to the Lindbergh case. Two days later, April 8, a Newark bank teller concluded that the serial numbers were from a ransom being paid for the baby. He relayed his hunch to an *Evening News of Newark* reporter, who put it into print. The story was picked up nationally, and the following day Lindbergh had Schwarzkopf publicly acknowledge that a fifty-thousand-dollar ransom payment had been made and that the kidnappers had failed to return the child.

— — —

Laura Vitray had spent almost six weeks covering the story for Hearst's *New York Journal*. She had followed the Jafsie ads with avid fascination but, like other reporters, knew nothing of John F. Condon. She read about John Hughes Curtis and Sam and heard rumors of a ransom payment's having been made in a cemetery. Like other elements of the investigation, none of it added up. Convinced that a conspiracy was in the making, she wrote a book that was rushed to print and entitled *The Great Lindbergh Hullabaloo*. In the introduction, datelined April 12, 1932, Vitray maintained that the missing child had not been kidnapped for ransom, nor was he being subjected to any danger. She believed that after the contents of her book were read, the child would be returned. She goes on to say that

> no one who has carefully examined the facts from day to day, can believe that the removing of this child from its home was the work of cheap, money-mad thugs, nor of any ordinary kidnappers, whether professional or amateur.

Vitray's conclusions come in the final two pages of the last chapter, which is called "I Accuse":

> I accuse the newspapers of this country of not reporting to the American people the true facts, as their reporters saw them, concerning the kidnapping of the Lindbergh baby.
>
> I accuse the hundreds of reporters who have worked on the story close to the centers where the news was breaking, and who were themselves convinced that the story was not wholly on the "up and up," of having kept that conviction hidden while writing the flood of sentimental slop that was heaved through the press since March first. A few days ago I was one of those guilty reporters myself, but I have stepped out of their ranks.
>
> I accuse the "powers" of the Underworld, who have become the powers which guide and move the financiers and the administration of our government, of having deliberately arranged the Lindbergh "kidnapping," not for ransom, but as a story, to divert public attention from the grave disaster that threatens this nation at their own hands today. It was the only story, bar none, capable of commanding the front page of every newspaper in the country throughout weeks, and perhaps until next fall.
>
> I accuse the American public and the voters of allowing this one unique issue of a stolen baby to turn their eyes away from those matters which must be solved at once, unless this nation is to be crushed beneath the weight of foreign tyranny, and of inner corruption.[17]

Two days later, on April 14, a five-dollar note from the ransom payment was discovered by a teller in a New York City bank. It was the second bill to have turned up since the money disappeared into St. Raymond's Cemetery. The first note, a twenty-dollar gold certificate, had also been recovered from a bank in New York City—a bill, it was later determined, that had been spent three days after the ransom payment was made.

14

A STAR IS BORN

CHARLES LINDBERGH WAS THE GREATEST NEWS GETTER OF THEM ALL. HENRY Breckinridge was as skilled a public relations man as existed. If their aim was to have the press, public, and police look in the wrong direction—as I fervently believe—no better helpmate could have existed than Dr. Condon. Condon was a runaway mouth who ordinarily would have been the last person in whom either Lindbergh or Breckinridge would have invested their trust. If, as I suspect, Lindbergh wanted done with the matter as quickly as possible, Condon would prove a bewildering impediment. The old doctor took on a life of his own, which was somewhat akin to riding a roller coaster.

On Monday, April 11, while papers across the land reproduced the list of serial numbers for the ransom loot, the *New York Times* and the *Bronx Home News* came up with the biggest scoop since the child disappeared.

A seventy-two-year-old former school principal named John F. Condon, using his initials, J.F.C., or Jafsie, had acted as Lindbergh's go-between and delivered the ransom to Cemetery John in the dead of night. The media descended on the Bronx. Condon was ready with a standing-room-only press conference in his parlor. It was a stirring performance, during which he cautioned that many facts must be withheld, opined that the large search effort may have scared off the kidnappers, and expressed hope that the abductors would honor their pledge and return the Eaglet. Reporters had finally come face-to-face with Jafsie Condon.

Whereas Lindbergh, Schwarzkopf, and official state-police spokes-men were guarded and usually terse in their comments to the fourth es-tate, John F. Condon inundated journalists with information. "Ask him a question and duck" was how one reporter described an early encounter with Condon. Jafsie's style was expansive, grandiloquent, and often buf-foonish, and the media wasted no time in criticizing Schwarzkopf and his troopers for having allowed Lindbergh to turn over money to the likes of the loquacious pedagogue. They also provided extensive profiles on Condon, as well as lapping up most everything he had to say. One of the things the venerable educator liked to do best at interviews was use an exaggerated Germanic accent when repeating what John had said to him. Garrulous and histrionic, Jafsie went beyond being hot copy; he was the first superstar to emerge from the crime, and he relished every moment in the spotlight.

Explaining that the swirl of press attention could impair Condon's effectiveness as the go-between, Lindbergh, through the offices of Schwarzkopf and Jimmy Finn, pressured newspapers into calling off their reporters. No sooner was the blackout imposed than the *New York Daily News,* which had already posted its own fifty-thousand-dollar re-ward for the return of the child, broke ranks, and all the other publica-tions followed. Accompanied by a pack of newsmen on his morning constitutional in the Bronx, or wherever else he chose to stride, Jafsie was a veritable Pied Piper—and a growing problem for most everyone with whom he had contact.

One of Jafsie's most recent screw-ups was discovered following the delivery of the ransom in St. Raymond's. At the strategy session at Mrs. Morrow's Manhattan townhouse, Jafsie boasted to a dismayed Elmer Irey of how he had beaten John down in price and only given him fifty thousand of the prepared seventy thousand dollars.[1] The additional ran-som that Condon had arbitrarily withheld meant there was twenty thou-sand dollars less by which to trace John and the gang—twenty thousand containing four hundred fifty-dollar gold certificates that would have been easier to spot than the five-, ten-, and twenty-dollar bills that made up the payment that disappeared into the graveyard.

During the furor that followed the disclosures as to who Jafsie was and what his role had been, Lindbergh and Breckinridge steadfastly stood behind him, as they had steadfastly stood behind Spitale and Bitz, Morris Rosner, and H. Norman Schwarzkopf. From a practical standpoint they had no choice. Neither did any of the other law-enforcement agencies now involved with the case. Whether he was part of an extortion scheme or for real, Condon was the primary channel of communication to whoever got the ransom money. He was the only person to have seen John, the only person who could identify him in the future. Or could he? Had the recipients selected him blindly as their go-between—or was he "in on it"?

What began to strike investigators and reporters who managed to interview Jafsie was that the old man seldom told the same story twice, and quite often his latest version of events contradicted what he had said in the past. Talking to Elmer Irey at the Morrow townhouse in the hours after the ransom had been paid, Condon described John as being between five feet eight inches and five feet ten inches, weighing 160 pounds, and having a triangular face with high cheekbones, almond-shaped eyes, thick and straight eyebrows, large ears, a straight nose, and slightly stooped shoulders.[2] He readily identified the sketch an IRS artist was making from his description as looking very much like John. The vital statistics he soon provided to other investigators and newsmen saw John get shorter and leaner and younger—thirty to thirty-four years old—standing straighter, stooping more, developing a growth on the inside of his left hand, talking in a thicker Germanic accent as well as in less of an accent, becoming more Scandinavian, using the expressions "smack me out" and "did you got my letter," pronouncing the words *perfect* as *pefect*, *colonel* as *kennel*, *five* as *fife*, and *where* as *vare*. Jafsie asserted that the drawing made by a second artist also looked very much like John even though it didn't bear that much of a resemblance to the previous picture he had identified. At least two newspaper reports would quote him as saying he never clearly saw John's face either in St. Raymond's Cemetery or in Woodlawn Cemetery.

Condon's earliest personal printed statements of what transpired had come on April 11, when the *Bronx Home News* published the as-told-to "True Story of Jafsie's Efforts to Locate Stolen Lindbergh Baby." Because this was the same day the *New York Times* revealed he was Jafsie and the day on which he later held the press conference acknowledging his participation in the case, certain law-enforcement officers suspected it was Condon himself who had leaked the story to either the *Times* or the *Home News* or both.

As for Condon's various early accounts of meeting with John in St. Raymond's, all were in agreement that he heard someone call out, "Hey Doc," or "Hey Doctor" and he turned in the direction of the voice, which came from inside the cemetery. In some of his statements, he claimed that he saw no one and called out, "Where are you?"; that he received no answer and went back to where the ransom message had said he should enter the cemetery, unlighted and unpaved Whittemore Avenue; that he walked up Whittemore and saw a man rise up beyond a bordering hedge; that as he continued to walk, the man moved along among the tombstones, keeping pace with him. In other narratives Condon related that on hearing the voice and turning toward the cemetery, he immediately saw a man stand up among the tombstones in the distance, gesture to him, and call out, "Hey Doctor, over here."

Wherever it was in the cemetery that they rendezvoused, most Condon narratives were in accord that the man, to reach the spot, had to scale a five-foot cement wall, cross a narrow, intercepting dirt road or lane, and jump another barrier, probably a fence. As he landed on the other side, one of the man's feet sunk into the soft dirt, and he was crouched behind a bush when Condon approached. In one version Condon asked, "What are you doing crouched down there?"; in another he was annoyed to find the fellow in that position, and the only thing he uttered was the command "Stand up!" When the man stood, Condon, in most accounts, recognized him to be John, who was wearing a dark suit and a fedora with a snap-down brim. But statements also exist in which Condon maintained that even though he knew it was John, he could not see his face in the dark. There is unanimity that John's first words were along the line of "Did you got it, the money?" which he spoke with a decided German or Scandinavian accent.

Condon provided an ample selection of his explanations to John for why he had not brought the money along, but most of them end with him saying the ransom is in the car. Abundant versions have John wanting to know who is at the car, and when he is told it is Lindbergh, he asks, "Is he armed?" Jafsie lies and says no, he isn't armed, and John tells him to retrieve the money. Diverse accounts make no mention of a gun or Lindbergh and state that John, after being told the money is in the car, simply tells Condon, "Get it!"[3]

The later renderings of the events always seem to have Condon insisting on seeing the baby before money changes hands, a demand that was missing from many of the earlier narratives. At least one version in which Condon asked to see the child has John refusing on the grounds that "my father won't let me." When asked if his father is a member of the gang, John replies, "Yes. Give me the money." Condon constantly tried to impress John with the fact that Lindbergh was not a rich man and got him to accept fifty thousand dollars rather than the full seventy-thousand-dollar ransom. Certain recapitulations tell of Condon going to the car to get the money and John walking away without further discussion. Others relate that before this occurred, Condon demanded his "receipt," the note saying where the child was. John replied that he had to go fetch the note and he'd be back with it in ten minutes. Later versions had Condon trying to use his wristwatch to estimate how far John was traveling when he walked off to get the "receipt." Condon walked to the car and was given the ransom by Lindbergh. How long it was before he returned to the cemetery and again met with John ranges from ten to fifteen minutes.

The most startling statement made by Condon is that when he went back and met John in the cemetery, he saw another figure lurking in the background. Later he would both deny that he had said this and insist that a third man definitely was there. In one retelling Condon had John counting the ransom money to make sure it was not marked, and he had him not counting it in another. Condon was given the envelope that said where the baby could be found, and in most instances John also told him about the *Nelly*. John disappeared into the cemetery, carrying the wooden box containing fifty thousand dollars. Condon returned to Lindbergh in the parked car.

A Condon tale that piqued the suspicions more than the curiosity of reporters and investigators was his alleged encounters with a woman he could never describe consistently.[4] Back on March 19, while awaiting new instructions from the kidnappers, Condon participated in a charity bazaar to raise funds for a new chapel at the Hart's Island jail. The event took place in a store at 394 East 200th Street, and while he was there displaying violins that were for sale, Condon was approached by a woman who told him, "Nothing can be done until the excitement is over. There is too much publicity. Meet me at Tuckahoe on Wednesday at five o'clock. I will have a message for you."[5] Before Condon could say anything, she was gone.

On Monday, March 21, he received the letter from the kidnappers in which they asked if Lindbergh got the package containing the baby's sleeping suit. The following day he inserted a newspaper ad confirming that the sleeping suit was received and found to be genuine. According to Jafsie, it was the evening after that, Wednesday, March 23, that he and Al Reich had driven to Tuckahoe, New York, in the hopes of meeting the woman who talked to him at the bazaar four days before. Once there, Condon proceeded alone to the New York Central Railroad depot. The woman was waiting. "You will get a message later," she announced. "Keep advertising until you hear more." Then, as at the Bronx bazaar, she beat a rapid retreat. Included among Jafsie's reasons for not following her from the depot was that he didn't want to imperil the missing child or do anything that would make the kidnappers distrust him. As had occurred with John in St. Raymond's Cemetery, Condon began to vary his accounts of meeting with the woman. One transcript has him saying he didn't see anyone at Tuckahoe connected to the case and that the reason he had gone there was to meet a relative.[6]

Trying to confront Jafsie with accusations of lying wasn't all that easy. Early on in the case, Harry W. Walsh, the Jersey City Police Department inspector assigned to the state-police manhunt, had publicly come under fire for having tried to implicate Red Johnsen and Betty Gow in the crime. With Lindbergh having been bilked out of fifty thousand dollars and critics insisting loud and clear that the state police never should have allowed the payment to be made and that the investigating team didn't have the talent to solve a crime of this magnitude, Inspector Walsh pursued his prime suspect, Violet Sharpe, a twenty-eight-year-old household maid at the Morrow estate who had been questioned back in mid-March regarding her whereabouts the night of the kidnapping. Certain that the nervous, often-hostile young woman had been lying to the officer who had talked to her at the time, Walsh, on April 18, began a series of interrogations intended to break down Violet. This led to one of the greatest tragedies of the case and to the most vehement outcries against Walsh and the state police in the entire investigation. But it was nothing compared with the personal humiliation he suffered when trying to break down Jafsie Condon. The old teacher, quite simply, had Walsh for lunch.

15

A MATTER OF JOHNS

AS THE LINDBERGH CAMP HAD PROBABLY HOPED WOULD HAPPEN, MEDIA AND public interest in the case began to wane. Part of this had to do with the mad-hatter antics of supposed go-betweens and contact men. The exhortations of Mickey Rosner and the headline-catching stunts of John Hughes Curtis and Gaston B. Means had begun to wear thin. Even Jafsie, the prince of print, had contradicted himself off the front page, though he still did have a following.

Lindy continued to express confidence that Cemetery John existed and was in possession of the baby. On April 18 at Sorrel Hill, he listened to an eyewitness account that placed John, or a man who certainly fit his description, in Newark's Hudson-Manhattan Railroad station the night after the fifty-thousand-dollar ransom was paid.[1] The Sorrel Hill meeting marked an upgrading for the New Jersey State Police, which had been excluded from Lindbergh's dealings with Jafsie Condon. H. Norman Schwarzkopf was in attendance, along with the officers in charge of the troopers' investigation of the case, Captain John J. Lamb and Lieutenant Arthur T. ("Buster") Keaten.

The man claiming to have seen John in New Jersey was the leading pretender to Jafsie Condon's throne as go-between, John Hughes Curtis. From a publicity standpoint, Curtis had come across lean days. He, Sam, and their contention that the baby was being held on a boat had been pushed to the sidelines by a fickle media that was focusing on Condon, who had also brought word that the Eaglet was aboard a boat. Boatwise, Curtis got to the press first. Accompanying him to Sorrel Hill and also sitting in on the meeting was his old friend Edwin B. Bruce, a well-to-do businessman from Elmira, New York. Missing was Lindbergh's adviser and confidant, Colonel Henry Breckinridge, who was theoretically committed to the authenticity of Jafsie Condon's John.

Curtis allegedly told Lindbergh, Schwarzkopf, and the two state-police officers that on April 3, a day after Condon had paid the ransom, he and Sam had driven to the Hudson-Manhattan Railroad station in Newark, where they met not only with John but with the rest of the gang of kidnappers: Eric, a Norwegian or Dutchman in his thirties; Nils, a five-foot-nine, 140-pound, thirty-two-year-old Scandinavian; and forty-ish George Olaf Larsen, nicknamed Dynamite and also Scandinavian, who was the captain of a schooner on which the child was being held.

The fourth member of the kidnapping team was its leader, John. Though the description Curtis gave of him jibed with what had become the standard portrait of Condon's John being reported in the papers at that time, differences existed. Jafsie at various times had said John's accent was either German or Scandinavian. Curtis's John was definitely Scandinavian. Jafsie's John was rather odd looking; Curtis's was handsome. The John that Jafsie described for reporters was thin and slightly stooped. The John of Curtis was endowed with an admirable physique. Jafsie had portrayed John as somewhat nervous and occasionally cowering. John, when Curtis had confronted him, was resolute and self-assured. On meeting at the Newark railroad station, Sam and the gang got into Curtis's car and drove across the state to Larsen's cottage in Cape May, New Jersey, where his wife, Hilda, was waiting for them. Hilda operated the two-way radio by which she kept in contact with the kidnappers when they were out to sea.

As Condon had used an accent when recounting what Cemetery John had told him, Curtis now did the same while telling Lindbergh and the state policemen of his John's conversations with him during their auto ride and subsequent stay at Larsen's cottage. John stated that he had contemplated kidnapping the baby for some time. Once in his possession, the stolen child would be kept with his girlfriend, who was German and a trained nurse. What his plan had lacked was inside assistance, collusion with a member of either the Lindbergh or the Morrow households. This had been achieved a month before the baby was actually taken, when he and his girlfriend had gone to a roadhouse near Trenton and bumped into just such a person, to whom he had offered a considerable amount of money. John had refused to divulge who the person was or in which of the two households he or she was employed.

The media had given special attention to a green Hudson sedan reported to have been seen in the Hopewell area the night of the kidnapping. Red Johnsen's green Chrysler, which contained what investigators deemed an incriminating empty milk bottle, had also received a good deal of print as possibly being the car sighted near the estate. Now, over two months later, in the den at Sorrel Hill, John Hughes Curtis alleged that John had told him that on March 1, he, his German girlfriend, Nils, and Eric drove to the Lindbergh estate in a green Hudson sedan. They drove onto a lane on the property and parked. Sam, who had followed them in his own car, parked on the main road so he could signal with his lights if danger arose. John and Nils removed a three-part ladder from the car along with a rag, a blanket, chloroform, and the ransom note that Larsen's wife had written, all of which they brought to the house. They went up the ladder and climbed through a second-floor window into the nursery. Rather than descending the unsteady ladder with the anesthetized baby, John and Nils brought him down the stairs and out the front door. During his confession to Curtis, John produced a twenty-four-inch by thirty-inch floor plan of both levels of the Lindbergh house and pointed to a specific part of it. "You see this here," he allegedly told Curtis, who recounted it for Lindbergh in the most compelling Scandinavian accent he could muster, "that's a pantry and it's a hallway between the kitchen and the front hall. We had this locked on the hall side, so if they got wise in the kitchen or servants' quarters they'd have to go all the way around through the dining room and living room to get to the front hall. You'll find that key on the hall side even now."[2]

Curtis contended that he had been taken to the garage by John and shown a green Hudson. Inside the car was a padded wooden box with blankets that John had stated had been used to carry the baby. Early the next morning, according to Curtis, he had driven to Trenton with Captain Dynamite Larsen, who had agreed to meet with Lindbergh. Dynamite had brought along a detailed description of the child, which Curtis was certain would convince the Lone Eagle that this was the authentic kidnapping gang. Dynamite had waited in the car while Curtis went to a pay phone and called Sorrel Hill, trying to reach Lindbergh.

Schwarzkopf and his two aides were unimpressed. Like the green Hudson sedan Curtis claimed he was shown, the fragility of the ladder had been widely reported by the media, and detailed floor plans of the house had been published in a great many papers and magazines. There was nothing new or unique about the use of chloroform by the kidnappers or of their leaving the nursery via the inside staircase. Journalists had speculated about both these possibilities for weeks. Curtis's description of John was in general accord with what the papers were reporting Condon had said, for the moment. The claim that one of the gang members was either Norwegian or Dutch and that three others were Scandinavian not only corresponded with Condon's well-reported statement that John's accent was German or Scandinavian, but it also rang of Henry ("Red") Johnsen, who had been born in Norway. Johnsen had also worked on boats—like Sam, Dynamite, and other gang members.

Schwarzkopf and his men would later insist they didn't believe a word of Curtis's story. They also did not inform Lindbergh of this, perhaps because the Lone Eagle seemed to be keenly intent on much of what was being divulged. There were compelling aspects to Curtis's story. He was, after all, on record as having said the baby was aboard a boat well before similar information was imparted to Condon the night of April 2.

According to Curtis's ongoing narrative, Lindbergh's delay in meeting him and Dynamite Larsen hadn't sat well with the already nervous sea captain–kidnapper. They couldn't reach Lindbergh by phone and to kill time had driven to Plainfield, New Jersey, where Dynamite took in a movie while Curtis had visited with relatives. By 6:00 P.M. they returned to a pay phone in Trenton, from which Curtis had called Sorrel Hill in another vain attempt to speak with Lindbergh.[3] It was too much for the edgy Dynamite, who had demanded to be taken home. Only after dropping Dynamite off at Cape May had Curtis realized he had left behind Larsen's letter, in which the baby was described. Later that evening Curtis had been called by a newsman, who informed him that Lindbergh had paid a fifty-thousand-dollar reward to the kidnappers through an intermediary named John Condon.

Curtis claimed that the next day he went to the Newark railroad station for a second meeting with the kidnappers. Everyone but Dynamite was waiting for him. They drove him to a three-story brick house, where John admitted he was the same man who had received fifty thousand dollars in St. Raymond's Cemetery. It was the first step in a shakedown scheme, "to chisel Lindbergh through Condon, then turn the boy over to you," he told Curtis. "That's why we are willing to let the kid go cheap." Lindbergh was rolling in money, according to John, who also stated, "If this gang of saps had any nerve, I'd sell the brat to the highest bidder." When asked the whereabouts of the crucial letter in which Dynamite Larsen described the baby, John smiled and told Curtis, "Torn up, of course. Do you think Larsen is a fool to keep something that hot?" After admitting that the baby was not in particularly good health, John said, "But we got a doctor to look after him, and my girlfriend, the nurse." How did John come up with a doctor they could trust? "You can get anything you're willing to pay for."[4] When Curtis demanded hard proof that John and the gang had the baby, he was shown fifteen hundred dollars in currency and a list of ransom serial numbers that appeared in a paper. Cross-checking, he found that the serial numbers on the bills corresponded to those on the list. This for Curtis was proof positive that he was dealing with the gang that had the child.

John Hughes Curtis seemed sympathetic, earnest, and certainly not the stripe of fellow to perpetrate a prank sadistic enough to involve a stolen infant. Besides his being a prosperous shipyard operator and respected businessman in his own right, such stalwart citizens as Admiral Burrage and Rev. Dobson-Peacock were confident that he was in touch with the authentic kidnappers. Lindbergh suggested that for the sake of expediency, the next time Curtis met with the kidnappers, he should be nearby. This occurred the very next night, April 19. Once again the state police were not informed of the plan of action or what transpired as a result.

Charles Lindbergh checked into a Cape May hotel, and around midnight Curtis brought him word that the gang had agreed to let Curtis go aboard Larsen's schooner on the condition that the Coast Guard be kept out of the area and that the serial numbers of the new ransom money not be recorded. Lindbergh agreed. Curtis returned at dawn, saying that John, Sam, and the other three kidnappers had taken him fourteen miles out to sea, where they boarded an eighty-foot-long freshly painted dark-green trolling vessel, whose name, *Teresa Salvatore,* was applied to a wooden surface that may have been covering up the ship's real name. Before Curtis debarked, the gang had instructed him to meet them in two days off Block Island. He would be called with the exact location. Should they miss one another at Block Island, Curtis could contact them through Hilda. Lindbergh asked if he had seen his baby aboard the *Teresa Salvatore*. Curtis said he had not.

Gaston B. Means had definitely seen the Lindbergh baby and held it in his arms. He assured Mrs. McLean of this the week before, on April 14. Reading reports that Jafsie Condon paid a fifty-thousand-dollar ransom, she had grown concerned and called Means in to find out what he had done with the $104,000 she had given him to pay the kidnappers.[5] And what about these people in Norfolk who were all over the papers negotiating for the child? Gaston had calmly explained that Jafsie, Curtis, and he were all dealing with the same gang.

According to Means, on discovering that the serial numbers of the ransom money had been recorded and on seeing all the Coast Guard boats near Martha's Vineyard, the kidnappers had lost faith in Jafsie and decided against giving him the baby. The gang had also come to mistrust John Hughes Curtis. The plain and simple truth was that the only person they now wanted to deal with was Gaston. It was after convincing Mrs. McLean of this that he let her know he had seen the baby. It had been hale and hearty and was being held near her summer home in Aiken, South Carolina.

As Condon had worked through John and Curtis through Sam, Means's contact was the Fox, who had already gone to Aiken and was now waiting for Mrs. McLean. She had barely reached her summer house when Gaston appeared with the Fox: a tubby, ferretlike little fellow with horn-rimmed glasses and a pencil mustache, who in reality was a disbarred lawyer by the name of Norman Whitaker. Despite having been a chess champion and having earned degrees at two prestigious universities, Whitaker was a convicted auto thief whose latest arrest had been for using slugs in a pay telephone. Mrs. McLean looked on as the Fox had searched the summer house for hidden microphones. The place was clean, and he told her nervously that he'd go confer with the gang. If she breathed a word of this, they would rub her out. A frightened Mrs. McLean vowed to keep silent.

The Fox showed up the next day, saying that the gang, fearing a trap, had left Aiken and was in Juárez, Mexico, just across the border from El Paso, Texas. Mrs. McLean, Means, and a professional nurse for the baby went to El Paso. After returning from an alleged meeting in Juárez with the kidnappers, Means told Mrs. McLean that because the ransom money they had received bore listed serial numbers and they couldn't spend any of it, the gang wanted her to give them thirty-five hundred dollars in bills that were not listed or marked. Mrs. McLean went straightaway back to Washington, D.C., where she tried to raise the needed funds by selling pieces of her jewelry to a friend so her bankers wouldn't know what she was about. The friend ratted to Mrs. McLean's lawyer. After listening to his client's story, the lawyer made her realize she was being swindled.

On April 17, the day before John Hughes Curtis went to Sorrel Hill and told Lindbergh about meeting with his John and the kidnapping gang, Gaston Means called Mrs. McLean from Chicago only to be informed that she had found out he was a fake and she wanted him to return the $104,000 he had taken from her. Means professed to be aghast at the accusation and vowed that if need be to protect his good name, he would rekidnap the child from the kidnappers. As for the $104,000, he would go dig it up at his brother's house in Concord, North Carolina, and bring it to her. Good to his word, he showed up at her house a few days later but without the money. He did have an explanation of why this was. Means definitely had the $104,000 in hand when he started back to Washington; however, along the way he had been flagged down by a man waving a lantern on a bridge. The man had whispered to him, "Number One." Knowing that this was the code name for a member of the kidnapping gang, Gaston had given the man the money, all of it! Mrs. McLean demanded he leave her home. Then she called her lawyer. Her lawyer called J. Edgar Hoover.

At dawn on Thursday, April 21, Lindbergh and Curtis were in a rented boat near East Quarter Lights, off Block Island, the location specified by the gang. Also aboard were Curtis's friend E. B. Bruce and Lieutenant George L. Richard, commandant at the Norfolk Naval Air Station, who had been assigned to assist the operation. The kidnappers' boat, the *Teresa Salvatore,* did not show up. Lindbergh, Curtis, and their party went to a New York City hotel previously agreed to by the gang. While the others slept and ergo could not hear, according to Curtis, he received a call from Hilda, who explained that the gang had aborted the rendezvous when they spotted fishing boats in the area. She said they wanted to meet them the next day and gave a location off the Virginia capes, near the Chesapeake Lightship.

Lindbergh, Curtis, and their entourage sailed for the rendezvous on the yacht *Marcon,* which had been lent to them for the duration of the search. Once at sea, Curtis informed the others of what he had obviously been informed of by Hilda: The boat they should now be looking for was a black-hulled Gloucester fisherman named *Mary B. Moss,* which had most probably been disguised as the *Teresa Salvatore.* The *Mary B. Moss* never appeared. Back in port Curtis received another late-night call from Hilda to which no one else was privy. Hilda said the *Mary B. Moss* and its kidnappers had developed engine trouble and returned to port for repairs but would be at the original rendezvous spot. Two days of bad weather kept the *Marcon* in port; sailing on the third day produced no sightings of the *Mary B. Moss.*

On Wednesday, April 27, with bad weather again keeping the *Marcon* idle and docked, Curtis flew to New York City on the pretext of meeting with Hilda. Who he actually saw was William E. Haskell, Jr., the assistant to the president of the *New York Herald Tribune.* Unbeknownst to Lindbergh, Schwarzkopf, and most everyone else, the seemingly prosperous shipyard operator was in serious financial trouble. The *New York Daily News* had already put in a bid for the story of his dealings with the kidnappers, with the proviso that he make the baby available only to them for photographs. What he was trying to elicit from the *Tribune* for these exclusive rights was a twenty-five-thousand-dollar advance. The *Trib* was willing to meet his price once the baby was returned and if Lindbergh agreed. Curtis accepted the terms.

— — —

Though there was generally consistent coverage of the Curtis-Lindbergh sea search for the baby, the media's interest in the case was on the wane. Jafsie's statements and activities still managed to get into print, but not many papers allotted space to the announcement by two previously well-publicized go-betweens, Salvatore Spitale and Irving Bitz, that it was flat-out asinine for Condon to have paid fifty thousand dollars to some clown in the dark before having the baby in tow. Pointing out that their professional opinions had been ignored, the two career gangsters publicly withdrew their services from the investigation.

A more discreet go-between was also about to end his association with the case and with liberty in general. Because Gaston B. Means had received the $104,000 dollars from Mrs. McLean within the boundaries of the District of Columbia, the jurisdiction to pursue the possible fraud went to J. Edgar Hoover's Bureau of Investigation. A review of the McLean complaint led to the issuing of a warrant for Gaston's arrest, which BI agents couldn't serve unless he was on D.C.'s turf. Means obliged them on May 5, by rolling up in a chauffeur-driven Rolls-Royce. The great car was promptly cut off by BI special agents, who arrested him. The smooth-talking and amusing Means, who had been dismissed from the BI years before by J. Edgar Hoover, was questioned by a man with absolutely no sense of humor: J. Edgar Hoover. Gaston professed profound shock that Mrs. McLean's money hadn't been returned to her. His lighthearted assurances that he wouldn't sue the BI for false arrest were wasted on J. Edgar, who had him locked up.

Charles Lindbergh not only knew that Mrs. McLean had given Gaston Means a hundred thousand dollars to pay the kidnapping gang, but he had tacitly endorsed the transaction. On Friday, May 6, while still aboard the *Marcon,* which bad weather had kept in port most of the week, he received word of Means's apprehension.

For the public at large, the Means arrest was one of the few stories to appear in the papers regarding the Lindbergh kidnapping that weekend. A lack of manhunt hard news had allowed local, national, and world events to reappropriate the country's headlines and front pages. As often as not, no mention at all was made of the crime.

The *New York Herald Tribune* continued to run daily boxes of two and three paragraphs on the inner pages that summarized the previous day's events in "The Lindbergh Case." The *Trib*'s Tuesday, May 10, recapitulation for May 9—"the sixty-ninth day since the baby was snatched from its crib"—reported that the sea-search negotiators who were trying to contact the kidnappers had "shifted their activities," and Vincent Ogle was apprehended and held for questioning after coming off a boat in Boston with his infant son, who bore a "faint resemblance to the Lindbergh child." Father and child were later cleared and released.

Because of the rough seas the week before, Lindbergh, Curtis, and their party had switched from the yacht *Marcon* to the more durable *Cachalot,* an eighty-five-foot ketch. On Monday, May 9, the *Cachalot* found no trace of the *Mary B. Moss* in the vicinity of Five Fathoms Banks off Cape May—the latest location where the gang was supposed to be waiting, according to what Hilda had told only Curtis. Back in port at Cape May the morning of May 10, Lindbergh, to avoid lingering newsmen, remained aboard, where he kept abreast of progress in other aspects of the investigation through coded cables from Schwarzkopf. Curtis had left the boat and gone to sort matters out with Hilda. The news he returned with was not good. Hilda had told him that a bitter dispute had split the gang into two groups. Her husband, Dynamite, headed the one that wanted to cancel their arrangement with Curtis and offer the baby to the highest bidder. John opposed him. Sam had worked out a compromise that kept the gang intact. The rendezvous would have to wait until the sea calmed.

The *New York Herald Tribune*'s May 11 two-paragraph Lindbergh-case summary reported that the day before, John Hughes Curtis and his aides were still absent from Norfolk, Virginia, another attempt to extort ransom money from Lindbergh had failed, and the unknown extortionist had eluded the trap set for him.[6]

A second extortion plot being more extensively reported in a different *Trib* story on May 11, as well as in other newspapers, involved new accusations against Gaston B. Means. Only a few hours after his being indicted for defrauding Mrs. McLean of $104,000, authorities were investigating allegations that he had bilked much more money out of Mrs. Finley Shepard, the daughter of robber baron Jay Gould, by claiming he could provide information on a Communist plot that imperiled her child and her fortune. By May 11, Mrs. McLean had heard from another would-be extortionist–go-between. His name was Arthur L. Hitner, a convicted con man who, under the alias of Markle, wrote a come-on letter to Mrs. McLean that ended up in the hands of the Bureau of Investigation.

16

EAGLES DEPART

- - -

LINDBERGH WAS AWAY MAY 12, 1932, WHEN THE NEWS REACHED SORREL Hill that put an end to the chaos surrounding his son's disappearance.

At approximately 3:15 P.M. that rain-swept afternoon, Orville Wilson stopped his truck along a section of the Princeton-to-Hopewell highway known as Mount Rose Hill so that his forty-six-year-old black helper, William Allen, could go into the woods and relieve himself. The two men had come from Princeton with a load of lumber destined for Hopewell. The spot where Wilson chose to park was on high ground one mile beyond Mount Rose, a tiny farming hamlet of twelve houses. Allen made his way up through the dense tangle of underbrush, thick stands of scrub oak, second-growth maple, and locust trees. If he had continued to the top of the rise and weather permitted, he would have had a clear view of the Lindbergh house some four miles across the valley. After passing a large, rotted stump of an oak tree, Allen ducked under a low-hanging limb, did a take, and cautiously approached what looked like a "skull lying in a hole."[1] It was a baby's skull, a section of which was broken.

Allen rushed to the truck, got Wilson, and brought him back. The body lay face down in a hollow, and except for a protruding foot was almost completely covered by leaves and dirt. What looked like a dress or underwear was bunched up on the child's back. Not all that far away in the underbrush was the auxiliary telephone cable from Princeton that led to the police command post in the Lindbergh garage and had been laid during the opening days of the manhunt.

Wilson and Allen drove down into nearby Hopewell where they found Officer Charles Williamson sitting in a barber's chair. Williamson, the first policeman to be informed that the Lindbergh baby was missing on the night of March 1, was now the first to learn of an infant's body in the woods on Mount Rose Hill. He brought the two truckers to Chief Harry Wolfe, who rang up H. Norman Schwarzkopf, who in turn dispatched a trooper and a Jersey City detective to Hopewell. Allen and Wilson led Williamson, Wolfe, the trooper, and the detective out to the hillside. Along the road was a burlap bag that contained tufts of blond hair. The truckers took the police to the grave site and gladly departed. After tentatively identifying the badly decomposed body as the Lindbergh baby, whom they had never seen, the trooper and the detective returned to Hopewell and phoned in their report to State Police Captain John Lamb, who informed them that three more officers were already en route: trooper Lieutenant Arthur T. ("Buster") Keaten, Inspector Harry Walsh, and Detective Robert Coar of the Jersey City PD.[2]

Walsh, Keaten, and Coar were taken to the dead baby in the woods by the trooper and detective at approximately 3:45 P.M. Frank Kelly, the state-police fingerprint expert, and a crime-scene photographer arrived soon after, and then Detective Warren Moffat of the Newark PD. Leaves and dirt were cleared away. The body was lying in a natural hollow. It was partially clothed and badly decayed. The left leg was missing, apparently devoured by small animals. The right forearm was gone, as was the left hand. Parts of the face were recognizable, and there was a tuft of curly blond hair on the head. It seemed to be the Eaglet, but Walsh wanted to be sure. He and Moffat drove across the valley to the Lindbergh estate. Without revealing that they had found a body, the two officers talked with Betty Gow and got a detailed description of what the baby was wearing the night it disappeared, as well as samples of thread and the flannel used in one of the garments.

Walsh and Moffat returned to the grave site. Walsh took a stick and attempted to maneuver the body so he could cut off the clothing. The stick slipped and punched a hole in the decomposing skull below the right ear. The garments were finally removed and laid out. They fit the description given by Gow, and the flannel sample seemed to match the material in a segment of one of the undershirts. It was 4:30 P.M. when Walsh reached the Lindbergh estate and presented the clothes to Schwarzkopf, saying that there was no doubt the little corpse was Charles Lindbergh, Jr.

The Mercer County coroner was ordered to the scene, and Betty Gow was brought to Schwarzkopf and shown the two flannel undershirts, which she identified as being the baby's. Gow refused to believe the child was dead, insisting that Lindbergh was about to meet the kidnappers' boat off Cape May, the boat on which the baby had been all along. Schwarzkopf telephoned the news to Henry Breckinridge in New York, and a procedure was decided on.[3] Schwarzkopf cabled Lindbergh that his baby's remains had been found; then he went into the main house and informed Anne Lindbergh and her mother, Mrs. Elizabeth Morrow.

Calls were placed to Gebhart's Hotel in Hopewell and the statehouse press room in Trenton, notifying media people of a 5:30 P.M. press conference to be held at the very place from which they had been barred since the second day of the investigation: the Lindbergh estate.

— — —

Big, bald Mercer County coroner and privately practicing mortician Walter H. Swayze arrived at the drizzle-logged grave site on Mount Rose Hill. He made an abbreviated examination of the corpse and the area, transferred the remains to a body bag, and headed back to the county morgue, which was located at his mortuary, on Greenwood Avenue in Trenton. After he left, troopers raked the area and collected ten barrels of material, which when later culled would produce tufts of blond hair, pieces of clothing, a toenail, and twelve small bones, four of which would be determined to have come from the baby's foot and six of which were not human.[4]

Reporters, who had assembled in the dining room of the state-police command post in the Lindbergh garage, were noisily speculating on what the press conference was about and why it was taking so long to get under way. During the delay Schwarzkopf called Governor Moore and informed him of the baby in the woods, as well as of the impending press conference. Moore relayed the news to a young statehouse reporter who was passing his office. The journalist, Francis Jamieson, telephoned the scoop in to his employer, the Associated Press—a scoop that would weigh heavily in his winning the 1933 Pulitzer Prize for reporting for his coverage of the Lindbergh case. After tipping off Jamieson, Moore made his own formal announcement to the media that the infant had been found.[5]

The baby's corpse reached the Swayze Funeral Parlor shortly past 6:00 P.M. Betty Gow arrived soon after. She spent no more than three minutes viewing the remains before identifying them as those of Charles Lindbergh, Jr., by means of an overlapping toe on the right foot.[6]

The first media announcement of the dead child's being found came at 6:12 P.M. over New Jersey radio station WOR. Minutes later a bulletin was traveling across the Times Square moving display board. By 6:30 P.M. NBC and CBS were broadcasting the word nationwide. At 6:45 P.M. H. Norman Schwarzkopf went before the press corps waiting in the garage command center. "We have to announce that apparently the body of the Lindbergh baby was found" was all he got out before pausing.[7] Gasps of disbelief filled the room as he returned to his written statement, saying that the body was discovered at 3:15 P.M. by "William Allen, Negro, of Trenton, who was riding on the Mount Rose Road toward Hopewell. He was riding with Orville Wilson on a truckload of timber. They stopped the truck so he could answer a call of nature." The *New York Times* would discreetly amend this sentence to read "They stopped the truck so Wilson [sic] could go into the woods on the Mount Rose Hill in Mount Rose, N.J."[8]

— — —

Henry Breckinridge and Dr. Philip Van Ingen arrived at the morgue shortly after Betty Gow made her identification. Van Ingen was the New York City pediatrician who had examined Charles Lindbergh, Jr., ten days before he disappeared from his crib. Now the highly esteemed doctor studied the tiny body on the morgue table. There wasn't that much left to go on. The sex organs were missing, along with other internal and external parts. Sixteen teeth could be counted, eight uppers and eight lowers. The pediatrician acknowledged that the corpse bore certain similarities to the Eaglet, but despite the overlapping toe he refused to identify it as that of Charles Lindbergh, Jr.[9]

Dr. Charles H. Mitchell, the official physician for Mercer County, reached the morgue at 6:45 P.M. Swayze, as county coroner, had authority to declare people dead and sign death certificates, but in the case of sudden, questionable, or violent death, the county physician was to conduct the examination. A large, windy man with small steel-rimmed glasses, dark gray hair, and a silver pompadour, sixty-year-old Charles Mitchell had once been the assistant surgeon at Trenton's St. Francis Hospital. For the last eleven years he had served as the Mercer County physician. Though he wasn't a forensic pathologist, Mitchell had performed over a thousand autopsies, a hundred of which had been done on children. Forensic expertise was available and nearby, but Mitchell never gave it a thought. He didn't dare.

When the autopsy began, Dr. Van Ingen was surprised to see the county coroner, Walter Swayze, rather than Dr. Mitchell, pick up the medical instruments. Only the three of them were present, and Mitchell confessed to Van Ingen that he suffered from severe arthritis and could hardly move his hands. If news of this got out, he told Van Ingen, he would lose his position as county physician. He and Swayze had worked out an arrangement whereby Swayze, who was a mortician with no medical or forensic training, would perform autopsies under Mitchell's direction. Van Ingen had four choices: leave and tell the world about the fraud, leave and tell no one, stay and later tell everyone, stay and tell no one. Van Ingen opted for the final choice. The deception, which would cause both Mitchell and Swayze to commit perjury, was to remain a secret for another fifty-eight years.[10]

Coroner Swayze began his superficial examination under the direction of Mitchell and with Van Ingen looking on. A leg, an arm, and a hand were missing. The lower portion of the body had been eaten away by animals. A section of skin on the right foot had kept its color—the victim was of the "white race."[11] The lips were swollen and pulled back on the teeth, sixteen of them. The large toe on the right foot completely overlapped the first and second toe. Van Ingen and Swayze assisted as Mitchell began the physical autopsy. The tiny mouth was pried open and the tongue and throat examined. The brains had turned to a stinking thick soup, which spilled out onto the autopsy table when the skull was sawed open.

Besides listing the missing body parts and saying that the sex of the dead child was undetermined, Dr. Mitchell's autopsy report stated that the abdominal organs except for the liver were missing, that the thoracic organs except for the heart were missing, and that the skin of the head, face, and right foot was discolored and decomposed. There was evidence of a hemorrhage on the inside of the skull along the left-side fracture line. A perforated fracture the size of a bullet hole was noted near the right ear. The autopsy report's final paragraph read, "Diagnosis of the cause of death is a fractured skull due to external violence."[12] Because no one present at the grave site had reported that Inspector Walsh accidentally poked a stick through the corpse's skull near the right ear, Dr. Mitchell was left to assume that the small hole could have been caused by a number of objects, including a bullet, which is what he said during a post-autopsy interview.[13]

— — —

A two-foot-high brick wall, constructed around the grave site by troopers, as well as continued state-police patrols, had effectively preserved the scene where the body had been discovered. Whatever the security measures at Swayze's funeral parlor–morgue in Trenton might have been, a reporter and photographer managed to gain entry, force open the casket, and take pictures of the body, copies of which would soon be on sale. For Lindbergh the ghoulish incursion was the media's ultimate affront to him, to his family, and to common decency.

— — —

Schwarzkopf had tried to spare Lindbergh the pain of viewing the body by assuring the Lone Eagle that the remains had definitely been identified as his son. Lindbergh's decision not to see the baby was widely reported. Then he changed his mind. Shortly before 4:00 P.M. Saturday, May 14, Schwarzkopf drove Lindbergh and Henry Breckinridge into an alley and up to the back door of the funeral home. The three men slipped in unnoticed by the crowd and newspeople around in front. Lindbergh was led to the room where the corpse lay covered. "Take that off," he requested. The cover was removed.

"Colonel Lindbergh, are you satisfied that this is the body of your baby?" asked Erwin E. Marshall, the Mercer County prosecutor, who was looking on.

"I am perfectly satisfied that it is my child."[14]

— — —

The finding of a dead baby in the woods posed questions that would fascinate future historians. Beyond the fact that the tiny corpse was five and a half inches longer than Dr. Van Ingen's measurement for the Eaglet ten days before his disappearance, an inference that it was older could be derived from an observation Dr. Mitchell, the county coroner, entered into his autopsy report under the category of "Special Characteristics": "Unusually high and prominent forehead and cranium, apparently greater in circumference than would be found in child of this age. The eight lower teeth and eight upper teeth were not only the normal number for a twenty-month-old child, but for a child up to twenty-four months of age."[15]

The possibility that the victim may have been dead longer than the seventy-two days since the Lindbergh baby had been first reported missing was contained in this autopsy sentence: "Body shows evidence of prolonged exposure and usual decomposition that would occur in the course of approximately two or three month's time."[16]

Arguably the manner in which the child was identified warranted reappraisal. Certainly Betty Gow had credibility. She had helped sew one of the garments by which she identified the body. Could she have lied in saying the corpse was that of the Lindbergh baby? Or was it possible she had mistaken the badly decomposed infant for Charles Jr.? Had someone removed the garments from the Lindbergh child and put them on the remains that were found in the woods? Assuming that County Detective Ellis Parker, Sr., was right and that the cadaver wasn't Charles Jr., how could this explain Betty Gow's final means of identification: the overlapping toes on the right foot? Wouldn't that be the definitive way of telling who it was? Apparently not.

According to County Prosecutor Erwin E. Marshall, Lindbergh had examined both the teeth and the overlapping toe and made his identification on the teeth alone. But how much could Lindy have known about teeth, even those of his own son? Was he that perceptive? He hadn't been in other things relating to the missing child's description early on. When he passed out pictures of the Eaglet in long, curly tresses, Lindbergh hadn't remembered that his son's hair had been cut. He had been contradictory in describing the child's habits. Or were these distortions conjured up by the press? Could Lindbergh tell by the teeth? Tell in three minutes—which, like Gow, is all the time he spent examining the corpse?

What of Dr. Philip Van Ingen's inability or refusal to identify the child he had examined ten days before he disappeared? Who would have known better than Van Ingen if it was the Eaglet in the morgue? The toes and teeth had made no difference to him. He didn't say it wasn't the Lindbergh baby, but he wouldn't say it was. Why had he been so reluctant, and why had Betty Gow and Lindbergh been so fast and sure? Gow had viewed the body immediately after it arrived at the funeral home from the woods, which meant it might still have been caked with dirt and grime. In that condition the only identifiable thing may have been the toes.

Breckinridge had brought Dr. Van Ingen from New York to the Trenton morgue. By all accounts they got there shortly after Betty Gow left, at 6:15 P.M., and before Dr. Mitchell arrived, at 6:45 P.M. Had Breckinridge tried to pressure Van Ingen into making a positive identification? Was that what Schwarzkopf was anticipating, why he kept the roomful of reporters waiting in the Lindbergh garage? Most of the newspeople had arrived for the press conference between 5:30 and 6:00 P.M., and Schwarzkopf could have read his statement regarding the discovery of the body then, or he certainly could have read it after Betty Gow made her identification at approximately 6:15 P.M. But Schwarzkopf didn't begin for another half hour, not until 6:45 P.M., the approximate time that Dr. Mitchell reached the morgue. It seems at least plausible that with Mitchell's appearance Henry Breckinridge abandoned attempts to elicit Van Ingen's identification and instructed Schwarzkopf to proceed with the press conference. Would Schwarzkopf have dared to proceed without Breckinridge's permission?

Why was it that Schwarzkopf didn't mention Betty Gow's positive identification of the body at the 6:45 P.M. press conference but did at a second meeting with reporters that evening? Sometime between 4:30 and 5:00 P.M., and based on Gow's earlier identification of the garments, he had told Mrs. Lindbergh and her mother that it was positively their baby in the woods, so why not mention Betty Gow's name at the 6:45 P.M. conference? Didn't he know that Gow had identified the body at the morgue? He was in touch with Breckinridge, who was at the morgue. Could it have been that Breckinridge didn't want to go with Gow's statement alone? Or, once again, was the delay in the initial press conference and the corresponding arrivals at the morgue coincidental?

What of Lindbergh's decision to view the body after he had announced he would not look at it? Was the change of heart that of a father desiring to see his child one last time? Or, as again seems likely, did Henry Breckinridge suggest that it would be better if someone in addition to Betty Gow vouched for the baby's being the Eaglet, particularly after Van Ingen's failure to do so?

For the doubting and suspicious the seeds of a conspiracy were easily culled from the events surrounding the May 12 discovery of a tiny corpse in the woods.

At 4:25 P.M., May 13, with flash lamps popping, newsreel cameras rolling, and several hundred onlookers watching, the gray hearse bearing a small oak coffin left the Swayze Funeral Parlor. Lindbergh, Breckinridge, and Schwarzkopf followed ten minutes later. The cortege of hearse and car reached the Rose Hill Cemetery and Crematory in Linden, New Jersey, at 5:30 P.M. Lindbergh and Breckinridge waited in the home of the cemetery superintendent while Schwarzkopf accompanied the hearse to the crematory. Reporters followed. No religious ceremony was performed, and by 6:15 P.M. the cremation was complete. Lindbergh drove home to Hopewell, leaving the ashes behind. A spokesman said that the family would provide an urn and that Lindbergh planned to spread the ashes over the Atlantic Ocean. It was also explained that the family had decided on cremation rather than burial because they feared that if the child were interred, the grave might be disturbed by souvenir hunters.

For all intents and purposes, Charles A. Lindbergh's interest in, and control over, the investigation of the crime had come to an end. Not until after the arrest of the case's first suspect, some two years and four months later, would a new group of investigators suspect that there may not have been a kidnapping, that the child died at Sorrel Hill on Saturday, February 27, 1932, three days before he was reported missing, that Charles and Anne Lindbergh and Betty Gow were not at the estate when the death occurred but the Whateleys were—and so was someone else.

Book Three

HOUSE OF CARDS

Prelude

IT SEEMED THAT THE METICULOUS SCENARIO CONCOCTED BY CHARLES LIND-
bergh had successfully established March 1 as the estimated date of the
child's death. The New Jersey State Police and a handful of local law-
enforcement operatives had blocked larger and more skilled agencies
from examining the facts firsthand. A smattering of media attention
focused on the whereabouts of the family and staff immediately prior to
the first, but nobody suggested, or ever dreamed, that the death had occurred on Saturday, February 27, as is quite likely the case.

The conspiracy scenario had another objective: that the crime be put
behind Lindbergh and his family as quickly as possible so they could
return to a normal life. For a brief moment that seemed possible. He and
Anne abandoned Sorrel Hill, taking up permanent residence at Mrs.
Morrow's estate in Englewood.[1] Anne prepared for the arrival of a second child, expected in August. Lindy returned to the experimental work
he was doing at Rockefeller Institute with the French biologist Dr. Alexis
Carrel—developing a blood pump for an artificial heart. He began chart-

ing new routes for both Pan American Airways and Transcontinental Air Transport, for whom he acted as an adviser.

Charles Lindbergh miscalculated. Time, he had hoped, would diminish the public's fascination with the crime. But the very artifice intended to shift attention away from the Lindbergh clan and staff helped perpetuate national interest: the ransom.

If Lindbergh had held firm to his original desire to pay the ransom in unmarked currency, chances of catching up to the extortionists would have been nearly impossible. But in a rare capitulation, he gave in to Irey and Jimmy Finn and allowed the recording of the ransom-loot serial numbers. Within days of its payment, bills from the fifty-thousand-dollar payment began to surface and went on surfacing for two and a half years. Public interest in the alleged kidnapping waned but never abated. Lindbergh was as far from the case as he would ever get.

— — —

The chapters to come present a greater logic, one that raises doubts about the guilt of the man who was charged with the extortion and kidnapping-death and points a finger at who the real extortionist probably was. It also renders Lindbergh, the master puppeteer, a lethal bystander, along with the New Jersey State Police. If a convincing case can be made for the innocence of the man executed for the kidnapping-murder of the child—and evidence was brought forward indicating that the extortionist in all likelihood was another—then two questions remain stronger than ever: Who murdered the baby, and who left the original ransom note on the windowsill?

The chase of ransom money moves into New York City, where the troopers had no authority to pursue the passers of bills, except at the sufferance of the NYPD. Hopes that the extortionist would not be found were dashed in September of 1934 with the first arrest made in the case since its onset. The suspect was in possession of almost fourteen thousand dollars in marked bills but had no direct links to the actual kidnapping, which meant he could only be charged with extortion. This was not good enough for many people, including H. Norman Schwarzkopf. New Jersey officials were intent on extraditing the suspect and trying him for the kidnapping and murder of the Eaglet. This might never have been possible save for Charles Lindbergh.

Lindbergh had stated that he would never be able to identify the voice he heard call out, "Hey, Doc," to Jafsie Condon in St. Raymond's Cemetery. The night had been dark, and Lindy was some two hundred feet away. Whatever his motives, Lindbergh reversed himself—identified the suspect's voice as being the same as the caller of "Hey, Doc."

The trial of the century got under way the first week of 1935. The small town in which it took place was overrun by tens of thousands of visitors each day. The press behaved abominably. "It was a sickness," television journalist David Brinkley would later comment. Time proved that the greatest abomination was the trial itself. Almost every bit of prosecution testimony and evidence was either false, contrived, or tampered with. The defense was at best mediocre, at worst inept and inane. The accused man was found guilty and sentenced to death.

Rigid, unbending, manipulative Charles Lindbergh came face-to-face with the reality that he had, by theory and with sworn testimony, helped condemn an innocent man to the electric chair.

17

MONEY TRAILS AND
OLD DOUBTS

CHARLES LINDBERGH HAD OPPOSED THE TWO PRIME MEANS INVESTIGATORS had for identifying and apprehending the unknown kidnapping gang. He insisted on keeping all law-enforcement personnel far away from the site selected to pay the ransom, thereby frustrating attempts to follow the felons. Nor would he allow the serial numbers of the ransom currency to be recorded.

Two members of the Sorrel Hill inner circle, Jimmy Finn of the New York Police Department and Elmer Irey of the IRS, had energetically urged Lindbergh to allow the listing of serial numbers. Charles Lindbergh had never changed his mind regarding an investigation decision. It didn't look as though he would in this instance, either. Elmer Irey was persistent in reminding Lindy that not recording serial numbers was a grave mistake—and one likely to evoke strong criticism. Public credibility was high on the Lindbergh-Breckinridge agenda.

Lindbergh did not particularly like or trust two Internal Revenue men assisting Irey: Frank Wilson and Arthur Madden.[1] Part of this may have had to do with the perception that, recorded or unrecorded, the IRS was obligated to track down the ransom loot after the money was paid—and would live up to this obligation. There was also pressure on Lindy from Jimmy Finn to list the serial numbers, but who was to say any of the bills would turn up in New York City, the only place Finn had jurisdiction. No, it was Irey who posed a potential credibility threat. But listing the bills could set off a nationwide treasure hunt that might heighten and prolong the case after the baby was found. Though perhaps not if only financial institutions and selected retail businesses were given lists of the numbers—lists that did not specify the bills came from the ransom, as Irey had been suggesting.

Lindbergh, for the first time since his son was reported missing, reversed himself on a manhunt decision. Serial numbers of the loot could be recorded. The following night, April 2, 1932, fifty thousand dollars of the seventy thousand dollars in recorded currency disappeared into St. Raymond's Cemetery.

Three days later, on April 5, the first bill of the ransom loot, a twenty-dollar gold certificate, was detected in New York City at the Ninety-sixth Street and Amsterdam Avenue branch of the East River Savings Bank of Manhattan. The man into whose account it had been deposited had no idea where he had got it. Four days after that, as the result of a news leak, Lindbergh had Schwarzkopf acknowledge that a ransom had been paid. By now papers around the world were reprinting a breakdown of the ransom-money serial numbers sent to banks and certain businesses—a breakdown that showed the fifty-thousand-dollar payment contained 4,750 bills, of which 2,000 were in the denomination of five-dollar bills, 1,500 in tens, and 1,250 in twenties. The five-dollar bills were U.S. Treasury notes, which bore red seals and red serial numbers. America was still on the gold standard, and the majority of ten- and twenty-dollar bills were U.S. gold certificates.

On April 14, a second ransom bill surfaced, this one a five-dollar note. Like the twenty-dollar certificate, it was discovered by a teller in a New York City bank. Not until after the body of the baby was found, nearly a month later, did more money appear: two five-dollar bills at different New York City banks on May 19, another five dollars, again at a Manhattan bank, on May 23. The May 19 money was traced to a Sinclair Oil Company in Brooklyn and a Bickford's Restaurant next to the bank where it had been deposited. The May 23 bill was tracked to a dry goods store on Orchard Street in Manhattan. No one at any of the establishments remembered who had passed the notes.[2]

The great American money hunt was on—and the New Jersey State Police's jealously guarded control of the investigation had all but eroded. So had Lindbergh's hope that the matter would quickly be forgotten. Adding to Lindbergh's despair, and prolonging and often escalating interest in the case, was the internecine competition among law-enforcement personalities.

New York City and its police department, not the New Jersey State Police, had the jurisdiction to track down whoever was spending the bills. The commissioner of the New York Police Department, no fan of H. Norman Schwarzkopf's, was only too happy to inform the media, loud and clear, that his boys in blue were on the trail. Named to head the unit of NYPD investigators assigned to the money chase was a fifty-one-year-old detective who had been the department's liaison with Lindbergh: Jimmy Finn.

Finn had been a fixture at Sorrel Hill from early on in the case and had learned firsthand he was on a one-way street when dealing with Schwarzkopf and the Jersey troopers. They accepted much of the information he and the NYPD gathered but shut them off from their own investigatory activities. With ransom bills surfacing only in New York City, the shoe was now on the other foot—Detective Jimmy Finn's. The state police could pitch in and help with the New York money hunt if they liked, but Jimmy intended it to be the NYPD's ball game. The troopers dispatched a twelve-man unit to New York, but submitting to someone else's guidelines wasn't always easy.

The Bureau of Investigation also had a presence in New York City. It had opened a Manhattan office at 370 Lexington Avenue, to which a detachment of fifteen special agents was assigned. The agent in charge was Thomas H. Sisk, who quickly established an amicable working relationship with Finn and the NYPD. Like the Jersey troopers, the bureau lads preferred doing things their own way when possible.

It was Elmer Irey and his T-men who were under the greatest strain regarding the money chase, but not from Jimmy Finn, with whom the IRS man had a practical working relationship. Irey had developed an antagonist as awesome as one could find: J. Edgar Hoover. It was nothing personal, just plain old terroristic interdepartmental rivalry à la the BI director. Back on Friday, May 13, 1932, a day after the child's body was found, President Herbert Hoover named J. Edgar to oversee and coordinate the activities of all federal agencies involved in the Lindbergh investigation. J. Edgar's first move was to kick the Internal Revenue Service and the Secret Service off the case. Lindbergh, taken aback by the arbitrary dismissal of Irey, who had become a Sorrel Hill insider, telephoned the secretary of the treasury. Irey and his operatives were reinstated, but J. Edgar Hoover remained in charge.

A March 18 meeting in Trenton between the New Jersey State Police, the county prosecutor, the IRS, and the BI saw J. Edgar again come up short. The troopers, it was announced, would continue to run the manhunt, and the federal agencies would provide whatever assistance was asked for by the state police. The final blow to Hoover's bid for jurisdiction came with the June 22 enactment of the Cochran bill, a federal statute against kidnapping, which was immediately known as the Lindbergh law. It was not retroactive. The kidnapping and murder of Charles Lindbergh, Jr., was still a state matter, with H. Norman Schwarzkopf and his troopers retaining control of the investigation.

J. Edgar Hoover had won more than he lost. His department finally had a significant criminal law to enforce and was well on its way to becoming a national police agency with teeth, or as it was usually called by the press, "a federal Bureau of Investigation," but the official name change would take time.

Due in part to Jimmy Finn's urging, Lindbergh had agreed to the Treasury Department's issuing a fifty-seven-page, two-columns-to-a-page list of ransom-money serial numbers on April 6, 1932—four days after the loot disappeared into St. Raymond's.[3] Before the month was out, the New Jersey State Police abandoned the Treasury booklet and issued their own modified list on a single printed page, which measured seventeen by twenty-five inches and included the troopers' phone number. One hundred thousand were distributed across the land—sixty thousand went to post offices—along with news of a twenty-five-thousand-dollar reward offered by the governor of New Jersey.

As the money chase ended its second month, May, only 6 of the 4,750 ransom bills had surfaced in New York in sixty days—a twenty-dollar gold certificate and a five-dollar note in April, three five-dollar notes in May, one five-dollar note in early June. Jimmy Finn seems to have feared the fifty-seven page Treasury booklet of serial numbers was too cumbersome to be used effectively by the bank tellers, but it was almost a full year before he took action.[4]

Finn, whose office was on the second floor of the NYPD's Greenwich Street station house, off Hudson Street in lower Manhattan, had over a dozen officers assigned to assist him in the dollar chase.[5] Even so, he personally followed up on every reported ransom bill. He also telephoned the Fed each day to see if any listed money had turned up. As an extra incentive for bank tellers to be on the alert, Finn helped persuade Lindbergh to offer a two-dollar bonus for each bill that was reported. Much later on he got the city of New York to do the same thing.

H. Norman Schwarzkopf had always smelled a conspiracy, if not necessarily to steal the baby, then certainly to extort ransom money. Another likelihood was that a horrible hoax had been perpetrated. His three candidates for these possibilities were John Hughes Curtis, Morris Rosner, and John F. Condon. Part of his reaction may have been borne out of frustration: being excluded from Lindy's dealings with the trio. Even if Lindy hadn't voluntarily abdicated from the manhunt, public outcry would have forced H. Norman to take some type of action. As it was, he told Lindbergh that he had to deal with the three go-betweens as prime suspects.

Late in the afternoon of May 12, the day the baby was found in the woods, the state police escorted John Hughes Curtis from Atlantic City, New Jersey, to Schwarzkopf's office at the Lindbergh estate. Waiting for him in addition to H. Norman were Captain Lamb and Lieutenant Keaten of the NJSP, Jersey City PD's Harry Walsh, Detective Warren Moffat of the Newark Police Department, IRS agent Frank Wilson, and Anthony M. Hauck, the Hunterdon County prosecutor who would most likely be trying the murderers when they were apprehended. The contentious welcoming committee made it clear to Curtis that they had questions to ask and that truth was the commodity they sought. His suggestion that they wait for Lindbergh to arrive was brushed aside. The grilling was harsh and direct. The men in the room had never been privy to the Lindbergh-Curtis activities; now they were. Detailed descriptions of Nils, Eric, John, Dynamite, Hilda, and the others deepened suspicions that Curtis was what Schwarzkopf, Lamb, and Keaten would later claim they had always believed: a fraud or worse. When Lindbergh finally reached Sorrel Hill, he asked Curtis what he made of the death. The bankrupt shipyard operator had no answers but suggested that he and the Lone Eagle hurry and catch up with Hilda and Sam, who might know. The advice was ignored. Captain Lamb took over the questioning of Curtis, whom the state police planned to keep away from the media as long as possible. On May 17, after five days of intensive interrogation, John Hughes Curtis confessed to having perpetrated a hoax on Charles Lindbergh and was taken into custody by the troopers.

John F. ("Jafsie") Condon was questioned the next day, Friday, the thirteenth of May. As always, he was garrulous and his statement slightly discrepant. The NYPD and the BI wanted time with him as well. So did the Bronx County attorney and, of course, the press. Whatever investigators may have been told by him, the public was reading of yet another encounter Dr. Condon claimed to have had, this one with four of the actual kidnappers. It occurred on a boat off City Island, a popular Bronx recreational park. Condon claimed he had gone there to expedite the ransom-release of the baby. On seeing that the four men were armed, he proclaimed, "Gentlemen, I come to you as an umpire of a baseball game. I am not armed and have no occasion to fire."[6] Three of the men put away their guns. Condon described the fourth man in great detail. His name was Doc, and he seemed to be Scandinavian. What exactly happened to Doc's gun was not mentioned, but there was no doubt that he was John.

On May 21, four days after the arrest of John Hughes Curtis, a Bronx grand jury began an inquiry into the ransom payment at St. Raymond's Cemetery. Among those slated to give secret testimony were Jafsie Condon, Henry Breckinridge, Max Rosenhain, Milton Gaglio, Al Reich, and Joseph Perrone, the cab driver who had been paid a dollar to deliver a ransom letter to Condon's home.

The New Jersey State Police left their initial questioning of Condon to Jersey City PD's Harry Walsh. Lindbergh and Breckinridge had publicly vouched for Condon, but after reading in one of the papers Jafsie's own account of meeting with Cemetery John, Inspector Walsh was convinced that the old man hadn't told the truth and that he was directly implicated in the kidnapping and murder.[7] The Jersey City cop was also confident he could get a confession from him. Jafsie was brought to the state-police barracks at Alpine, New Jersey, on June 2, 1932, where Walsh's blunt, accusatory style resulted in a raucous four hours of confrontation but no admission of guilt from the imperious former school principal.[8] Subsequent searches of Condon's Bronx home and summer shack, phone taps, and mail surveillance resulted in the old man's receiving a clean bill of health from the state police, but he remained the target of a great many skeptical lawmen, a number of whom suspected he was nothing more than another Gaston Means, John Hughes Curtis, or Morris Rosner.

Schwarzkopf had not been privy to most of what had transpired between Lindbergh and the various go-betweens. Now, as interrogators began to elicit the facts, many a lawman was startled, if not alarmed, by what was learned. One of the most troubling disclosures came from Morris Rosner. Like John F. Condon, he was interrogated on Friday, April 13, at Sorrel Hill. The unnerving fact revealed by Mickey was that copies had been made of the original ransom note found in the nursery the night the child disappeared and that these copies were then circulated in the New York City underworld. The avowed motive for this was to try to identify the unknown author of the messages that Lindbergh and Breckinridge had so ardently denied existed. According to Rosner, many criminals had viewed the reproductions, including forgers and bunco artists. The possibility now existed that someone other than the actual kidnappers may have sent the last twelve ransom notes, that this someone had examined a copy of the nursery message and forged the writing style to extort fifty thousand dollars from Lindbergh.

On May 27, after having analyzed the handwriting evidence the New Jersey State Police had sent him, seventy-one-year-old Albert Sherman Osborn submitted his findings. He was the second, and by far the best-known, expert on questioned documents with whom the troopers had checked. Eleven of the thirteen messages contained "signatures" of three interlacing colored circles dotted by three perforation marks, and according to Osborn's findings, all thirty-three perforations seemed to have been made by the same instrument, perhaps a nail. The inks used in drawing the circles were commonplace and provided no clues as to where they had been obtained. The same was true of the paper and envelopes. Osborn felt that a German-English dictionary had been referred to while the messages were being composed. He found characteristics of German sentence structure and phraseology throughout the text. The addressee on one of the envelopes, "Mr. Doctor John F. Condon" was distinctly German.[9]

Like that of the previous expert from whom the state police had received an opinion, Osborn's general conclusion was that only one person had written all thirteen messages. But this was not unequivocal. Osborn did concede that there was a difference between the writing in the first note, found in the nursery, and that in the subsequent twelve—as would be elaborated on at the trial. He felt this may have been due to the author's intentional attempts to disguise his handwriting in the first note or perhaps because it was composed under difficult physical conditions, such as in an automobile.

Despite the state police's acceptance of Osborn's single-writer theory, another body of thinking held that an extortionist had got hold of a copy of the first ransom note, imitated the writing style, and in an effort to obtain the money, had sent the next twelve messages received by Lindbergh, Breckinridge, and Condon. Put in simpler terms, two different criminal elements were involved with the tragic death: the kidnapper-murderers and the extortionists. There was nothing unique about this in 1932. Several newspapers pointed out that the burgeoning rash of kidnappings for money over the past several years had been accompanied by a dramatic rise in the interception of ransom payments by sharp-eyed forgers and con men. In years to come, newsmen as prestigious as Edwin Newman would cite the two-different-party theory regarding the Lindbergh ransom notes and payment.

Ellis Parker, Sr., Burlington County detective and arguably New Jersey's greatest crime buster, was leaning toward a single-writer, single-kidnapper theory. He was pretty certain who it was, but he wanted confirmation. He had samples of his suspect's penmanship, and on August 22 he wrote to H. Norman Schwarzkopf, requesting a photostatic copy of the original ransom note, which he promised to show to no one. The trooper boss wrote back on August 24:

> My Dear Mr. Parker
> Permit me to acknowledge receipt of your esteemed communication of recent date and with reference thereto, would state, that we are not authorized to give out any copies of any of the ransom notes other than those officially released for publication.
> If you have any documents which you wish to compare with the original note, if you will submit them to us we will

have the comparison made by the experts working on the case and inform you of the findings.

Regretting that we cannot comply with your request, I beg to remain,

> Very truly yours
> H. Norman Schwarzkopf
> Colonel and Superintendent,
> New Jersey State Police[10]

Two days after that, on August 26, Parker sent a letter to Governor A. Harry Moore, in which he enclosed a copy of H. Norman's response to his request. The state's chief executive was reminded that early on in the investigation he had urged Parker to study the Lindbergh case. Parker wrote that he had and that he now knew the "calibre" of the kidnapper. He then complained that

> it looks to me as though the State Police do not intend to let any officer, outside of their own, have any information that might clear up this case, as they will not release anything for fear some one else will solve the problem and they are using this method to get them to bring any information to them.
>
> Early in this case, the various police organizations and County Detective organizations appealed to me. I did not want to do anything that was unethical and felt the State Police should have full sway.
>
> If I had a photostat copy of the ransom note, that I might study it, I would know for certain whether my deductions are right.
>
> You will note in the Colonel's letter, where he says, "that we are not authorized to give out any copies of any of the ransom notes other than those officially released for publication." I don't know who he means by "we" and that is the reason I am writing to you.
>
> If this case is in charge of some other individual, I would certainly be pleased to receive a communication from you, informing me who they are, that I might get in touch with them.
>
> I have always labored under the impression that the State Police were conducting this investigation.

> Trusting you will use your power to see that I get a
> photostat copy of the original ransom note and I assure that
> it will not be given out to anyone. I only want to study it.
> I remain,
>
> At your service.
> Ellis Parker Sr.[11]

There is nothing to indicate that Parker was given a copy of the original note. The man he now suspected to be the kidnapper-murderer, as well as the author of the ransom notes, was the go-between he himself had recruited: Paul Wendel.

— — —

Charles Lindbergh emerged from private life and once again became involved with the crime, this time at a federal courtroom in Washington, D.C. It was June 8, and Gaston B. Means was on trial for extorting $104,000 from Mrs. Evalyn Walsh McLean. The BI was in charge of the case and didn't seem much concerned that Gaston was now claiming he had returned all the money. Lindbergh testified as to the kidnapping, for dramatic effect more than for substantive purposes. He attended every session of the trial and resided at Mrs. McLean's sumptuous home during his stay. On Monday, June 13, the jury retired. It took only two hours for it to find Means guilty. On the fifteenth of June 1932, the judge sentenced him to fifteen years in prison.

A dozen days after that, the trial of John Hughes Curtis began at the Hunterdon County Courthouse in Flemington, New Jersey. Curtis was charged with obstruction of justice in the Lindbergh case. Defending him was a local lawyer by the name of C. Lloyd Fisher. As had been the situation at the Means trial, Lindbergh was present. He sat at the table of the prosecuting attorney, Anthony Hauck, the Hunterdon County district attorney. Since the act of reporting false information was not a crime in New Jersey, the state would have to link it to a circumstance that was prosecutable. Hauck did this by claiming that Curtis, rather than perpetrating a hoax, was in touch with the actual kidnappers and in an effort to frustrate their apprehension had provided authorities with false information. The media made it blatantly evident that Curtis had concocted the story about a gang, but the prosecution dealt with the mythical criminals as if they were flesh and blood. Two and a half days later the jury found Curtis guilty as charged. The judge sentenced him to a year in jail and fined him a thousand dollars.

If Lindbergh estimated the crime was now finally behind him, he was wrong.

— — —

H. Norman Schwarzkopf and Inspector Harry Walsh were certain that Violet Sharpe, a Morrow household maid, was connected to the kidnapping-murder. Mrs. Morrow's entire twenty-eight-person contingent of maids, cooks, chauffeurs, grounds keepers, and others had been brought from Morrow's New Day Hill in Englewood to the Lindbergh home at Sorrel Hill in the weeks following the disappearance. The chauffeur Henry Ellerson was one of the first to be interviewed because he had driven Betty Gow to Sorrel Hill on March 1. Like Ellerson, almost all other Morrow employees passed their interviews with flying colors. Not Violet Sharpe. She had not told the truth in the opinion of Harry Walsh and Schwarzkopf. Why else would she lie about her whereabouts the night of the kidnapping, unless she was implicated? Well, not exactly lie, just not be able to remember the name of the man whom she went out with that night and the other couple who was along. There were other inconsistencies as well. And what about her hostile attitude at being questioned about her private life? They thought she was guilty. Of what, Walsh wasn't all that sure. But he was not about to let her get away with it. Lindbergh was reported to have been incensed at the suggestion Sharpe had premeditatedly abetted the kidnapper-murderer, but he did allow that this might have happened without her knowledge.

Violet underwent her third state-police interrogation on May 23. It was conducted by Walsh with Lindbergh and Schwarzkopf looking on. Little was accomplished. Lindbergh noted that Violet was scared and upset but did nothing to stop Walsh from having at her again.[12] Seventeen days later, on Thursday, June 9, Walsh resumed his questioning— and would later admit that he was "shocked" by Violet's deterioration since their last encounter. She had lost fifty pounds and was generally wasted. This did not keep him from grilling her, ostensibly about one Ernest Brinkert, whose business cards had been found in her room. Violet became hysterical. Walsh resented the fact that a doctor was called, and he refused to leave. The doctor attested that Violet was on the verge of a breakdown and ordered the questioning to end. Walsh was incensed. To him she was faking.[13]

At 10:00 the next morning Walsh phoned the Morrow house with news that Lieutenant Keaten would pick up Violet and take her to the state-police barracks at Alpine for further interrogation. Panicked at the prospect, she hurried upstairs to her room, took a can down from her wardrobe closet, and poured some of the white powder it contained into a glass, which she filled with water and drank. She made her way downstairs and collapsed. A doctor was there in a matter of minutes. It was too late. Violet Sharpe was dead from the cyanide chloride she had ingested.

Walsh was unrepentant about the death. Schwarzkopf, in an effort to downplay the incident, distorted some facts, held back on others, and tried to point the blame anywhere but at himself and his organization. Violet's demise, in the opinion of the trooper boss, was confirmation of her possible involvement in the crime. A tribute to Schwarzkopf's sublime shortsightedness in regard to public relations was his confidence that the distortions and half-truths had vindicated his actions and effectively stemmed any criticism that might have been raised against him and the trooper investigation.[14] H. Norman was wrong again.

Headlines across the nation and in many European countries condemned the state police for killing Violet Sharpe and demanded the organization be held accountable and punished. The banner of the *London Daily Telegraph* saw the death as a DISGRACE TO AMERICAN JUSTICE. Anne Lindbergh was moved to wonder what a crude and imperfect world we live in—that we understand nothing.[15] Publicly, Lindy and Henry Breckinridge stood behind Schwarzkopf.

Evidence that the business cards found in Violet's bedroom—the pretext Walsh had used for grilling her the day before her death—were probably planted did not help the troopers' cause. The three people whose names she could not remember came forward and identified themselves. None was connected with the kidnapping-murder. The state police still wouldn't concede Violet's innocence, a posture they maintained until they were able to perform a slight bit of character assassination and contend that she had lied to them to cover up a series of sexual affairs with various men. History was to show little sympathy for the troopers' point of view. Sharpe's death remains a despicable black mark against the New Jersey State Police.

Good news for the Lindberghs arrived Tuesday morning, August 16, at Mrs. Morrow's New York City apartment. Anne gave birth to her second child, a seven-pound, fourteen-ounce boy to be named Jon. Few in the media commented that Jon was not all that dissimilar from John, the infamous presence who allegedly received the ransom money in St. Raymond's Cemetery.

18

MONEY CHASE

FIVE-DOLLAR RANSOM NOTES CONTINUED TO APPEAR THROUGHOUT THE SUM-
mer of 1932: an additional two in June, one in July, three in August, one
in September. Again the bills were passed in New York City, and most
were discovered in banks. Whenever the joint task force of the NYPD,
the BI, and NJ troopers was able to trace a bill to its original source, the
recipient was unable to say how he or she had come to have it.

With banks closing throughout America as the Great Depression continued to worsen, a beaming new face emerged on the national political
scene, that of a man with one hell of a gift of oratory. It had taken three
ballots before Franklin Delano Roosevelt, the governor of New York,
was nominated as the presidential candidate of the Democratic party.
His running mate was old, crusty John Nance Garner. Roosevelt's hand-
picked candidate to replace him in the governor's mansion in Albany was

Herbert Lehman. The GOP nominee to oppose Lehman in the November election was one of the earliest advisers to Lindbergh after the disappearance of the baby, William J. Donovan. Among FDR's first presidential-campaign promises was a pledge to end Prohibition. Herbert Lehman also came out for the repeal of Prohibition. So did William J. Donovan, which put him in direct conflict with his party's platform. Oddly enough, it would be one of Donovan's campaign leaflets that coined the phrase New Deal and pledged just that in Albany. Months later FDR's forces came up with the same rallying cry of a New Deal in Washington.

— — —

The first ten-dollar gold certificate from the ransom loot was discovered on October 22, the same day that Herbert Hoover, running for reelection, cited ten indications that the degenerating economy was getting better. October also saw the recovery of a twenty-dollar gold certificate, two additional ten-dollar gold certificates, and three five-dollar notes, for a total of sixty-five dollars, the largest monthly tally yet registered. Only five five-dollar notes were recovered in November, the month in which Franklin Delano Roosevelt defeated Herbert Clark Hoover for the presidency by a landslide vote and William J. Donovan got soundly thrashed in the New York State gubernatorial race by Democrat Herbert Lehman. In December a five-dollar note and a ten-dollar gold certificate surfaced.

— — —

Nineteen thirty-three began with no money being recovered in either January or February, and a solitary ten-dollar gold certificate turned up in March. The fourth day of March saw fifty-one-year-old Franklin D. Roosevelt sworn in as the thirty-second president of the United States. In his inaugural address he asserted a firm belief that the only thing he and the populace had to fear was fear itself. On March 5, FDR ordered the nation's banks closed for a four-day "holiday," in the hopes of saving the entire system from collapse. It didn't take long for opponents of FDR to raise the cry that he was trying to set himself up as a dictator, just as Adolf Hitler had in Germany.[1]

— — —

Every ransom bill to date had been found in deposits made at various New York City banks. With the exception of that traced to a candy store and an Edison Company office in Brooklyn, a cigar store in Queens, and two people living in Irvington, New York, all the recovered money was spent in Manhattan. Unlike his counterparts heading the state-police and BI detachments in New York, Jimmy Finn insisted on going into the field and talking with each recipient of a bill. He did this accompanied by a Jersey trooper, and in most instances with a special agent from the Bureau of Investigation. The modus operandi they followed was Finn's: to conduct the interview without revealing that the currency was from the ransom loot. This was accomplished by claiming that the money was counterfeit and inquiring as to how the interviewee had come into possession of the bogus note. Most people could not remember. But two did.

In December of 1932, a salesman in a lower Manhattan men's sportswear shop recalled receiving a listed five-dollar note from a six-foot tall, light-complected man who spoke with an accent. On March 1, 1933, a ten-dollar gold certificate was spent at a downtown cigar store by a light-complected man who had a long, thin face, was approximately six feet tall and forty years of age, and wore a soft hat and dark clothing. Both descriptions were similar to a police profile that had appeared in the papers and on circulars regarding Cemetery John.

＊ ＊ ＊

Investigators differed as to how many people were passing the money. Some, like Finn, thought there was only one. Several bills discovered early in the ransom hunt had been spent at restaurants, which for Jimmy, at least, indicated that the passer was using the loot to supplement his ordinary income, something a well-organized gang would not allow its members to do. There were other clues as to the behavior of the passer or passers. A few bills were traced to New York burlesque houses. Other bills showed severe crease marks, which indicated that at least one of the passers had the habit of folding a ransom note tightly in three: lengthwise through the center, then through the center crosswise, and crosswise again through the center. Such a folded note could easily fit into a watch pocket.

＊ ＊ ＊

On April 5, 1933, in preparation for the United States' going off the gold standard in two weeks, President Roosevelt ordered that all gold coin, gold bullion, and gold certificates be turned in at banks of the Federal Reserve system before May 1. With gold certificates comprising the bulk of outstanding ransom money, updated lists of their serial numbers were reissued. During the remainder of April, the Federal Reserve Bank in New York retrieved twenty-eight ten-dollar gold certificates from the Condon payment, twenty-four of which had been exchanged at the Chemical National Bank at Cortlandt Street and Broadway in New York City. On May 1, the New York Fed came across twenty-six more listed ten-dollar gold certificates that had been turned in at the same Chemical National Bank. On May 2, going through the receipts for the exchanges made the last week of April at the Manufacturers Trust Company, 149 Broadway, the New York Fed found fifty ten-dollar gold certificates of ransom loot. It was another discovery that same day that made headlines.

An exchange transaction conducted directly at the New York City branch of the Federal Reserve Bank contained 297 gold certificates, all from the ransom. One of the bills was a twenty; the remaining 296 were tens, for a total value of $2,980. The teller, who had received the money the day before, May 1, could not recall who had made the exchange, but a deposit slip was attached to the currency, on which the customer had written his or her name and an address: J. J. Faulkner, 537 West 149th Street, N.Y.C. The NYPD, Jersey troopers, and Bureau of Investigation's special agents descended. No J. J. Faulkner existed at 537 West 149th Street.

The Lindbergh case returned to the headlines, and copies of the bank-deposit slip bearing J.J.'s signature appeared on many a front page. Searching the records, investigators found that twelve years earlier a Faulkner family had resided not at 537 West 149th Street but at number 547. A marriage license was located that revealed that on February 17, 1921, Jane Emily Faulkner of 547 West 149th Street had married Carl Oswin Geissler of nearby Larchmont. New York handwriting expert Albert D. Osborn, who by now had devised a test by which it could be determined if someone was the author of the Lindbergh ransom messages, compared Geissler's signature on the marriage license with that of J. J. Faulkner's on the deposit slip and proclaimed that they were similar.[2] Samples were sent to the BI's handwriting expert in Washington, who said the same person had written the two signatures. After an exhaustive probe, Geissler, his relatives, and friends were found innocent of any complicity with the crime. With what would be the organization's most extensive manhunt, the BI continued the search for anyone whose name sounded like that. Included among those investigated by special agents was the author William Faulkner.

A battle was brewing between a pair of supreme egomaniacs who didn't have much use for each other: J. Edgar Hoover and H. Norman Schwarz-kopf. Hoover's special agents had pursued the mysterious J. J. Faulkner with a far larger effort than both the NYPD and the New Jersey State Police could have mounted; then the BI all but dropped out of the New York money chase, ostensibly to follow other channels of investigation. The troopers, who also were searching for clues to the kidnapping-murder in other places, never abandoned the money trail. When by August of 1933 the best lead any agency had was still the passing of ransom money in New York City, the Bureau of Investigation returned to the hunt with a vengeance and a tactic. Only now the organization had a new name and was officially the Division of Investigation, or the DI.

In a letter dated September 18, 1933, Hoover reminded Schwarzkopf that the DI had the legislated license to assist in any other law-enforcement effort to find the abductors of the Lindbergh child, and he also invited the state police to provide his organization with a summary of their investigation to date.[3] For H. Norman, J. Edgar's reemergence in the case created a public relations dilemma. Hoover was as skillful at manipulating the media as Schwarzkopf was inept. When J. Edgar withdrew most of his special agents from the New York City investigation, reporters seemed not to notice. Listening to him speak and reading many of his organization's press statements now that he had decided to get back into the money chase, one might get the impression that he and his Division of Investigation had taken over the Lindbergh case. As J. Edgar, amidst ample media coverage, tried to forge an alliance between the Jersey State Police, the DI, and the NYPD to apprehend the passer or passers of the ransom bills, Schwarzkopf was hard-pressed. To say no would eliminate his troopers from the New York City manhunt, as well as provoking even more ire from antagonistic journalists who were hailing Hoover's assistance and plan.

In October of 1933, Schwarzkopf publicly joined and praised the joint state-police–DI–NYPD effort orchestrated by J. Edgar. Privately he told Special Agent Sisk that he had no intention of opening his files to the DI, and he never did.[4] Two of Schwarzkopf's top aides and staunchest loyalists on the state-police force, Captain John J. Lamb and Lieutenant Arthur T. ("Buster") Keaten, were openly hostile to the arrangement. Lamb and Keaten had supervised the troopers' handling of the Lindbergh case since the onset, but in the opinion of the author and BBC investigative reporter Ludovic Kennedy, they were "third raters" when it came to standard police work.[5] Keaten was in direct command of the twelve troopers dispatched to New York City. His claim to fame as a crime buster was that he had worked on the troopers' end of the sorry investigation of the Hall-Mills murders.[6] Keaten told Special Agent Sisk that " 'Roosevelt and his gang' were dangerous Communists and that when the Republicans were elected, 'Schwarzkopf goes in.' "[7]

Captain John Lamb also listed the state police's minimal participation in the Hall-Mills case as his top credit. An excitable, not too clever, red-faced man, Lamb joined Keaten in criticizing Scotland Yard and launching tirades against almost everyone else who had tried to help in the case, including the Northwest Mounted Police, the New York Police Department, and investigators and inspectors for the Department of Labor and the Treasury Department. Lamb as well as Keaten bragged that their men had been ordered not to give any information to the NYPD or special agents of the DI. Lamb referred to Detective Jimmy Finn as a "nitwit" and to New York City's new police commissioner John F. O'Ryan as an "old broken-down general."[8] Lamb resented the DI as much as the NYPD. Luckily for the trooper interest, Detective William F. Horn had established an affable working relationship with Finn, Sisk, and Special Agent William F. Seery.

The police, DI men, and troopers of the joint task force were provided with a sketch of Cemetery John made by the cartoonist James T. Barryman from descriptions given to him not only by Jafsie Condon but by Joseph Perrone, the taxi driver who had carried a message from the kidnapper to Condon. There were qualms about this. Perrone had gotten only a fleeting glimpse in the dark at the man wearing a brown topcoat and brown felt hat who had paid him one dollar to deliver a ransom message to Condon, and he originally stated that he would not be able to identify him.[9] Under the glare of continued press coverage and notoriety, he began to recall in great detail the face he hadn't seen clearly enough to describe at the time, and it didn't differ all that much from what, thanks to Jafsie, had already been printed in the papers. Perrone, once his memory returned, identified quite a few suspects as being John.

Even though the DI, like most other agencies, was suspicious of Condon, its special agents met with him regularly and displayed mug shots of people who might be Cemetery John. None ever was. Once the New York City money chase got under way, DI as well as NYPD investigators paid specific attention to neighborhoods in New York City where German and Scandinavian languages were spoken, whose accents Condon attributed John as having.

- - -

Locations where ransom currency was recovered were marked with pins on large maps in the offices of both Finn and Sisk, and a pattern emerged:[10] More money was being spent in a triangular section of the Bronx than anyplace else, an area that contained no German-speaking communities. Then ransom bills appeared in Albany and Cooperstown, New York. Several showed up in the state of Maine.

- - -

On the clear and cold evening of Sunday, November 26, 1933, at Loew's Sheridan Square Theatre on Seventh Avenue and Thirteenth Street in Greenwich Village—over two hundred blocks south of the Bronx triangle—a man handed a tightly folded bill to cashier Cecile M. Barr. The feature for the evening was *Broadway thru a Keyhole,* which starred Paul Kelly and Constance Cummings. The script had been written in part by the most powerful gossip columnist in the world, the acerbic Walter Winchell, who was an avid chronicler of the Lindbergh crime and investigation. On opening the compact bill—it was folded once lengthwise and twice across—the young movie-house cashier saw that it was a five-dollar Federal Reserve note. The customer seemed puzzled when she explained that there were three different admission prices. He bought a forty-cent ticket and went inside.

The next morning the theater's assistant manager deposited the creased five-dollar note with the other receipts at a Seventh Avenue branch of the Corn Exchange Bank. A teller by the name of William Cody spotted it as coming from the ransom loot. When cashier Barr came on duty at 5:00 that night, she was confronted by Special Agent Manning, Detective Horn, and Jimmy Finn. They wanted to know if she could describe the person who gave her the bill. Indeed she could. He was in his mid-thirties, and even though it was cold out, he hadn't worn a top-coat over his dark suit. He was of medium height and weight and had a wiry build. A dark slouch hat was pulled down over his forehead, and his blue eyes unwaveringly returned her look from a triangular face formed by high cheekbones, flat cheeks, and a pointed chin.[11] Barr claimed that the customer was American and made no mention of his having an accent. She did, however, identify Barryman's drawing of Cemetery John as being the man who gave her the folded five dollars.

The excitement prompted by the Sheridan Square Theatre find was short-lived. The second anniversary of the money search came and went with bills continuing to pass but no identifying descriptions of the passer being made. The same was true through the spring and summer of 1934, during which time investigators tracked listed bills to as far away as Kobe, Japan, without developing a relevant lead. For Jimmy Finn, at least, answering a call from a bank was no longer the thrill it had been in the past. Nor was it any fun talking to reporters anymore. Finn and the NYPD, as had the Jersey troopers for a long while, were feeling the bite of impatient and critical journalists. The lack of progress was even putting the DI under fire.

New territorial spending patterns of ransom money began to appear on the pin-dotted maps in the offices of the DI and the NY police. The elusive passer seemed to have run out of five-dollar bills and was drawing more regularly from his backlog of twenty-dollar gold certificates, which were easier to spot. A flurry of listed twenties had been retrieved in the Yorkville section of upper Manhattan, between East Seventy-ninth and East Eighty-ninth streets. There were fewer but consistent discoveries of ransom bills being paid for merchandise between Fifty-ninth Street in Manhattan and 161st Street in the Bronx along the Lexington Avenue subway line and along the Second Avenue and Third Avenue elevated lines. As far as Finn could project, the passer had taken to traveling between midtown Manhattan and the Bronx in an effort to change ransom loot, but he was concentrating this effort in the business and restaurant district of Little Germany, as Yorkville was known, where German was spoken as frequently as English.

A second eyewitness was developed when on September 6, 1934, Finn, Horn, and Special Agent Seery traced a ten-dollar gold certificate from the Lindbergh ransom loot to a food and vegetable store on Eighty-ninth Street and Third Avenue in Yorkville. A young Italian American clerk by the name of Levatino remembered that the bill had been given to him as payment for a six-cent head of lettuce by a man who was not a regular customer. When the proprietor of the shop chewed Levatino out for making $9.94 worth of change for a ten-dollar bill, the surly stranger had got into an argument with the owner and shaken a menacing finger at him. Levatino's description of the passer closely fit that of Cecile Barr, the movie-theater cashier. But whereas Barr thought he was American and hadn't seen the color of his hair, the young clerk said he seemed to be German and that his hair was light brown.

To Finn's way of thinking, the same man had given ransom money to Barr and Levatino, a person who in the course of the nine-month lapse of time between the two incidents had evolved from a retiring, unsure, suspicious criminal into an aggressive, self-confident, and somewhat arrogant one.[12] Finn and Special Agent Sisk, confident they were breathing down the passer's neck, agreed that the time had come for extreme action. Five DI special agents, five trooper detectives, and five NYPD plainclothesmen, including Finn, infiltrated the area between East Seventy-ninth Street and East Eighty-ninth Street, where bills were most frequently passed. Each man was assigned a post and given a report-in time. When more ransom surfaced in the area, Sisk pushed for an escalation of manpower and volunteered to send in more special agents. This was the final straw for Captain Lamb of the state police, who feared that Sisk, a man he had never cared for, was conniving to exclude the troopers from the final capture of the passer. " 'Sisk, you and your outfit want to run the whole thing,' Lamb fumed. 'You make me sick . . .' Sisk replied, 'What did you contribute to this case except to knock everybody and everything? You do nothing but sit around and make everybody think you're smart.' Lamb yelled, 'Don't talk to me like that,' " only to be shouted down by other officers of the state police.[13] Admitting that he might be jittery, Lamb apologized.

The number of investigators operating on the streets was upped from fifteen to fifty and bumped again to sixty-four. Twenty-five were from the NYPD, twenty from the DI, and nineteen from the New Jersey State Police. Besides infiltrating the Yorkville terrain, mobile patrols kept a tight watch on vegetable stores and stands along the Lexington Avenue subway and the Second Avenue and Third Avenue elevated railroad stations between Fifty-ninth Street in Manhattan and 161st Street in the Bronx. Other lawmen were stationed at each of the subway and elevated stations along the route; still others walked the blocks between stations, looking for someone who fit the passer's description. Fat men were eliminated; so were those over five feet ten inches tall. Middle-aged prospects were passed by, along with anyone who didn't speak German or a Scandinavian language.

Earlier in the investigation, when Finn and Sisk had noticed that no bills were passed for days or often a week after the local papers reported the recovery of ransom loot, they prevailed on the city's editors not to mention the finding of future currency. By August of 1934, with the news blackout still in force, a steady stream of ransom bills was turning up. Then Jafsie Condon called both Finn and Sisk—and breathlessly reported that he had been riding on a bus and had seen John walk past on the street, and by the time he got off and gave chase, John was gone.

As DI, NYPD, and trooper investigators flooded the specified area, Condon went public with the information, thereby shattering the news blackout. Even so, ransom money continued to surface. The Finn-Sisk attempt at censorship received another setback on Sunday evening, September 16, when a listening audience of millions heard Walter Winchell berate New York City bank tellers on his popular evening radio show by saying, "Boys, if you weren't such a bunch of saps and yaps, you'd have already captured the Lindbergh kidnappers."

On the afternoon of September 18, 1934, two days after Walter Winchell's public scolding of New York City bank personnel, the chief teller of the Corn Exchange Bank at 125th Street and Park Avenue in Manhattan reported the finding of two ten-dollar gold certificates from the ransom loot. The DI was notified, and Jimmy Finn, Special Agent William F. Seery, and John J. Lamb of the New Jersey State Police responded. Printed in pencil on the back of one of the two bills they were shown was this notation: "4U-13-41, N.Y."[14] The ten-dollar gold certificate was quickly traced to the Warner-Quinlan filling station at 127th Street and Lexington Avenue, only four blocks away from the bank. Walter Lyle, the station manager, recognized the bill and identified the printing on the back as his. He remembered very well who had given it to him.

Lyle related that the previous Saturday night, September 15, just before 10:00 P.M., a dark-blue 1930 Dodge sedan had pulled into his gas station. An attendant, John Lyons, unscrewed the radiator cap to see if water was needed while Lyle, pump hose in hand, asked the driver if he should fill her up. The driver, a man with a German accent, said no, he only wanted five dollars worth of "ethyl." While Lyle pumped the gas and Lyons cleaned the windshield, the man got out of the car. He wore mechanic's garb and had a V-shaped face with high cheekbones, flat cheeks, and a pointed chin. "That's ninety cents," Lyle said after hanging up the hose and replacing the Dodge's gas cap. The man took an envelope from his inside jacket pocket and withdrew a ten-dollar gold certificate, which he gave to Lyle. The owners of the station had cautioned against accepting gold certificates, which were no longer legal tender. Lyle had also received a New York Police Department circular asking that they be on the alert for Lindbergh ransom money. Until recently he had kept the accompanying list of serial numbers beside the cash register in the office. Seeing Lyle study the bill, the man had said, "They're all right. Any bank will take them." Lyle told him that you didn't see many gold certificates anymore, to which the man replied, "No. I only have about a hundred left." After giving the man his change and watching him drive off, Lyle jotted down the license plate number on the back margin of the ten-dollar gold certificate before putting it into the register.[15]

Subsequent to interviewing Lyle and leaving the filling station, Jimmy Finn telephoned a friend at the New York State Motor Vehicle Department, read him the license number, and waited on the line while a search was made. Finn was told that the name and address for license plate number 4U-13-41 was Richard Hauptmann of 1279 East 222nd Street, the Bronx.

— — —

Lawmen cautiously infiltrated the area. Two- and three-story wood-and-stucco houses backed by a thick stand of woods and fronted by well-tended lawns and flower beds lined the north side of the twelve-hundred block along East 222nd Street, a distinctly blue-collar neighborhood. Number 1279, the address given for Richard Hauptmann, was something of an exception. The house was ordinary enough, a two-story frame structure coated in tan stucco, with the second floor set back slightly. But the front lawn and ample side yard were tainted with weeds. The side yard ended at a narrow, unpaved, rutted road named Needham Avenue, directly across from which was a ramshackle wooden garage whose double doors were painted red and padlocked. Running along Needham Avenue and on into the woods behind the property were venerable oak and poplar trees. Six and a half blocks to the west, and within hiking distance of the house, 222nd Street ends at Woodlawn Cemetery—the place where Jafsie Condon claimed the first of his two meetings with John had occurred.

Excited investigators worked through the night amassing whatever information they could on Hauptmann and trying to devise a strategy for apprehending him. He was thirty-five years old and rented the five-room apartment on the second floor of number 1279, where he lived with his wife and young son. Two other families occupied the pair of apartments on the first floor. A search of police files produced no arrests. License-bureau records showed that he had registered the same 1930 Dodge for the past four years and that in 1931 it had been described as dark green, rather than its present dark blue. Jimmy Finn and Special Agent Sisk were more than optimistic that they had finally found their man. Hauptmann had been born in Germany, which meant he probably had an accent.

The frenzy increased as the lawmen tried to formulate a plan of attack. Should they invade the house and take him there? What if Hauptmann were armed and prepared for this? Should they let him lead them to his accomplices, assuming he had accomplices? Should they let him lead them to the rest of the ransom money? Should they risk him spotting their surveillance and escaping? One thing was certain, he must be taken alive. A strategy was finally worked out. It was agreed that the operation be kept secret from the press.

That the atmosphere among the sixty members of the joint task force now involved with the case was electric is understandable.[16] The first bill from the ransom payment had been detected in a New York City bank back on April 5, 1932. During the ensuing thirty months, money-chase investigators had traveled seventy-six hundred miles to 716 locations, where bills had been passed and five thousand people had been questioned.[17] Now for the first time since the baby disappeared, a suspect was about to be apprehended.

- - -

At 8:15 A.M., Wednesday, September 19, 1934, a wiry five-foot-ten, blue-eyed man emerged through the front door of the house at 1279 East 222nd Street. He weighed approximately 180 pounds and wore a dou-

Charles A. Lindbergh and the Spirit of St. Louis *shortly before his historic May 20, 1927, trans-Atlantic flight to Paris* (Bettmann Archive)

Lindbergh and his mother, Evangeline, prior to the flight (Library of Congress)

Charles and Anne Morrow Lindbergh in Washington, D.C. (AP/Wide World Photos)

Charles A. Lindbergh, Jr. (AP/Wide World Photos)

The ransom letter allegedly left in the nursery the night of March 1, 1932

Two views of the Lindbergh estate in Hopewell, N.J. Top photograph shows police examination of kidnapper's apparent route of entry into nursery. (Library of Congress)

*William J. "Wild Bill"
Donovan, who may have been
at the Lindbergh estate on the
night of the disappearance*
(Library of Congress)

Betty Gow and Ollie Whateley (AP/Wide World Photos)

*Col. H. Norman Schwarzkopf, Anne
Lindbergh, and Mrs. Dwight Morrow*
(AP/Wide World Photos)

Charles Lindbergh and Henry Breckinridge
(UPI/Bettmann)

If the kidnappers of our child are unwilling to deal direct we fully authorize "Salvy" Spitale and Irving Bitz to act as our go-between. We will also follow any other method suggested by the kidnappers that we can be sure will bring the return of our child

Charles A. Lindbergh
Anne Lindbergh

The announcement of a change in go-betweens, which was reproduced in many newspapers (Library of Congress)

Salvatore Spitale and Irving Bitz (UPI/Bettmann)

Left to right: Henry Breckinridge, Jafsie Condon, and an unidentified man, in the Bronx, April 1932 (UPI/Bettmann)

Al Capone and an unidentified detective (Library of Congress)

Gaston B. Means (Library of Congress)

Rear Admiral Guy Burrage, spokesman for go-betweens Rev. H. Dobson-Peacock and John Hughes Curtis (UPI/Bettmann)

Mrs. Evalyn Walsh McLean (Library of Congress)

Violet Sharpe (AP/Wide World Photos)

William Allen and Orville Wilson, the two men who discovered the remains of the Lindbergh baby, being interviewed by the press shortly after they reported their find (AP/Wide World Photos)

Remains of baby found in the woods on Mount Rose

LINDBERGH RANSOM RECEIVER SEIZED;
$13,750 FOUND AT HIS EAST BRONX HOME;
THE MYSTERY SOLVED, POLICE DECLARE

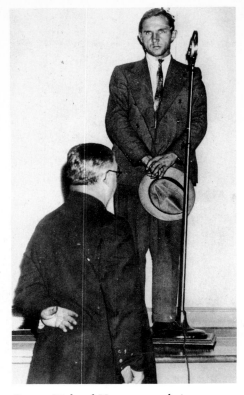

SUSPECT SELDOM TALKED

Jobless Carpenter Had No Close Friends but Bore Good Name.

CAME HERE AS STOWAWAY

Told Neighbors in Bronx He Quit Job After 'Making Money in Wall St.'

HAS A 10-MONTH-OLD BABY

His Home Furnished Simply Despite $400 Radio—Known as an Ardent Hunter.

MAN WHO GOT LINDBERGH RANSOM.
Bruno Richard Hauptmann, Alien German Resident of the Bronx.

KEY CLUE PROVIDED BY CHANCE REMARK

'I've Got a Hundred of Them,' Hauptmann Told Attendant, Giving Him $10 Gold Note.

AUTO LICENSE RECORDED

Gasoline Station Employe Says He Suspected Customer of Being a Counterfeiter.

HELD AS EXTORTIONIST

Alien Is Identified by Taxi Man as One Who Dealt With 'Jafsie.'

WORKED NEAR HOPEWELL

Handwriting Similar to That in Ransom Notes—Ladder Also Points to Suspect.

ONE-MAN CRIME, IS THEORY

Gold Note Spent at 127th St. Gave Clue—Jersey Ready to Push Murder Charge.

DETAILS OF ARREST GIVEN BY O'RYAN

Capture of Suspect Result of Tracing of Lindbergh Ransom Money.

MERCHANTS AID POLICE

Commissioner Lays Capture to Close Cooperation by 3 Enforcement Agencies.

Bruno Richard Hauptmann being questioned in police lineup, September 21, 1934 (AP/Wide World Photos)

Hauptmann's garage, where ransom money was discovered (Library of Congress)

ble-breasted blue suit and brown shoes. A soft hat rode on his blond hair. His flat cheeked, V-shaped face resembled somewhat the sketch that cartoonist Barryman had drawn of Cemetery John. The man crossed the front lawn and the rutted road known as Needham Avenue, went to the wooden garage, unlocked the red doors, and entered. A dark-blue 1930 four-door Dodge sedan with license plates that read 4U-13-41 backed out and stopped. The man left the car, closed and padlocked the garage, returned to the Dodge, and drove off. Members of the joint NYPD-DI-trooper arrest team, who had been watching from a distance, scrambled for three black, unmarked Ford sedans.

Nine lawmen tailed the blue Dodge south through Bronx Park and on along Park Avenue: Detective Jimmy Finn, Special Agent Seery, and Trooper Horn rode in one of the black Fords; Sisk, Buster Keaten, and NYPD detective Chester Cronin were in another; New Jersey Troopers Denis Duerr and John B. Wallace occupied the third, which was driven by Detective Sergeant William Wallace of the NYPD. As they neared the busy intersection at East Tremont Avenue, one of the tailing cars feared they might lose the Dodge. With a city street-cleaning truck blocking the way, the Dodge sedan slowed. Before being able to pull around the truck, it was pinned in by one of the black Fords. Trooper Duerr, gun in hand, rushed to the driver's window of the Dodge and shouted for the car to pull to the curb. Sergeant Wallace threw open the passenger's door, slid onto the seat, and poked a gun into the driver's ribs. A second Ford moved up beside them; a third blocked the rear.

Richard Hauptmann stared at the lawmen inside and outside his automobile, then pulled to the curb and shut off the engine. He was jerked from behind the wheel, handcuffed, and led onto the sidewalk, where, in a nervous voice marked by a strong German accent, he complained of his treatment.[18] Sisk and Keaten stood studying him and made no reply. There on the sidewalk, with traffic rolling past and the lawmen still not talking, he was frisked, and no weapon was found. His wallet, taken from his back trouser pocket and examined, contained twenty-nine dollars: a five-dollar bill, four singles, and a twenty-dollar gold certificate. Special Agent Seery checked the serial numbers. The twenty was from the ransom loot.

The silence was broken with a flurry of questions regarding how he came to have the gold certificate, which they told him was counterfeit. Dick Hauptmann calmly explained that he had initially collected gold notes as a hedge against inflation and that at one time he had three hundred dollars worth. When his inflation fears abated, he began to spend the hoard. The gold certificate they had taken from his billfold was the last he possessed. They asked why he told the filling station attendants that he still had about a hundred dollars in gold money. Dick now admitted that he had just fibbed. Yes, he did have about a hundred dollars worth left. At his house. In a tin box. While Finn went to telephone his superior to inform him of the apprehension, the prisoner was kept in the back of a Ford and handcuffed to Sergeant Wallace. According to one version, Wallace looked at the German carpenter in distaste and said, "So you're the Lindbergh kidnapper."[19] In most other accounts Hauptmann wouldn't be told the true reason for his seizure until later.[20]

Another team of DI, NYPD, and trooper investigators was energetically searching the second-floor apartment at 1279 East 222nd Street when Hauptmann was brought back. He showed them the tin box. It contained $120 worth of gold coins. He was berated. They wanted gold certificates, not coins. He was shoved down onto the bed, then ordered up so the bed could be stripped and searched. The mattress was taken away and cut open. Hauptmann stoically watched lawmen ransack his apartment in their quest for evidence. They found family photographs, a German-English dictionary, seventeen memorandum books written in German, letters, and a pile of Hudson Bay sealskins. The most suspicious items recovered were not necessarily incriminating: a pair of high-powered binoculars and service station give-away maps of many states, including New Jersey and Massachusetts. Dick explained that he was a nature lover—and later he admitted that on occasion he had hunted small game in New Jersey not all that far from Hopewell but insisted he had never been at the Lindbergh estate. His young wife, Anna, who was with their baby son, Manfried, in the backyard, came upstairs. Shaken by the sight of her husband in handcuffs and the apartment in near ruin, she asked him if he had done something wrong. He told her no. She was ordered out of the premises.

An electric wire was found that ran from a bedroom window to the small frame garage just beyond the rutted road at the edge of the property. Hauptmann told investigators it was part of an improvised alarm system he had installed to scare off burglars who might try to steal his car. By way of demonstration, he pressed a button by his bed, and an electric light went on in the garage. Sisk, who had noticed Richard glancing in the direction of the garage, went downstairs with Buster Keaten and Inspector Lyons of the NYPD and checked out the structure. Neatly stored in the fifteen-by-eleven-foot interior were a baby carriage, trunks, folding chairs, and other household articles. Nearby was a workshop area replete with a carpentry bench. The garage floor was composed of oil-stained eight-inch-wide wooden planks that appeared to have been burned or charred. A pair of middle planks was loose. The trio of lawmen pried them up. The dirt beneath looked freshly leveled. They took a spade and dug down. A foot below something metal was hit. After exhuming it and cleaning it off, they saw it was a metal jar. A heavy jar. The lid was forced off. Nothing was inside except water.

A break developed in the front apartment on the first floor of the house, which was occupied by the landlady: a ten-dollar gold certificate from the ransom loot, which Hauptmann had given her the day before as partial payment of his September rent. An eyeglasses case that she used as a hiding place produced another listed ten-dollar bill, this one received as part of Hauptmann's January rent. By then Hauptmann had been spirited off to the police station in Greenwich Village where Jimmy Finn had his office. No one knew he was there, and the police intended to keep it that way as long as possible.

A rhythm of its own was taking over the investigation, a fervor and blindness. The optimum goal of the task force members was to implicate the suspect directly in the kidnapping-murder, as well as in extorting ransom money from Charles Lindbergh. The line between these two objectives became blurred in the rising enthusiasm. Like Finn, others at the scene would later contend that they were already certain Hauptmann was both the abductor and the killer of the child even though the extent of his culpability at the moment was that he had passed three ten-dollar bills of ransom money, had been in possession of a listed twenty-dollar note, and generally resembled the sketch of John. The cleanest and surest approach was to get Hauptmann to confess. NYPD brass was en route to lower Manhattan. So were H. Norman Schwarzkopf and J. Edgar Hoover.

— — —

NYPD's Second Precinct station house was at 130 Greenwich Street, a block away from the noisy Hudson Street elevated tracks. Dick Hauptmann arrived sometime after midday and was fingerprinted but not charged. It was the era of the third degree. Hauptmann was slapped into a straight-backed wooden armchair. The initial grilling was left to a New York City cop, with Schwarzkopf looking on. Investigators had been saying that the gold notes were counterfeit; now they came right out and accused the German of extorting ransom money from Lindbergh.

Hauptmann denied the charge and insisted all he knew about the Lindbergh crime was what he had read in the papers. He rattled off his background and openly admitted that he had twice tried to enter the country illegally before succeeding. Asked if he had a police record in Europe, he lied and answered no.

Dick Hauptmann readily took the handwriting test devised by Albert D. Osborn, knowing that it was intended to expose the true author of the ransom messages. Somewhere along the line investigators learned that his full name was Bruno Richard Hauptmann. Finn took credit for starting to address him as Bruno. Hauptmann objected to this. He wanted to be called Dick or Richard. Thus did he become forever Bruno. By 2:00 P.M. interrogators were openly accusing him of having kidnapped and murdered the Lindbergh baby.

Dates became the thrust of the interrogation—where Bruno was on three specific evenings: March 1, 1932, when the baby was reported kidnapped; April 2, 1932, when Jafsie Condon handed fifty thousand dollars to Cemetery John; and November 26, 1933, when Cecile M. Barr, the cashier of the Greenwich Village movie house, received a tightly folded five-dollar bill from the ransom loot.

Hauptmann recalled that on Tuesday, March 1, 1932, he spent the day working as a general handyman at the Majestic Apartments at Seventy-second Street and Central Park West in New York City. Between 5:00 P.M. and 6:00 P.M. he took the subway back home to the Bronx, got into his car, and by 7:00 P.M. was at Fredricksen's bakery-lunchroom in the Bronx, where his wife, Anna, worked every Tuesday and Friday and where every Tuesday and Friday he had dinner with her. After dinner on Tuesday, March 1, 1932, they drove home and went to bed. The next morning he left the car in the garage, as he always did when he didn't drive Anna to the bakery, and took the subway to work at the Majestic. On the way he read about the Lindbergh kidnapping.

Hauptmann flatly denied he was John or that he knew Jafsie Condon other than by reputation and by seeing his name and picture in the papers. Why could he remember so well where he had been on April 2, the day the fifty-thousand-dollar ransom was paid to John in St. Raymond's Cemetery? For two reasons. It was his last full day of employment, the day he quit his job at the Majestic Apartments. It was also the first Saturday in the month, the evening of which was always reserved for music and his friend Hans Kloppenburg. Kloppenburg played the guitar, Bruno the mandolin. On April 2, 1932, like every other first Saturday evening of the month, Kloppenburg arrived at Bruno's house after 6:00 P.M. They played their instruments and sang old German songs. As always, Kloppenburg left around midnight.

As for Sunday evening, November 26, 1933—when a man bought a movie ticket from the cashier Cecile M. Barr with a tightly folded five-dollar Federal Reserve note—it happened to be Bruno's birthday, which he was celebrating at his home in the Bronx with a few friends.

Anna Hauptmann was brought to the station house and interrogated in a different room from her husband. Except for the few moments' encounter at their apartment earlier in the day, she hadn't seen or spoken to him since his apprehension. Asked the same questions he had been asked regarding the three dates, she gave essentially the same answers as to his whereabouts. When Anna finally learned Richard was being accused of the kidnapping and killing of Charles Lindbergh, Jr., a stunned slow take and her hand rising to cover an open mouth were enough to convince most observers she wasn't in on it.

By midnight it was beginning to look like Bruno himself might not be in on it. Preliminary follow-ups failed to disprove his alibi, and the possibility loomed that he was not John, that he was telling the truth about buying up gold certificates, which meant he couldn't even be charged with extortion. So far he hadn't been cited for any crime and was being held incommunicado.

As the grilling approached its twelfth uninterrupted hour, investigators received their worst news yet. After analyzing the handwriting test Bruno had taken earlier, Albert D. Osborn refused to confirm that the German carpenter was the author of the ransom messages and asked to see additional and specific samples of his penmanship. Hauptmann was once again given pen and paper and instructed to write what Osborn had requested. The results were rushed over to Osborn's apartment. The interrogators also had Bruno write verbatim what they dictated: entire passages from the ransom notes, in which the idiosyncratic phrasing and the misspelled words were copied exactly as they had appeared in the original text. At 4:00 A.M. Osborn telephoned Schwarzkopf, who was still at the Village station house, with his final conclusions: Hauptmann had not written the ransom messages. H. Norman told the expert in false documents that they had obtained additional writing samples that might change his mind. A none-too-enthusiastic Osborn replied, "Well, send them over."[21]

According to Hauptmann's account, the beatings got worse at dawn. His alibi hadn't changed, which created a dilemma for the New York City police. They alone had Bruno in custody, and a growing number of senior city cops felt that since there was nothing of which to formally accuse him, they had better let him go before word reached the press that an uncharged suspect was being held incommunicado. Schwarzkopf and the state police would not hear of it.

There was a reluctance to have witnesses identify Hauptmann. One reason for this was that the mere act of bringing six or so people to the station might alert the press and thereby limit the investigators' time with Hauptmann, not to mention their interrogation techniques. Another cause for caution was the reliability of the available witnesses. The state police claimed to have turned up at least two men who might be able to place a suspect near the Lindbergh estate on March 1, 1932, thereby tying him into the kidnapping and murder. Condon and, to a lesser degree, Perrone, could say if Bruno was Cemetery John, thus establishing the charge of extortion. Several other people would know if the suspect had passed them money from the ransom loot. But for a good many officers on the joint task force who would later deny it, each of the witnesses seemed to have his or her own individual flaws. Taxi driver Joseph Perrone, whom Schwarzkopf himself had already called unreliable, was a case in point.

Just when Perrone identified Hauptmann is questionable. One usually accurate source puts it around midnight,[22] but it was most likely the following evening. Perrone had originally stated unequivocally that he would never be able to recognize the man who had paid him a dollar to deliver a ransom letter to Condon on Saturday, March 12, 1932.[23] Since then he had identified several suspects as being that person. At the Greenwich Street station house Perrone was given a pep talk by officers, then taken in to a three-man police lineup, in which Hauptmann was flanked by two burly detectives, to whom he bore very little resemblance. Perrone picked Hauptmann out as the man who gave him the dollar and the envelope.

By midmorning, September 20, Hauptmann, who was still in the chair undergoing interrogation, showed the effects of having been awake for nearly thirty hours. This was not random procedure. Policemen of the 1930s had long been practicing what the mind-bending experts of the decades to come would consider the linchpin of brainwashing: denial of sleep. Interrogators continued to carp on the fact that despite his not having had a job since the day the ransom disappeared into St. Raymond's, he always seemed to have more than enough money. Bruno explained that he had been lucky with speculations in the stock market and in animal furs, such as the sealskins that had been found at the apartment. His partner in the fur business was a man named Isador Fisch. Investigators already had Hauptmann's papers that seemed to reflect the stock market transactions. According to Bruno, the accounts for the fur trade were with Fisch, who had returned to Germany and died.

As the morning wore on, the matter of charging the suspect grew critical. The continued police presence at the Hauptmann apartment, no matter how low-key, would eventually attract reporters. Then, at approximately 11:30 A.M., while searching the wood-frame garage with other task force officers, Detective James J. Petrosino of the NYPD noticed that a board had been nailed across two uprights above Bruno's workbench. He tapped on it, then pried it off. Revealed in the recess behind was a narrow shelf. Resting on the shelf, wrapped in newspapers, were two bundles. Petrosino removed and opened one of the packages. Inside were one hundred ten-dollar gold certificates. The second package produced eighty-three ten-dollar notes. The serial numbers were checked. All $1,830 came from the ransom payment.

Detective John Wallace of the New Jersey State Police hurried from the garage, drove to the nearest pay phone, rang up the downtown station house, and got Schwarzkopf on the line. Learning of the money, the trooper boss ordered, "Go back to the garage and find the rest of it. And when you find it, put it back like it was and bring the wife to the garage." Wallace didn't understand. Schwarzkopf elucidated. "I want the money found in the wife's presence, to get her reaction."[24]

The packages were rewrapped and returned to their hiding place. At 12:40 P.M. another secret shelf was discovered. This one supported a one-gallon shellac can. Beneath several rags inside the can were twelve packages containing a total of $11,930, also from the ransom payment. The stash was wrapped in pages of the June 25, 1934, and September 6, 1934, editions of the *New York Daily News*. The $11,930, like the previous $1,830, was restored to its secret niche. Mrs. Hauptmann was brought down to the garage and watched as the officers feigned the search and discovery of the first two packages and the shellac can. When the contents of each were revealed—a grand total of $13,760—the astonished young woman again put a hand to her mouth. After the inspectors sat her down, she asked, " 'Where did this money come from?' It was Lindbergh's money, where did she think it came from? 'I know nothing of this,' she told them. Was she certain of that? 'I am certain! I know nothing!'

" 'Well, your husband knew about it, that's for sure.' "[25]

19

THE MOST HATED MAN

IN THE WORLD

- - -

ANY THOUGHT OF BRUNO RICHARD HAUPTMANN NOT BEING IMPLICATED IN the crime vanished. Dispelled along with this, in the mind of most investigators, was a concept that had been embraced since the child was reported missing: that a gang, not an individual, had perpetrated the kidnapping. Others would continue to believe that it required more than one person to steal the child and that, therefore, Hauptmann had accomplices. But for the majority of Bruno's captors, it was suddenly a one-man show. Hauptmann was the kidnapper-killer, the writer of the ransom notes, the receiver of fifty thousand dollars—a super criminal. All that was left was to prove it.

- - -

Several investigators were confident a mathematical case could now be made for him being the sole recipient of the fifty-thousand-dollar ransom. In addition to the $13,760, a third cache of bills was found,

amounting to $840, along with a tiny hand gun, concealed in his garage.[1]
They estimated he had put $25,000 into the stock market and made
enough other expenditures since he quit his job two and a half years
before to account for almost all the money given to John in St. Raymond's.

At 2:00 P.M. Hauptmann, bleary-eyed and mussed after spending
more than a full day and night in the wooden armchair, was confronted
by Inspector Lyons, H. Norman Schwarzkopf, Buster Keaten, and Special Agent Sisk. Lyons, addressing him as Richard, asked that he think
before he answered and then wanted to know, "Have you told us everything?" Hauptmann answered that yes, he had told all he knew. "You
don't have any gold notes hidden away, do you?" No, sir. "Are you
sure?" Yes. "Well you're a liar! You're a goddamned lying son-of-a-
bitch, aren't you?" I am not! "You are, you are, you're a lying son-of-a-
bitch because we found the money, the Lindbergh money, in your
garage. What do you say to that? And goddamnit, no more lies. We're
not going to listen to any more of your lies. We want to know everything
and now! Do you hear me?"

Bruno said that he heard and that he was not going to lie—and that he
could explain the money. "You can explain the money?" Yes, he could.
"Well, let's hear."[2]

Bruno now told them that it had to do with his partner in the fur deals,
Isador Fisch. The previous Christmas, Fisch had taken a trip back to his
native city of Leipzig, Germany, to visit his parents. Just before sailing,
he stored a trunk, several suitcases, and a cardboard shoe box with the
Hauptmanns. The shoe box, which was tied with string, was put on a
high shelf in the kitchen broom closet and forgotten. Fisch was tubercu-
lar and in poor health and died in Leipzig on March 29, 1934. During a
heavy rainstorm just three weeks ago, the roof of the broom closet developed a leak. While taking drenched articles down from the shelf, Bruno
rediscovered the shoe box, which he had never opened. Now that it was
wet, he opened it. Bruno didn't deny his surprise on viewing the contents:
approximately fourteen thousand dollars in gold certificates. Without
telling Anna of his find, he brought the damp currency to the garage,
divided it into several piles, each of which he wrapped in newspapers,
and created hiding places for them. Since Fisch had owed him seven
thousand dollars, Bruno saw no reason not to even their financial account and appropriate half the money for himself. He intended to spend
no more than the rightful seven thousand dollars, which he began to do
sometime in August.

At the time no one believed the Fisch story, as it became known, but several of the most cynical officers grudgingly marveled at Bruno's ability to come up with such a yarn after undergoing nonstop interrogation without sleep and food.

— — —

Word swiftly spread that fourteen thousand dollars in ransom money had been seized in the Bronx and that the police had taken a suspect into custody. This was what America and the world had waited so long to hear, and the media bore down with a fury. By 4:00 P.M. the name Bruno Hauptmann was being flashed over the airwaves. Extra police were rushed to his home in the Bronx to contain reporters and neck craners. The scene at the Greenwich Village station house was approaching riot proportions. Crowds jammed the narrow streets, and many of the curious had walked out along the nearby elevated tracks to catch a better view of the action. As 5:00 P.M. approached, the corridors inside the precinct were packed with frantic news personnel boisterously intent on getting a peek at the greatest confrontation of the decade: Jafsie Condon was on his way over to identify Hauptmann as Cemetery John. By now the handwriting expert, who had learned that fourteen thousand dollars in ransom money had been recovered from the garage, revised his previous opinion and said that Bruno had used a clever device to mask his penmanship. Osborn and his equally expert father weren't fooled. Hauptmann, they asserted, was the true author of the ransom messages.

J. Edgar Hoover, H. Norman Schwarzkopf, and General John F. O'Ryan, commissioner of the New York Police Department, were on hand as Richard Hauptmann, his wrists handcuffed in front of him, was led into the office of the second deputy police commissioner at the Greenwich Street station house and made to stand between NYPD detectives Martin Monahan and Benjamin Rosenberg in a fourteen-man police lineup. Like Rosenberg and Monahan, the other eleven suspects were members of the New York PD and wore civilian clothes. The time was 5:30 P.M., and the man who seemed to be watching most intently, and being intently watched by many others in the room, was John F. Condon. The lineup was for him, Jafsie, the indomitable showman and the surest news copy of the entire case, the only intermediary so far not to end up in jail or publicly disgraced, a man most investigators still didn't trust.

Inspector Lyons, who was in charge of the event, explained the ground rules. "Dr. Condon, start at the head of the line, look at all these men, and if you can identify the man to whom you passed the money to on the night of April 2, 1932, you just go over and put your hand on his shoulder."

"May I ask for a favor?" Condon said. Of course he could, and what was that favor? "To speak to each man for one minute on something nobody else has heard but me?"

Lyons agreed. Condon walked back and forth along the line three times. On the last pass he stopped in front of suspect 3a, Richard Hauptmann, studied him for a moment, moved on down to suspect 13, and asked, "May I eliminate several men from the line now and have them come forward?" The request was granted, and he had 2, 3a, 11, and 12 step forward: a detective, Hauptmann, and two patrolmen. "Can I speak to them?" Condon asked. "You don't mind do you?" Nobody minded, and he stood in front of Hauptmann and addressed the four suspects who had come forward. "When I saw you I gave you my word I would do all I possibly could for you if you gave me the baby. The only way in the world I think you can save yourself at all is to tell the truth. I gave you a promise heard that day. Follow that promise."

At Jafsie's request Inspector Lyons ordered the four suspects to hold out their hands, palms up. Condon examined all eight supinated palms, then asked suspect 2 his name. "James J. Kissane," the detective answered. The same question was posed to 3a. "Richard Hauptmann," Condon was told. On being asked, 12 and 11 answered respectively, "Herman Schwartzberg" and "Francis Mershon." Condon walked back to Hauptmann, handed him a slip of paper, and told him to read it aloud. Hauptmann, in his thick German accent, read, "I stayed already too long. The leader would smack me out. Your work is perfect." Condon said that he could not quite hear the last three lines. Hauptmann read them again, "The leader would smack me out. Your work is perfect."

Condon asked if Hauptmann had ever seen him before. "Never," Bruno told him. You never saw me before? "Never." What is your name? "Richard Hauptmann." What is it, again? "Richard Hauptmann." Condon handed him another slip of paper and told him to say what was written on it. "John," Hauptmann read. And you didn't see me before? "No, I never saw you before." Bruno was ordered to hold out his hands again and did. Again Condon looked them over; then once more he asked each of the four suspects their names. The four complied with the request.

Jafsie had all the men but Hauptmann step back. "I gave the money. I promised to help out in case the baby was restored to me," he told the German. "Do you remember that?" Bruno did not. "And I said I would help out?" No, Bruno had never talked to him. "I never broke my word in my life. What is your name?" Richard Hauptmann, Bruno said. "Where were you born?" Germany. "What place?" Saxony. "You don't remember me—speaking to me?" Bruno couldn't say that he could.

Condon talked to Hauptmann in German for a bit, then switched back to English saying, "That's what I meant—you didn't understand me. Listen. You never saw me before?" No. "Didn't speak to me?" No. "You live in the Bronx?" Yes. "Do you know 233rd Street?" 233rd Street? Yes, Bruno knew it because he lived at 222nd in the Bronx. "You have nothing to say to me at all?" asked Condon, who now was studying the carpenter's profile. No. "Why?" Because Bruno didn't know what to say. Jafsie had him put on his hat, put it on to one side. "You didn't speak to me about the baby?" No. "Never said a word?" Never said a word. "You didn't speak to me about the baby at all?" No. "You are positive of that?" Positive.

Inspector Lyons broke in and asked Condon, "Would you say that he was the man?"

Condon replied, "I would *not* say that he was the man."

"You are not positive?"

"I am not positive," Jafsie confirmed.

"Do you recognize the voice?" asked the inspector.

"The voice was husky. I'd like him to say this quick. When it's a man's life, gentlemen, I want to be careful. May I write something?" Bruno read what Jafsie wrote on the paper: *What would your mother say? She would not like it. She would cry.* "Louder, I am not able to hear," Jafsie declared. Bruno read it again, louder. "Still a little louder." Hauptmann obeyed. "Whom were you afraid of up there besides your mother? Do you remember Number Two?—that you could not wait any longer because they would smack you out?—the leader?" Bruno didn't know what he meant. "All right, say, 'Number Two.' " Number Two. "Your name is what?" Richard Hauptmann. "How long do you live in the Bronx?" Nine years. "Nine years up there. You don't know me?" No. "Never saw me?" No.

The most consistent statistic in Condon's various descriptions of John was his weight, approximately 160 pounds. Now he asked Hauptmann, "How much do you weigh?" Around 180 to 182. "Have you gotten a little stouter lately than you were? Did you increase in weight lately?" No, he was practically the same. "In two years?" Yes. "How much did you weigh then, about? A little lighter?" No, he guessed that he was the same. A slight difference in summertime or wintertime, that's all. "Did you ever run in races?" No. "Did you ever take exercises in German turning school?" Not here, over there. "In the old country?" Yes. "You can climb pretty well with your hands?" He used to do it in school as a child. "In a gymnasium?" Yes, gymnastic school.

Inspector Lyons wanted to know, "Is that the man?"

"He is the one who would come nearer to answering the description than anybody I saw," Condon replied. "You gave me no hint and I picked him out. He is a little heavier. Can I go over and talk to him? I couldn't say that he is not the man."

"It looks like him?" asked Lyons.

"Yes."

"But you cannot identify him?"

"No. I have to be very careful. The man's life is in jeopardy."[3]

Despite the fact that few investigators trusted Jafsie, many of them were still stunned by his failure to make the identification. Some were angry. Others openly speculated as to whether he was in cahoots with Hauptmann. The quirky pedant left the station house besieged by reporters and photographers. His comment to Inspector Lyons, "You gave me no hint and I picked him out," would lead generations of case scholars to believe that the police had given him every hint as to which of the fourteen suspects they were certain was John.

───

Other witnesses were brought into the lineup room, and this is most likely when Perrone, the taxi driver, picked out Hauptmann. Cecile M. Barr, the Greenwich Village movie-house cashier who described the customer who gave her the folded ransom bill the night of November 26, 1933, as being American, identified him as being that man. Levatino, the greengrocer clerk, and Lyle, the filling station man, also identified him as the passer of ransom money.

The rudiments of an extortion charge were in place, but this was not good enough for H. Norman Schwarzkopf, who was playing for the highest stakes of any law-enforcement official connected with the crime. Only by establishing a link between the suspect and the kidnapping-murder could he regain control of the investigation—by having Hauptmann extradited to New Jersey to stand trial for the death of the child. If H. Norman was unable to make such a connection, New York could try the suspect for extortion. Later that afternoon the NYPD officially accused Hauptmann of just that.

A near riot occurred when a crowd tried to break through police lines and get at Hauptmann as he arrived at the Bronx Supreme Court. Prompted by Schwarzkopf and the state's attorney general, Governor Moore of New Jersey called Governor Lehman of New York and asked that the prisoner be extradited. The extortion trial was set aside, but Hauptmann's Brooklyn-based attorney, James M. Fawcett, blocked extradition with a writ of habeas corpus.

Fawcett was confident he could keep his client from being sent to New Jersey. What didn't help his cause was that Hauptmann had lied about not having a previous criminal record. The authorities now knew—and undoubtedly would try to use the information in court—that Hauptmann had been convicted of grand larceny, petty theft, receiving stolen property, and armed robbery and had served over three years at the Bentzin Prison in Seconsen, Germany. The grand larceny convictions had come as the result of several burglaries, which included his breaking into the home of a country mayor—using a ladder and entering through a second-floor window. The armed-robbery conviction resulted from Hauptmann and an accomplice stealing groceries from two women at gunpoint—two women who were wheeling a baby carriage. Three months after his release from prison, he was picked up and charged with another series of burglaries. To avoid prison, he fled to America. The record indicated that Bruno was an inept and amateurish crook at best. He fared better as an escape artist. Bruno was credited with a jailbreak as well as jumping out of a police van.

Fawcett remained certain he could block his client from standing trial for murder in New Jersey. He planned to show that since arriving in America, Hauptmann had been an honest and hard-working family man, even if he hadn't bothered to take out citizenship. Of far more relevance to the case was that Fawcett had the testimony of alibi witnesses as to where his client was the night of the crime and on the night the ransom was paid. He also had physical proof—employment records from the Majestic Apartments—that Hauptmann was at work in New York City on the afternoon of the March 1 kidnapping.

New York's Bronx County grand jury convened on Monday, September 24, 1934, and heard thirty-two witnesses before indicting Bruno Richard Hauptmann for having extorted fifty thousand dollars from the Lindberghs. Hauptmann himself testified to what he had already told lawmen: He was not John, and he hadn't been given the ransom in St.

Raymond's Cemetery. The German carpenter insisted that he was at home with his wife and their friend Hans Kloppenburg at the time the money was paid and continued to maintain that he hadn't discovered the shoe box belonging to Isador Fisch that contained $14,600 until August.[4] Testimony was given by the Osborns that Bruno was the writer of the ransom letters. Also of importance were the statements by the pair of service station employees who received the bill by which Hauptmann was traced, Walter Lyle and John Lyons, as well as the taxi driver Perrone and Cecile Barr, the movie-house cashier.

By now investigators had found John Condon's telephone number written on a wooden beam in Hauptmann's closet. A somewhat muddled Bruno didn't deny to the grand jury having put it there and explained that like everyone else he was interested in the case. He would later refute the confession and rue having made it.

The Condon number was a harbinger of the manipulations and tampering to come in regard to physical evidence and witnesses. In a 1989 television documentary on the case, author Anthony Scaduto would ask, "Why would a man write on the inside of dark closet the phone number of the intermediary with whom he is dealing in a kidnapping case, if he doesn't have a telephone in his house?"[5] According to Ludovic Kennedy, the journalist Tom Cassidy of the *New York Daily News* wrote Condon's address and telephone number in pencil on the closet beam, ostensibly as a joke. Kennedy maintains that three people confirmed Cassidy was the writer.[6] Former newsman Frank Fitzpatrick was to tell Scaduto in 1976, "Tom Cassidy himself told me he wrote it there. Hell, he bragged about it all over town. He even showed us how he wrote it." Russell Hopstatter, another veteran scribe, said to Scaduto, "Sure, Cassidy wrote that phone number—he admitted that to me and Ellis Parker, he told everybody about it." Russell M. Stoddard, a one time *Camden Courier-Post* reporter, is the last source cited by Kennedy: "[Cassidy] told a bunch of us he did it to get a new lead for the story the next day."[7]

Whether as a joke or new story approach, the number and address in the closet was to have an indelible and grievous effect on the fate of Bruno Hauptmann.

As had happened at the trials of Gaston B. Means and John Hughes Curtis, Charles Lindbergh was on hand to testify at a legal proceeding, and it was he as much as any one person who would seal the fate of

Bruno Hauptmann. Following a brief appearance before the Bronx grand jury, Lindy was asked if he would recognize the voice he had heard say, "Hey, Doctor, over here," at St. Raymond's Cemetery back on April 2 of 1932. The Lone Eagle, already on record as having said he could not, now modified his position and said that perhaps he might. The next day Lindbergh, wearing a disguise, was placed among a group of observers who were seated in the prosecutor's office. Hauptmann was brought in and compelled to walk back and forth and call out in a variety of fashions, "Hey Doctor, over here." The Lone Eagle departed without making an official comment.

What exactly made Charles Lindbergh reverse himself remains speculative. But he did. In no uncertain terms he told the Bronx County district attorney, Samuel J. Foley, that Hauptmann's was the voice of Cemetery John—an identification the DI and J. Edgar Hoover would forever deem untrustworthy because of the manner in which it was elicited and because they didn't believe that Lindbergh, or anyone for that matter, could remember after nearly two and a half years, a voice he had heard utter a handful of words from a distance of two hundred feet.[8] What Hoover or anyone else thought was of no consequence. Charles Lindbergh had spoken. The noose was drawn.

In a rare reversal of legal procedure, the Bronx grand jury indicted Hauptmann before he was arraigned. The arraignment came on Thursday, September 27, before Judge Lester J. Patterson. Hauptmann pleaded not guilty to extortion. The judge set a trial date of October 11 and denied the motion by defense attorney James M. Fawcett to reduce the hundred-thousand-dollar bail to five thousand dollars. The prisoner was returned to the Bronx County jail, where he had been kept on a twenty-four-hour-a-day watch since being brought uptown from the Greenwich Street police station. That afternoon, under the guise of routine interviews by an assistant Bronx County DA, investigators went to work on friends and acquaintances of Hauptmann who might have been able to corroborate where he was on critical dates. Nearly everyone but his wife would eventually change what he or she had to say or would refuse to testify in his behalf. Later many of them would claim they had been intimidated, openly threatened, and continually harassed by the interrogators. Officers such as Jimmy Finn and Buster Keaten would avow they had done nothing but be polite and ask routine questions in their often-prolonged follow-up for the truth.

The media were having their day. This was the event they had promoted from the moment the baby was reported missing. For nearly three years newspapermen and radio broadcasters had relentlessly beat the drum and built the suspense in their demand that the perpetrators be found. Now the fiend was in custody and about to be tried. Anxiety was worldwide. So was a passion to mete out capital justice. Justice was not always uppermost in the mind of individual reporters, but a hot story was.

The press weighed heavily on a potential witness's decision as to whether to testify for Hauptmann. Every turn of events, even that occurring behind the closed doors of supposedly secret grand juries, had a way of making the newspapers and radiocasts. The media were not friendly toward Bruno. A witness who considered speaking up for him faced public ridicule as well as intense police scrutiny, which may have been the reason that several handwriting experts who had agreed to appear in court and say that Hauptmann had not written the ransom notes resigned from the case before testifying. The state police would contend the experts dropped out because they realized the accused man was indeed the author of the messages.

— — —

Another pattern took shape: the emergence of physical evidence helpful to the prosecution and the disappearance of evidence helpful to Hauptmann. Two examples of the former were the finding of Condon's telephone number written in pencil on a beam inside a closet of the Hauptmann home and the September 26 discovery by NJSP Lieutenant Lewis J. Bornmann of a missing section of wood flooring in Hauptmann's attic, wood that investigators would contend had been used in the construction of the ladder. As we have seen Tom Cassidy of the *New York Daily News* was subsequently credited with writing Condon's phone number in the closet,[9] but Bornmann continued to defend his discovery and further stated that he was the first investigator to examine the attic, even though a review of the records reveals that nine searches of the attic by some thirty-seven law officers had occurred before his September 26 exploration.[10] Additional doubt was shed on Bornmann's claim when it was learned that he had written three drafts of his report for that day and hadn't bothered to mention the critical discovery of missing wood until the second draft. At the opposite end of the evidence spectrum was the mysterious disappearance of the employment records for the building where Hauptmann claimed he was working the day of the kidnapping.

If, as H. Norman Schwarzkopf had told the media the day of Hauptmann's arrest, he intended to extradite the prisoner to New Jersey and
try him for the kidnapping and murder of the child, proof would have to
be presented that implicated the German carpenter in the deadly event. It
arrived at the Bronx County Courthouse in the person of Millard
Whited, a thirty-five-year-old illiterate, dirt-poor hillbilly who lived with
his family in a shanty just up the road from Sorrel Hill. Whited had been
wakened the night of the kidnapping by a search party that included
Lindbergh and Buster Keaton. He told them he had seen nothing and no
one suspicious. In a formal statement taken seven weeks later, he reaf-
firmed that he had seen nobody suspicious in the area of the Lindbergh
estate.

According to those who knew him, Millard was thoroughly dishonest
and a congenital liar.[11] His sudden recollection of having noticed a stranger in the neighborhood on February 18, 25, and 27 seems to have occurred subsequent to his being informed that useful information might
result in him receiving part of the twenty-five-thousand-dollar reward
posted by the state of New Jersey. He would later assert that he had been
promised three hundred dollars if he would say everything investigators
told him and that after he complied, he received only thirty dollars.[12] The
state police contended that Whited had first identified Hauptmann from
two photographs shown him by Captain Lamb and Corporal Wolf. The
troopers also provided an explanation as to why Whited wasn't brought
to the Greenwich Village police station in New York City when Hauptmann was first picked up back on September 19: the almost perpetually
unemployed laborer was on a logging trip in Pennsylvania.[13]

Millard Whited was the glue with which H. Norman Schwarzkopf
intended to bind his extradition case against Bruno Richard Hauptmann:
an eyewitness who would place the accused man near the scene of the
crime on or about the time of its commission. Captain Lamb of the NJSP
escorted Whited to the Bronx County Courthouse on Saturday morning,
October 6. Hauptmann was placed in a lineup without his lawyer's
knowledge. Whited picked him out as the man he had seen near the estate in the days before the kidnapping. When brought to the Bronx
County DA's office and told of the identification, Hauptmann yelled, "I
was never at the Lindbergh house, never! I will not confess. I am innocent
of any crime!"[14]

That afternoon Schwarzkopf convened a press conference at which he violated the confidentiality of the New Jersey secret grand jury system by publicly stating when and where he would present the twenty-three witnesses whose testimony he was certain would lead to a murder indictment against Bruno Richard Hauptmann.

－－－

On Monday, October 8, alerted by H. Norman's pronouncement of two days before, the media were waiting in force as a cheering crowd of locals greeted the grand jurors who arrived at Flemington's Hunterdon County Courthouse for their supposedly secret hearings. It was the second official inquiry into Hauptmann's relationship to the crime and ordinarily would have been headed by Anthony M. Hauck, the balding thirty-five-year-old county DA who had successfully prosecuted John Hughes Curtis for the Lindbergh scam over two years before. Hauck was downgraded to main assistant to the man who named himself chief prosecutor, thirty-eight-year-old David Theodore Wilentz, the attorney general of New Jersey. Wilentz and Hauck were aided by four other prosecutors.

Shouts and applause from outside the ancient courthouse echoed the arrival of Charles Lindbergh. Once inside and duly sworn in, he told the secret conclave that the voice he had heard call out, "Hey, Doctor!" in St. Raymond's Cemetery belonged to the man whom the Bronx County DA had forced to repeat the cry several weeks before: Bruno Richard Hauptmann. The day's hearing was rounded out by testimony from Schwarzkopf, eight troopers, two DI agents, an IRS man, and three NYPD officers. At an evening press conference attended by Wilentz and Governor A. Harry Moore, Schwarzkopf told reporters that Lindbergh had positively identified Hauptmann as the man whose voice he'd heard in the cemetery. News of Lindy's ID was instant and worldwide. The trapdoor of the gallows had all but snapped open on the accused but untried German.

Grand jury proceedings for October 9 focused on legitimizing the jurisdictional right of Hunterdon County to prosecute the murder case. Since under New Jersey law the maximum punishment for kidnapping was a prison term of thirty years, David Wilentz had decided to try Hauptmann on a statute that stipulated that if during the commission of a felony a victim is accidentally killed, the perpetrator can be convicted of first-degree murder. Wilentz intended to invoke this felony-murder law by claiming that Hauptmann had entered the Lindbergh nursery to steal the Dr. Denton worn by the child and that in the commission of this burglary he had killed the infant, who still happened to be inside the night garment.

On that October 9 Tuesday, to establish Hunterdon County's right to the trial, Wilentz had Dr. Mitchell, the presiding physician of Mercer County, testify before the Hunterdon County grand jury that the baby had been killed by a blow to the head inflicted either during the theft of the Dr. Denton or shortly after, thereby implying that the tiny victim was dead before leaving the territorial boundaries of Hunterdon County, something neither Mitchell nor anyone else knew for a fact. This exercise in truth bending was added to by an out-and-out prevarication when Mitchell described an autopsy that he credited himself with having done but in fact never performed.

Assisted by physical evidence, such as ransom notes and handwriting specimens, the father-and-son team of Osborns assured the jurors that Hauptmann was the author of the messages. A Madison, Wisconsin, wood expert by the name of Arthur Koehler, who claimed to have traced wood from the ladder to the Bronx, testified that the missing board in Hauptmann's attic floor was a section of the kidnapper's ladder known as rail 16. Millard Whited again swore he had seen Hauptmann near the Lindbergh estate a week before the kidnapping. Reinforcing Whited's testimony was a student by the name of Benjamin Lupica, who said he saw Hauptmann's car in the area of Sorrel Hill around the time of the child's disappearance. Subpoenas had been issued to two more men who allegedly saw Hauptmann near the estate prior to the kidnapping, but neither one was called to testify. Movie-theater cashier Cecile Barr was on hand to repeat her accusation that Hauptmann had given her a five-dollar ransom bill on the night of his birthday, some nine months before he supposedly discovered the money left in a shoe box by Isador Fisch.

It took thirty minutes for the Hunterdon County grand jury to indict Hauptmann for the murder of the baby. Before Tuesday was out, Governor Moore had an extradition warrant sent to New York's governor, Herbert Lehman, who agreed that it would be honored.

- - -

H. Norman Schwarzkopf had prevailed. He was already the official spokesman for the case and would soon be in total control of the pretrial arrangements. J. Edgar Hoover wasted no time in letting it be known that since his special agents had successfully completed the majority of work in the Lindbergh investigation and because he estimated that the New Jersey State Police were probably competent enough to handle the remaining details on their own, the DI was officially withdrawing from the case.

The effort by Hauptmann's attorney, James M. Fawcett, to quash the extortion indictment was dealt a setback when he was denied a usually routine courtesy: access to the notes of the secret Bronx County grand jury. The defense lawyer and his client fared better in petitioning for a writ of habeas corpus with which to block Hauptmann's removal to New Jersey. On Thursday, October 11, a day when the scheduled extortion trial was postponed to accommodate the extradition proceedings, Hauptmann was back before a Bronx court for the fourth time since his arrest and learned that his transfer to New Jersey had been stayed, pending a formal review at the beginning of the week.

- - -

On Monday, October 15, with crowds surging outside the spanking-new seven-million-dollar Bronx County Courthouse building and with security at a maximum, some four hundred members of the press and public who were admitted to the ninth-floor hearing chamber got the first public view of Bruno Richard Hauptmann. A pair of motion picture news cameras that was allowed to film the proceeding helped provide the world with a vivid preview of what was to come after the first of the year in New Jersey. Not only was the defendant present at the extradition hearing—seated at his counsel's table, guarded by fifteen detectives and deputy sheriffs—but he took the stand and in direct examination testified that on Tuesday, March 1, 1932, he had spent the time from 7:00 A.M. to 5:00 P.M. in New York City, either working as a carpenter at the Majestic Apartments on Central Park West or looking for a job at an employment agency on Sixth Avenue. Between 5:00 P.M. and 6:00 P.M. he returned home. Since his wife, Anna, worked as a waitress at Fredericksen's bakery-lunchroom in the Bronx every Tuesday and Friday, he changed clothes and did what he normally did on Tuesday and Friday nights: had dinner with her at Fredericksen's after she got off work, usually between 9:00 P.M. and 9:30 P.M. After dinner they went home.

In an accusatory and confrontational cross-examination New Jersey's attorney general, David Wilentz, hammered away at why Hauptmann had previously claimed only that he was working at the Majestic Apartments on March 1, and now admitted he might have been at an employment agency instead. Hauptmann contended that when initially questioned, he hadn't been given the time to think out clearly where he was on that date. As a result, he had repeated the first thing that came to mind. Now that he had time, his best remembrance was that he had been at one or the other place.

Wilentz, in an ongoing jab of questions, made the most of Hauptmann's having first lied about being in possession of additional ransom money and then having switched to the alibi that Isador Fisch left it with him. Subsequent to the discovery of the initial $13,760 in listed bills, investigators searching for even more currency dismantled Hauptmann's garage and at the edge of one board discovered six drilled holes. Five of the holes contained a total of $840 in rolled-up ten-dollar gold certificates from the ransom payment. The sixth and largest hole produced a miniature German-made pistol, which Wilentz homed in on. Hauptmann asserted that he had purchased the weapon on Eighty-second Street in New York City and hid it in the garage because he didn't have a gun permit. The last time he fired the weapon was on a trip to California in the summer of 1931.

Displeased that Wilentz turned to his police record in Germany, Hauptmann somberly conceded that he had been convicted of grand larceny in Europe on June 3, 1919, and that fifteen days later, on June 18, he was convicted of robbery with a gun as a result of having held up two women. He also acknowledged that when he had been discovered stowed away on a German liner and was dropped off at Ellis Island, he gave authorities a false name: Pellmeier. Caught stowed away a second time, he went by his own name, Richard Hauptmann. On the third try he succeeded in illegally entering the United States and never took out citizenship papers. Wilentz was unsuccessful in trying to make Hauptmann say he could climb better than most people. The prisoner admitted to having visited New Jersey in 1931 and to having been in Flemington just a few months before his arrest. Hauptmann maintained that he had only been circulating the ransom money for three or four weeks but conceded that he was afraid to deposit any of the bills in the Federal Reserve Bank because they could link him to the crime. Wilentz finished his cross-examination having highlighted a great many contradictions in Hauptmann's statements but without having got the prisoner to alter his alibi one iota.

Hauptmann's testimony neared an end with his lawyer, James M. Fawcett, asking him, "Were you in the state of New Jersey on March 1?"

The prisoner, who for two hours and fifteen minutes on the stand had maintained his equanimity, answered no in a polite and respectful manner.

"Did you murder the child Charles Augustus Lindbergh, Jr.—"

"No," Hauptmann interrupted, as composed as ever.

"On March 1, 1932, or any other time?" Fawcett continued.

David Wilentz leapt to his feet and in one breath shouted, "Didn't you build a ladder and put it up against the Lindbergh house, and didn't you go up that ladder into the house and murder the child?"

"No," Hauptmann shouted, rising halfway out of his chair.[15]

Away from the courtroom Wilentz was not reluctant to express his personal feelings about Hauptmann. "He's guilty as hell," the attorney general was quoted as saying in the following day's edition of the *New York Post*. "I've never prosecuted anyone before," he told the reporter. "I hate to prosecute. I've always tried to have a tolerant attitude. I've defended hundreds of criminals charged with all sorts of crimes. But this case of the Lindbergh child cries aloud for justice. The murder of a helpless little baby is such a revolting crime."[16]

On the second day of the hearing, Fawcett had Hauptmann's wife, Anna, testify that in the early evening of Tuesday, March 1, 1932, her husband had come to Fredericksen's bakery-lunchroom in the Bronx, where she was working. They had dinner there and then went home. Fawcett brought Christian Fredericksen and his wife, Katie, to the stand to confirm that Anna waitressed at their bakery-lunchroom every Tuesday and Friday and to offer corroboration, to the best of their memory, that Hauptmann had dinner with her there the evening of March 1, 1932. Wilentz, in questioning Anna and the Fredericksens, astutely established that they remembered the event not because it occurred on March 1, 1932, a day that none of them specifically recalled, but because it happened on Tuesday, a day Mrs. Hauptmann always worked as a waitress and when Hauptmann usually came by for dinner before driving her home.

Wilentz called on Albert S. Osborn, who testified that he was reasonably certain Hauptmann had written the ransom messages.[17] When during cross-examination Fawcett caused the expert in false documents to contradict himself, the hearing took on the aspects of a David-and-Goliath battle that pitted an obscure Brooklyn lawyer and his handful of private detectives against a high-visibility attorney general and the combined forces of the New York and New Jersey law-enforcement establishments. Unhappily for the defense attorney, no one was rooting for David. On entering the fray, Fawcett had no doubt he would win. His most important witness, the secret weapon with which he intended to demolish the extradition action and save his client from being tried for murder, would present evidence from the Reliant Property Management Company—evidence Fawcett had seen—verifying that Hauptmann had worked at the Majestic Apartments on March 1, 1932, and therefore couldn't have been in New Jersey at the time of the baby's disappearance.

The witness was Reliant's timekeeper, Edward F. Morton. Fawcett had subpoenaed him to appear as the defense's first witness and bring along the company time sheets. When the court attendant called Morton's name, the timekeeper failed to respond.[18] Fawcett began with a different witness, then had the court again call for Morton. Morton never appeared. Compounding Fawcett's dilemma was Wilentz's unexpected witness: Howard Knapp, the assistant treasurer of the same Reliant Property Management Company for which Morton worked. Knapp brought a time sheet with him, all right, but not for the first half of March 1932. The record was for the second half of the month and established what was to become a cornerstone in Wilentz's case against Hauptmann: that the German carpenter hadn't begun to work at the Majestic Apartments until March 21, 1932. And what of the time sheet for the first half of the month, including March 1? "Our records do not indicate that any such record exists at this date," Knapp stated on being cross-examined by Fawcett.[19] Under more pressure he held out the possibility that Joseph P. Furcht, a former superintendent at the building, might have additional information.

Wilentz called Millard Whited to the stand and had him swear to having seen Hauptmann near the Lindbergh estate. Though Fawcett was visibly dejected over the time sheet matter, he got Whited to admit that Captain Lamb had shown him photographs of Hauptmann before he picked the suspect out on the lineup. When asked if he was getting part of the reward, Whited lied to Fawcett and said no. Fawcett produced a cousin of Whited's and two neighbors, all of whom attested to Millard's bad character and unreliability. Wilentz paraded out James Petrosino, Inspectors John Lyons and Henry D. Bruckman, Buster Keaten, and Captain Lamb. It was Wednesday, October 17, and by late afternoon the presiding judge, Earnest E. L. Hammer, had heard enough. He ordered that Hauptmann be extradited to New Jersey, then granted Fawcett a forty-eight-hour stay in which to appeal.

Tom Cassidy of the *New York Daily News* was closing in on Joseph Furcht. Cassidy was the reporter who had admitted to his fellow newsmen that he had written Jafsie Condon's telephone number on the wooden beam in Hauptmann's bedroom closet. Furcht had indeed been Hauptmann's supervisor at the Majestic Apartments, only the German carpenter couldn't for the life of him remember Furcht's name. Cassidy had been present when Hauptmann was first being interrogated and recalled this lapse in his memory. After Furcht was mentioned at the extradition trial, Cassidy tracked him to the lunchroom of his current place of employment, the Department of Public Welfare on New York City's Eighth Avenue.

Furcht remembered Hauptmann and told Cassidy that in late February of 1932 he needed to fill a pair of positions suddenly vacated by workmen who had originally come from the labor-contracting company for the Majestic, Reliant Property Management. He turned to another contractor, E.V.C. Pescia, proprietor of Pescia's Reliable Employment Agency at 779 Sixth Avenue, who sent him Gus Kassens and Richard Hauptmann. Furcht had no records, but he took Cassidy to see Pescia. Pescia did have records, ones that showed that on Saturday, February 27, Hauptmann and Gus Kassens had gone to the Majestic Apartments, where they were hired for a job that was to begin on March 1, 1932. Cassidy had photostatic copies made and took the statements of both Furcht and Pescia. Fawcett was informed and got Furcht's affidavit and a statement from Pescia.

That evening, October 18, Fawcett went to Judge Hammer and received permission to bring the new information before Justice Francis Martin of the appellate division of the state supreme court. Furcht accompanied Fawcett to Justice Martin's office but was not called into his chambers. He did, however, talk to reporters who had gathered there to interview him and assured them that Hauptmann was at work until 5:00 P.M. the night of the kidnapping. Judge Martin agreed to let Fawcett appear and make a motion to introduce his new evidence at 2:00 P.M. the next day, when the appeals court was scheduled to consider Judge Hammer's recommendation for the dismissal of the habeas corpus action and the extradition of Hauptmann to New Jersey. The *Daily News* beat the competition to press with its scoop, which thoroughly stunned David Wilentz and Bronx County DA Sam Foley. Foley said he had never heard of Furcht and Pescia. He later conceded that Hauptmann had worked at the Majestic Apartments on March 1 but tempered his admission with an unsubstantiated opinion that the German carpenter had left the job at

1:00 P.M., thereby allowing himself ample time to drive to Hopewell and perpetrate the crime.

Wilentz, for whom the Furcht-Pescia revelations were near catastrophic, masked his agitation with a bold face as he assured reporters that their information would have had no effect on Judge Hammer's decision to extradite Hauptmann, even if it was introduced as evidence at the appellate level. The next day at the courthouse, waiting for the appeals session to begin, Wilentz confronted Furcht in a hallway and demanded, "What do you mean by this? We don't want to condemn innocent men in New Jersey. If you had any evidence, why didn't you come to me?" Bristling with indignation, Furcht shot back that because his wife was in the hospital seriously ill, he didn't even know his name had appeared in the papers or that he had some connection to the case until a *Daily News* reporter approached him. "I was willing then and I am willing now to answer any and all questions," he told Wilentz heatedly, "and I resent any reference that I have held something back!"[20]

The five-judge appeals court spent the afternoon and early evening of Friday, October 19, reviewing Furcht's affidavit, listening to Pescia's statement, and hearing Fawcett's argument for introducing the new information as evidence. The justices unanimously refused the request on the grounds that the information was "merely accumulative and not contradictory" and that a clear-cut issue of fact should not be evaluated at an appeals hearing but at the trial of action, to wit, the impending murder trial.[21] It was 7:05 P.M. when the justices handed down their decision and ordered that the temporary stay of extradition be lifted.

At approximately 10:20 P.M. that same night, October 19, a convoy of seven cars and escort motorcycles entered Flemington, New Jersey, and stopped at the jailhouse. Along with a host of reporters and cameramen, an estimated one thousand local citizens were waiting, many holding burning white flares by which to see. They watched silently as New Jersey detectives got out of six of the cars. From the seventh, manacled and impassive, came thin, sullen, five-foot-ten Bruno Richard Hauptmann. He was turned over to the five-foot-tall county sheriff, John H. Curtiss, and to the jail warden, Harry O. Macrea. After being frisked, Hauptmann asked for a cigarette. He was given an entire pack. Then he was led into the jailhouse. Twelve state troopers deployed and took up sentry outside.

Police investigators had extensive interviews with Pescia and Furcht and, later, with Gus Kassens, whom it took time to locate. Before long Pescia's records vanished, never to be found. Even though photographs of them had appeared in the *Daily News,* Pescia became disinclined to verify that they had ever existed or to discuss the matter. Kassens signed an affidavit saying Hauptmann had not started work until several weeks after March 1. Joseph Furcht was persuaded to refute his first affidavit with a second one, in which he stated that he did not know if Hauptmann worked at the Majestic on March 1, and implied that the *New York Daily News* had distorted what he told them.[22]

The time sheets and payroll records of the Reliant Management Company, the prime labor contractor for the Majestic Apartments, would forever cast a shadow on the veracity of David Wilentz and the investigators who assisted him. Information surfaced that showed that just before the extradition hearing got under way, the supposedly nonexistent time sheet for the first half of March was hastily removed from the Reliant office. So were company payroll records that might have reflected that Hauptmann had worked on March 1. It soon came to light that the missing payroll records had been placed "under lock and key" in the office of a Bronx County assistant district attorney. At the end of October, with Hauptmann already in New Jersey waiting to be tried for murder, the assistant DA turned them over to Detective Cashman of the NYPD, who dutifully signed a receipt for them.[23]

Edward F. Morton, the Reliant timekeeper Fawcett had subpoenaed as his first witness, blamed his failure to appear at the hearing on the fact that the time sheet for the first half of March was not available to him. The man the company sent in his place, Howard Knapp, had testified not for Fawcett but for Wilentz. Knapp misled the court about the existence of a time sheet for the first half of the month and brought with him a time sheet for the second half, which ostensibly showed that Hauptmann hadn't begun work until March 21. Later, when this time sheet was carefully examined, several curious aspects were evident. The names of thirteen handymen and carpenters who had worked at the Majestic Apartments during this period were listed in a column down the left side of the page, with Hauptmann's name on the bottom. Beside each name, stretching horizontally to the opposite end of the sheet, were sixteen boxes designating the last sixteen days of the month. The day an employee worked was noted by a check mark. The box for a day he didn't work was left blank. But not in Hauptmann's case. The boxes for March 16, 17, 18, 19, and 20 on Hauptmann's line were each filled with a roundish inkblot large enough to mask any check mark that may have existed underneath, inkblots the court had been told meant that he hadn't been employed on those days.

If Hauptmann had worked at the Majestic from the sixteenth through the twentieth, as the seemingly doctored payroll record indicates, then Wilentz's contention that Hauptmann hadn't been hired on at the apartment house until March 21 would have been discredited. In the half century to come, a majority of scholars would suspect that tampering had occurred, and attendant perjury. It made little difference for the defendant.

For Ellis Parker, Sr., the arrest of Bruno Richard Hauptmann was a travesty. He told his old friend and former manhunt boss Harold Hoffman that the crime had been perpetrated by a local disbarred lawyer by the name of Paul Wendel. According to Parker, Wendel was on the verge of cracking, and it was only a matter of time before he confessed.[24] Harold Hoffman had other things on his mind, but single-handedly he would add a new and terrifying dimension to the Lindbergh case.

On December 3, 1934, a month before Hauptmann's trial got under way, Anne's older sister Elisabeth—who had married Aubrey Morgan in December of 1932—expired in Pasadena, California.

20

HULLABALOO

— — —

IN THE VIEW OF THE AUTHORS ALAN HYND AND ANTHONY SCADUTO, WHO
would write about the event much later, three trials were actually occurring: the trial in the courtroom, the trial in the newspapers, and the trial
on radio.[1] Almost from the time of his arrest, newspapers and radio had
been proclaiming that the defendant was guilty. Since every juror knew
what the media had been saying, the only question left open seemed to
be, How guilty was guilty? It really didn't matter. The media had mes-
merized the nation with technology and hoopla. This was just the beginning. Matters of law and justice would come at a later time and in
different courtrooms.

— — —

Because Sheriff John H. Curtiss was only five feet tall, his legs didn't
quite touch the floor as he sprawled in his chair at his Hunterdon County
Courthouse office in Flemington. The pudgy lawman toyed absently

with a watch chain, stroked his fox terrier, Buddy, chewed on an un-lighted cigar, and announced to the reporters who had come to interview him that, yes, he would happily take "donations" of five and ten dollars for choice seats to the upcoming Hauptmann murder trial. Curtiss, a Republican, was reported to have already collected twelve hundred dol-lars in donations to help offset "expenses." When news of his scalping activities reached Trenton, he received a telephone call from the Demo-cratic governor and soon-to-be U.S. senator, A. Harry Moore, who forcefully reminded Curtiss that the state of New Jersey, not Hunterdon County, was bearing the cost of the trial. In rebuttal Curtiss pointed to a $150 bill for lumber to build press seats. No one is quite sure what the governor said to this, but it seems to have been persuasive. "All right, all right," the wee law officer grunted, "I'll return every cent of it."[2]

Sheriff Curtiss grievously underestimated the marketplace. Though the main trial room of the hundred-year-old Hunterdon County Court-house was uncomfortably small, poorly ventilated, and exceedingly hot, by the beginning of 1935 it was host to the most publicized criminal proceedings in the history of the republic. Scalpers in New York City were asking from one hundred to three hundred dollars a ticket for re-served seats to a so-so session, on the rare occasions when one was avail-able. When and if the popular Jafsie Condon took the stand, the price was expected to soar to five hundred dollars. A section of the gallery was available to the public on a no-charge first-come, first-served basis, and eager spectators formed long lines each morning, hoping for admittance. Just waiting in the perpetual throng outside the courthouse and observ-ing who was entering or leaving were usually worth the trip that sight-seers made to be there. Many of the faces they saw were world renowned. Charles Lindbergh attended every session. Mrs. Lindbergh was often with him, as was Colonel Henry Breckinridge. Other well-known personalities were usually in possession of scalped tickets or were admitted by the prosecution or defense under the guise of being wit-nesses: Douglas Fairbanks, Ginger Rogers, Jack Benny, Jack Dempsey, Moss Hart, Lowell Thomas, and social-register types galore. Often all a visitor had to do to find a famous man or woman was turn from the courthouse and look directly across Main Street to the four-story Union Hotel. A celebrity might be outside on one of the porches that ran along the building's facade or in the hotel dining room, which had become the prime gathering place for out-of-towners.

The conversion of Hopewell—population nine hundred plus with a police force of two—into a rip-roaring Forty-second Street in the wake of the Lindbergh kidnapping on March 1, 1932, was tepid tea in comparison with the transformation that Flemington—population twenty-seven hundred with only one full-time policeman—underwent in January of 1935. The first weekend of the Hauptmann trial, an estimated twenty thousand automobiles and sixty thousand sightseers descended. The average speed on the roads into town was three miles per hour, and traffic was backed up an average of ten miles in all directions. Once in Flemington, the legions of visitors found it next to impossible to get out. On Sunday a restless mob of five thousand swarmed past the guards who were trying to keep them out of the county courthouse and went on a rampage: They cavorted in the jury box, shouting out their names; waited their turn to pose in the judge's banc or in Lindbergh's seat or in the prosecutor's or on the defendant's chair; searched every nook and cranny of the building for souvenirs, many of which they fought over; took as mementos almost anything that wasn't nailed down and quite a few items that were, including spittoons, mops, bars of soap, toilet paper, pieces of chairs and tables; cut their initials into wooden surfaces; invaded the attic communication center and tried to tear out cables.

The population of Flemington doubled, and massive traffic jams became commonplace as the trial proceeded. For the depression-racked quiet little town, bumptious outsiders were part of an economic windfall. Retail prices soared, and any home owner with a spare bedroom or bed could rent it out at a handsome price. If board was offered as well, exorbitant charges could be extracted by the meal. The only hostelry in town, the Union Hotel, was completely booked, (nine hundred requests had been received for its fifty rooms when the trial was announced back in October) but management had hired on additional help so the dining room could be kept open until midnight. The hotel also converted a main-floor storage area into a tap room, which the media not only appropriated as their preferred watering hole but named after Nellie, the stray pooch that a New York reporter had adopted. Business at the nearby Blue Bowl Tearoom rose dramatically. The same was true for the Candy Kitchen, which featured a Lindbergh sundae, a Hauptmann pudding, and baked beans bearing the name of the prosecutor. To help meet the demand for meals, the Woman's Council of the Methodist Episcopal Church prepared a lunch, of which many a lawyer and reporter availed himself or herself. One farsighted press organization had rented an entire country club in the area to house and feed its staff. Another paper had taken whatever apartments could be found. The balance of reporters were on their own. Hotel accommodations in Princeton, fifteen miles southeast of Flemington, were heavily booked, and quite a few newspeople stayed in Trenton, which was twenty-one miles to the south. Several scribes braved the awesome traffic and commuted the sixty plus miles from New York City each day.

The streets of Flemington became a gouger's paradise as out-of-town hawkers vied with local shopkeepers in peddling every kind of souvenir imaginable, from "autographed" photos of Lindbergh to "certified" locks of the dead infant's hair. Among the best-selling novelty items was a miniature replica of the kidnapping ladder that was being built and sold by a local lad and his brother.[3]

The trial seemed to mark a milestone in the long and strenuous relationship between Charles Lindbergh and the media. If Lindy had sent the press on a bogus chase, hoping the interest in the death of his son would abate, he had miscalculated. The media had persisted and triumphed. Lindbergh had accepted the reality that the timetable of his scenario had been upset—extended far longer than he desired. He had done all he could not to get anyone implicated in the crime. These efforts failed. Lindy's decision to identify the voice from the graveyard may have been a last resort to end the tragic ordeal his family had endured. Many legal experts believed that even if Hauptmann was convicted, he would be spared the death penalty.

Lindbergh resigned himself to becoming a supporting player in the Flemington spectacular. He maintained his dignity and cut a heroic figure. Many a Lindy watcher thought he or she detected signs of relief in the Lone Eagle. He was just as inaccessible to reporters as in the past and just as much the target of journalists' gossip, but there appeared to be a certain mellowness about him.

The press on the whole behaved despicably, as David Brinkley would incisively document in his 1962 program on media deportment at the trial of the century, which was subtitled in part " 'It Was a Sickness.' "[4] Four hundred fifty reporters and photographers were estimated to be in Flemington, a healthy percentage of whom seemed to be strident and rowdy, hard drinking, and insensitive to the town. Almost every major paper in the country, as well as a great number from around the world, was represented, and the Hearst syndicate alone had sent a staff of fifty. The attic rooms over the trial chamber had been converted into a communications center replete with forty telegraph and cable operators,

Noon recess outside Flemington court-house, January 3, 1935 (AP/Wide World Photos)

Lindbergh leaving the courthouse, January 3, 1935 (AP/Wide World Photos)

Local Flemington boys selling their homemade souvenir ladders, which became the symbol of the trial (UPI/Bettmann)

David Wilentz (center)
(UPI/Bettmann)

Attorney Lloyd Fisher (hand in pocket), who replaced Reilly as defense attorney, faces reporters as the clock runs out on Hauptmann's life
(UPI/Bettmann)

Hauptmann and defense attorney Edward J. Reilly. Nicknamed "Death House," Reilly spent less than half an hour conferring with his client during the entire pretrial and trial period. (UPI/Bettmann)

Mrs. H. Norman Schwarzkopf accompanying Anne Lindbergh from the court-house (Library of Congress)

Charles Lindbergh testifying at the Hauptmann trial, January 3, 1935 (Library of Congress)

Hauptmann (standing, extreme left) hears the jury deliver a verdict of guilty (AP/Wide World Photos)

Jafsie Condon (right) with his friend and ex officio bodyguard Al Reich (Library of Congress)

The convicted Hauptmann in his cell, February 14, 1935. After a year of appeals he would be electrocuted. (AP/Wide World Photos)

Harold G. Hoffman, the forty-first governor of New Jersey, with his family (AP/Wide World Photos)

Ellis Parker, Sr., who worked on Governor Hoffman's reinvestigation of the Lindbergh case (UPI/Bettmann)

New Jersey's court of pardons on their way to deliberate Hauptmann's final fate, January 11, 1936. Governor Hoffman is third from the left. (Library of Congress)

Jacob J. Nosovitsky, "international spy" and master forger, fit most of the physical descriptions Condon gave regarding "Cemetery John." (Journal American Morgue, University of Texas)

Naval credential (possibly a forgery). The author found over 60 aliases for Nosovitsky, a third of which used the initials J.J. (Journal American Morgue, University of Texas)

Clyde Tolson (left) and J. Edgar Hoover. The bureau boss insisted that his friendship with Nosovitsky was not professional. (AP/Wide World Photos)

DAILY NEWS

J.J. FAULKNER 'CLEARS' BRUNO

Story on Page 9

'J. J. FAULKNER' AIDS HAUPTMANN DEFENSE

Gilbert, 'Great Lover' of Films, Is Dead on Coast

Expert Identifies Handwriting In Letter Sent to Hoffman

By ROBERT CONWAY

(Staff Correspondent of The News)

Trenton, Jan. 9.—The mysterious J. J. Faulkner, unidentified depositor of $2,980 Lindbergh ransom money, has absolved Bruno Richard Hauptmann in a two-page letter to Gov. Harold G. Hoffman. The handwriting on the sensational document, mailed two weeks ago from New York City, was reported by a handwriting expert today to be identical with that on the Faulkner deposit slip from the Federal Sub-Treasury Building on Wall Street.

This important development was disclosed a few hours after Prosecutor Anthony M. Hauck Jr. of Hunterdon County announced that a conference would be held Saturday to decide what action to take on a farmer's story that Anna Hauptmann was near the scene of the crime on Sourland Mountain in the Spring of 1931.

The dejection of Bruno's

PROBE OF DAD'S DEATH ASKED BY ANN HEWITT

San Francisco, Jan. 9 —

Ambassador to Mexico, Dwight D. Morrow, and his wife, Elizabeth. (AP/Wide World Photos)

The Morrow children: Elisabeth, Anne, Dwight, Jr., and Constance. (Bettmann Archives)

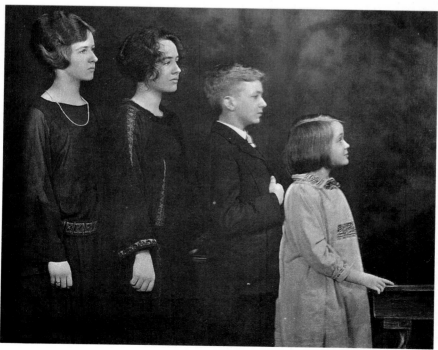

Lindbergh with Ambassador and Mrs. Morrow and their daughter Constance in Mexico City during the Christmas and New Year's holiday of 1927–28. (Bettmann Archives)

Elisabeth Morrow arriving in New York aboard the S.S. Olympic, *November 21, 1928. Newspapers circulated the rumor that she was to marry Lindbergh. The caption read "To wed Lindy?"* (UPI/Bettmann)

Elisabeth returning from Europe on June 13, 1932, after the death of her nephew. The physical changes to which Harry Green referred are evident. (UPI/Bettmann)

who, according to the wireless companies, were capable of transmitting a million words a day. The mass of telephone and telegraph wires leading from the tall utility pole on the sidewalk through the upper windows of the courthouse included forty-five direct lines to such places as Paris, Berlin, London, Buenos Aires, and Sydney, Australia. Motorcycle messengers roared through the narrow streets, many of them heading for the improvised airfield at the edge of town, from which film of the day's events was flown to New York and other cities and developed in time for late-night or early-morning editions.

Inside the thirty-by-forty-five-foot courtroom, a hundred reporters, fifty cameramen, and twenty-five communications technicians had somehow managed to operate in a fraction of the space they usually required. Among them were star journalists and special writers whom the more affluent publications had hired on, such as Walter Winchell, Arthur Brisbane, Edna Ferber, Fannie Hurst, Damon Runyon, Alexander Woollcott, Kathleen Norris, Heywood Broun, and Dorothy Kilgallan. The ace reporter for Hearst's *New York Journal* was Adela Rogers St. John, whose father was one of America's most prestigious lawyers. Adela had a direct line not only to the prosecuting attorney, David Wilentz, whom she often advised, but also to the defense attorney, Edward J. Reilly. William Randolph Hearst and his twenty-four papers had been openly declaring that the accused man was guilty, but this did not deter the Hearst organization from paying Reilly seventy-five hundred dollars in advance to represent the defendant in return for the exclusive rights to the story told by the defendant's wife. During the proceedings it was not unusual to see Adela St. John conferring with Reilly or Wilentz or to observe Winchell passing Wilentz a note.

Walter Winchell, who, like Hearst, had already pronounced Hauptmann guilty, was one of the most popular and powerful columnists of his day. Not only did he write about the trial, but he tersely reported his views on radio to a listening audience that was larger than that of any of his broadcasting competitors. And his competitors were also there and reporting: Gabriel Heatter for station WOR, Boake Carter on WABC, Hans von Kaltenborn for WCBS. Each evening WHN had the respected lawyer Samuel S. Leibowitz provide a summation of the day's testimony. On another wave length actors dramatized the proceedings. Whether the court knew that newsreel cameras were being brought into the trial room and quietly condoned it is moot, but cameras were there, poorly disguised and with the microphone for one of them concealed at the end of the jury box.

Radio was coming of age with the trial. An estimated forty million Americans were listening to on-the-scene broadcast reports from Flemington hours before the first headlines could hit the street. In addition to regularly scheduled newscasts, New York City alone had nine special reports on eight different stations in just the afternoons of each trial day. Even in the area of "special features," radio held its own with print. The papers had contracted a series of experts, including psychiatrists and legal scholars, to write about the trial. Their commentaries had proved to be very popular with the readership, and very influential. Radio was putting on its own specialists with equal success, particularly in the case of Samuel S. Leibowitz.

Radio interviews with the key participants in the trial created yet another order of stars and credibility. H. Norman Schwarzkopf, whose rigid posturing and personality ruffled many a newspaper reporter and who didn't come across all that well in motion picture newsreels, had a perfect voice for radio. In a fledgling medium where if you sounded good, you were good, he spoke with a staccato authority that convinced a large segment of the listening audience that if H. Norman said so, it had to be so. For the first time in the protracted and turbulent investigation, he and his state troopers gained a popularity all their own.

In 1932, the New Jersey State Police and H. Norman Schwarzkopf had been instrumental in restricting the media's access to the news of the kidnapping. Over the ensuing two years and ten months the superintendent and his men had suffered journalism's continued barbs about their having been inept in their initial investigation of the crime and ineffectual throughout the manhunt that ensued. Much of the media had argued that it had been the New York Police Department and federal agents who apprehended the suspect, even though the troopers had participated. The trial at Flemington offered Schwarzkopf the opportunity to vindicate himself and his organization. The state police were providing the majority of the evidence and witnesses on which the prosecution was basing its case. The smallish, ramrod-erect trooper boss still seized every opportunity to be photographed, particularly beside lanky Slim Lindbergh, but the old animosities between him and the print media seemed to have been laid aside. So was the long-held view that the crime had required more than one person in its perpetration. Walter Winchell's manifesto that the defendant had acted alone in the kidnapping and murder of the infant was the prevalent view. The betting odds were overwhelming that the jury of twelve tried-and-true local citizens, who had only the highest regard for their famous former neighbors, Charles and Anne Lindbergh, would find the defendant guilty.

The state police had an additional and thankless task at Flemington: trying to maintain law and order inside and outside the courthouse. Keeping the massive flow of traffic moving was next to impossible. By the second week of the trial, it was estimated that fifty thousand visitors were coming to town each day. Regulating the crowds that consistently congregated on Main Street in front of the courthouse was equally trying. The multitude had a propensity for knocking aside barricades and restraining ropes. Troopers often had to form flying wedges to get key personnel in and out of the building.

As required by New Jersey law in a capital case, the jury had been sequestered, but this did not prevent the jurors from hearing news, rumors, and opinions about the trial. Four times a day they had to run the gauntlet through a mob that usually spread from the Union Hotel, where the jurors were billeted, to the courthouse, directly across the street. As they passed, the crush of spectators often shouted helpful hints at them: "Burn the Dutchman!" "Send him to the chair!" "Give the murderer what he deserves." Wherever there was a crowd, ubiquitous newsboys were usually nearby, yelling out the latest extra-extra-read-all-about-it headlines.

The jurors, eight men and four women, occupied six rooms on the top floor of the Union Hotel. They took their meals in a sectioned-off area of the hotel's dining room, where the conversations of nearby reporters, who were forever discussing the case and exchanging information, could be clearly overheard. The media folk often shouted at one another to make sure the eating jurors knew what they thought of the day's testimony. The jurors were allowed no radios in their rooms, but an emergency broadcasting station had been installed on the floor below their rooms, and they could not help but hear the newscaster's on-air reports and comments about the proceedings.[5]

The trial, once under way, exceeded all expectations. This was due in part to the compelling array of new personalities involved with the proceedings. No Hollywood casting agent could have found a better type to play the presiding judge than the man who was trying the case, seventy-one-year-old Justice Thomas W. Trenchard. Childless after forty years of marriage and beginning his sixth seven-year-term on the bench, the white-haired, quiet, conservative, ultradignified Trenchard had the reputation of being scrupulously fair.

The media's new white knight was black-haired David T. Wilentz, who had an uncanny knack of playing to the hidden newsreel cameras no one was supposed to know were in the courtroom. Wilentz was consistently besting that patriarch of pomp, defense attorney Edward J. Reilly, also known as the Bull of Brooklyn, who was the self-professed veteran of fifteen hundred homicide cases and the loser of but six. He was also nicknamed Death House. Reilly insisted that was because he took on so many hopeless cases and saved so many clients from the gallows. His detractors claimed it was the other way around: that he sent them to their death. Reilly had replaced James M. Fawcett on November 2. Among the team of lawyers assisting the Bull was C. Lloyd Fisher, the local attorney who had represented John Hughes Curtis in the same courthouse back in 1932.

Embossed in red on Ed Reilly's stationery and business cards was a ladder along with the announcement that he was chief counsel of "The Lindbergh-Hauptmann Trial." His courtroom note-pads bore only the red ladder. A tall, imposing figure with thinning hair and prominent jowls, whose once-brilliant career had given way to booze, busty blondes, meaningless courtroom dramatics, and quirky lapses due to an advanced case of tertiary syphilis, Death House not only admired Charles Lindbergh but also kept a photograph of him on his desk. He was on record, off-the-cuff, as saying that his client was the killer and deserved the chair.[6] The fifty-one-year-old, four-times-married, honey-voiced orator had wasted no time in trying to make friends beyond the courtroom. On his arrival in Flemington, Reilly announced to the local citizenry that he would like to live there among them. He addressed the Rotary Club and the American Legion, and as an homage to the town's down-home simplicity, he occasionally wore a plain blue serge suit and vest in court rather than his traditional cutaway jacket and carnation, striped trousers, and spats. He had been paid his entire legal fee in advance and often seemed to be more interested in promoting himself than in defending his client. Death House, like David Wilentz, was forever giving interviews to reporters and posing for the cameras. Despite a strenuous effort to grab the spotlight whenever possible, Reilly was able to command only a fraction of the attention being showered on Wilentz, Lindbergh, or his client. Instead of preparing his case the night before the trial began, he was still passed out from the New Year's party of the day before.

Once the proceedings were under way, Reilly did frequent radiocast analysis of the day's testimony. In the courtroom he had the same unerring ability to play to the concealed newsreel cameras that Wilentz had. His bid for judicial sympathy included placing the defendant's wife and their easy-to-cry three-year-old son, Manfried, in view of the jurors. He managed to keep spectators on the edge of their seats with intimations that not only would he have the defendant testify in his own defense but that he might very well call Al Capone to the stand, among a great host of others.

21

TRIAL OF THE CENTURY

FEW EVENTS IN MODERN COURTROOM HISTORY HAVE EVOKED THE PASSION and controversy of Bruno Richard Hauptmann's aptly named trial of the century. In this author's mind it was a legal mockery and media sideshow of the highest order. The jury and judge appeared blatantly biased. Many of the witnesses and much of the evidence, under the stewardship of the New Jersey State Police, strike this author as flat-out fraudulent. But how can standards of propriety be applied to a farce? Legalistically, ethically, and morally, that's what the trial of Hauptmann approached, a farce—as black a comedy as American jurisprudence could muster.

Hauptmann's trial got under way on Tuesday, January 3, 1935, with the prosecutor, Attorney General David Wilentz, in unassailable form and a well-rehearsed cast backing up the three superstars who were slated to testify for the state: Charles and Anne Lindbergh and Jafsie Condon.

Since no one had seen the child kidnapped or murdered, Wilentz's case was to be based on circumstantial evidence. His strategy had already been previewed at the Hauptmann extradition trial at this same courthouse. First he would try to establish that the child had been kidnapped from his nursery and that ransom money was paid for his return—a ransom of which some fourteen thousand dollars ended up in the possession of Bruno Richard Hauptmann. The additional witnesses scheduled to testify in this phase included the gas station attendant who took down Hauptmann's name and the movie-house cashier who claimed he gave her a tightly folded ransom bill. The cashier was of particular importance because the prosecution expected Hauptmann to say the ransom bills belonged to Isador Fisch and he didn't discover he had them in his possession until after a rainstorm flooded his closet, forcing him to clear the shelves. The movie-house cashier had received a ten-dollar ransom note well before the rainstorm. Drawing the extortion noose even tighter was a battery of handwriting experts, led by the Osborns, who would claim that Hauptmann was the sole author of the thirteen ransom notes. The most damning testimony was expected to be Lindbergh saying he heard Hauptmann's voice at the passing of the ransom money.

The second phase of the attorney general's case would attempt to establish Hauptmann's physical presence near the Lindbergh's estate at the time of the kidnapping. At the extradition proceedings, testimony to this effect had been heard from two men, both of whom were expected to take the stand again. Reporters felt this portion of Attorney General Wilentz's case was particularly vulnerable, since the witnesses might easily crumble under the withering cross-examination anticipated from defense attorney Death House Reilly.

His buffoonery to the side, Reilly had admirers who expected him to "crack" a few other key prosecution witnesses. One thing was certain: Death House was a grandstand player who loved to put on a good show.

Anne Morrow Lindbergh was among the first prosecution witnesses called by Wilentz. She quietly established that her child had been stolen, then brought many in the hushed room to tears as she identified, item by item, garments taken from the baby in the woods as being those her son was wearing when last she saw him on the night of March 1. Attorney Reilly told the court, "The defense feels that the grief of Mrs. Lindbergh needs no cross-examination."[1]

Charles Lindbergh was the next to be called. He seated himself easily, crossed his legs, and leaned attentively forward, with his elbows resting on the arms of the wooden chair and his hands folded on a knee.[2] Reporters' eyes "popped wide with amazement" to see he was wearing a revolver in a shoulder holster under his rumpled, loose-fitting coat jacket.[3] Had they been looking at Hauptmann, they would have seen the defendant lean forward as well, peer hard at Lindbergh, then sit back.[4] Lindbergh related what had taken place the night of the kidnapping and identified the ransom note found in the nursery.

Charles Lindbergh, during the course of negotiations with the kidnappers, usually let others read the incoming ransom messages aloud to him. In the Flemington courthouse this January day, he left the reading to Dave Wilentz. While recounting the discovery of the ladder and a man's footprint as well as ladder holes in the soft ground beneath the nursery window, Lindy managed to get a dig in at the media's bad deportment. The session ended with his identification of the second ransom message, which had been mailed to the estate, and with Wilentz again reading the text aloud.

The next day on the stand, Lindbergh linked the prosecution's case to physical evidence, such as the chisel and dowel pin, identified ransom messages sent to Henry Breckinridge and John F. Condon, told of driving Condon to St. Raymond's Cemetery on the night of April 2, 1932, and related that after Condon had walked up to the corner along St. Raymond's and started back across Whittemore Avenue, "I heard very clearly a voice coming from the cemetery, to the best of my belief calling Doctor Condon." Wilentz asked what the words were. Lindbergh responded, "In a foreign accent, 'Hey, Doctor.' " And has the witness heard this same accented voice again? Wilentz asked somewhat later. "Yes I have," Lindbergh answered under oath. Wilentz wanted to know whose voice it was that called out "Hey, Doctor" that night in the cemetery. Lindbergh said, "That was Hauptmann's voice."[5] Then, for the first time, the Lone Eagle looked at the prisoner.

The world had its first superheadline of the trial.

A moment of expected confrontation arrived with Death House Reilly's cross-examination of Charles Lindbergh. Rumors had been spreading lickety-split that Lindy was wearing a gun in the courtroom because he had initially intended to shoot Death House should the defense attorney's cross-examination of Anne prove too harsh. With Lindbergh himself on the stand, one of the first questions Reilly asked was, "Are you armed, Colonel?" Wilentz objected. The judge didn't know to what, since he hadn't heard the question.[6] Lindbergh, having been warned that Reilly might inquire as to the weapon, gratuitously announced he wasn't armed and opened his jacket to demonstrate the point. The first great confrontation had fizzled. Worse was to come.

During a radio broadcast the night before, Reilly had proclaimed that he would reveal the identities of the actual kidnapper-murderers. Rather than starting off the next day's cross-examination by challenging Lindbergh's damning but vulnerable "Hey, Doctor" testimony, Death House befuddled even his own colleagues by obliquely proposing a theory as to the true perpetrators of the crime: hostile neighbors who had conspired with a disloyal member, or perhaps members, of the Lindbergh's household staff. He suggested that the homicidal neighbors, angered by Lindbergh's closing of a long-used lumber road on his property, had not only been informed the baby would be there on a Tuesday night by the treacherous employee or employees but had also been told how to leave the nursery with the stolen infant, which was not by the ladder but down a staircase in the Lindbergh home. Reilly implied that because household staff members were involved with the kidnapping, the family dog did not bark when the nursery was entered and the child brought down the stairs. Reilly had the witness describe the staircase locations in the house. While Lindbergh allowed that it might have been physically possible for him and his wife to have been eating in their dining room without seeing or hearing someone descending the main stairway, he deemed it very unlikely. There was another way down from the nursery, a servant's staircase going to the kitchen, which opened onto a gravel parking area at the rear of the house. Reilly got an admission from Lindbergh that no one had bothered checking this possible route of exit the night of the crime.

Death House alluded to the New Jersey State Police as having bungled the investigation, which would be a continuing theme, but he concentrated on the hiring procedures that had led to the employment of Betty Gow and the husband-and-wife team of Aloysius (known as Oliver) and Elsie Mary Whateley as well as their activities the night of the crime. Ollie Whateley had died back in 1933, and Reilly targeted him as the prime inside betrayer without specifically saying so. Death House also brought up Violet Sharpe and Mrs. Morrow's chauffeur Henry Ellerson, who had driven Betty Gow to the estate that fateful Tuesday. Lindbergh dismissed the defense supposition and avowed his complete trust in all the staffers. Reilly elicited a review of the child's death and touched on Lindbergh's connections with John F. Condon and two other go-betweens, Mickey Rosner and John Hughes Curtis. Lindbergh saw nothing suspicious about Condon's having offered his services as a go-between in a paid advertisement or in the fact that Jafsie always seemed to be alone when critical events occurred.

At no time during his cross-examination did Reilly challenge the witness's identification of a voice that two years and nine months earlier had spoken at most four words from a distance of over two hundred feet. Lindbergh left the stand virtually uncontested by the defense lawyer.

On cross-examining Elsie Mary Whateley, the Lindberghs' former cook and housekeeper, Reilly attempted to establish that her late husband, Ollie, knew Jafsie Condon and was extremely friendly, if not intimate, with Violet Sharpe. Elsie Mary, who had wept openly when the defense attorney had pressed Lindbergh for details on the death of his son, repulsed Reilly's assault on her dead husband with forced calm and poise, and she prevailed. The Bull of Brooklyn fared somewhat better when he cross-examined Betty Gow and probed her relationship with Henry ("Red") Johnsen, one of the few people who had known the Lindberghs were still at the estate on Tuesday, March 1. His bellowing suggestions that on the day of the kidnapping Johnsen had called her not from Englewood but from Hopewell and that the motive of the call was to see if the coast was clear created a furor in the courtroom and ultimately led nowhere.

Reilly did get Gow to say that the family dog, a chronic barker that was usually given the run of the house, had been kept in the Whateleys' apartment the night of the kidnapping and was not heard to bark. Reilly also established that between the Lindbergh house and Mrs. Morrow's home in Englewood there were another four or five sleeping suits similar to the one the child was wearing the night he disappeared. Reilly's suggestion that in April, a month after the infant disappeared, Gow and Whateley had intentionally dropped the infant's thumb guard next to the driveway, which had been thoroughly searched by investigators, was vehemently denied by Gow.

Death House and his associate defense attorneys—C. Lloyd Fisher, Egbert Rosecrans, and Frederick A. Pope—were the most effective in negating testimony from New Jersey state troopers, many of whom seemed to have let various investigatory details go undone. Their carping at statements by troopers Bornmann and Kelly, as well as by wood expert Arthur Koehler, frustrated the prosecution's efforts to have the ladder entered as evidence. Wilentz, though enraged by this, continued to pursue the extortion phase of his prosecution by calling to the stand a tried-and-true witness who had picked Hauptmann out of a police lineup in Greenwich Village and identified him for the Bronx County grand jury: taxi driver Joseph Perrone. Wiping clean his glasses, he told Wilentz and the Hunterdon County court that Bruno Richard Hauptmann was the man who paid him a dollar to deliver a ransom message to Condon. When instructed to point Hauptmann out, Perrone confidently strode from his chair and placed a hand on the German's shoulder, announcing, "This is the man."

"Liar," Hauptmann said quietly.[7]

Though the defense attorney's continual and booming objections during direct questioning unnerved the cab driver, Perrone managed to survive Reilly's boisterous cross-examination.

By dawn on Wednesday, January 9, an estimated one thousand people were lined up in the drizzle, hoping to hear Jafsie Condon's testimony. Condon was one of the great crowd pleasers of the Lindbergh case and one of the most outrageous publicity seekers. Jafsie still never missed an opportunity to speak and still rarely told the same tale twice. Many waiting in line, as well as in the gallery, didn't care what he said. They adored Jafsie almost as much as they despised the accused.

Dave Wilentz had not wanted to use Condon as a witness. The attorney general had been frustrated and angered by the old man's failure to identify Hauptmann in the police lineup in New York City back in September. At one point he even threatened to have Jafsie arrested. Wilentz had avoided calling on Condon to testify before the Hunterdon County grand jury as well as at the Bronx extradition hearing. But Jafsie had made headlines by managing to interview Hauptmann alone. He had also dropped hints to reporters that he was ready to say he had given the ransom money to the prisoner but would not definitely confirm this to Wilentz. Whatever the pressures or reasoning, Wilentz relented. From all reports he was uneasy. If ever a witness was potential lion meat for Death House Reilly, it was Jafsie Condon—and the media were playing it to the fullest.

Called to the stand by Wilentz, Jafsie wasted no time in rattling off his many credits and contradicting himself. He was also about to provide one of the most memorable moments in modern trial history. Wilentz asked to whom he had given the wooden box containing the ransom money, and Jafsie answered, "John."

Almost as an afterthought Wilentz queried, "Who is John?"

A dramatic pause ensued. Then Condon raised a bent finger toward the defendant and said, in resounding and accentuated syllables, "John is Br-uno Rich-ard Haupt-mann!"[8] Hand raised and fingers pointed, he repeated it twice more.

Reilly's cross-examination of Condon was being anticipated by many newsmen as the trial's penultimate confrontation. Other reporters were touting it as the Battle of the Windbags. Several of the prosecuting attorneys feared Reilly might very well discredit the eccentric Condon. When Death House and Jafsie finally locked horns, it was all Jafsie. Not only did the agile-tongued former principal counter almost every thrust the defense attorney tried, he usually put the courtroom in stitches doing it.

Associate defense attorney C. Lloyd Fisher acquitted himself far better than Reilly. The prosecution, in a bid to enter into evidence documents written by Hauptmann at the New York Police Department's Second Precinct the night of his apprehension, called on four law officers to testify and produce exhibits. The specimens were allowed as evidence, but not before Fisher, on cross-examination, got one officer's admission that Hauptmann had been interrogated fifteen straight hours prior to the samples' being taken, and not before he made another officer reveal that he had dictated what Hauptmann was to write. When Wilentz called Internal Revenue Service agent Frank J. Wilson to the stand, Fisher blocked the prosecution from entering into evidence the $14,600 found in Hauptmann's garage. Wilentz scored points by getting Wilson to agree that since Hauptmann's indictment not one more dollar in ransom money had turned up. Fisher rallied during cross-examination when Wilson confirmed that the Treasury Department had carefully investigated the $2,980 of ransom money deposited at the Fed Bank in New York by J. J. Faulkner and that the handwriting on the deposit slip was not that of Hauptmann.

Wilentz called on his battery of handwriting experts—which helped to run up costs in what would become the most high priced trial in New Jersey's history, an estimated $130,000, as opposed to the $50,000 spent on the entire Hall-Mills murders, the most expensive New Jersey trial to date. Albert S. Osborn and his son, Albert D. Osborn, who would put in expense bills for $12,000 and $9,655 respectively, again gave testimony that Hauptmann had written the ransom letters. Their opinions were reinforced by a battery of additional authorities, whose expenses, when added to those of the Osborns, brought the prosecution's total outlay for handwriting testimony up to $46,661.15, or better than a third of the hearing's total expenditures.

Coroner Walter Swayze recounted seeing the body in the woods and removing it to the county morgue, where it was identified by Betty Gow and Colonel Lindbergh. He admitted signing the death certificate, which over strenuous defense objections was entered in evidence. On being cross-examined by Reilly, he conceded that he was an undertaker, not a physician, and that he had signed the death certificate on information furnished to him by someone else.

Dr. Charles H. Mitchell, the Mercer County physician, perjured himself by testifying under oath that he had performed the autopsy on the body while Swayze looked on. It was just the opposite: Swayze had performed it with Mitchell looking on. Mitchell told the court that the child died of a fractured skull. Because he had found traces of a blood clot along the fracture line, it was his professional opinion that death had occurred either instantaneously or within a very few minutes following the blow—thereby implying that the child had been killed during the kidnapping and reinforcing the prosecution's contention that the murder had been perpetrated while the victim was still in Hunterdon County.

For a time it appeared that Death House Reilly was finally on track. During cross-examination he pounded away at Mitchell's examination of the corpse as well as at his general competence. Mitchell asserted that the child could not have died from what appeared to be a bullet hole in the skull—a possibility he was on record for having suggested to the press at the time of the autopsy. When asked if any other doctor assisted him, the county physician answered in the negative, even though Dr. Philip Van Ingen was there observing the autopsy being performed by Swayze. Mitchell insisted he had allowed no one to see the body but couldn't explain how the Movietone News people had managed to take pictures of the operation. He knew at the time that the autopsy was important but still saw no need to have called in a forensic specialist, which he was not. The reason he hadn't taken a photograph of the blood clot that had allowed him to estimate the time of death was that he felt his memory was as good as any picture. The doctor bridled when Reilly suggested that if he had died before a suspect was arrested, no one could have testified to the autopsy from a medical viewpoint. Reilly returned to Mitchell's conclusion about the cause of death: Indications of a blood clot and evidence of a cracked skull had led the physician to believe the child died of a blow to the head. Then Reilly dismissed the witness.

Wilentz supporters would later contend that because Reilly hadn't followed through on Dr. Mitchell's shaky medical conclusions, the prosecution was able to anticipate that the defense might be trying to establish that the baby in the woods wasn't the Lindbergh child. Hauptmann advocates would insist that the state police had eavesdropped on Death House and his associates. Doubts as to the tiny body's identity were indeed part of the defense strategy, or so Lloyd Fisher thought when earlier in his cross-examination he got truck driver Orville Wilson to testify that the dead infant was found in Mercer County and that the adjoining land was owned by St. Michael's Orphanage.

Dave Wilentz, to counter any thoughts that the corpse belonged to one of the children of St. Michael's Orphanage, called to the stand Elmira Dormer, the woman in charge of St. Michael's, who testified that in the months of February and March 1932 no children were missing from the institution. Wilentz offered to produce the ledgers Dormer had brought along, should the defense have any dispute as to the attendance. They didn't, and Wilentz made doubly sure by asking, "There is no claim that the child in the woods came from the orphanage?" Reilly, in a surprise reversal, declared that the defense had never doubted that the tiny body was that of the Lindbergh baby, thereby enraging Lloyd Fisher, who leapt to his feet and before striding from the chamber, shouted at Death House, "You are conceding Hauptmann to the electric chair."[9]

Among those prosecution witnesses testifying to the trail of ten-dollar gold certificates that resulted in Hauptmann's apprehension and to the subsequent discovery of ransom money in his garage were gas station employees John Lyons and Walter Lyle, DI agents William F. Seery and Thomas H. Sisk, Trooper John Wallace, and New York police officers James J. Petrosino and Maurice W. Tobin. Inspector Henry Bruckman of the NYPD gave direct testimony that Hauptmann had confessed to having written Condon's phone number on an exposed board in his unlighted closet—and during cross-examination he admitted that the closet was unlighted and conceded that to read the number, you would have to have your back up against the closet wall.

Edward F. Morton, the Reliance Property Management timekeeper who had failed to appear as James Fawcett's first defense witness in Hauptmann's extradition hearing because the proper documents had not been available to him, now testified in behalf of the prosecution—and presented evidence that Hauptmann had not begun work at the Majestic Apartments until March 21, 1932. Cecile Barr identified Hauptmann as the man who had paid for a movie ticket with a folded five-dollar ransom bill on November 26, 1933, the night of his birthday. Her testimony was particularly critical to the prosecution, which counted on it to negate the defense claim that Hauptmann didn't discover Fisch's money-filled shoe box until August of 1934.

The second phase of Wilentz's strategy, placing Hauptmann near the scene of the crime, was left not only to Millard Whited but to a pair of additional witnesses for the prosecution: seventy-four-year-old Amandus Hochmuth, who lived near Sorrel Hill and was almost blind with cataracts, and Charles Rossiter, a salesman for the Perfect Foods Company. All three expected a share of the reward money, something that would not be all that easy for them to collect.

A series of recalls set the stage for Wilentz's final witness, Arthur Koehler, the wood expert from Madison, Wisconsin, who was being heralded in the press. Koehler claimed to have traced an almost imperceptible blemish on one of the rails in the ladder, rail 16, to a defective knife in a plane at the J. J. Dorn Company lumber mill in McCormick, South Carolina, and, subsequently, to have tracked a shipment of one-by-four-inch Southern-pine boards from the Dorn mill north to the National Lumber and Millwork Company in the Bronx, where Hauptmann was known to have worked as well as to have purchased lumber. Aided by charts, diagrams, and photographs, Koehler testified that as the result of a careful study of rail 16 in the ladder and the remainder of the missing board in Hauptmann's attic, "I have come to the conclusion that those two pieces [of wood] at one time were one piece. That they have been cut in two."[10] One reason for his reaching this conclusion was that four nail holes in rail 16 fit perfectly into the nail holes in a remaining joist in the attic floor.

To explain why rail 16 was narrower than the missing attic board, Koehler produced a plane that had been recovered from the workbench in Hauptmann's garage and contended that the groove marks on the ladder section left no doubt that the board had been shaved down by Hauptmann's plane. Following many objections by the defense, the court allowed Koehler to demonstrate by clamping a piece of onionskin paper over the edge of a strip of ponderosa pine and rubbing it back and forth with a pencil. After shaving the edge with the plane from Hauptmann's garage and applying a fresh sheet of onionskin, he made another rubbing. He placed a third onionskin page over the edge of rail 16 and again rubbed the pencil over it. The impressions on the first sheet of onionskin revealed the grain of the wood. The second and third sheets showed identical ridges made by the plane. Koehler applied the onionskin test to cleats he made in a sample piece of wood with the chisel that had been found near the abandoned ladder the night the child disappeared. They matched the pattern of the onionskin rubbing of the chiseled cleats on the actual ladder. Koehler finished off his testimony by asserting that the three-section ladder, when contracted, fit easily into Hauptmann's car, and that whoever constructed the ladder knew a good deal about carpentry. There was no doubt that the jury, as well as the courtroom, had been intrigued by this witness.

Attorney Frederick Pope took up the defense cross-examination by challenging most everything the wood expert had said. Koehler could not be shaken.

The prosecution rested its case. It was now January 24, the seventeenth day of the trial, and defense counsel Egbert Rosecrans asked permission to make a motion for a verdict of acquittal.

Rosecrans's action would be cited and sided with for decades to come as it was contended, among other things, that there was no evidence that the alleged crime was committed in Hunterdon County rather than in Mercer County, where the corpus delicti was found, and therefore the Hunterdon County court did not have the jurisdiction to try the case. Without such proof of venue, according to Rosecrans, the legal presumption must be that the fatal blow was struck and the death occurred in Mercer County. The defense also challenged the felony-murder statute under which the prosecution was attempting to find the defendant guilty. Rosecrans wondered aloud if burglary—in this case the stealing of the baby's sleeping garment—even qualified as a felony. He argued that all the state had proved was that someone had entered the Lindbergh house with the intent to kidnap the child. The defense further maintained that under the very felony-murder statute to which they were adhering, the state could not convict Hauptmann of murder until it had established that he had committed the felony that incidentally led to the murder: in this instance, burglary.

Wilentz passionately defended the court's legality and the prosecution's case. Justice Trenchard denied the motion for acquittal. The defense was ordered to proceed.

— — —

C. Lloyd Fisher's opening statement on behalf of Bruno Richard Hauptmann that same day expressed confidence that he and his fellow counselors would convince the jury that their client had a complete alibi, especially for the critical dates of March 1, 1932, the night of the kidnapping; April 2, 1932, the night the ransom was paid in St. Raymond's Cemetery; and November 26, 1934, the evening the movie-house cashier Cecile Barr received a folded five-dollar bill from the ransom loot. Pleading poverty and simultaneously taking a swipe at the money expended by the prosecution for handwriting testimony, Fisher promised to produce his own experts who would attest to Hauptmann's not having written the ransom notes. He and his colleagues would account for every cent of Hauptmann's money and prove that his business relationship with Isador Fisch was what the client always contended it was. They would show the jury that the witnesses Hochmuth and Whited—both of whom put Hauptmann near the Lindbergh estate at the time of the crime—were unreliable.

" 'Now, I want to come down for a minute, if I may, to the manner of the conduct of the police in this case,' " Fisher told the jury.

> "I want to show you what we will prove about it. We believe that we will be able to show that no case in all history was as badly handled or as badly mangled as this case, and we refer specifically to the witness Kelly and his testimony about the ladder. Now after Kelly had played around with that ladder—and we will prove this—for days and days and days, and couldn't find a print of any kind or description, after he had gone over the entire inside of the house and couldn't find a print, even of the people who put the baby to bed, they called in an expert, Doctor Hudson, of New York City, and in the sight of Kelly, we will prove to you, Hudson took off some eight hundred fingerprints."[11]

The jury was not convinced by the defense witnesses, many of whom were blatantly questionable. Death House Reilly, who would spend a grand total of only twenty-six minutes conferring with his client during the entire trial, had not only gone public and announced over the radio and in the papers that he was searching for witnesses who could aid the defendant, but he had actually put several of these volunteers on the stand—to the delight of the prosecution.[12] Even reliable witnesses seemed to be sorely unprepared, and minor debacles could not be averted.

Among those swearing under oath that they had seen Hauptmann in or near Frederiksen's bakery-lunchroom on the evening of March 1,

1932, were Elvert Carlstrom, Louis Kiss, and August Van Henke. The prosecution easily established that Carlstrom had never left his job in New Jersey the evening of March 1 and that Kiss—a self-professed silk-painter artist and part-time brew-it-yourself rumshiner who allegedly got lost in the Bronx while delivering two pints of his product—had been at Frederiksen's on a different night. The credibility of Van Henke—he attested to having seen Hauptmann walking a police dog near the restaurant—was put in doubt when it was revealed he had two aliases and had operated a speakeasy.

Lou Harding testified for the defense that on March 1 he had directed two men in a dark-blue suburban automobile with a ladder inside it to the Lindbergh estate but that neither of the men was Hauptmann. When Wilentz suggested that the witness had once been convicted of assaulting a woman, Harding set the record straight by insisting the charge was "carnal abuse."

Defensewise, things didn't go all that swimmingly for April 2, when the ransom was passed in St. Raymond's. Benjamin Heier took the stand and told of having seen Isador Fisch jump over the cemetery wall that night, but it turned out that Heier had been in an automobile accident eight miles away at the precise time he said he had seen Fisch. Heier was later indicted for perjury.

Lawyer Reilly didn't give up on his attempt to link the crime to a member of the Lindbergh-Morrow household staffs. Peter H. Sommer told the jury that on the night of March 1 he was on the Weehawken ferry from New Jersey to Manhattan and saw two men, one of whom resembled the photograph he was shown of Isador Fisch. After the ferry reached New York City's Forty-second Street pier, Sommer saw the two men help a woman with a baby in her arms onto a trolley car. The witness identified a photograph of Violet Sharpe as being that woman. On cross-examination Sommer became so addled and contradictory that the courtroom was thrown into chaos, particularly when he was reluctant to either reidentify the photographs he had previously said were Fisch and Sharpe or refute his earlier testimony. Resuming his cross-examination the next day, Wilentz established that Sommer was a professional witness who had testified in such cases as the Hall-Mills murders and had once threatened to change his testimony unless he was paid the fifteen dollars he insisted was due him.

Reilly's most grievous miscalculation was putting Bruno Richard Hauptmann on the stand. As Death House had hoped, it added to the drama of the trial—and to the cliff-hanging question of whether the stoic

German would "crack" or "thaw" under Wilentz's cross-examination, whether he would not only confess but possibly name his accomplices, if they existed. Hauptmann did not possess the sort of personality that engendered either trust or compassion. A lean, dour illegal alien, he spoke with a pronounced guttural accent and betrayed a pomposity and an arrogance that reporters referred to as typically Germanic in an age when isolationist America watched with mounting distaste and trepidation the bloody antics of Adolf Hitler. Hauptmann, like Hitler, had been a corporal in the German army during World War I, a machine gunner in an army that had fought and killed United States doughboys. Though not an unbright man, the defendant displayed a glaring contempt for the intelligence of others. He relished being the center of attention and often seemed to gloat over what he considered to be his own mental superiority. He appeared particularly proud of the fact that Wilentz had not been able to make him crack as he was caught in this exchange during his cross-examination:

"You think you are a big shot, don't you?" Wilentz asked.

"No, should I cry?" Hauptmann answered.

"You think you are bigger than anybody, don't you?"

"No, but I know I am innocent."

"You are a man that has the will power, that is what you know isn't it?"

"No."

"You wouldn't tell if they murdered you, would you?"

"No."

"Will power is everything with you, isn't it?"

"No, it is—I feel innocent and I am innocent and that gives me the power to stand up."

"Lying when you swear to God that you will tell the truth. Telling lies doesn't mean anything!"

"Stop that!"

"Didn't you swear to untruths in the Bronx courthouse?"

"Stop that!"[13]

Hauptmann had taken the stand at 3:09 P.M. the same day the defense attorneys began to present their case. Sitting no farther away than fifteen feet, his eyes firmly set on the accused, was Charles Lindbergh. Reilly led Hauptmann through an account of his whereabouts on March 1 and April 2. Hauptmann repeated his dealings with Isador Fisch, who he still maintained had left the ransom money with him. One by one he was shown the ransom messages. He studied each of them, one by one, before denying he was the author. The day's testimony ended with Hauptmann swearing he had not built or owned the ladder nor had he given a folded five-dollar bill to a Greenwich Village movie cashier on the night of his birthday.

Though a severe snowstorm hit Flemington that Thursday night, the largest and most unruly crowd to date was jammed into the courtroom the next morning—seven hundred people filling a chamber that could barely accommodate the usual gathering of two hundred.[14] Every aisle and nook and cranny was filled with sitting and standing men and women, a great many of whom chatted away or aggressively tried to better their location. Despite repeated warnings from the bench, the gallery giggled and guffawed at the slightest opportunity. Bailiffs' shouts of "quiet" added to the din. One outburst of raucous laughter finally provoked Justice Trenchard to lose his temper and proclaim that any future laughers were to be brought to the bench for sentencing. The reason for the overflow turnout was twofold: Hauptmann was to give his second day of testimony, and there was a possibility that Wilentz's cross-examination might begin. But the session started off with Death House Reilly questioning his client.

Shown the sleeping suit worn by the dead baby in the woods, Bruno denied ever having seen it before. Then, with Reilly's help, he went into a discursive explanation of his financial dealings. Following the noon recess, he was back on the stand to relate his arrest and mistreatment while at the NYPD's Greenwich Village station house. In response to Reilly's query, Bruno related how he had been forced to write exact copies of the ransom message, inclusive of the misspelled words. Reilly ended his direct examination late in the afternoon of Friday, January 25. Hauptmann had acquitted himself quite well while denying any complicity in the kidnapping-murder, had been self-assured and even relaxed in responding to the questions, often smiled—occasionally joked. With only a half hour left before the day's session ended, David Wilentz began his cross-examination.

As Hauptmann had a habit of smirking, so did Wilentz. Both were aliens: The accused had entered the country illegally as an adult; the prosecutor had been brought here legally at the age of one from Lithuania. What heightened the confrontation for many observers in the overcrowded courtroom was the fact that Hauptmann was German and Wilentz was Jewish. In general, the confrontation was an expanded replay of their prior meeting in the extradition hearing at the Bronx federal courtroom the previous September, which it now appeared had benefited Wilentz more than Hauptmann.

The attorney general began casually enough, listening to Hauptmann's gratuitous clarification of testimony he had just given on his financial dealings. After posing a routine series of questions regarding the defendant's criminal record in Germany, Wilentz walked up to the witness chair and shoved a dark-red memorandum book in front of Hauptmann. The book had been taken from the defendant's apartment the day of his arrest. "Take a look at this word particularly," the prosecutor demanded. "Tell me if that is your handwriting, that one word there."

Hauptmann squirmed in his chair but gave no answer. Alluding to the German's earlier assertions that he was being framed and that a policeman may have put Condon's telephone number in his closet, Wilentz asked, "Or did some policemen write it?"

Hauptmann said he could not remember every word he had written in the book. "Just the one word, that's all," Wilentz pressed. "There are only a few words on the whole page. That one word, tell me if that is in your handwriting?"

Hauptmann conceded that the word looked like his handwriting, but he did not remember putting it in the book. The German sighed; his pale face was flushed. No longer did he sit defiantly erect in his chair, sweeping the overcrowded courtroom with his eyes. His gaze was fixed on the floor. He tried to laugh off the attack.

"Well now, this isn't a joke!" shouted Wilentz. "You know either it is your handwriting, or it isn't! Is it your handwriting?" The German mumbled that it looked like his handwriting. "Now, tell me, how you spell 'boat'?" Hauptmann brightened and spelled it b-o-a-t. "Yes," Wilentz agreed. "Why did you spell it b-o-a-*d*?"

Hauptmann reached for the book, saying, "You wouldn't mind to tell me how old this book is?"

"I don't know how old it is. You know; I don't know."

"Let me see it." The book was given him.

"Why did you spell 'boat' b-o-a-d?" insisted Wilentz.

"This book is probably eight years old," Hauptmann objected.

"All right, why did you spell b-o-a-d?"

"Well, after you make improvements in your writing—"

"All right," the prosecutor interrupted, "so that at one time you used to spell 'boat' b-o-a-d."

"Probably eight or ten years ago, and I'm not quite sure if I put it in."

"At one time you used to spell 'boat' b-o-a-d, didn't you? Isn't that right?"

"No, I don't think so."

"Eight years ago, six years ago, ten years ago, whenever it was, you used to spell 'boat' b-o-a-d; isn't that right?"

"I don't know."

"You spelled it in there, didn't you?"

"I—"

"You tell the truth now! Didn't you spell it in there?"

"Now listen. I can't remember I put it in there."

Wilentz continued to pound away at the word *boad*. Hauptmann desperately maintained he couldn't recall writing it in the book.

"The reason you don't say yes or no," Wilentz finally concluded, "is because you wrote 'boad' when you got the fifty thousand dollars from Condon, isn't that right?"

To a *New York Herald Tribune* reporter Hauptmann looked obviously frightened while replying, "No sir."

Wilentz handed Hauptmann the final ransom message Condon had received. "Do you see the word 'Boad Nelly'?"

"I see it."

"B-o-a-d?"

"I see it."[15]

Pressed sharply by Wilentz, Hauptmann refused to agree that the word *boad* in his book and the word *boad* in the ransom note were formed alike. By now the defendant had taken out a handkerchief and was wiping away his perspiration. The prosecutor linked the *boad* spelling to Hauptmann's native Saxony, then shifted and hammered away at the defendant's business records and partnership with Isador Fisch. "The only man who knows about any monies between you and Fisch, so far as the stocks are concerned, is that man that is dead, Fisch; isn't that right?" Wilentz asked. A moment later he asked, referring to Fisch, "Did he help you kidnap this Lindbergh child and murder it?"

"I never saw—" Hauptmann started to say.

"You never saw?"

"Mr. Lindbergh's child!"

"But Fisch didn't help you, did he?"

One of Hauptmann's attorney's, C. Lloyd Fisher, entered a shouting match with Wilentz and was chided by the judge for shouting. Wilentz homed in on the two-by-four wooden board found in Hauptmann's garage. The board contained drilled holes in which a small gun and rolls of ransom money had been found. Wilentz suggested that the round holes had some connection with the circles that formed the symbol on the ransom notes. Hauptmann admitted that if you drill a hole, it's usually round. The prosecutor shifted to the defendant's illegal-entry attempt into the United States and the fact that on one occasion he used the alias Perlmeier. Was Perlmeier's first name John? Bruno didn't remember.

"Are you the Cemetery John who was up at Woodlawn Cemetery?" Wilentz demanded.

"Positively not!"

"Are you the Cemetery John who was in the other cemetery?"

"No, I never was in the cemetery."[16]

The day's session was over. Hauptmann, visibly shaken by the ordeal, told reporters that he felt fine. Was he worried? "Why should I be worried?"[17] Then he was led back to his cell. After three more days of equally searing cross-examination, Hauptmann was slightly less enthusiastic. But he hadn't "broken" or "thawed" under Wilentz's onslaught, and he was very proud of that.

— — —

On February 2, when the trial was in the fifth week, David Wilentz was "shocked" to learn that newsreel cameras had been smuggled into the courtroom and were illegally filming the proceedings. Attorney Reilly and Justice Trenchard were equally surprised.[18] None of them, it would seem, had noticed the additional glare and heat created by the high-powered bulbs with which someone had replaced the courtroom's ordinary socket lights. The cameras were ordered removed, but somehow the proceedings went on being secretly filmed under the high-powered photo lights.

— — —

After twenty-nine days of hearing testimony, the jury retired to consider a verdict. The prosecution's case had been circumstantial. No one had seen Hauptmann at the Lindbergh estate, and the witnesses who placed him near the area in the approximate time frame of the crime were highly questionable. No fingerprints had been found, and the one footprint the police had sketched wasn't introduced. No concrete evidence was offered as to where or exactly how the baby had died, but the state had maintained that the blow that inflicted death was intentional and that it was obvious the kidnapper never meant to take care of the child while negotiating for the ransom. There was no question that Hauptmann was in possession of ransom money. Jafsie Condon's testimony that Hauptmann was Cemetery John, the man to whom he paid the ransom, did not establish that Hauptmann either kidnapped or killed the baby. Albert D. Osborn, the handwriting expert who originally said Hauptmann had not written the ransom messages, was insistent that Hauptmann was the author of all the communications. A "wood expert" traced a piece of wood in the ladder to a board in the attic of Hauptmann's home. That essentially was the state's case.

There was a good deal of prosecution testimony that Reilly could have challenged, but he chose not to. On the occasion when he seemed to be on the verge of discrediting a state's witness, as in the case of Jafsie Condon, he suddenly had no more questions. His defense, all in all, was disorganized, and it often flagged. Instead of calling many credible witnesses who might have helped establish that his client was not in New Jersey the night of the kidnapping or at the cemetery when the money was passed, he put out a public call for new witnesses who could help save Hauptmann. He brought to the stand at least one tried-and-true professional witness he had used in the past. His biggest mistake may have been in allowing Hauptmann to testify. Bruno didn't fully comprehend the legal process but pretended he did. The defendant apparently believed that if he could show that his expenditures for the previous years had come from money he had earned, not from the ransom loot, he would be vindicated and the charges dropped. Wilentz conducted a withering cross-examination, pointed, and shouted accusations of "You killed the baby!" Death House Reilly's objections were few and usually tepid. To some in the gallery, he seemed indifferent to the bashing being suffered by his client.

An estimated seventy-five thousand to one hundred thousand people were visiting Flemington each day by the time the jury retired to consider a verdict.[19] Justice Trenchard ordered that everyone without an accredited seat be removed from the courthouse and that the doors be locked. The crowds outside began to chant for Hauptmann's death. The judge retired to his chambers, by all accounts to read. Activities in other parts of the building were less sedate. A noisy crap game got under way in the law library adjoining the courtroom. Media people, court stenographers, lawyers, law students using the library, and Broadway characters took their turn at the dice for stakes that ran as high as eight hundred dollars a roll. In the courtroom games of checkers and tic-tac-toe were being played. People wandered about with paper bags in their hands, munching sandwiches or cakes, drinking coffee, milk, beer, or applejack. The floor was littered with papers, cigarette stubs, and remnants of discarded food. Dave Wilentz sat in the jury box and quipped to reporters, "This is where I should have been in the first place."[20]

— — —

Death House Reilly luxuriated in the witness chair, reading a paper and smoking his cigar. At one point he good-humoredly burlesqued the testimony of state's witnesses for a group of reporters by shooting questions at himself, then cupping a hand to his ear and pretending he was too deaf to hear them. "What was that? What? Repeat the question?"[21] Overcome by a melodic impulse, Reilly and a lady reporter stood before the judge's banc and sang "When Irish Eyes Are Smiling." An alert was flashed that Justice Trenchard was on his way to the library. The crap game instantaneously broke up, and many of the gambling attorneys and law students began reading law books or briefs. Trenchard entered, recovered the volume he was after, and left with a quizzical smile on his face. The game resumed.

— — —

Many of the reporters waiting for a verdict across the street in Nellie's tap room at the Union Hotel were drinking hard and heavy and intermittently giving forth with raucous renditions of what they called their "schnitzel-bank song":

> *Ist das nicht ein ransom box?*
> *Ja, das ist ein ransom box.*
> *Ist das Fisch ein clever fox?*
> *Ja, Fisch ist ein clever fox.*
> *Ransom box?*
> *Clever fox!*

> *Ist das nicht ein dowel pin?*
> *Ja, das ist ein dowel pin.*
> *Fitted das not nicely in?*
> *Ja, it fitted nicely in.*
> *Dowel pin?*
> *Nicely in!*

Ist das nicht ein ransom note?
Ja, das ist ein ransom note.
Ist das nicht ein Nelly Boad?
Ja, das ist ein Nelly Boad.[22]

The reference to "Nelly Boad" was not the Union Hotel's Nellie's tap room, but the boat *Nelly* on which the final message from the kidnappers had said the baby could be found, safe and well.

At 10:00 P.M. word spread inside the courthouse that the jury had reached a verdict. The scramble into the trial room was accompanied by shouts and hysterical singing. Someone threw a stone that shattered a portico window. Suddenly the lights went off. Matches were lighted and the pandemonium continued. Inexplicably the lights were restored. Wilentz shouted to the state police, "Close and lock those doors. I want every man in this room seated. I want the noise stopped."[23] An AP reporter who had smuggled a shortwave radio inside in his briefcase flashed the wrong signal number to a wire-room operator, who interpreted it to mean that Hauptmann had been convicted and was sentenced to life imprisonment. AP relayed the false information across the country.[24]

At 10:28 P.M. the tiny bell in the courthouse steeple tolled, signifying that the jury was ready with its verdict. Crowds spilled out to join the throng already waiting on Main Street. As they stood jammed together and silent under the glare of newsreel-camera floodlights, the police fought to keep open the lane through which news messengers would leave the building.

At 10:29 P.M. Hauptmann was led into the courtroom, manacled to his guards. The jury entered and took its place at 10:30. Fourteen minutes later Justice Trenchard appeared. The defendant was ordered to stand and did, clutching the hand of one of his guards.[25]

The county clerk said, "Ladies and Gentlemen of the Jury, have you arrived at a verdict?"

"We have."

"Who shall speak for you?"

"The foreman."

"How say you, Mr. Foreman? Do you find the defendant guilty or not guilty?"[26]

"The foreman spoke in a whisper, 'Guilty.' There were shouts of approval and laughter, and applause. The foreman's hand fumbled in his pocket. His fingers shook as he brought out a folded piece of paper, which he had trouble opening. The clerk suggested he read in a louder voice and he did. 'We the jury, find the defendant, Bruno Richard Hauptmann, guilty of murder in the first degree.' "[27]

A first-degree murder verdict without a recommendation for life imprisonment meant an automatic penalty of death. The jury made no recommendation for life imprisonment.

Ed Reilly polled the jurors, and the court asked if the prosecution wished to make a motion for sentencing. David Wilentz, who had expected a much harder courtroom battle and possibly a more lenient verdict had to be reminded by the judge of the next step to be taken: "Do you wish to make a motion for sentence, Mr. Attorney General?" After a start Wilentz said he did, and Hauptmann was ordered to stand again.

"Bruno Richard Hauptmann, you have been convicted of murder in the first degree," said Justice Trenchard. "The sentence of the Court is that you suffer death at the time and place and in the manner provided by law."[28]

The time was in the coming month, Monday, March 18, 1935. The manner and place of death was the electric chair at Trenton State Prison.

Guards rushed the manacled prisoner out as clapping began in the jury room. A roar of cheers and applause was heard as word of the decision reached the crowd in front of the courthouse and was relayed on into the dining room and Nellie's tap room at the Union Hotel. Somewhat later two drunken reporters staggered out onto the hotel porch. One played the kazoo, and the other danced a jig to a familiar ditty:

Ist das nicht ein ransom note?
Ja, das ist ein ransom note.

Book Four

THE FORTY-FIRST
GOVERNOR

Prelude

BRUNO RICHARD HAUPTMANN WAS ON DEATH ROW AT TRENTON STATE Prison, and all the legal procedures were in play to keep him alive.

Not far away, at the New Jersey Statehouse, popular Harold G. Hoffman was the new governor of the state. Hoffman had no particular interest in the Hauptmann trial, which was in progress when he took office. Ellis Parker, debatably New Jersey's greatest county detective, remained certain that the baby was alive and in the possession of Paul Wendel. The governor placed great trust in Parker but refrained from getting involved with the Hauptmann affair—until, ostensibly, he ran into political trouble.

Harold Hoffman was a Republican in an age and land of Democrats. And those in charge of the kidnapping-murder trial—particularly the governor's long-time rival, David Wilentz, attorney general of the Garden State, who was acting as state's prosecutor—were Democrats. The hard-hitting Wilentz had failed to get Bruno Hauptmann to "thaw" or "crack"—to confess to the crime and name his accomplices. Made aware of the political advantages should he be the one who got Hauptmann to talk, the governor discreetly, if not clandestinely, interviewed Bruno on death row—and came to believe that the doomed prisoner was not implicated in the child's demise and probably had no part in the extortion plot. But what of the trial that convicted Hauptmann—the witnesses and the evidence? How much of this could have been altered? Tampered with?

Ultimately three things combined to get Hoffman involved in the Hauptmann case. His proposed tax legislation ran into trouble, his political base began to erode, and he was told the identity of the true killer of the Lindbergh baby. Which course of action he would follow and for what reason seemed dependent on the crisis of the moment—and for the combative Little Captain there was no end to reversals and cliff-hanging.

When it came to the Hauptmann matter, one thing was certain: Caution must rule the day—secrecy. And secretly he launched a reinvestigation into the kidnapping and trial.

For Charles Lindbergh a probe of the facts was unnerving, and assuming he had concocted the kidnapping-murder scenario, it could reveal the true happenings over the weekend of February 27, 1932. On learning of Harold Hoffman's investigation and the assertion that the case would be reopened, Lindbergh covertly fled the country, taking up exile with his family in England, tacitly blaming the governor for his disaffection.

Condemned and blocked at every turn, Harold Hoffman became nearly as unpopular as Hauptmann. When all else failed to establish Hauptmann's innocence, the governor issued a thirty-day reprieve from execution, and the heavens thundered with disapproval. The race was on to save Hauptmann. Funds were short, and the quality of his investigators second-rate. Harold Hoffman could not, and would not, give up. He was certain he had learned the secret of Sorrel Hill, that he knew who the actual killer was and Lindbergh's part in the cover-up. But was there time enough to prove it?

Why would a man as active as Harold Hoffman risk his entire political career on this issue? The scenario we are about to sketch provides virtually the only explanation.

22

HAROLD GILES
HOFFMAN

A DESCENDANT OF THE SCOTTISH SANDSTONE SCULPTOR JAMES CRAWFORD
Thoms and of the original Dutch colonizers of New Amsterdam, Harold
Giles Hoffman was born in South Amboy, New Jersey, on February 7,
1896. A fascination with journalism began in high school when he became a reporter for the *South Amboy Citizen* and an occasional stringer
for the *New York Times* and the *New Brunswick Daily Home News*.
After graduation he took a full-time job at the *Perth Amboy Evening
News,* where he quickly rose to assistant city editor and then sports editor. His career was terminated by a disagreement with the paper's owner,
one of many altercations and feuds that would mark his life.

With America's entry into World War I, Hoffman enlisted in a New
Jersey National Guard infantry company that became part of the American Expeditionary Force's Blue and Gray Division. He graduated third in
his class at officer's training school, saw action in the Meuse-Argonne
offensive, and at the age of twenty-one received a battlefield promotion
to captain. Returning home a war hero with the nickname Little Captain,

he became the treasurer for the South Amboy Trust Company and during the ensuing decade was vice-president of his own bank, president of the Hoffman-Lehar Real Estate Corporation, president of the Mid-State Title Guaranty and Mortgage Company, treasurer of the National Realty and Investment Corporation, and the director of the Investor Building and Loan Association. In 1919 he married Lillie May Moss, the daughter of a prominent South Amboy dentist.

A Republican, young Harold made his debut into elected politics in 1923, when he became Middlesex County's assemblyman. As a 1925 write-in candidate, he won the fall election for mayor of South Amboy. The following November he invaded a traditionally Democratic stronghold, New Jersey's Third District, and handily defeated the candidate for the U.S. House of Representatives. His congressional record was hardly stellar, but the Republican leader of New Jersey awarded him the powerful party chairmanship of the Middlesex County organization. In 1930 he was appointed to a four-year term as commissioner of New Jersey's Department of Motor Vehicles. It was a high-visibility position, which Hoffman wanted, and it paid ten thousand dollars per annum, which he needed. Controversy erupted when Harold refused to give up his seat in Congress. He finally did rebate his congressional salary, but he served out the balance of his elected term on Capitol Hill while simultaneously running the DMV.

As commissioner of the Department of Motor Vehicles, Hoffman had been provided with a statewide platform for showing off his rhetorical skills. It was on this circuit that he gained national attention as the spokesman for a new concept in America: highway safety. An indefatigable showman who loved a crowd, he also used these speaking engagements to campaign energetically for local and national Republican candidates, which obligated them to him. It paid off splendidly when he called in old debts to help win the governor's race.

A cuddlesome bear of a man and a snappy dresser who seldom could resist making a pun or playing a practical joke on a pal, Hal Hoffman was infectiously amiable and lucid, characteristics that made him a perfect ringmaster for the frequent galas given at New York's Waldorf-Astoria Hotel by the Circus, Saints and Sinners Association, a power club that boasted some of the most famous names in the land among its all-male membership and put on the Waldorf fetes to raise money for a retirement home for the circus performers it sponsored. The highest honor that an individual Saint and Sinner could receive came once a year at a roast-type initiation in which the inductee took to the stage and publicly made a fool of himself before being dubbed a Fall Guy. William Randolph Hearst, Frank Buck, Robert Ripley, Eddie Rickenbacker, Mayor Fiorello La Guardia, Rudy Vallee, and Gene Tunney were among the elite group that made Fall Guys. A CS&S bash wasn't something the press could overlook. Most of the media liked Hoffman.

Harold Hoffman's gubernatorial win proved particularly humiliating for Frank Hague, mayor of Jersey City and head of the powerful Hudson County Democratic machine. A record-breaking number of Americans to vote in an off-year election voiced their approval of President Franklin D. Roosevelt's New Deal policies and provided an overwhelming victory for Democratic candidates. In New Jersey's Senate race, ex-governor A. Harry Moore easily defeated the incumbent Republican. But Moore's former governorship had been filched from the pocket of the Democratic machine by an ebullient GOP charm merchant. Media speculation that Hague's power and influence were in a state of permanent remission was immediate.

Adding insult to injury for local Democrats was not only that Hoffman had been one of the rare Republicans to win a significant contest in America this election but that the popularity of the ubiquitous governor-elect continued to soar. Hoffman seemed to be everywhere at once, talking, gibing, glad-handing, and being feted, photographed, and interviewed. National magazines and radio made him into a major political figure, a GOP golden boy who stood a chance of being his party's standard-bearer in the coming presidential election. The Democratic National Committee was concerned, but as the trial of Bruno Richard Hauptmann grew closer, New Jersey's party leaders thought they might possibly have the person to counteract the high-riding governor-elect, a man who had once bested Harold Hoffman in an election: Attorney General Wilentz.

Thirty-nine-year-old David Theodore Wilentz was a long-time friend and rival of Harold Hoffman. Both men had grown up in the Amboys area and knew one another since boyhood. Both had been reporters for the *Perth Amboy Evening News,* and when Hoffman left as the paper's sports editor, Wilentz had replaced him. Hoffman had been manager of a local basketball team, and when he quit, Wilentz had taken over. They had both served in the army during World War I: Hoffman reached the rank of captain; Wilentz, the rank of lieutenant. Both men entered politics at approximately the same time. Wilentz was elected chairman of the Middlesex County Democratic party and carried the county for the first time in ten years. The chairman of the vanquished Middlesex Republican party was Harold Hoffman, suffering the first defeat in his political career. During the 1934 state election Wilentz helped his old friend and adversary Harold Hoffman in his bid for the governorship.

Hoffman and Wilentz were both married and fathers; the governor had three young daughters; the attorney general, two sons. Each man was extremely ambitious. In appearance, style, and public appeal they were strikingly different: Hoffman was a short, round-faced, big-bodied man who had a tendency to overeat. His attire, though tasteful, was usually casual. He was enormously outgoing and likable and quick to laugh. He made friends easily and kept them. David Wilentz was small, slim, and swarthy—and looked a little like John Cassavetes. His dress was on the flashy side: tight, Broadway-style double-breasted suits, a white silk scarf, a velvet-collared chesterfield overcoat, and an off-white felt hat worn at an angle. He was a serious, shut-off type of fellow who, though quick-witted, had trouble smiling and disliked perfunctory conversation. Wilentz trained like an athlete, was in excellent physical condition, and lived a religious and disciplined life.

Governor Harold Hoffman was not unaware of the Lindbergh trial. Ellis Parker, an old friend, was among those who kept him posted. And Ellis didn't give a hoot what Dave Wilentz and the Democrats were saying; Hauptmann had nothing to do with the kidnapping, and the child probably wasn't dead.

Ellis Parker, Sr., was county detective of Burlington County. Skeptical that the baby in the woods was Charles Lindbergh, Jr., he had a pretty good fix on where the Eaglet was and how to have the child returned to his parents. Right or wrong, Parker's involvement in the affair would have long-term and dire consequences for himself, H. Norman Schwarzkopf, and the new governor of New Jersey, Harold Hoffman.

The Old Chief, as Ellis Parker, Sr., was known, came from an era in which most towns and rural villages in the state of New Jersey, whether they had a constable or not, relied on the county detective in matters of serious crime. No one had fared better under the system than Ellis. During forty years of service, he had solved hundreds of cases and gained a national reputation as New Jersey's premier detective. The Old Chief was also in the forefront of those who had opposed the formation of a state-police organization and was one of the earliest to complain of its inefficiency after the first troopers took to the roads in December of 1921. He relished the difficulty the troopers—or anyone, for that matter—had in coping with New Jersey's thriving bootlegging industry. Parker did amazingly well intercepting shipments of illicit whiskey and tracking down remote distilleries, an achievement he attributed to his ability to develop underworld informants. The Old Chief's critics suggested that he himself was a bootlegger who was putting the competition out of business.

Parker and Schwarzkopf had been antagonists for as long as most people could remember. Each did what he could to discredit and embarrass the other. Parker, who was good with the press, had a distinct advantage in this department—and with choosing assignments. Parker refused an invitation to get involved with the infamous Hall-Mills murders of 1922, a case in which Schwarzkopf and his troopers were ordered to participate. Hall-Mills went unsolved, becoming an albatross for investigators who were part of it.

In 1932, with the ghosts of Hall-Mills barely a decade old, H. Norman Schwarzkopf assumed nominal control of the Lindbergh kidnapping investigation. At the onset no lessons seemed to have been learned from the Hall-Mills incident. As with Hall-Mills, the scene of the crime was not preserved, and vital physical evidence, such as footprints, were destroyed. Once again reporters were allowed to roam the area of the crime and talk to almost anyone they wanted other than the Lindberghs and the household staff—until Schwarzkopf's men overreacted in evicting them from the grounds of Sorrel Hill and, as best they could, isolating them from the facts. As blunder followed blunder in the Lindbergh disappearance, H. Norman again appeared not to know how to respond when he came under fire from the press. The Hall-Mills killings still ranked as one of the most bungled investigations in modern history—but the New Jersey State Police, for some obscure reason, seemed to take pride in being involved with the case.

— — —

Ellis Parker very much wanted to be included in the state's official investigation of the Lindbergh snatch. On March 11, ten days after the child disappeared, George M. Hillman, a Democratic committeeman from the Old Chief's home county, wrote to Governor A. Harry Moore's secretary, suggesting that it might be to the governor's advantage to get in touch with Parker. Moore did just that in a letter dated March 13, 1932. While encouraging the Old Chief to work on the "Lindbergh matter," as he assumed Parker was doing, the governor failed to invite him to join the manhunt officially. Parker profusely thanked the governor for his letter and pledged to do what he could in the matter.[1] He did pursue the case on his own, only to be denied requested information by H. Norman Schwarzkopf. Not long after, he took over then-commissioner Harold Hoffman's investigation of the crime on behalf of the Motor Vehicle department. Like that of Parker, the destiny of Hoffman was to be intrinsically linked to that of H. Norman Schwarzkopf and the Lindbergh case.

In 1932, the commissioner of New Jersey's Department of Motor Vehicles, Harold Hoffman, was outraged that the state's number-one family had been victimized. The thirty-six-year-old war hero was a man in a hurry. His position as head of the Motor Vehicles department provided a power base in an already-promising political career known for brash and dramatic moves. Tracking down the infant's abductors excited the adventure-craving Bulldog Drummond–aspect of his character, but competition and politics came first. Nothing could have better suited Hoffman, a Republican, than coming up with the Lindbergh baby before anyone else did, especially the state-police boss, H. Norman Schwarzkopf, who had been installed in his position by a Democrat.

One perk available to a New Jersey motor vehicle boss, which few of Hoffman's predecessors had taken full advantage of, was having a small but private investigatory force available. Automobiles were a new phenomenon. Even newer were the ordinances regarding their use. The department's team of inspectors usually concentrated on investigating auto-related crimes, such as theft, but the events of March 1, 1932, saw Harold Hoffman broaden those parameters.

In the wake of the Eaglet's disappearance, the DMV erected roadblocks throughout New Jersey, inspected cars and trucks, and put traces on all out-of-state license plates. A file search was initiated that provided the state police with lists of license plate numbers of missing or stolen cars. The troopers readily accepted the information but displayed a cavalier indifference to helpful hints from the Motor Vehicle boys. This was fine with Commissioner Harold Hoffman, who hadn't bothered to check with Superintendent H. Norman Schwarzkopf before expanding his investigation of auto thieves to include other criminals.

Harold Hoffman rather liked Schwarzkopf, but he did think the West Point graduate would be better served shaving off his Charlie Chaplin mustache. H. Norman hadn't appreciated the grooming hint. Hoffman hadn't relished what he considered the high-handed manner in which he and his personnel were being treated by the state police and their boss during the early stages of the Lindbergh crime. Nor was Hoffman blind to the vote-getting potential should he, the commissioner of motor vehicles, rather than the superintendent of the state police, capture the kidnappers. Harold was a team player as long as it was his team. What better man to add to your manhunt roster than New Jersey's greatest detective? Ellis Parker, his services snubbed by Governor Moore and H. Norman Schwarzkopf, accepted the commissioner's offer and joined Motor Vehicle's investigation. Hoffman assigned his most trusted aide to assist the Old Chief, Inspector Gustave ("Gus") Lockwood, who the state police claimed was the governor's part-time driver.

- - -

Installed with the DMV's inquiry, Ellis Parker wasted little time putting out feelers to various underworld contacts, particularly in the area of the Lindbergh estate. The ominous Sourland Mountain provided a safe haven for the area's moonshine and bootlegging industries, not to mention an ample variety of other nefarious pursuits. No one knew the individual criminals involved in these activities better than Ellis, whose favorite tactic was to infiltrate illicit societies with a network of well-placed informants. One of his earliest contacts on behalf of Harold Hoffman's department was Sam Cucchiara, owner of the Hopewell barbershop, who arranged for Gus Lockwood to buy a stolen car from one Caspar Oliver.

The Oliver farm was on Rocky Hill Road in Blawenburg, only two miles from the Lindbergh estate. Auto parts littered the ground. Lockwood, posing as a gangster, was grilled by the craggy Caspar. Satisfied that Gus was a genuine illicit article, he agreed to sell him a 1929 Buick sedan. When and where Gus could take delivery was vague. Oliver, believed to have served ten years in Sing Sing, was suspected of working as a henchman for a Brooklyn bootlegger called Liddle, who had connections with Chicago's Capone mob. Groups of men from New York often gathered at the Oliver farm, and on one occasion over the summer as many as forty had arrived in a bus. There was more. At 4:00 P.M. March 1, an auburn sedan with New York license plates and three men inside had been seen at Oliver's farmhouse. The shades were pulled down at 7:00 P.M. and had remained down until March 4.[2]

On Wednesday, March 16, after several days of waiting, Gus Lockwood had been shown where the car he wanted to purchase was being kept: in Oliver's barn—under a ton of hay. On March 19, a strike force from the DMV swept down on the farm and barn. Caspar took to the woods, where he was found hiding. The car under the hay was not connected to the Lindbergh kidnapping case, but it led to a protracted investigation of an auto-theft ring that had been operating in the area.

Ellis Parker was a past master at public relations and dealing with the media. Harold Hoffman was even better at it than Parker. The commissioner wasn't sure exactly what political office he would be running for next, but he knew that good press never hurt. On March 20, 1932, to the surprise of H. Norman Schwarzkopf and the state police, the *Trenton Evening Times* reproduced a photograph of the automobile concealed under the ton of hay only two miles from the Lindbergh estate. Also included was an insert picture of Caspar Oliver. The caption gave Inspector Gus Lockwood sole credit for the discovery. The story and pictures had been supplied by the Associated Press, but Harold Hoffman was also in direct contact with many newspapers regarding the progress of his department's search, including the *New York Sun*. So was the greatest detective in New Jersey.

— — —

Nearly three years later, on January 15, 1935, while standing outdoors on a snow-swept platform, making his inaugural address before a chilly crowd of seven thousand, the newly sworn-in governor of New Jersey, Harold Giles Hoffman, suggested a 2-percent excise tax to help the depression-racked state. He was in immediate, and big, political trouble. Taxes were anathema to Jerseyites—they had brought down politicians more unbeatable than this governor of less than a day.

— — —

Politics in New Jersey, Chicago mayor Big Bill Thompson once said, is like being a whore with bad eyesight: You're never sure who you're in bed with. Boss Frank Hague provided proof that Big Bill was prescient. Hague, a pro-tax advocate, immediately began to rally support against the governor's impending tax bill. In this he found himself in bed with a majority of the state's old guard Republican leaders.

The Little Captain had a reputation for bold strokes when confronted by crisis. Cutting a deal with boss Frank Hague and the Democrats to get his tax bill passed in June of 1935 was an example of this. But the wildfire objections to the law, particularly among his fellow GOP pols, was something he had not expected, nor was it something he seemed to know how to cope with. Old political allies abandoned him. Other sources of support eroded.

On October 9, 1935, Bruno Richard Hauptmann's appeal was turned down by the New Jersey Court of Errors and Appeals. The following day, during a special session of the New Jersey State Legislature, the assembly voted fifty to three, and the senate ten to zero, for repeal of the governor's four-month-old sales tax law. Harold Hoffman had suffered the greatest defeat of his political career.

Governor Hoffman desperately needed to reestablish his popularity and political power base. But dare he try another bold stroke? He had come a cropper with the last one, and this had contributed to his being in the mess he was in. Did another potential grand design even exist? Was it the Lindbergh-Hauptmann case? Possibly. With local GOP pols viewing the Hauptmann trial as a political defeat, what could be bolder than proving that Wilentz and the Democrats had convicted the wrong man? This was a perilous path to travel. The public and the media overwhelmingly wanted Bruno Richard Hauptmann electrocuted and the Lindbergh affair done with. The governor was on record as saying that he trusted David Wilentz and believed the Flemington jury had rendered a fair and considered verdict. Whatever was to be done in this direction must be done with discretion.

In early October, Colonel Mark O. Kimberling, principal keeper of the New Jersey state prisons, had come to the governor with a private and fateful message. Kimberling was a founding member of the New Jersey State Police and a political ally of Hoffman's. The word he brought was that Bruno Richard Hauptmann wanted to see the governor. Hoffman, plagued by continuing mass political defections and a hostile press and fighting tooth and nail to save his doomed tax law, ignored Hauptmann's request.

During the trial it had been hoped, if not expected, that the defendant would "crack" or "thaw" under prosecuting attorney David Wilentz's searing cross-examination and admit to the crime and reveal his accomplices. But the dour German carpenter had stuck to his alibi and conceded nothing. Now, in mid-October, reconsidering the condemned man's request for an interview and speculating that Hauptmann might have "thawed," the benefits of receiving Bruno's confession took on new dimensions for a governor desperately in need of a little bit of magic.

23

BOLD STROKES AND
BRUNO

HAD HAROLD HOFFMAN ARRANGED FOR THE SECRET MEETING IN A LESS IM-
petuous fashion and gone to see the prisoner alone, the political hurri-
cane that was to follow might have been avoided. He did neither. The
governor was by legislation a member of the court of pardons, the jury of
last resort should all Hauptmann's appeals be rejected, as appeared
would be the situation. There was a precedent for individual court members' visiting condemned men, but not in the dead of night, timing that
gave the impression of secrecy, or under circumstances that might be
considered capricious.

According to Hoffman, the opportunity to see Hauptmann arose on
October 16, 1935.[1] "My recollection is that there had been a last minute
cancellation of an evening engagement," he stated.

> I know that it was not until after dinner on that evening
> that I thought of visiting Hauptmann that night.
> From my suite in the Hotel Hildebrecht I called Colonel

Kimberling. "Mark," I said, "I'm coming down to see that fellow. Will tonight be O.K.?" Mark Kimberling answered in the affirmative.

I had been given to understand that Hauptmann could not express himself very well in English, and I thought I might need an interpreter. And of course I figured I might need a stenographer, particularly if he wanted to make a confession. My first thought therefore had been of Mrs. Bading. She was an expert stenographer, spoke German fluently and could be depended upon to maintain the confidence that I thought essential to my plan."

Mrs. Bading was Anna Bading, Ellis Parker's longtime secretary and sometime investigator, on whom a local chapter of the Eastern Star organization had conferred the honor of Worthy Matron. When she received the governor's call on the night of October 16, saying to meet him within the hour at Mark Kimberling's residence adjoining the state prison, she had been in Mount Holly, New Jersey, at another Eastern Star function. Stopping only long enough to grab a steno pad and several sharp pencils, Mrs. Bading reached Kimberling's residence still in her party garb: an evening gown and silk slippers. Told she was to accompany Kimberling and Hoffman to death row to an interview with Bruno Richard Hauptmann, she protested, " 'Governor, I simply can't go in there dressed like this.' " Mark Kimberling gave her one of his overcoats, which she put on.

Kimberling drove Bading and the governor around to the Third Street gate of the prison, where he had posted Deputy Warden George Selby, a World War I lieutenant colonel who had served overseas with Hoffman's 114th Infantry Regiment. Once through the gate, they turned to the right and followed a prison guard to the death house. As the door opened, the guard's flashlight picked up the muslin-covered electric chair.

Bading took a seat on a small bench near the white-shrouded chair and waited, should she be needed inside to take dictation and translate. On Kimberling's order the iron door separating the death chamber and death row was opened. He ushered Governor Hoffman through. A quick turn to the right, and they were standing before the bars of cell 9. " 'Richard,' " Kimberling said softly to the occupant, " 'the Governor to see you.' "

A guard unlocked and opened the metal door. Harold Hoffman entered. The door was shut and locked behind him, with Kimberling saying from outside, " 'Call me, Governor, if you want me.' " Then he walked down the corridor and joined the guard.

The most hated man in the world wore a blue-gray shirt open at the neck and dark prison trousers. The governor told him to sit down on his cot, and he did. A pitcher and basin rested on a stand nearby. There was a table in the cell that was covered with papers and books—a Bible, several works of philosophy and astronomy, and the transcripts of the trial. Also on the table was a photograph of the prisoner's wife and young son, Manfried. Fifteen feet away, on the other side of the cell's wall, stood the electric chair.

A New Jersey governor could temporarily stay an execution but did not have the power to commute a death sentence. The only power that could do that at this stage was New Jersey's court of appeals, of which the governor was the president.

"I sat down beside him," Harold Hoffman explained, "I said something, just what I don't recall, designed to put him at ease; but I did not then, or at any time during my visit, promise him aid or make any expression of sympathy or belief in his statement to me."

Jafsie Condon and John Hughes Curtis had each used an ersatz German accent in relating to the media what their respective Johns had said to them during ransom negotiations. When later writing of his visit to Bruno Richard Hauptmann on death row, Governor Hoffman utilized the same technique.

" 'Governor, vy does your state do to me all this?' " he reported that the condemned man asked him in cell 9. " 'Vy do they vant my life for something somebody else have done?' "

Replied the governor, " 'Well, you have been found guilty. The courts—' "

" 'Lies! Lies!' " Hauptmann pointed to one of the trial records. " 'All lies! Vould I kill a baby? I am a man. Vould I built that ladder? I am a carpenter.' "

Hauptmann's most "earnest plea" had been to take a lie detector test. " 'Vy vont they use on me that? And on Doctor Condon also use it? They haf too some kind of drug, I haf heard. Vy don't they use on me that drug? And on Doctor Condon use it too?' "

Harold Hoffman was now certain that Hauptmann hadn't thawed, that he would not be confessing. "Here was no cringing criminal pitifully begging for mercy," the governor wrote, "but a man making a vehement claim of innocence, bitter in his denunciation of the police and of the prosecution and their methods." And bitter, too, in his excoriation of his former chief counsel, Death House Reilly.

" 'Could a man do for dollars vat Reilly haf don to me?' " Hauptmann asked. " 'Only once, for about five minutes, did I haf a chance to explain my case to him, really. Sometimes he came to see me, not often, for a few minutes. How could I then talk to him?' "

Hauptmann's complaints against the police began with his footprints, which apparently didn't match the one found under the nursery window or the one found at the graveyard where the ransom was paid.

"Vy do they take from me all my shoes? When I was arrested they took from me, among many things, my shoes. Vot for I could not imagine, but now I have found out. Because they have a footprint—a footprint of a man, who according to the prosecutor, climbed the ladder to get the unfortunate child. . . . Vy did they not produce at the trial the impression of which they cast a model? Vy? They cannot say that my foot has become larger or smaller—

"So too the footprint which was found in the graveyard from where Doctor Condon swore that he gave to John fifty thousand dollars. Also here my shoe certainly did not fit. Vy did they not produce here the plaster model that they made?"

Following his meeting with Cemetery John, Jafsie Condon also made a phonograph recording of the conversation, which was widely reported in the press but was not entered in evidence by the prosecution and which the state police in one instance denied existed. " 'Does any one think that these footprints and this record have been held back out of pity for me? Oh no. For me, not pity!' "

As for fingerprints,

"Is it not true that in every case when a person is arrested they take his fingerprints? So they did vith me [at the NYPD station house in Greenwich Village]. A few days after, two New Jersey state police came to me in a Bronx prison and vanted further prints. I told them these had already been taken. These men replied the ones they took haf not been clear enough, so they take firmly about six sets. Then one or two days later they come again with the statement that still there are several spots not plain enough. So they took more—and also the sides of my hands, which they did not take before, and then especially the joints of the fingers and the hollow parts of my hand. . . . Then at the trial, when my counsel asks about fingerprints the prosecutor say simply, 'There are no fingerprints.' If that is so, no fingerprints on the ladder, on the letters, on the window sill, in the room, vy they want so many times my fingerprints? I can only think they haf fingerprints, but they are not like mine, so they say they haf none. . . .

"But they invent another story. They say I haf worked vith gloves. Is this not a worthless lie? Because since in that room they found no other fingerprints—not of the parents, or the child's nurse or the other servants—can't this statement be possible? It is even said that Mrs. Lindbergh and the nurse Betty together pulled down the window which was stuck, but there are no fingerprints found on the window frame. Do the parents, then, ven they go to the room to take joy in their child, and all the servants, also wear gloves?"

Hauptmann focused on Dr. Erastus Mead Hudson, whose silver nitrate processing of the ladder had developed many usable latent prints. " 'But, there were nowhere any of mine. The jury would not believe this expert because he would not say anything to convict me.' "

Governor Hoffman subsequently learned that not only had fingerprints been recovered by Dr. Hudson, but photographs had been taken of them, the negatives of which had been held in the possession of the state police. J. Edgar Hoover would inform the governor that the New Jersey State Police never sent copies of the photographs to the DI's fingerprint identification center, the most extensive and authoritative file of this sort in the land.

Regarding the prosecution's attempt to link the chisel found near the ladder the night of the kidnapping to the tool kit discovered in Hauptmann's garage two and a half years later, Hauptmann said this:

"Among my carpenter's tools they found a chisel which looks in part like the one found at the Lindbergh place near the ladder. That my chisel is ground differently, is a different size, and has quite a different handle, made no difference. They simply said, 'No, this is Hauptmann's chisel,' and the jury believed them. They do not believe when I say that my chisel set is an entirely different one from the one they found. For my set was a Stanley set, one

fourth inch to one and one half inch. They must haf taken
out some sizes and put among them others like the one they
found, except the three-quarter inch chisel. For the one they
found is a Bucks Brothers chisel."

The governor would discover that the factory that manufactured the
chisel found at the Lindbergh estate had estimated the instrument had
been made thirty years before. He would also become convinced that the
chisel was not Hauptmann's and that documents had been altered in
order to give the appearance that it was.

An accusation had been made that the prosecution withheld Hauptmann's correspondence with Isador Fisch, the man who the defendant
still insisted had given him the shoe box containing some fourteen thousand dollars in ransom money. " 'So all of these letters—I think six or
seven—I have saved and put in a large envelope in my desk from which
the police took them.' " Hauptmann had risen from the cot and picked
out a volume of the Flemington transcript.

> "But when we ask for these letters at the trial I receive
> the answer, 'Ve haf none.' God in heavens! All the letters
> vere together. One of the letters I never could get clear, for
> it said that shortly before Isador died he called for me and
> seemed to want to say something about me. But he was too
> weak or did not vant to. So he took to his grave that vich
> would be of great help to me now. . . .
>
> "Vye did Vilentz say that he did not have these letters,
> when my letters answering them were there? No, those
> letters did not fit the state viewpoint, so they had to
> disappear. But they took precautions and had the Fisch
> family and the nurse [who attended Isador at his death]
> come to America. They surely expected that I would insist
> more on these letters and say what vas in them. But ven I
> could recall only in parts the contents and the jury vould
> not haf believed me, I was obliged to say nothing. For if I
> told vat I had remembered, vould not the Fisch family, who
> vere paid for coming here, haf said the opposite upon the
> suggestion of the prosecutor?
>
> "For vat else was the family brought here? So Pincus
> Fisch [i.e., Isador's brother] vas not called to the stand, and
> so, too, the nurse vas not called. Thus all direct evidence
> vich might haf freed me disappeared."

Harold Hoffman would soon gain possession of copies of the letters referred to by Hauptmann, including a pencil draft of Pincus Fisch's correspondence, which corroborated that Isador, on his deathbed, kept calling for Hauptmann and "wanting to tell us something" about him.

Harold Hoffman had been skeptical that Isador Fisch would have left some fourteen thousand dollars of ransom money in Hauptmann's custody and that Hauptmann wouldn't have ascertained until after Fisch's death in Leipzig that the package contained currency. The condemned man addressed the subject in a protracted recounting of his relationship with Isador, which ended with the question, " 'Could I haf known dot the money vas the Lindbergh baby money? No! How could any sensible person think dot?' "

Harold Hoffman had considered himself a sensible man and seemed to find credence in the prisoner's accounting, as well as in his denial of having told Walter Lyle that he had about a hundred gold notes left. " 'For vas it not testified at the trial, and truly so, dot to the gasoline station man I haf said, vhen I gave him the bill, "I have a hundred more like dot"? Vould I say dot if I knew dese bills maybe could take my life some day?' "

Hauptmann had talked rapidly and without excitement about the circumstances of his arrest. He admitted he had lied about the additional money in the garage, not because it was ransom money, which he didn't know, but because he feared he would get into trouble if they knew he had so many gold certificates on hand. " 'Besides,' " he added, " 'near the money I haf hidden also a pistol vich I know I am not suppose to have.' "

He had told of a beating he received in a New York City police station:

> "I vas handcuffed in the chair and the police give me such a terrible licking dot I fall downvard to the floor. Dey showed me a hammer and den dey put out the lights and started to beat me on the shoulders, the back of the head, and the arm. Den, too, dey kicked my legs with the feet and kept yelling, 'Where is the money? Vhere is the baby? Ve'll knock your brains out!' "

The governor subsequently obtained a copy of the oral and physical examination Dr. Thurston H. Dexter made of Hauptmann in the presence of James M. Fawcett and Louis L. Lefkowitz, the assistant medical examiner. It was dated September 25, several days after the alleged third degree. After detailing bruises, lumps, swellings, and discolorations, Dr. Dexter concluded that Hauptmann, " 'had been subjected recently to a severe beating, all or mostly with blunt instruments. The injuries resulting from this are general and include the head, back, chest, abdomen and thighs.' "

The ladder had come up, along with the so-called wood expert.

> "Listen, Vilentz says I am smart criminal. He says on dese hands I must haf vorn gloves, because dere are not fingerprints. He says on dese feet I must haf vorn bags, because dere are no footprints. If I was a smart criminal, if I vould do all dose things, vy vould I got in my own house and take up half one board to use for one piece of the ladder—something dot always would be evidence against me?"

Governor Hoffman found logic in Hauptmann's argument and would later come across information that made him gravely distrust the wood expert's findings. There was a matter of location, the fact that Hauptmann and Jafsie Condon, who lived within a few miles of one another, were both regular visitors to City Island, a local recreational area. Condon, according to Hauptmann, had a real estate office there. To get to it, he had to pass the Dixon Boat House, where Bruno kept his canoe. Condon continued to pass the boathouse throughout the summers of 1932, 1933, and 1934, a time when he and the police were hunting for John.

> "How could anybody believe dot vhen Doctor Condon vas looking as he says all over the country for 'John,' who he now says is me, vidout coming face to face vith me. Condon says dot he could identify 'John' vhen 'John' vas valking along a street and he vas on the top of a bus, yet on City Island, nearly every day he vould not see me and pick me out as 'John.'
>
> "If I vas the kidnapper and I got the money from Condon, vould not I know, too, dot the Doctor vas in City Island many, many times? And vould not I have stayed away from City Island because I vould haf been afraid of being identified by Condon?
>
> "The man who vas talking vith Doctor Condon at Voodlawn Cemetery vas said by him to veigh between 155

to 160 pounds: for did not the Doctor say he could tell, and he felt the arms of 'John'? But my veight at about that time vas 175 pounds—it shows so on my automobile license."

Hauptmann had appeared confused by Jafsie's activities, including the visit paid him by the aging educator when he was being held at the Hunterdon County jail pending his trial.

"Doctor Condon vas vith me on a bench in the cell and vas asking me if haf any athletic training. I said yes. Den he asked me if I haf von any prizes, and I told him sixteen or seventeen in Germany for running and jumping. Den it looked like he was going to cry. He took a piece of paper and marked it in four parts and said he divided the case in four parts. Von part he said vas the baby, and in another part he made a little house vith a bench. He called me 'John' many times. He pointed to the first square and said, 'Dot is the baby—dot come first.' Den he pointed to the second space and said, 'Dot is the man I spoke vith—the go-between.' I asked him vhat was a go-between and he explained. . . .

"He said if I know anything I should confess, because there vas no connection between the money and the kidnapping and I vould clear myself and himself. He said the police vere treating him roughly. But he never said I am the fellow—and vhen he left he asked could he come see me again, and I said 'yes.' "

Bruno swore to the governor that he had never written Dr. Condon's phone number in his closet and suggested that perhaps a policeman or reporter had put it there. He also objected to the jury's having believed Cecile Barr rather than the defense witnesses who testified he was home celebrating his birthday at the time she said he bought a movie ticket with ransom money in Greenwich Village.

"Den dere is the old man, Hochmuth, eighty years old and more, who says he sees me go by his house at Hopewell in a green car vith very red face and eyes like a ghost looking out of the automobile vindow. Dis man can hardly see. He admits on the vitness stand dot the police haf him in the jail at Flemington looking at me in the cell for over half an hour, but he says he could not see me—only a figure—and further dot he untruthfully said he live in New York vhen he really lived in New Jersey so he could get money for relief. Yet my vitnesses are not believed—the five people who saw me in New York in the bakery vith Annie at the time dot the crime was committed. . . ."

Harold Hoffman would obtain New York City Public Welfare documents showing that at the approximate time in 1932 Hochmuth said he saw Hauptmann in the area of the Lindbergh estate, Hochmuth was "partly blind" and had "failing eyesight due to cataracts."

The governor had been anxious to end the interview, but Hauptmann was reluctant to let him.

"Vy don't the police keep on looking for the man Faulkner who deposit nearly $3000 of the Colonel's money? . . .

"Vy is it just von—me—dey vant to get for the death of the poor child? . . . Vy do dey believe the fairy tale about the support from the child's sleeping garment [thumb guard] by the nurse Betty Gow and the housekeeper a month after the crime, right vhere it vould haf been seen so many times by hundreds of people? . . . Vye do they try to prove I haf had and spent $50,000 vhen only maybe $15,000 has been found?"

The governor ended the interview and called for Mark Kimberling, who came down the corridor and unlocked the door of cell 9. " 'Vot harm could I do anybody behind dese bars?' " asked Hauptmann. " 'Vhen dey kill me dey kill an innocent man. But I know—dey think vhen I die, the case vill die. Dey think it vill be like a book I close.' "

The governor stepped into the corridor and heard the cage key click in the lock behind him. Within a few steps he was at the steel door to the death chamber, and he looked back at the pale face behind the bars of cell 9. " 'Good night, Governor—and thank you for coming.' "

Harold Hoffman said goodnight back, entered the electrocution chamber, and told a waiting Mrs. Bading, "Come along, Anna—it's over."

The governor returned to his rooms at the Hotel Hildebrecht and wrote far into the night and early morning, recounting what Hauptmann had said. He had very few answers to the questions posed by the prisoner and in many instances wasn't sure to what the German was referring. "An atrocious crime had been committed," he stated. "Justice, to my mind, was not to be found merely in the execution of a single convicted criminal.

"There had been a crime that must never recur; a case that must never be repeated; a challenge that must, in the interest of society, be effectively met.

"My duty it seemed, was clear."[2]

The next day, October 17, Governor Harold Hoffman had a copy of the eleven-volume trial transcript sent to him; then he traveled to New York City for a busy day of appointments. Early in the evening he talked with a member of the May 1932 Bronx County grand jury and got a firsthand account of possible evidence tampering by police and elected officials.

After the baby had been found in the woods, the Bronx grand jury had conducted an investigation into the death and surrounding circumstances, including the participation of a local resident many police officials looked on with grave suspicions, John F. ("Jafsie") Condon. When called before the panel, Jafsie had spent a goodly portion of his time at a blackboard, drawing symbols such as Indian "high" signs and secret Italian Trigamba and simultaneously lecturing his listeners on them. The juror the governor spoke with saw no relevance in this and had said to Condon, "What we are interested in, Doctor, is a description of the man to whom you paid the $50,000.00."

"I am not sure," Jafsie had snapped back. "His hat was pulled down and his coat collar was turned over his face."

The juror now told Governor Hoffman that later in the inquiry Condon had given a partial description. "I remember him [i.e., Condon] saying that his eyes were 'separated a little from the bridge of his nose, such as a Chinese or Japanese, and they were almond shaped and bluish gray in color.' "[3]

The juror-informant further related that subsequent to Hauptmann's conviction in Flemington, he'd gone back to the Bronx district attorney and asked to read the record. It was given to him, but he could find no reference to the Chinese-eyes description. The informant allowed that in the excitement of the examination, Condon's remark might have gone unrecorded.

Two days later, on October 19, Bruno Richard Hauptmann, who had been in jail thirteen months, was granted a stay of execution so his attorney could appeal to the U.S. Supreme Court.

Governor Harold Hoffman received a surprise phone call from Washington, D.C., which served as a tacit reminder that there were political benefits of a national dimension for himself and the Republican party should he prove that the condemned man was innocent. On the line was Charles Curtis, the vice-president of the United States under Herbert Hoover and still a rallying point for a small, influential group of GOP national leaders. Curtis and Hoffman had known each other slightly when the governor served in the House of Representatives. Then as now Harold Hoffman was flattered to be singled out by the former vice-president.

Curtis, in his unsolicited call, asked if the governor had been looking into the Hauptmann case. Hoffman took on a noncommittal stance and said he hadn't been especially interested.

> "I mentioned, I think, that Hauptmann had been convicted and the conviction sustained by the Court of Errors and Appeals, but that the matter would shortly be before the Court of Pardons, of which I was a member.
>
> " 'I think,' said Mr. Curtis, 'that there are a lot of funny things about that case.' He went on to tell me some of the doubts he entertained and he expressed the opinion that, as governor, I should go carefully into the matter before Hauptmann's final appeal for life was made. 'I've read a lot of the testimony,' he added, 'and it doesn't seem to me that he was adequately represented—or that he got a very fair deal.' He closed with a request that I 'see Mrs. McLean.' "[4]

Mrs. Evalyn Walsh McLean, the gadfly Washington, D.C., hostess who had given Gaston B. Means a hundred and four thousand dollars with which to secure the return of the Lindbergh baby, wasn't satisfied with the Hauptmann trial. One of the things she did about this was hire her own private detective to pursue the truth. Another had occurred at a dinner party for some forty or fifty people at her elegant Washington home, Friendship.

After dinner, eight or ten of the older, more important men were standing in one corner of the room. I asked them if they were fully satisfied over Bruno's conviction. Some said they thought he was "in on it," but they one and all agreed that it could not have been a one man job.

I told them I was very worried about it, and if and when the supreme court turned down the appeal I planned to go see Governor Hoffman and tell him everything I had picked up.

They all laughed at me and said: "Why Evalyn, you are crazy. Governor Hoffman is too smart a politician to touch this with a ten foot pole. He knows only too well it would ruin him if he did."

I grabbed the phone for Charlie Curtis and asked him to get in touch with the governor to learn when I could go up and see him at the end of the week. Charlie called back and said the governor would be down the next day to see me at eleven o'clock.

At eleven the next morning a taxicab drew up at Friendship and I went downstairs to meet a quiet, smiling, dignified man with a very determined face.

I told him everything I knew about the case. He remained perfectly quiet, listening. He thought for a few minutes and then said: "Well, all this fits in with what I have up in New Jersey." And then he looked at me and said, "You know, Mrs. McLean, if I go on with this thing it will quite likely ruin me politically."[5]

In later writing of the meeting with Mrs. McLean, Harold Hoffman included the fact that Charles Lindbergh had been her houseguest during the trial of Gaston B. Means. He also revealed that "she told many interesting things in a spirit of confidence that I may not violate. These things may some day be part of Mrs. McLean's story." The governor returned to New Jersey with, as he put it, "new information to check."[6]

Two men and their secrets approached one another: Charles Augustus Lindbergh, the calm, precise, ultimate planner, and the hyperactive, impulsive Harold Giles Hoffman. The governor had interviewed Bruno

Richard Hauptmann and come away believing that the doomed prisoner was not implicated in the death and probably had no part in the extortion plot. He was already suspicious of the legal proceedings that had tried Hauptmann and found him guilty. There were witnesses he believed had perjured themselves, physical evidence he suspected had been tampered with. Added to this was new information, some from Mrs. McLean, and far more devastating statements from members of the Morrow household staff.

Action must be taken—that was the nature of Harold Hoffman. Which action and for what reason, he wasn't sure. Reassessing the Lindbergh case would be sticky business and dangerous. The Lindbergh-Morrow clan was as well connected and powerful a family as existed. Lindy himself was manipulative. Vengeful. A head-on confrontation must be avoided. But could it?

For Charles Lindbergh a probe of the facts would open old, painful wounds of the child's death. It might also expose a plot he had concocted to obscure the truth regarding that demise—assuming there was such a plot and the truth had been altered. Would the obdurate, self-assured Lone Eagle tolerate another investigation into the case and, possibly, into his involvement? Did he still have the power to stop such a challenge if he chose? Lindbergh at this juncture appeared to have no warning that this was about to happen—or that his antagonist, Harold Hoffman, was every bit as compulsive and flawed as the Lone Eagle.

24

THE BUBBLE BURSTS

ON OCTOBER 29, 1935, THE NEW JERSEY COURT OF PARDONS MET FOR THE final session of its current term. Governor Harold Hoffman, the nominal president of the body, was there and in passing mentioned that he had visited death row and talked with the condemned prisoner Bruno Richard Hauptmann, a dubious but technically not proscribed practice under the rules of the court. "This case will soon be in our laps," he told the others. "Frankly, I'm puzzled about a lot of things in connection with it. I wish that some of you judges, when you are at the prison, would talk to this man. I'd be interested in having your opinions."[1]

By now Harold Hoffman had read the trial transcripts as well as having discussed the matter with Ellis Parker, Sr., and C. Lloyd Fisher, the assistant defense attorney who had taken over as Hauptmann's main lawyer. What the governor didn't mention to the other members of the court of pardons that October 29, or to almost anyone else, was that he had given his OK for the formation of a secret task force to look into the crime and conviction.

One of the principal figures in the governor's investigation was the Old Chief, Ellis Parker, Sr., the county detective of Burlington County. His office was at the county court building on Main Street, Mount Holly, directly across from the grand old house in which he resided. Parker's staff included his secretary–sometime sleuth, Anna Bading, and his son Ellis Jr.

Parker was unwavering in his belief that Paul Wendel, a disbarred New Jersey lawyer and ex-convict, had stolen the Lindbergh baby and that the child might still be alive. One of the first people he personally recruited for the governor's operation was Murray Bleefeld, a dapper New York City underworld character with connections to Trenton's dyeing and cleaning trades. When Bleefeld's brother was sentenced to jail in New Jersey, Murray sought out Parker for assistance. The Old Chief arranged a meeting between Bleefeld and the keeper of the prisons for New Jersey, Colonel Mark O. Kimberling, at Kimberling's residence.[2] Murray tried to discuss his brother's situation, but Parker insisted on talking about the Lindbergh-Hauptmann case. Bleefeld's brother was transferred from a prison to a prison farm. Murray agreed to help Parker in the investigation.

Bleefeld was taken to the Hotel Hildebrecht in Trenton and introduced to Governor Hoffman, who swore him in as a special deputy. The assignment given Bleefeld by Parker was to locate Paul Wendel. Wendel, wanted on a check-kiting rap, had disappeared and was believed to be hiding out somewhere in New York City. Bleefeld was encouraged by Parker to recruit his brother-in-law, Martin Schlossman, a laundry owner, and a friend, cab driver Harry Weiss, to assist in the search.

Liaison between Parker and the governor was left to Mark O. Kimberling and Gus Lockwood. Kimberling and Lockwood, who was still an inspector with the Department of Motor Vehicles, also acted as the chief recruiters and operation heads for other aspects of the investigation, which were far broader than Parker's obsessive quest for Wendel. Because of his mobility Lockwood also had a major hand in the surreptitious recruitment of investigators.

Since there were no official funds available for man power, and because day-to-day expenses for the secret probe were paid from the governor's pocket, the coin of the realm became cronyism and outstanding political debts, many dating back to the days when Harold Hoffman ran the Department of Motor Vehicles, an organization that boasted its own detective corps. Quite a few of these former investigators now worked for one or another of New Jersey's numerous private detective agencies, an active field that fed on the ongoing strife between industry and a labor movement revitalized by the support of the pro-union Roosevelt administration. When scabs or goons were needed to break a strike or resituate sit-ins, management could count on detective agencies to provide them. Despite his connivance with several of the state's most powerful Democratic bosses, Harold Hoffman was a pro-management Republican and, ergo, partial to a private detective industry that curried favor.

One expert hired to assist the governor's investigation, Erastus Mead Hudson, was neither a crony nor a private detective. During Hauptmann's trial Dr. Hudson had been frustrated by the defense's inability to sway the jury with his fingerprint findings. He also did not take kindly to what he considered to be attempts at private intimidation and public humiliation by the police and prosecution. In today's legal climate he might have brought suit for libel or defamation of character; back in the winter of 1935, his best way to reinstate his reputation was by proving that his silver nitrate system was valid and, therefore, his conclusion was correct: Since Hauptmann's fingerprints had not been among those he found in the nursery or on the ladder, chances were Hauptmann was not implicated in the kidnapping.

Dr. Hudson had taken Hauptmann's cause a step further by delving into the handwriting of the ransom notes, but for expertise in this area he suggested that the governor get hold of Jesse William Pelletreau, a Jersey City private detective who had served as an investigator for defense attorney James M. Fawcett when Hauptmann was being charged with extortion by the Bronx County district attorney in September of 1934 and who had copies of all the handwriting connected with the case.

In the early part of November, Gus Lockwood delivered a letter to Bill Pelletreau, wanting to know if the gruff, round-faced private eye had any interest in becoming a member of the governor's investigatory team. Bill's answer was affirmative, and the next day Lockwood picked him up in Jersey City and drove him to Mount Holly for an interview with Ellis Parker, whom Pelletreau had first met when working on the Bradway Brown murder case.[3] The Old Chief questioned the Jersey City PI on his investigation for Fawcett as well as on his views on the crime. Then as later Bill Pelletreau was certain that Hauptmann had not authored the ransom notes. He was equally certain that his ability to analyze handwriting would prove this. Following the interview with Parker, Lockwood drove him to Trenton, where he met with Mark O. Kimberling and repeated what he had told the Old Chief. Kimberling made an appointment for Pelletreau to meet the governor at the Hotel Hildebrecht on November 29. As per schedule, Bill arrived at Harold Hoffman's suite with display charts and blowups.

"I understand that you don't agree with the experts that Hauptmann wrote the ransom notes," the governor said.

"That is my finding," Pelletreau answered.

"Do you have any idea who did write the ransom notes?"[4]

Pelletreau did not, but for him a possible answer lay with the mysterious J. J. Faulkner. During the kidnapping trial the state's handwriting experts had agreed that Hauptmann had *not* written Faulkner's name on the bank deposit that had been used to exchange $2,980 in ransom loot for non-gold-certificate currency. In Pelletreau's mind this proved that at least one other person was involved in the case.

Governor Harold Hoffman invited Jesse William Pelletreau to join his team of investigators. The Jersey City private eye accepted.

Mrs. Evalyn Walsh McLean's contribution to the governor's highly discreet inquiry was Robert W. Hicks, a Washington lawyer and well-thought-of criminal theorist, whom she had hired to reexamine the crime—and whom she agreed to go on paying while he was on loan to the Hoffman inquiry. Hicks had once submitted a ballistics report to H. Norman Schwarzkopf that projected, but did not prove, that the dead baby found in the woods might have been killed by the tiny Lilliput gun found hidden in the work area of Hauptmann's garage. Since that time Hicks had come to believe, as Parker did, that Hauptmann had nothing to do with the crime.

Other investigators participating in the secret probe, or soon to be recruited, and who the governor would subsequently acknowledge had helped his cause included Harold C. Keyes, a former government operative recently in the employ of Mrs. Bruno Richard Hauptmann, who was given the code name K-4; George Foster, who along with Pelletreau had been an investigator for James M. Fawcett during Hauptmann's extortion and extradition trials; Leon Ho-age, a meticulous paper chaser who would scrutinize the state-police files for discrepancies, contradictions, and irregularities vis-à-vis the investigation and trial; Samuel Small, a career penman and lay handwriting specialist with dubious professional standing in the field of disputed documents.

There were others whom the governor, for whatever his reasons, did not acknowledge but who played, or were to play, an active role in his investigation: Elizabeth J. McLaughlin, his private secretary; R. William Lagay, an aide-de-camp; his press secretary, William S. Conklin; his friend and sometime attorney Harry Green; Dr. Hudson's secretary, Mary McGill; private investigator Winslow P. Humphrey, code-named C-D-1; private eyes William Lewis and Leo F. Mead of the Mead Detective Bureau; and Max Sherwood of the Sherwood Detective Agency.

Another unmentioned set of allies, and possibly the governor's prime covert source of information, was to be found among the ranks of the New Jersey State Police. The troopers, though seemingly united in the belief that Hauptmann alone committed the crime, were not in agreement. Some members of the force even suspected he might be innocent but never dared say so openly. No state cop liked the accusations that his organization had mishandled the investigation and rigged evidence, but one or two quietly allowed that it might be so and expressed the opinion that H. Norman Schwarzkopf, if not directly responsible for this, had afforded a clique of favored subordinates the free rein with which to disgrace the organization. More than one trooper was troubled by the fact that rather than examining new information objectively, the state police had lapsed into a defensive stance and seemed willing to go to unspeakable lengths to discredit anyone who challenged their findings and conclusions. Factionalism had always existed in the ranks, just as some had always been disenchanted by Schwarzkopf's posturing and pomp. Then, too, there was the political practicality of staying on the good side of Governor Harold Hoffman, who had the power to replace H. Norman when the superintendent's term as state-police boss expired in June.

Back on January 17, 1935, in an effort to dispel the contention that the corpse found in the woods was not that of the Lindbergh infant but most likely the remains of a child from St. Michael's Orphanage, which owned the adjoining land, the prosecution at Hauptmann's trial had elicited testimony from Mrs. Elmira Dormer, the custodian of St. Michael's. Dormer had told the jury that in February and March of 1932 all of the institution's children were accounted for. Ten months later Ellis Parker still wasn't buying this and assigned Bill Pelletreau to check out the enrollment of the orphanage in early 1932 and learn which of the children had died.

Whereas Parker seemed unclear as to the fate of the Lindbergh infant after he was kidnapped, he was quite positive as to what became of the ransom Wendel received in St. Raymond's: Wendel gave it to a former client of his: Isador Fisch. According to information developed by Parker, when Paul Wendel was still practicing law in New Jersey, he had successfully defended Fisch in a smuggling case, which most likely involved narcotics. Not knowing what to do with the fifty thousand dollars in gold notes that Jafsie Condon had given him in the cemetery, Wendel sought out Fisch. He lied about the origin of the currency and said he wanted to get rid of a stash of counterfeit bills. Fisch, who immediately recognized samples of the money as being ransom loot, lied in return and said yes, for a stipulated percentage he would sell off the counterfeit. Wendel delivered some twenty thousand dollars in gold notes. Later, when Wendel demanded his money from the sale, Fisch told him to get lost, letting him know that he knew the bills were ransom loot.[5]

Robert Hicks agreed with Ellis Parker that Isador Fisch had ended up with ransom money, but for a set of reasons different from those subscribed to by the Old Chief. Hicks was convinced that Fisch, not Wendel, had written the ransom messages and that Fisch, not Wendel, had been given the fifty thousand dollars by Jafsie Condon. At five feet five and a half inches, Fisch was shorter than what had come to be the generally accepted pre-arrest description Jafsie provided of John. Hicks opted for believing Condon's earlier statements to the Bronx grand jury: that he had never clearly seen John's face. Fisch's protruding ears and hacking cigarette cough fit the profile provided by Condon at the time. Jafsie had also said John had a Scandinavian or German accent. Fisch, a Polish Jew who was raised in Germany, spoke with a German Yiddish accent. One statistic supporting the possibility that Fisch also kidnapped and killed the baby was his lightness. Isador tipped the scale at 150 pounds, a far better weight at which to climb and descend the rickety ladder than the 160 pounds John was estimated to be by the contradictory Condon.

Isador Fisch was born in Poland in 1905, and when he was still very young his family moved to Leipzig, Germany, where he grew up. Leaving school at seventeen, he spent three years apprenticing to a local fur company. Like many young people in those days, Fisch and a fellow apprentice, Henry Uhlig, worked on the black market to make ends meet. Uhlig raised the fare for a steamship ticket, came to New York City, and stayed with their former foreman at the fur company, who had become a bootlegger. Uhlig got a job and sent Fisch the money to join him. Once in New York, Fisch found employment as a fur cutter and soon was making a hundred dollars a week. Uhlig was as large and outgoing as Fisch was small and withdrawn. They shared an apartment and, due mainly to the gregarious Uhlig, developed a small circle of friends, many of whom Fisch persuaded to invest in shaky, if not fraudulent, speculations.

In addition to cutting furs, Isador Fisch was developing into a small-time con artist. Speculation in pelts was one of his hustles; another was eliciting investments in a pie factory, of which he himself had been conned into becoming president by a convicted gambler and a fugitive hoodlum. Uhlig later estimated that Fisch had fleeced nearly thirteen thousand dollars from their friends with his investment schemes. Fisch's brother thought the amount was closer to seventeen thousand dollars.[6] What became of the money was anybody's guess. By the time Fisch and Hauptmann grew friendly and started doing business together in 1932, the penurious little German-Pole had given up his job in the fur industry and was spending $3.50 a week rent for the cheapest room in a boardinghouse. Many of his friends believed he was destitute.

One of the joint ventures with which Hauptmann and Fisch involved themselves was playing the stock market, Hauptmann's specialty. Another was purchasing furs, conceivably stolen pelts, Fisch's forte. By the summer of 1933, they had formed a partnership in which each man was to put up $17,500 for the purchase of furs and stocks. Hauptmann claimed that their speculation in furs alone that year netted more than $6,000. Fisch died in Germany of tuberculosis in 1934, leaving Hauptmann with four hundred sealskins and a shoe box full of ransom money.

— — —

Robert Hicks's scenario, in which Isador Fisch was John and had received the ransom, generated few supporters from the ranks of investigators working for the governor. It is questionable how many actually knew what Hicks was about. Though accessible and good-natured, Harold Hoffman was an extremely secretive man, a past master at not letting one group of trusted aides know what the next group was up to. The true measure of this clandestine bent was to come in a stunning posthumous confession that would shock a nation. Thus in the ongoing investigation, Ellis Parker, Sr., and Bleefeld's people pursued Paul Wendel without the knowledge of other probers. Hicks tended to go his own way.

- - -

The discreet investigation accounted for only a small part of Governor Harold Hoffman's hectic schedule in the early winter of 1935. First and foremost he had to run the state and try to find the money needed to do so. With his tax law rescinded on October 10, 1935, one solution he came up with to solve the financial crisis facing New Jersey was the legalization of racetrack betting, which in itself was tempestuously controversial. Besides the governor's administrative and legislative problems, there were official functions he had to attend in and out of New Jersey and the speeches he had to make. Just as important was mending the political fences the tax battle had caused within his own Republican party. This wasn't all that easy, because in most of his speeches Harold Hoffman couldn't resist berating anyone who had voted against his ill-fated law or who was now opposing his racetrack measure. As had been the case with the tax bill, his own Republican party was against the legal-betting action. Among the governor's growing number of media critics was New Jersey's influential *Trenton Evening Times,* which seemed never to miss a chance to write an uncomplimentary editorial on the state's chief executive.

Try as Harold Hoffman might, he was not the sort of man who could hide what was on his mind—or sit still for very long. Over a five-day period in early November, he attended election-night festivities in his home state, visited Cleveland, Ohio, spoke before a Buffalo, New York, teacher's group, and dropped in on the Niagara Falls, New York, Chamber of Commerce. His favorite away-from-home events were the raucous Circus, Saints and Sinners bashes in New York City, where he found time to don his ringmaster's costume and emcee at least a portion of the evening's high jinks.

- - -

Time was running out on the life of Bruno Richard Hauptmann. December had begun, and the governor's hope that Hauptmann himself would thaw and name a conspirator had not been realized. Ellis Parker was no more successful at establishing that Paul Wendel was the kidnapper or that the baby in the woods was not Charles Lindbergh, Jr. Investigators had gathered a considerable amount of information that discredited much of the prosecution's case against Hauptmann, but it could hardly assure that a retrial would result.

Other aspects of the secret inquiry had reached a point where the governor might soon have to step in, at the risk of considerable public outcry, and interview the Lindberghs. He might even have to interview Betty Gow and possibly Jafsie Condon.

— — —

Ellis Parker, with a strong assist from Lloyd Fisher, had homed in on the two prosecution witnesses whose testimony had been particularly detrimental to Hauptmann at the Flemington trial: Amandus Hochmuth and Millard Whited. He was hellfire certain they had lied under oath by testifying to having seen Hauptmann near the Lindbergh estate at the time of the crime. The Old Chief was equally sure he could discredit them. What he wasn't able to achieve when he set about to do this was secrecy. Word got out around New Jersey that Parker was investigating the crime—at the governor's behest. Confronted by the accusation, Harold Hoffman issued a press statement, which was released from Parker's Mount Holly headquarters.

"When I went into the office, the first thing Mr. Parker did was to come in and talk over the matter with me," the governor was quoted as saying. "I am interested in it, naturally, because I am a member of the Court of Pardons, which is a court of mercy." The governor denied directing Parker to reinvestigate the Lindbergh case but allowed that "all along, since I have been in office, [Parker] has discussed the matter with me whenever there were new developments."[7]

— — —

Following a speaking engagement in New Jersey on Wednesday evening, December 4, 1935, Harold Hoffman traveled to New York City and dropped in at Madison Square Garden, where a six-day bicycle race was in progress. He accepted an invitation by one of the race officials to visit "the boys" in the press room and was soon ensconced among the sports writers, listening to their tales and trading gibes. He was caught off guard when one scribe abruptly turned the conversation away from athletics. The writer had covered the Hauptmann trial and, predicated on the evidence he had seen produced, expressed doubts that the German should have been convicted. He went so far as to say that some of what he observed in the courtroom was *"phony."*

"I replied that Ellis Parker had expressed the same thing to me," Harold Hoffman related. "The writer asked me if Parker was investigating the case, and I told him that he had been working on it since a few days after the commission of the crime."[8]

The governor returned to his New York City hotel and went to sleep. Of the next morning, December 5, he wrote, "I was handed a metropolitan newspaper containing a two paragraph story and the rather modest headline, 'Lindbergh Case Reopened.' "[9] The text quoted Hoffman as saying that Parker was investigating the Lindbergh matter and implied that the governor had engaged him to do so.

The luncheon–speaking engagement Hoffman had come to town to attend took place on schedule at the New York Ad Club. Seated at the head table along with the governor was Henry Breckinridge. Hoffman gave a speech on the influence of advertising on the nation's economic situation and avoided any reference to the Lindbergh case. Leaving the dais, he was surrounded by ten or twelve reporters from the New York newspapers as well as the national press services who wanted to know if the governor had indeed engaged Parker to reinvestigate the Lindbergh case and what had been found out so far. An impromptu press conference was arranged in a nearby room, at which the governor tried to field an onslaught of questions. Amid the barrage Pat Grady of the Associated Press posed a fateful query: "Governor, have you ever seen Hauptmann?"

"Yes," Hoffman answered.

"Where?"

"In the State Prison."[10]

After a few more questions the reporters scrambled to the phones. Despite having worked on a newspaper during his youth and having adroitly manipulated the press for years as a politician, the governor headed away without paying much mind to the brief exchange with Pat Grady.

By the time Harold Hoffman returned home that night, front pages across the land had announced that he had secretly seen Hauptmann in jail and that the case had been reopened. The press corps, which was heading for New Jersey in numbers reminiscent of the original kidnapping night, was one manifestation of the immediate and nationwide public outcry against the governor's actions. Mark O. Kimberling exacerbated the matter by first denying that the visit to death row took place, then claiming he did only what he was ordered to do—by Harold Hoffman. Nor did the governor help his own public relations cause by explaining that his only interest was ensuring that justice was done but refusing to tell reporters exactly why he had gone to see Hauptmann or what he had learned. The chief executive of New Jersey repeated, as he had done before, that Ellis Parker had always believed Hauptmann was innocent and that he found some merit in this.

What dismayed the governor as much as the extent of the protest was the rancor with which it was leveled. He complained that he was being treated like a national villain. In retrospect, that isn't surprising. Americans, who had agonized over the disappearance and death of Charles Lindbergh, Jr., for almost three years and who trusted mightily in the courts of the land, sincerely believed that justice had been served with the guilty verdict and death penalty. They wanted the matter closed and done with and had expected it would be. Now Harold Hoffman was denying them this.

The national surge of criticism against the governor was nowhere more biting than in the *Trenton Evening Times,* which along with extensive hard-news coverage of the continuing controversy, ran scathing editorials on him for the better part of two weeks. Among other things suggested by the *Evening Times* was that his visit to Hauptmann was illegal and unethical; a publicity stunt to help gain the prisoner a new trial; a decoy meant to distract the public from his impending racetrack-betting referendum; a ploy motivated by other political considerations; a defamation of the entire judicial system of New Jersey; and a smoke screen for his imminent firing of H. Norman Schwarzkopf. "What a tragedy it would be," proclaimed the *Evening Times* editorial of Friday, December 6, 1935, "if the slayer of the Lindbergh baby should receive the undeserved mercy of maudlin sentimentality because of superficial publicity-seeking and a gubernatorial flair for Broadway theatricals." The next day's editorial ended by saying, "Once more Hoffman's administrative actions have done nothing but cause thoughtful Jerseymen to hang their heads in shame." Adding insult to injury for Harold Hoffman was that even the *Perth Amboy Evening News,* where he had worked as a young man, was critical of him—for having broken the story to New York City reporters rather than the New Jersey press.

On December 7, bowing to pressure on him to make a public statement on his position, the governor said in part:

> The case of Bruno Richard Hauptmann is one with which the dimensions of American justice will be measured by all Americans and the world. Because of the unprecedented prominence given to the trial of this man, there have been thousands of rumors in circulation. Some of these allege other conditions disadvantageous to either the prosecution or defense. The offense charged was a dastardly crime, threatening our whole system of living in mutual confidence. No person participating in this crime can be allowed to escape the full penalty. . . .
>
> If the defendant in this case is guilty beyond a reasonable doubt, he must pay the penalty demanded by the law. That is required for the protection of society against the criminal. If he is not guilty, he should not be punished. That is required for the protection of society against itself.[11]

Though his comments did little to counteract the massive flow of criticism, there was an increase in the letters of support he had been receiving.

On Monday, December 9, the U.S. Supreme Court refused to review Bruno Richard Hauptmann's conviction. December 13 was Justice Trenchard's seventy-second birthday, and the venerable jurist set a new date for the execution: January 17, 1936. December 13 also saw leaders of the New Jersey State Legislature refuse to call a special session, thereby dooming the governor's proposed referendum to permit race-track gambling.

Three days later, on December 16, the governor received a letter from the condemned man:

> With clear conscience I have fought my case. In my heart I can not believe that this state will break the life of an innocent man. I would be very thankful for permitting any able person, who are free of any opinion in this case, to take a test with so-called lied detector, serum or whatever science may offer. I hope for myself and in the course of justice that this, my wish, may inspire Dr. Condon to do the same. I have a deep interest in what kind of force made him

change his saying. Because when he was visiting me in my Flemington cell, he said all excited to the prosecutor, "I can not testify against this man. . . ."[12]

The timing of the letter was not good. Besides the fact that the race-track legislation had been defeated, a battle had been shaping up in Trenton over whether Frederick Brodesser, an ally of the governor's, would continue on as clerk in the house of assembly for 1936. On December 20, as an ominous certification of the governor's political downslide, his own Republican party rejected Brodesser.

It is doubtful that word of a reinvestigation made Charles Lindbergh happy. Not only would it put him and his family back in the spotlight, but it might also jeopardize something else. Assuming his cover-up plot was an actuality, Lindy had been lucky until now, but close scrutiny of the facts at this late date might very well pick up what had previously been overlooked. An even worse possibility existed: that the governor had already learned the secret of Sorrel Hill; that he knew the child had died on Saturday, not Tuesday; that he knew why.

Lindbergh, ever clear-eyed and methodical, made his move—in a clandestine act that was truly catastrophic for the beleaguered Harold Hoffman. It occurred the next evening at 11:30 P.M., when Charles and Anne Lindbergh, with their young son, Jon, secretly boarded the freighter *American Importer* in New York Harbor and sailed off for England and self-imposed exile. The covert exodus was announced with headline fanfare on December 23. The Lindberghs did nothing to refute the statements of their friends and allies that Harold Hoffman's capricious opening up of old wounds had caused their flight. Their destination was exile in England, where Elisabeth Morrow's widowed husband would act as Lindy's spokesman.

A savage new round of headline stories and editorials berated the governor and his investigation for having driven America's royal couple into exile.[13] Impeachment rumors circulated around Trenton. Hate letters poured in, and threats. Harold Giles Hoffman, who less than a year before had been among the most popular young politicians in the country, was gaining on Bruno Richard Hauptmann as being the most disliked man in America. Worse was to come.

25

THE ROCKY ROAD TO

REPRIEVE

— — —

ON DECEMBER 23, 1935, THE DAY THE LINDBERGHS' EXILE FROM THE UNITED
States broke into the headlines, Bruno Richard Hauptmann filed an application with the court of pardons, in which he asked for clemency and
stated that he was not guilty of the crime charged.

Since the U.S. Supreme Court had already rejected the prisoner's appeal and because a New Jersey governor was not invested with the power
to commute a death sentence, the court of pardons was Hauptmann's
last practical hope of avoiding the electric chair. As far back as Monday,
December 9, the *Trenton Evening Times* had warned against Governor
Hoffman's trying to manipulate this court into reversing Hauptmann's
death sentence. With the new year approaching, anti-mercy hard-liners
contended that the state's constitution did not grant the court of pardons
the specific right of commutation. The *Evening Times* was among them,
and it also spearheaded a protest meant to discourage Harold Hoffman
from invoking the primary legal right he did have in the matter: a guber-

natorial reprieve with which he could stay the execution for up to ninety days in three increments of thirty days each.

A majority of the governor's supporters not only wanted him to heed the pressures and back away from a reprieve, which if issued, was bound to result in a national protest, but they also desperately urged him to abandon the investigation. Only when Bruno Richard Hauptmann was dead would the dust settle, and only then could they busy themselves with trying to rebuild his political base. But Harold Hoffman wasn't letting that many friends know what he was about. A few who did know suspected that his career had been so badly damaged that the only chance to salvage it was by sticking to his guns and regaining credibility by proving that Hauptmann was either innocent or hadn't acted alone. Others of the inner circle felt that even this wouldn't be good enough. For them the only hope was a long shot: coming up with the actual kidnapper-murderer. Hoffman's investigators were intent on doing just that, and in the opinion of Bill Pelletreau the true perpetrator had already contacted them.

— — —

Back on December 13, 1935, a letter mailed from Brooklyn and addressed to Dr. E. M. Hudson, Gotham Private Hospital, 30 East Seventy-sixth Street, New York City, was delivered. The text was written in disguised handwriting:

> Mr. Dear Dr. Hudson
> You whant know about Lindbergh boy please going or got to
> 440 1st Brooklyn. Please do not tell police the boy is dear
> an ist Blonde blue eyes   you see a big man in the basement
>   Hautpman is not guilty
>
> a friend of
>   Dr. Condon
> Jhon

On the back of the page was this:

> (Keep this to yourself or . . .)

The following day, December 14, Mary McGill, Dr. Hudson's aide, summoned Pelletreau, who checked the handwriting in the letter against samples of the ransom messages he had as well as against a copy of J. J. Faulkner's signature.[1] Ever since working for Brooklyn attorney James M. Fawcett as part of Hauptmann's extortion and extradition defense team, Pelletreau had been on the alert for a *k* similar to the distinctive one that the mysterious Faulkner had written on the bank-deposit receipt for $2,980 in ransom currency on May 1, 1933. Now the Jersey City private eye found what he considered to be an identical *k* in the message to Dr. Hudson. After further comparisons and analysis, particularly with the letter *m* and the transposition of the *h* in the name Jhon, Pelletreau was certain that the author of the Hudson letter had also written the ransom notes received by Lindbergh, Breckinridge, and Jafsie Condon. No blue-eyed baby was found at 440 1st, but as the message urged, the matter was kept quiet.

Bill Pelletreau puzzled over why the authentic author of the ransom letters would bother to write to Dr. Hudson only to lead him on a wild-goose chase regarding the Brooklyn address. In late December, after returning from a lead he had checked out in Texas, Pelletreau came up with a tentative answer. "It was my opinion that this letter had been written primarily so as to reach the hands of the authorities and cause doubt as to the guilt of Hauptmann."[2] This may have been hindsight.

On January 2, 1936, with fifteen days left before Bruno Richard Hauptmann's electrocution and as insistence that the death occur per schedule became a nationwide cry, Pelletreau was called to Harold Hoffman's suite in New York City's New Yorker Hotel. The governor took the private detective into the bedroom, produced an envelope, and said, "I would like to have you read this letter, Bill, and tell me what you think of it."[3] Then he left.

New-York, Jan. 1.st 36

To his Excellency
the Governor of the State of N.J.
Mr. Harold G. Hoffman.

Sir: As the Zero hour in the Hauptmann Case draws near, I feel impelled to direct these few lines to Your Excellency in order to dispell the preconceived idea of the guilt of Hauptmann or rather to sustain and affirm you in your own and rightly-so formed idea of his innocence.

In spite of all the confusion and artificially created hateful atmosphere attending his trial, you seem to have been the only person, who was capable of preserving an objective view of the case, notwithstanding all the animosity and antagonistic feeling and outside pressure which factors combined were able to sway a Jersey Jury of twelve good but spine-less people to return a Verdict of guilt against an innocent man in a Capital Case on purely superficial-yea-artificially created evidence.

Hauptmann, an expert carpenter, made the kidnap ladder, the work of which an apprentice boy of one months standing would be ashamed of. Hauptmann, guilty of this crime he stand convicted of ?

Does Your Excellency believe that, in the own words of the most famous judge in the case, who exercised undue and unconstitutional control over 12 simple minded good people. Of course, I know you don't. I cannot help but admiring you for the fact that you are about the only person in dominant position who was capable of sustaining an un-biased and wide perspective of the case. Hauptmann is not guilty, not of the crime he stands convicted of.

All the poor bum is guilty of is his money madness, which made him risk a Thousand Dollars or so of his own good money, in the belief and greedy notion, that he could get independently rich and by hiding this cheaply acquired hoard he brought himself in all this trouble, nearly causing him to lose his life, which I hope will now be spared.

Now that I have communicated to Your Excellency and given you some of the inside dope, You will readily understand that for personal reasons I am not interested to go into further details and your Honor will also believe me that these lines are not dictated by a desire to be an informative.

All I intend to do is to follow the impelling power of my conscience and the desire to friendly assist you to prevent the State of N.J. from committing a legal blunder and murder, and you will not rue the day when you granted commutation, for clemency I cannot possibly invite, because I cannot come out in the open.

You are comparatively young yet and you might live to

see the day when the whole truth will likely come out perhaps as a death-bed story. As far as Condon is concerned . . . You would be well advised to take his assertion with a grain of salt. He has reasons.

Having done my duty as I see it before me, and assuring your Excellency of my highest regards and my firmest belief in your highest integrity, who will know how to act in matters Hauptmann,

I am closing
most respectfully
J.J. FAULKNER[4]

Analyzing the two-page Faulkner letter, Pelletreau found the signature to be identical with the one J. J. Faulkner had left on the 1933 bank-deposit slip. More important, the writing was the same as in the ransom messages, as well as in the letter to Dr. Hudson. Despite the fact that photographic copies of the bank-deposit signature and the ransom communications had been reproduced in the newspapers, Pelletreau was convinced that the hand that had written them had also written the letter to Harold Hoffman. For the "poor bum" paragraph of the letter strengthened a theory that had been debated off and on since Hauptmann's arrest: that one of the illegal enterprises the German carpenter may have speculated in, with or without Isador Fisch, was the buying up of "hot" currency at a fraction of its worth and hoping to exchange it at full value on the street.

On January 3, Governor Hoffman, in his capacity as president of the court of pardons, sent H. Norman Schwarzkopf a letter in which the trooper superintendent was directed to deliver to the clerk of the pardons court "documents, exhibits or articles of evidence in connection with the murder of Charles Augustus Lindbergh Jr." The list of material the governor wanted from the state police took up four pages and covered thirty specific categories.[5]

The following day the first shipment of requested evidence was turned over to the governor by the state police. It included some seventy individual items plus twenty photographs and also the complete files on Betty Gow, the Whateleys, and seven other people. The second delivery of the day contained the troopers' complete Condon file, three other files, and thirty-six additional items. Inspector Harry Walsh, it turned out, did not write up reports on his investigatory findings, so all the troopers could provide regarding the Jersey City policeman's part in the Lindbergh investigation was newspaper coverage or statements made by his co-workers. More requested material was sent to the governor on January 6.

The next day something else was being sent out. Mark O. Kimberling, principal keeper of the New Jersey state prisons, issued invitations asking eighteen people to attend the January 17 electrocution of Bruno Richard Hauptmann, with instructions that "The hour of 8:00 P.M. has been designated by me for such execution and you will kindly be at my office in this Prison not later than 7:15 P.M."[6]

The court of pardons had scheduled Saturday, January 11, for hearing Hauptmann's petition for clemency. His attorneys and the governor's investigators had been working hand in hand on a presentation, and to date their strongest case for commuting the death penalty was eclectic and occasionally bizarre. They had grounds on which to claim that the state police had bungled the investigation and that false testimony had been given at the trial, particularly in regard to placing Hauptmann at the scene. They were also confident they could disprove much of what the wood expert had testified to at the trial, thereby negating the importance of the ladder. Jafsie Condon was certainly a target. Ellis Parker's claim that the baby in the woods was not Charles A. Lindbergh, Jr., had Dr. Van Ingen's prekidnapping examination and a good deal of hearsay evidence to support it but nothing that was unassailable. Even so, the Old Chief, who had gone public with the theory back in 1932, was insistent that the wrong-baby issue be brought up.

The governor's investigators were busy elsewhere. Robert Hicks rented the Hauptmanns' former apartment in the Bronx—Lieutenant Bornmann of the NJSP had done the same thing months earlier—and microscopically studied the attic from which the prosecution's wood expert had claimed a runner on the ladder had come. Hicks also spent time at St. Raymond's Cemetery, taking measurements and timing, with a stopwatch, a reenactment of Jafsie's ransom payment to John.

Other information sent the governor's men to a spot in St. Raymond's Cemetery where the Westchester Creek flowed. Digging began along the muddy bank for the wooden box in which Jafsie had delivered the ransom money to John. Data was also developed that linked a male German who was the keeper of a rooming house on West Ninetieth Street with the mysterious woman who was supposed to have talked to Condon at the charity bazaar. Investigators put him under surveillance and instigated an extensive background check, which included discreetly examining a bank account that was in his wife's name. Still another lead brought Hoffman's agents to a salesgirl in a Bronx store, who insisted that her sister, living on Long Island, could name at least one person who purchased four thousand dollars in ransom bills.

Probers found no wooden box in Westchester Creek, surveillance on the man who ran the rooming house proved unproductive, and on being questioned, the sister of the Bronx salesgirl claimed to have forgotten the name of the buyer of four thousand dollars in ransom notes. They fared no better following up on a letter from a friend of Fisch's from Leipzig, which was written in German and asked a New York furrier to sell the 220 dressed skins left there by Fisch. The letter authorized the furrier to deduct his sales commission, asking to remit whatever was left because his family needed the money. On being confronted by investigators, the furrier explained that since dress furs of that type brought a dollar each, he had ignored the request.

It was debatable whether any or all of the information on hand and its corroborating evidence would persuade the court of pardons to stay the death sentence and call for another trial. Nor could this likely be achieved by the letter from J. J. Faulkner to the governor, which was now being examined by additional partisan experts. What was needed was either the actual living Lindbergh baby or J. J. Faulkner himself. The *New York American* had a hunch who the latter might be: a German-speaking Russian Pole.[7] At the same time the Old Chief received a letter from Dennis Doyle, a sneak thief claiming to be a relative of Jafsie Condon's.[8]

On January 10, the day before the court of pardons was to meet, the final edition of the *New York Daily News* exclusively reproduced photographed segments of Faulkner's January 1 letter to the governor under the headline J.J. FAULKNER "CLEARS" BRUNO. That night John F. Condon, whose upcoming articles in *Liberty* magazine, "Jafsie Tells All," had been widely quoted as saying that Hauptmann had not acted alone, suddenly sailed for South America. An incensed governor let it be known he wanted Jafsie arrested and brought home.

Standing at the entrance of the New Jersey Statehouse the next day and facing a crowd of the curious while movie-newsreel cameras mounted on trucks swept the scene, Harold Hoffman, referring to the impending *Liberty* magazine revelations, proclaimed, "Condon makes the flat statement that more than one person was involved in the plan. He goes so far as to write he knew two of those involved. If Dr. Condon knows these things, I feel the authorities should have the information."[9]

The governor said that Attorney General Wilentz was the man he would ask to take Condon into custody.

When told of the governor's statement, Dave Wilentz, who was in conference with his prosecution staff, replied that he had not yet been informed of the apprehension request and that he "would not anticipate what the Governor will do."[10] He and his office, like most of the reporters and cameramen gathered at the statehouse, had something else on their mind: the court of pardons's consideration of Hauptmann's final petition for clemency, which was slated to begin at 10:00 A.M. The attorney general and his aides were preparing their arguments against its being granted.

— — —

That Saturday, January 11, 1936, a *New York American* reporter, Sanford E. Stanton, accompanied Governor Hoffman's most trusted lieutenant, Gus ("Popeye") Lockwood, to the New York City jail at 100 Centre Street, known as the Tombs, to meet Wally Stroh, who was serving time for a burglary conviction.[11] Also in attendance was Dennis Doyle, a convict incarcerated at the Riker's Island Penitentiary. With Doyle was a Mr. Badian, secretary to the warden of Riker's Island, who acted as stenographer for the interviews.

Lockwood wanted Stroh to repeat the story regarding the German-speaking Russian Pole Jacob Nosovitsky's involvement in the Lindbergh kidnapping that he had given to the *American* nearly three and a half years before. Stroh would later claim that Lockwood told him they hoped the information he supplied could be presented to the court of pardons on the coming Monday, even though the court was meeting that day. The motive for the information, in any case, was to "secure a reprieve or some consideration" for Bruno Richard Hauptmann or, if that failed, to provide a sufficient basis on which the governor could issue a stay of execution.[12]

Stroh did not perceive Nosovitsky as merely an extortionist who had somehow intercepted a copy of the original ransom note.[13] For Wally he was the kidnapper-killer as well. Stroh had met Nosovitsky when they were inmates at the Hart's Island jail in New York City. He stated that the Doc, as Nosovitsky was known, was an authentic doctor who had often mentioned the possibilities in the "snatch racket." After their release from Hart's Island, Nosovitsky persuaded Stroh to finance him in the ill-fated manufacture of a dermatological panacea called the Skin Peeler. When the venture went belly-up, Nosovitsky found them work as private detectives with the Eagle Detective Agency at 1440 Broadway. Eagle was run by Max Sherwood, also known as Max Schlansky, who Stroh believed was a relative of Nosovitsky's. This was back in 1931. By 1936, Max Sherwood was investigating for Governor Hoffman.[14]

Stroh recalled Nosovitsky's continual chat about scams and snatch jobs they should pull. At one point he went into detail, and revealed that he had teamed up with a New Jersey gang. Nosovitsky's plan, according to Stroh, was as follows: "Information obtained from this New Jersey bunch, whose part it was to do the actual kidnapping and our part was as he put it, would be collecting the ransom money."

Nosovitsky had fallen on unhappy days and was desperately in need of money. Stroh helped him out as best he could. The last time they saw each another, Stroh paid for a cab so Nosovitsky could go and meet a friend he was sure would lend him money "if he explained what he intended to do the next morning." A week before the Lindbergh kidnapping Stroh received a card from Cleveland, in which Nosovitsky said everything was all right and that he would be in touch later.

There was another thing Stroh mentioned: Nosovitsky had used the initials J.J. not only in front of his own name but as part of his favorite alias, J. J. Shannon. J.J., just as in J. J. Faulkner.

The matter of Condon's lurid past—charges of his impairing the morals of minors when he conducted a kindergarten for young girls—Stroh left to his associate, Dennis Doyle. Doyle claimed to be related to Condon, whom he suspected of lying about the Lindbergh kidnapping. Doyle let it be known that he had never been an informant, that he wasn't about to start now, and that his motive was establishing the innocence or guilt of Hauptmann. He made no mention of the reward money. Doyle didn't want to get into the rumors and printed newspaper accounts that his cousin Jafsie molested young girls and had actually been arrested for it. Though he stated that the family never discussed the young girls, he did recall once asking his mother about it. She told him, "It was just some girl looking for publicity."[15]

Stroh's and Doyle's statements to Gus Lockwood and the *American* reporter had been taken down as they talked. Affidavits were prepared, which both prisoners signed.

— — —

The pivotal legal event of that Saturday took approximately six and a half hours to unfold. The eight members of the New Jersey Court of Pardons—five judges, a retired butcher, the publisher of the *Jersey City*

Journal, and Governor Hoffman—four of whom were Republicans and four of whom were Democrats, began hearing Hauptmann's petition to commute his death sentence to life in prison at 10:37 A.M. Five of the members had heard most of the case when they sat on the court of errors and appeals, and they were expected to again refuse Hauptmann's request. The secret session took place around a long conference table in a room behind the court of errors and appeals chamber in the statehouse annex with Wilentz, Schwarzkopf, and the defense lawyers in attendance. Two of the most detrimental witnesses to Hauptmann at the Flemington trial were not available: Charles Lindbergh and John F. Condon. Because Jafsie had fled the country, there was speculation that the court might grant Hauptmann's request on a temporary basis until he could be talked to. Many "experts" felt that if the defense lived up to its promise of introducing irrefutable new evidence, there was an outside chance Bruno might just win.

Wilentz began the session with a summation of the Flemington trial; Schwarzkopf then reviewed the state-police investigation that preceded it. Lloyd Fisher took over for the defense. Since the court had rejected an earlier suggestion of hearing directly from Hauptmann, either on death row or in the hearing chamber, Fisher would have to rely on the two suitcases of reputedly new evidence that had been brought to support his claims.[16]

Damon Runyon, who reported on the court of pardons session in his syndicated newspaper column, found the event to be a "small time revival" of the original Hauptmann trial, which he had also covered.[17] The newsreel cameras, gawkers, and hawkers were certainly reminiscent of the carnival spirit back then, and the nostalgic Runyon even paid a visit to Nellie, the pooch, after whom Nellie's tap room in Flemington had been named. She was now fat, lazy, and happily snoozing her days away in the luxurious surroundings of Trenton's Stacy-Trent Hotel.

At 4:05 P.M., after hearing almost five and a half hours of testimony, the court of pardons began its vote in executive session. The rejection for clemency was handed down shortly after 5:00 P.M. Bruno Richard Hauptmann would die in the electric chair as scheduled, the coming Friday, January 17 at 8:00 P.M.

–– –– ––

The court proceedings had been secret, but it became common knowledge that Governor Hoffman was the lone member of the eight-man body who voted to keep Hauptmann alive.[18] Word also leaked out that the governor "went far afield to search out new evidence in the case."[19] Newspapers reported that advance copies of Condon's forthcoming magazine series had been introduced before the official proceedings got under way, not after. The two suitcases of "new" evidence the defense had brought into the hearing room was said to have been nothing more than old evidence. The *New York American* wrote that Lloyd Fisher had cited an affidavit by John Hughes Curtis claiming that a gang of seven men had committed the crime.[20] Wilentz had countered this by insisting that the matter of accomplices was not relevant to Hauptmann's conviction. He further argued that evidence that the condemned man had written the ransom notes tied him to the crime; and this being so, regardless of whether Hauptmann was alone or had many accomplices, he was guilty, and the nature of the crime warranted his execution. The Faulkner letter to Governor Hauptmann was also said to have been introduced, along with the opinion of the defense's document expert that the handwriting matched that of the ransom notes. Nothing establishing who Faulkner was seems to have been brought up.

The posthearing interviews that newsmen had requested with the usually cooperative governor were rejected, not by Harold Hoffman, who hurried away a vision of displeasure, but by his press secretary, William S. Conklin.[21] The question on the media's mind, which already appeared in print, was whether the governor would now grant Hauptmann a reprieve so that his private investigation could continue trying to develop information. The matter of whether new evidence could affect the prisoner's destiny was muddled. New Jersey's legal establishment generally concurred that either the trial judge or the court of pardons still had the power to reverse Hauptmann's death sentence if new information warranted such an action. A vociferous minority of judicial scholars doubted that such a right existed.

— — —

As newsboys in America shouted Hauptmann's fate from street corners, newspeople who had gathered outside the Llandaff, Wales, estate of Aubrey Morgan waited patiently to speak with the Lindberghs, who were staying there. Aubrey Morgan had been married to Anne Lindbergh's older sister, Elisabeth, who died December 3, 1934. Since going into exile, the Lindberghs had made no public statements concerning the events in Trenton, and Morgan informed reporters that the Colonel intended to keep it that way.

In Kamenz, Germany, told of the American court's refusal to commute her son's death sentence, Frau Pauline Hauptmann collapsed in her chair and moaned, "That's terrible. How can it be." She declared, "Colonel Lindbergh will take a terrible responsibility on himself if he permits the execution."[22] Back in Trenton, Frau Hauptmann's daughter-in-law, Anna, did what she could to tolerate reporters, went to church, conferred with her lawyers, and sent a cable to her mother-in-law: "Beloved mother, don't despair. There is still hope. The truth will come to light before it is too late, for Richard is guiltless. With love, Annie."[23]

Ralph Hacker, John F. Condon's son-in-law, couldn't understand Governor Hoffman's eleventh hour decision to question Jafsie. "Why, he has been willing to be questioned at all times," Hacker told reporters. He explained that the ocean voyage was Condon's regular vacation, coupled with a desire to get sea air for his daughter, Hacker's wife, whose health was not good. "Before leaving on this trip he had an inquiry made of the attorney general if there was any reason why he should not go at this time and was assured there was not." Hacker revealed that his wife and Jafsie had not taken along passports, which meant they wouldn't be visiting any foreign country. He said they were staying with friends in the Canal Zone, and he had no idea how long they would be away.[24]

Confronted by the press, Attorney General David Wilentz admitted he knew that Condon, a potentially crucial witness for the defense's case for clemency, planned to leave the country the night before the court of pardons was to hear Hauptmann's petition. "I saw no reason then," Wilentz told a reporter, "why he shouldn't go and I see no reason now."[25]

By the morning of January 12, the media were reporting that during the court of pardons hearing, a confrontation had occurred between Hoffman and Wilentz over the apprehension of Jafsie Condon, as well as over the governor's power to invoke a reprieve as he saw fit. The disagreement carried into the next day, and Hoffman, in a pique of anger, was said to have told Wilentz that if he had to, he would continue to reprieve Hauptmann until the end of his term as governor, some two years hence.[26]

The governor's trip to New York City that evening was accomplished with an unusual degree of secrecy, considering that he was continually dogged by newsmen. He was a regular commuter to Manhattan, where his usual pied-à-terre was the New Yorker Hotel's gubernatorial suite, number 2200, better known as the Huey Long Suite, since it had been favored by the Kingfish when he'd been in town. The ostensible reason for the trip was to attend a Circus, Saints and Sinners bash that night, a usually high-profile event that was well covered by the media.[27] But it wasn't until the next morning that reporters got wind he was in town. Arriving at suite 2200, they found the governor poring over his upcoming budget message to the New Jersey legislature. Not lost on the newsmen was the fact that Bruno Richard Hauptmann's defense attorneys occupied suite 2600 in the same hotel, where they were trying to devise last-minute strategies for saving their client's life.[28] The governor denied having met with them during his current visit, refused to commit himself on the matter of granting a reprieve, said he still intended to have Condon arrested and brought back to America, and in response to questions about the criticism being heaped on his intervention in the Hauptmann case, he said,

> Politically I've always had the ball on my own five-yard line. I'm in the position that had I done nothing, I would have been blamed for negligence in duty, and when I do try to do something, I'm charged with seeking publicity.
>
> Hauptmann means nothing to me personally. I have had no object in this case but to see that justice is done. I think every one will admit that the death of Hauptmann will leave the case still not completely solved.
>
> There are still many angles of this whole thing to which we do not know the answer. When the relatives or lawyers of any man condemned to death come to me with information which may aid the prisoner, I consider it my duty to investigate that information. I have done no more or less in this case.[29]

Exemplifying how the governor's behavior had frustrated and outraged a great many Americans was Congressman Blanton of Texas. On Monday, January 13, Blanton rose on the floor of the U.S. House of Representatives and attacked the "yellow newspapers" he accused of creating sympathy for the condemned prisoner. He ridiculed the governor and told his Capitol Hill colleagues, "Hoffman has no more right to order the arrest of Dr. Condon than I have. If Hoffman authorized the statement in the headline he ought to be impeached."[30]

In France, *Paris Soir* published a copyrighted interview with Charles Lindbergh, the first such story the Lone Eagle had granted since going into exile. "I want silence and peace," he was quoted as saying. "I want to be forgotten. I should like people to forget even my name."[31]

With the clock ticking for Bruno Hauptmann, the mounting suspense as to whether the governor would grant a reprieve was added to by political enemies in the New Jersey State Legislature who claimed that no such right existed and that they would block any attempt by the chief executive to try to delay the execution. Then, too, there was another legal technicality to exhaust, which if by itself couldn't save the condemned carpenter's life—and few expected this to happen—might provide the governor with one more pretext for issuing the reprieve: a writ of habeas corpus to be filed with the U.S. Supreme Court on the grounds that Hauptmann's constitutional rights had been violated during the kidnapping-murder trial in Flemington. Hauptmann's chief counsel, Lloyd Fisher, brought in two constitutional-law experts to initiate the process of a federal appeal.

On the morning of January 14, the *New York American* reported on its front page HOFFMAN TO GIVE REPRIEVE IF ABLE. The paper attributed the information to an unnamed reliable source and also printed that should anti-reprieve forces, led by the Democrats, make good on their threat to legally challenge the current statute pertaining to the matter, the governor's allies were ready to introduce a new bill for immediate passage by the legislature that would ensure his right to issue a reprieve. The *American*, like other papers, also wrote that the Democratic members of the state legislature were prepared to demand that the body launch an official investigation into the governor's conduct vis-à-vis the Hauptmann case.

One particularly sticky wicket that the governor's detractors hoped to make an issue of was expressed by Mercer County assemblyman Crawford Jamieson: "We are informed that Governor Hoffman was accompanied by one or two women when he made the secret visit to Hauptmann's cell." Jamieson also demanded to know on what evidence the governor based "his friendly attitude" toward Hauptmann. There was more: "We want to know why he has consulted the defense counsel so often and ignored the Attorney General, the legal adviser of the state government."[32] From Chicago, where the report of a special American Bar Association committee bitterly criticized the tactics used at Flemington, Lloyd Fisher and his fellow defense lawyers received unexpected support for their contention that Hauptmann hadn't received a fair trial.

— — —

At 6:02 P.M. the evening of January 14, after a stormy ninety-minute hearing in a federal courtroom in Trenton's new Post Office Building, Judge J. Warren Davis denied Hauptmann an application for a writ of habeas corpus. A moment later he denied a second motion for a federal stay of execution. Journalists, wanting to know the governor's next move, were told by his press secretary that no steps would be taken to force Jafsie Condon to return from his cruise. This, to the media, sounded like final confirmation that a reprieve was imminent.

The next day the electric chair at the Trenton State Prison was tested and found to be in working order. The media were told that Hauptmann's spiritual adviser, Rev. John Mathis, would accompany him to the execution room, along with the prison chaplain, Rev. John Goorly.

That evening Harold Hoffman was back in New York City, this time accompanied by his secretary and aide-de-camp, William Lagay. Once more he checked into the New Yorker Hotel unnoticed by the press. He was, from all indications, exhausted and despondent. Despite the fact that much of the media and many antagonists pictured his investigation as a well-financed and pervasive undertaking abetted by the powers vested in the office of the chief executive, the opposite was more accurate. His staff was composed mainly of volunteers—and a ragtag lot at that. The inquiry had little or no available cash and in the governor's own estimation was also "handicapped by merciless ridicule, blocked at every turn by the police agencies who should have been aiding in the search. Progress is feeble."[33]

As much as anything, the night of January 15 in the New Yorker was meant to be a cathartic, and Hoffman would later write,

> Harassed and tired after weeks of abuse, my office swamped with the daily receipt of thousand of letters and wires, almost worn out with efforts to dodge reporters, photographers, private detectives, and "cranks" who seemed to encounter me at every turn, the evening held promise, in spite of the few appointments I had made, of being fairly free for relaxation and thought. I needed it. In

the following day I knew I would face the necessity of making an important decision.[34]

The governor was scheduled to meet at the hotel with Ellis Parker. Since the Old Chief wanted Murray Bleefeld's brother-in-law, Martin Schlossman, to be sworn in as a deputy, Schlossman may have been invited to join them, something that never occurred, probably due to an unexpected guest. While chatting with the governor, Vernon Taylor, the assistant manager of the New Yorker, mentioned that David Wilentz was downstairs in the hotel's Terrace Room, having dinner with friends.

Harold Hoffman would later write that he wasn't sure whether he asked Taylor to tell the attorney general that he was in the hotel or whether Wilentz learned on his own. One way or another, and "without prearrangement," the governor stated,

> we got together and talked about Hauptmann.
>
> It was a long, earnest, important talk. The Attorney General and I have known each other for years. We managed the same basketball team at different times; we worked for the same newspaper; he became Democratic County Chairman of Middlesex County; I became Republican County Chairman of that county at the same time. Wilentz became Attorney General; I became Governor. There is little difference in our ages. I respect his ability, his successful fight against odds to make a place in the world. He has done many things that reflect friendship for me.
>
> Dave Wilentz and I do not have to "pull our punches." . . . We have disagreed in politics; we have certainly disagreed, without any personal feeling, on the Hauptmann case. . . . That night I expressed to the Attorney General the doubts I entertained about the case. I gave him frankly my appraisal of the value of the testimony of the state's identification witnesses, the things that I considered evidence that should have been presented, the position I had been placed in by misrepresentation.
>
> There were some things I could not tell him—[35]

Wilentz, for the sake of argument, assumed that the key defense witnesses were untruthful. He was still convinced by the physical evidence—

Condon's phone number on a closet beam (which a reporter had all but confessed to printing there), the spelling of *boat* as *boad* in the ransom note as well as in an old diary—that Hauptmann's conviction was warranted.

"But that evidence," the governor argued, "would support only the crime of extortion. Even if it were unanswerable, it would not put Hauptmann at the scene of the kidnap and murder."

Wilentz replied, "Then why in hell doesn't he tell the truth?"[36]

According to Harold Hoffman, the two old adversaries agreed that it was more important "to society" to get the complete story—how a man could conceive and execute such a ghastly plan single-handedly—than it was to take his life. They evolved a plan to secure a confession, if there was a confession to be had.

"Wilentz left, and I had another visit to make," Hoffman wrote. "J. Edgar, I had learned, was in the hotel."[37] The director of the Division of Investigation was in suite 2716-17, and the governor visited him there.[38] The two men talked until well after midnight. It was now January 16. The following evening Hauptmann was to die.

⁃ ⁃ ⁃

With less than three hours' sleep Harold Hoffman left New York City on the 7:00 A.M. train to Trenton. It was January 16, and he went straightaway to his suite at the Hotel Hildebrecht and dispatched Colonel J. Fred Margerum, his military aide-de-camp, to arrange for an immediate, and discreet, meeting with the condemned man's wife, Anna Hauptmann. The governor was soon en route to the Stacy-Trent Hotel, where Mrs. Hauptmann was staying. To avoid the lingering battery of photographers and newsreel men in the lobby, he entered through a rear door, took a freight elevator upstairs, and went to the hotel manager's private suite, where he was left alone with the doomed man's wife. "Mrs. Hauptmann," Harold Hoffman said with an assumed air of finality, "tomorrow is the day when, under the law, your husband is to die. I wanted to help him, but he has not been telling me, or anyone else, the truth."

"No! No! No!" screamed Anna Hauptmann. "Dot isn't so! Richard did tell the truth! He is telling the truth!" With clenched fists she began beating against the governor's chest. "Listen to me, Gofe'nor, listen to me!"

"Things look bad for your husband," Hoffman continued. "Every one seems to believe that he is guilty. There is only one way in which he can save his life."

The distraught wife wanted to know what that way was, and the governor explained the understanding he and David Wilentz had come to the night before: If Hauptmann agreed to tell the whole story, the governor and the attorney general or an aide of the attorney general's, would go to the prison and listen; if they were convinced he was telling the truth, even if he had acted alone in perpetrating the crime, they would petition the court of pardons to set aside the death penalty and change his sentence to life imprisonment—and there was no doubt that the court would honor the request from both the governor and the attorney general.

"You must go to the prison this morning," Hoffman told her. "You must see your husband. You must tell him he can save his life. You must tell him that you want him to tell the truth."

Anna Hauptmann screamed that she could not, that he would turn his back on her. "He vould think dot the last von in the vorld to know that he is innozent should think, too, dot he haf commit this crime!"

More emotional give and take ensued, and finally the woman agreed to a compromise suggestion: that she would ask her husband if he would be willing to be seen by the governor and the attorney general and answer their questions. She stipulated, however, "I vill not say to him—his vife—dot at last he should tell the truth, van alvays I know dot he has told the truth dot he did not do dis terrible thing."

An hour later, back in his rooms at the Hotel Hildebrecht, Harold Hoffman received a call from the keeper of the state prisons, Mark Kimberling, who put Mrs. Hauptmann on the phone. Richard, she told him, would see him and Wilentz. "But Gofe'nor, the story is just the same; he haf told eferything he knows—nothing more he can tell."[39]

Hoffman called Wilentz and informed him of Hauptmann's response.

"To hell with it, Harold," Wilentz declared. "If that's still his attitude, I'm damned if I'm going to do anything to help him."[40]

Bruno Hauptmann was not interviewed.

At approximately 2:33 P.M. in Washington, D.C., the U.S. Supreme Court wasted only twenty-one words in refusing Hauptmann's attorneys the right to petition for a writ of habeas corpus and a stay of execution. The condemned man's final legal tactic had failed.

At 3:25 P.M. Governor Harold G. Hoffman, accompanied by the attorney general, David Wilentz, and the Hunterdon County prosecutor, Anthony Hauck, arrived at the executive chamber of the statehouse. The crush of waiting spectators, reporters, photographers, and newsreel cameras was invited into the governor's conference room, where at 3:29 P.M. they were told by Hoffman, "The Attorney General and I just have been in a conference on this matter, and I have decided to issue a reprieve for thirty days."

Newsmen rushed for telephones and temporary telegraph facilities, causing the governor to comment, "They apparently don't care what the Attorney General says about this." The governor went on:

> "My intention is to grant just this one reprieve. There will be no further reprieves. I had held that with fourteen different reprieves given by six different governors since 1906, there existed ample executive precedent for the issuance of a reprieve by the governor even though the ninety day period had expired since the conviction at Flemington.
>
> "On a strict interpretation of the law, the Attorney General feels that a reprieve cannot be granted. But he has agreed by reason of the fact there is ample precedent that the right of the Governor will not be challenged."[41]

Questions followed.

With the none-too-cheery Wilentz and Hauck looking on, Harold Hoffman signed the order that extended Hauptmann's life—and his own efforts to prove who had killed the Lindbergh baby—another thirty days.

26

COUNTDOWN

THE RACE WAS ON. HAROLD HOFFMAN HAD THIRTY DAYS TO SAVE THE LIFE OF Bruno Richard Hauptmann and salvage what he could of his crumbling political fortunes. Legal recourses were running out. A confession by Hauptmann that he had not acted alone would help the governor's cause. A confession that he alone was guilty would also be welcomed. Governor Hoffman fervently believed that Hauptmann's complicity in the crime was negligible, if not nonexistent, and proving it had become a passion—proving it anyway he could, with any gambit possible. Enter Jacob Nosovitsky.

On January 17, 1936, as word of the previous day's reprieve for Hauptmann made headlines, Nosovitsky also was front-page news, but only in the *New York American* and not under his own name. The *American* ran a two-column article, BREAK SEEN NEAR IN MYSTERY, that carried the by-line of Sanford E. Stanton, the reporter who accompanied Gus Lock-wood and investigator Mary McGill to the December meeting at the Tombs with Wally Stroh and Dennis Doyle.[1] Like Nosovitsky, Stroh and Doyle weren't mentioned by name in the text, only as two New York prison inmates, but Stanton credited them with providing information that unearthed the latest prime suspect in the governor's attempt to determine who actually perpetrated the Lindbergh crime: a Russian Pole—that is, Nosovitsky. The mysterious suspect was said to speak German fluently and bear a striking resemblance to Hauptmann. Back in 1932 he had a hacking cough, an affliction Jafsie Condon had attributed to John.

The Stanton article asserted that the mystery man, who was no minor criminal, had a record of burglary, forgery, and bigamy; that he had boasted of having fooled the Justice Department into employing him as a confidential investigator and that one of his dupes was J. Edgar Hoover; that he had tried, a short time before the Lindbergh kidnapping, to extort money in a scam where St. Raymond's Cemetery was used as the drop off. Back in 1932, he had been working with a woman accomplice. Three days before the Eaglet disappeared, they dropped out of sight.

Stanton recounted that in the wake of the two inmates' having fingered the Russian Pole, the governor's experts worked all night and concluded that his handwriting bore a striking similarity to that in the ransom notes as well as to J. J. Faulkner's signature. The governor was said to have been impressed by this and other information indicating that the mystery man, and possibly his woman accomplice, were the true culprits. An all-out search for the suspect had been initiated the week before. Hauptmann's reprieve came on the heels of these discoveries and with the governor stating that the new lead "holds dramatic possibilities which may overshadow anything that has thus far occurred in the case." Though the apprehension of the mystery suspect might establish that Hauptmann was innocent and save his life, an aide to the governor allowed that it could also, evidentially, tie Bruno closer to the crime than ever. If the Russian Pole was the perpetrator, Hauptmann might turn out to have been an accomplice.

The *American* article detailed additional activities and frustrations of the governor's investigators in recent days that could have been obtained only by someone privy to inside information, such as Stanton. It would be half a day before most competing papers would have any statement as to why Harold Hoffman had decided on granting the reprieve. Stanton bared it on January 17: The governor wanted the whole truth, and after studying every available record, including the new information, he was not convinced that Bruno had acted alone.

The following day Stanton still had the exclusive on Nosovitsky, as his page-one three-column report in the *New York American* announced, HOFFMAN TRACES NEW SUSPECT IN WEST AS HE DEFIES CRITICS; OFFICIALS GET DEATH THREATS: "Suspect Search Involves Woman; Police Chiefs Told Name of Lindy Case Accomplice." The text revealed that the governor's investigators, working independently of the New Jersey State Police, had sent information regarding the new prime suspect to police departments in several midwestern cities. Their mystery man's description was, of course, a description of the still unnamed Jacob Nosovitsky:

Age 47–49
Hgt 5' 10½"
Wght 160
Eye Gray
Hair Sandy streaked with gray
Prominent cheek bones
Speaks with strong Teutonic accent.

The *American* let it be known that the governor's operatives, who had been on the case for two months, believed they were weaving together a strong chain of circumstantial evidence that implicated both the Russian Pole and the woman accomplice. The suspect's trail had already led investigators near where Hauptmann lived in the Bronx as well as to Yorkville, where Bruno had spent much of his time. It was discovered that an associate of the wanted man lived on the sixth floor of a walk-up apartment building in the Bronx. The investigator assigned to follow up, in this case a woman detective, had rented a room in the building and waited for the suspect to show up, which he failed to do.

According to the *American,* the governor had initially requested a review of every step of the case from the night of the kidnapping on, including channels of investigation followed by the New Jersey State Police, the New York PD, and the G-men. Crack sleuth Gus Lockwood was quoted as saying, "My orders were simply to clean up the case. Particularly, I was told to dig up Hauptmann's accomplices, if he had any."

By Sunday, January 19, the *New York Daily News* and the *New York American* both proclaimed that the trail of J. J. Faulkner—they both acknowledged him as being the Russian Pole—had been picked up by the New Jersey State Police and federal agents and that his capture appeared imminent. The *American*'s exclusivity regarding Nosovitsky had ended.

— — —

The two-party theory, so circumspectly embraced by the governor and a select group of aides, exploded into print the following day, when several newspapers made a startling revelation: The Russian Pole might only have intercepted the ransom payment and had nothing to with the taking of the baby. It was reported that the suspect may have seen the ransom note that Rosner, Spitale, and Bitz had shown around the New York City underworld in the wake of the child's disappearance back in March of 1932 and then copied the style to send his own counterfeit notes, which ultimately brought Jafsie Condon—and fifty thousand dollars—to a meeting with him in St. Raymond's graveyard.

Not one newsman, or paper, speculated that if this were true, if in fact the note had been copied, who was it, then, who had written the original message, and who had left it in the nursery, where Lindbergh claimed he had found it on a windowsill?

— — —

On January 16, the day the reprieve was granted, the *Trenton Evening Times* printed a special edition, in which a front-page editorial box called for the governor's impeachment. Nearly every other paper in the state condemned his action, though few of them echoed the impeachment demand. Even publications usually partial to Hoffman found little merit in granting a reprieve. The national and international media were no more consoling.

Harold Hoffman struck back at his critics and, in particular, at the *Trenton Evening Times*, by saying:

> I expected it. It is typical of the editorial abuse I have received since November 1934 when I committed the unpardonable sin of being elected when the Trenton Times and several other New Jersey newspapers said that I couldn't.
>
> If impeachment is the price that must be paid for daring to follow the dictates of my own conscience, I am ready to

pay it. A good investigation of the Lindbergh case might be a healthy thing. If an investigation is started I will not run away.

I have never expressed an opinion upon the guilt or innocence of Hauptmann. I do share, with hundreds of thousands of other people the doubt as to the value of the evidence that placed him in the Lindbergh nursery the night of the crime. I do wonder what part passion and prejudice played in the conviction of a man who was previously tried and convicted in the columns of many of our newspapers.[2]

Word that Harold Hoffman would command him to reopen the Lindbergh investigation sent Schwarzkopf running to Wilentz, from whom he sought a definition of his legal rights and obligations regarding such an order. The attorney general was not duty bound to the governor in this matter. But the superintendent of the state police, who was flat out against the reprieve, had to obey the chief executive's dictates. After conferring with Wilentz, Schwarzkopf announced that he would do as the governor bade. Hoffman had reason to believe that H. Norman's compliance was not wholehearted when on January 19 he learned that Lieutenant Keaten of the state police and three more top trooper officers were discreetly monitoring the progress of his investigation.[3] The governor had already added to the state police's and Wilentz's discomfort with a report that he was inviting J. Edgar Hoover's Division of Investigation to join the reopened inquiry. Wilentz was able to pay Hoffman back in kind regarding Jafsie Condon, who was still in Panama and whom the governor urgently wanted to interview. Jafsie wired Wilentz on January 17, saying he was willing to come back. The attorney general answered that he saw no reason, under the prevailing conditions, for the old man to cut short his vacation.

The open break between Harold Hoffman and H. Norman Schwarzkopf as well as David Wilentz, which many newsmen were predicting, never quite occurred. But animosity ran high, and brinkmanship was the rule of the day. H. Norman managed to get a lick in by asserting that even though he would do as ordered by the governor, Hauptmann was guilty.[4] The governor saw to it that an open letter he had received was circulated around the state office building; it urged that Mark O. Kimberling be named the new superintendent of the New Jersey State Police when H. Norman's five-year term ended in June. Schwarzie's defenders accused Hoffman loyalists at the Department of Motor Vehicles of writing the letter. The governor demanded that Wilentz turn over to him material in his possession concerning an alleged illegitimate son of the late Dwight W. Morrow. The attorney general did so on January 22, with a stern warning for the chief executive not to follow this course of investigation.[5]

On Thursday, January 30, Schwarzkopf received a sharply worded letter from the governor, instructing him to renew the investigation of the Lindbergh case and saying in part that the state-police boss was to "continue a thorough and impartial search" and that "you will acknowledge receipt of this letter and will report to me, in writing, at least once weekly, the steps you have taken."[6] The text also contained nineteen questions the governor demanded be answered, many of which were accusatory in regard to the state-police investigation and the prosecution's handling of the trial.[7] In a telephone discussion regarding the order, Schwarzkopf asked Wilentz, "How do you respond to something like this?"

The state's attorney general replied, "You don't. Hauptmann has been tried and convicted and he's exhausted his appeals. As far as I'm concerned the governor's investigation is irrelevant."

The trooper boss explained, "But he wants a weekly report—on our progress."

Wilentz countered, "All right. So you look around and what do you find?"

The answer Schwarzie came up with was "Nothing."

"So that's your report," the state's ranking law-enforcement officer explained.

The following day Schwarzkopf responded to the governor in writing, pledged his full support of the renewed inquiry, and added, "Please turn over to me any and all information you may possess which may support the doubts you have expressed."[8] David Wilentz, the same day, publicly criticized the governor for reopening the case, reiterated his firm belief that Hauptmann alone was guilty of the crime, gave assurances that Colonel Schwarzkopf would cooperate with the governor, and left for a three-week vacation in Florida.

Harold Hoffman and David Wilentz did share one new and common experience: In the wake of the reprieve's being issued, they had each received death threats for their respective stands on the issue. So had prosecutor Anthony Hauck, whose children were threatened as well. All three officials and their families were assigned bodyguards.

J. Edgar Hoover's public posture subscribed to the guilt of Bruno Hauptmann, but just prior to the reprieve he had met with Harold Hoffman in the New Yorker Hotel, a meeting that might have given the governor an impression that the director of the bureau was sympathetic to his views. J. Edgar liked Harold Hoffman. But he certainly didn't care much for Jacob Nosovitsky, who had conned him into writing personal endorsements for an ongoing scam back in the 1920s. His principal bête noire, however, was H. Norman Schwarzkopf, who had not only excluded the bureau from the original Lindbergh investigation but had made no secret that he intended to take J. Edgar's job. Hoover and his organization had systematically done what they could, within the confines of questionable taste, to discredit the state-police handling of the Lindbergh case. The difficulty here was that they had so effectively been cut off from the inquiry that much of the information the G-men obtained was second- and thirdhand and inaccurate. Even so, there was little the troopers had done that one bureau expert or another couldn't take to task.

Subsequent to the reprieve, Hoover provided the governor with solicited as well as unsolicited information regarding the case,[9] such as a copy of a letter he received on January 5 and passed on to David Wilentz on January 23 that declared the Lindbergh kidnapper to be one Mike Sololiski, a Russian Pole who had killed five women.[10] The same shipment of documents included a letter from the lawyer representing an ex-convict who claimed that Gaston Means handed him twenty-five thousand dollars.

J. Edgar Hoover was no political novice. The Lindbergh case was poison PR medicine. He didn't mind helping his pal the governor twit Schwarzkopf's nose, or even Wilentz's, for that matter, but ultimately he wasn't going to open up a full investigation into the affair. When on February 4, Harold Hoffman, a Republican, finally got H. Norman Schwarzkopf, the appointee of a Democratic governor, to request formally the DI's participation in the renewed investigation, Hoover let his boss, U.S. Attorney General Homer Cummings, another Democratic appointee, extend a polite refusal.

Harold Hoffman didn't fare any better with the coalition administration of New York City's mayor, Fiorello La Guardia, a fusion candidate.

Schwarzkopf's February 4 letter to the commissioner of the New York Police Department, now James Valentine, requested that the NYPD reinstate its original team of Lindbergh investigators and revive the case. In his reply Valentine lauded the renewed inquiry and flatly refused to participate.

The governor was forced to go it alone, using a group of predominantly volunteer investigators, whom the *New York Herald Tribune* consistently referred to as amateurs. Since Justice Trenchard had agreed to Wilentz's request to set a new execution date only after the thirty-day reprieve ran out, it was expected that Hauptmann would be given an additional four or five weeks to live. The task before Harold Hoffman's probers was profound. Locating the elusive Nosovitsky was already more difficult than had been expected. Reviewing the state-police case files—there would be an estimated forty thousand pages accumulated by the governor before the matter was concluded—was in itself a monumental undertaking. Coordinating the activities was often impossible, and many of the operations, like runaway trains, sped off in their own direction.

On January 16, the day the reprieve was signed, the *New York American* announced that Governor Hoffman had moved his investigatory headquarters to a midtown New York City hotel. This was partially true. He continued to visit Manhattan's New Yorker Hotel for political as much as investigatory reasons and also to be near his favored Circus, Saints and Sinners organization. There is nothing to indicate that he didn't confer on the progress of two New York City–related channels of investigation. Wally Stroh was still being interviewed at the Tombs by Gus Lockwood's team, which included Mary McGill and William Pelletreau. Stroh, who had approximately sixty days left to serve in jail, agreed to stay at McGill's home on his release so he could be available as he was needed by the governor's people. His information had already sent at least one investigator to Nosovitsky's brother in Cleveland. The brother acknowledged that his notorious sibling had been there a week before the kidnapping but claimed not to know his present whereabouts. Lockwood's unit continued to contact out-of-state agencies and try to locate and interview people who might know where Nosovitsky had gone, such as Mollie Schneiderman, his bigamized third wife.

Ellis Parker also had a New York City operation under way: zeroing in on the man he stubbornly considered to be the sole culprit, Paul Wendel. Murray Bleefeld and several associates had managed to trace Wendel to the Stamford Hotel on Manhattan's Thirty-second Street and were keeping him under surveillance.

The bulk of the investigation remained in New Jersey, with command posts in either the governor's suite at Trenton's Hildebrecht Hotel or in his offices at the statehouse. It was at the statehouse that on January 18, two days after signing the reprieve, Hoffman conferred with another group of his operatives, a meeting at which Dr. Erastus Hudson gave additional weight to the possibility of Lindbergh's manipulations by claiming that shortly after the kidnapping someone in the Sorrel Hill household had carefully wiped the nursery clean and that "it was ludicrous to imagine that the kidnapper had gone down the ramshackle ladder with a pail of water and rag in one hand, and the baby in the other."[11]

The governor at this juncture had been contacted by a young woman from Boston named Zoe Hobbs, who was petitioning to become a volunteer investigator. They had exchanged several letters before she wrote to him on January 17, saying in part that he was a great man for his stand on the Lindbergh-Hauptmann case. Zoe enclosed a personal biography that claimed she had been a court reporter for the *Boston Evening Record*. On the second page it stated, "If an investigation is to take place, why not let it include members of the Lindbergh and Morrow family."[12] The governor accepted her application.

— — —

The slapdash manner in which the governor had recruited investigators, and the quality of this personnel, began to take its toll. Many of these operatives bore code names. K-4, for example, was Harold C. Keyes, the private detective who had come to the governor via Bruno Hauptmann's attorney, Lloyd Fisher. Keyes, among other self-assigned tasks, was currently investigating a reputed sweetheart of Isador Fisch's as well as the possession by a New York man of eight thousand dollars that might have come from the ransom payment.

R-9 was Robert Hicks, the vaunted criminologist whom Mrs. McLean had contributed to the cause and whose salary she was still partially paying. R-9 was also receiving funds from another booster of the governor's investigation, Paul G. Clancy, editor to the *American Astrology* magazine.

Hicks had a remarkable ability to get his name in the papers, where it had already been reported that he went to St. Raymond's Cemetery and reenacted the ransom payment and had Hauptmann's attic examined in conjunction with his own wood expert, Arch W. Loney of the Public Works Administration. Another well-reported assignment being investigated by Hicks was a claim that Betty Gow had been seen at the Elarno Hotel in Coney Island, Brooklyn, just prior to the kidnapping. His most imaginative bit of press agentry occurred just before the issuing of the reprieve. He was aboard a train when two trunks crashed through the window of his compartment and knocked him unconscious. Railroad personnel told reporters it was an accident; Hicks swore it was a plot.[13]

Zoe Hobbs had also begun to display a knack for getting her name in the papers, so far and luckily in out-of-town papers. When it came to major media mischief, not to mention tampering with the investigation's top source of information, Hobbs and Hicks could take a lesson or two from the private eye and handwriting maven Bill Pelletreau.

The *New York American* had helped steer the governor's investigators to Wally Stroh and as a result received an exclusive on the story. It was only time before other papers would learn who the *American*'s, and Gus Lockwood's, source was. Warned of this by the governor's men, Stroh agreed to make no statements to other media people. He was good to his word, telling inquiring journalists that if any information was wanted, they should contact Mary McGill's boss, Dr. E. M. Hudson, at 30 East Seventy-sixth Street.

Like McGill, Pelletreau was one of the investigating team's members who continued to visit Stroh. Stroh was broke. Pelletreau arranged a deal for Wally with the *New York Daily News*—and a deal for himself as the *News*'s representative. Stroh was working on a story that would present all the facts—and name Nosovitsky. His asking price was five thousand dollars, which the *News* agreed to place in escrow. If Nosovitsky turned out to be the malefactor, Wally could have the money and the *News* could have his story. Until then, to maintain the investigation's confidentiality, the paper could not publish the suspect's name. Though it was not part of the arrangement, on Sunday, January 19, the *News* broke the *New York American*'s stranglehold on the story by announcing, along with the *American*, that the trail of J. J. Faulkner had been picked up by the New Jersey State Police and federal investigators and that his capture appeared imminent.

Wally Stroh and William Pelletreau were not the only ones concerned with dollars. The Great Depression still gripped the land. People needed money. In the crunch Harold Hoffman would pay a needy investigator out of pocket, and the source of some of these funds would come back to haunt him. Harold ("K-4") Keyes focused a good part of a January 20 letter to the governor on his own particular financial bind. Keyes claimed that he was still owed over twenty-one hundred dollars by Lloyd Fisher and Mrs. Hauptmann, who hadn't paid him for the twenty-one weeks that he was in their employ. To do his current work for the governor, he had to borrow and pawn. Now he was behind by at least two hundred dollars and needed to keep on renting a car. K-4's suggested solution to his predicament was for Harold Hoffman to put him on the state payroll.[14] Zoe Hobbs, via a series of desperate telegrams, would soon be putting in her requests for expenses also.[15]

As February began, Hobbs was industriously following up leads on the Morrow and Lindbergh families. The search for Nosovitsky had been unproductive, and Ellis Parker's only concern seemed to be Paul Wendel. Others in the investigation focused on more esoteric clues as well as on reexamining the trial and the state-police investigation. Many of their objectives were set down by the governor in his January 30 letter to Schwarzkopf, which ordered the state-police boss not only to reopen the investigation but also to answer nineteen questions regarding the troopers' investigation.

Despite the fact that the press had printed his claim of having received ten thousand letters regarding the reprieve and that 80 percent voiced approval of his decision, Harold Hoffman's action in behalf of Hauptmann had triggered a bitter in-house battle over his right to lead his own Republican party. Rumors that the state legislature, which had never impeached a governor, was about to impeach him proved false, but in a rare action the state committee of Jersey's GOP requested that he attend their January 21 meeting in Trenton.[16] Hoffman appeared and was roundly criticized for granting the reprieve. Warnings were issued that his activities in behalf of Hauptmann were unpopular with voters. Some committee members suggested that he not attend the party's upcoming national convention at Cleveland. The governor insisted on being a delegate.

The same day as the GOP meeting in Trenton, the *New York American,* which had initiated the search for Nosovitsky and given more linage to the reinvestigation than any other New York City newspaper, printed an editorial condemning Hauptmann's reprieve and accusing the governor of PLAYING A LONE HAND—FOR WHAT STAKES, HE ALONE KNOWS. Twelve days later, on February 2, Henry W. Jeffers, chairman of the New Jersey Republican State Committee, emphatically denied that the GOP intended to repudiate Governor Hoffman for his policies. Jeffers, a close friend of the governor's who had become head of the committee when Hoffman was elected, made no mention of the reprieve or investigation but did admit that some committee members were at odds with the state's chief executive over policy and patronage. "In spite of these personal differences," said Jeffers, "I think I speak for all members of the committee in saying that the Governor has been fearless and sincere and probably has devoted more time and thought to State problems than any chief executive in the history of New Jersey."[17]

Three days later, and seventy-two hours shy of his fortieth birthday, on February 7, in a devastating political setback Governor Harold Hoffman, with a vote of fourteen to nine, was stripped of his party's leadership by the New Jersey Republican State Committee. His supporters were quick to insist that this drastic action was not due to the Lindbergh case but to intraparty fighting, a condition the governor helped exacerbate when he came out swinging during the sixth annual HGH Birthday Club banquet at New York's Commodore Hotel. It was Thursday night, February 6, and Hoffman told a spirited gathering of a thousand-strong dinner guests that if his political enemies wanted war, war he would give them. He had particular venom for the *Evening News of Newark* and a New Jersey state senator named Everett Colby, whom he accused, in so many words, of possessing a society Blue Book mentality and of never having gotten over the fact that the people elected Hoffman governor. Colby, Hoffman told his delighted guests, was no newcomer to ruining the GOP in New Jersey; it was a skill he had begun perfecting way back in 1906.[18]

The *Trenton Evening Times*'s birthday message to the governor was contained in yet another editorial attacking him, which was headed DEATH BEGINS AT FORTY![19]

On February 9, the governor checked into the Mercer Hospital in Trenton—for what was called a minor nasal operation. Rumor spread that it was a heart attack or a nervous breakdown. It could have been neither, or both. But Harold Hoffman needed the rest.

The reality of execution had begun to affect Hauptmann. He had already seen seven of his death row cellmates walk past on their way to the electric chair. Richard, as he still wanted to be called, cried more often, got on well with the guards, and seemed to have lost a good deal of his arrogance. There was one point on which he remained uncompromising and intransigent: his innocence. Deals to save his life had been offered—some including money, which he desperately needed—if he would only name his accomplices. Richard would not hear of it. Then, in a surprise move, he dismissed Lloyd Fisher, who had believed in his innocence, and replaced him with forty-three-year-old Samuel Simon Leibowitz, the high-profile defender of the Scottsboro boys and Al Capone who was acclaimed for his daily radio analysis during the Hauptmann trial and who was certain Bruno was guilty.

The action came as a result of Mrs. Evalyn Walsh McLean's avid belief that Hauptmann hadn't acted alone and that his trial had been a mockery. It was at her recommendation that Harold Hoffman had taken on Robert Hicks as one of his investigators. McLean continued to pay a portion of Hick's salary; now she conferred with him to see what action could be taken in Bruno's behalf. She met with Leibowitz at her Washington abode. The New York lawyer was cocksure of Hauptmann's complicity but considered it nonsense to believe that only one man perpetrated the crime. He would take the case and obtain a confession and agreed to a ten-thousand-dollar retainer plus a bonus of fifteen thousand dollars if successful, all to be paid by McLean. McLean was also willing to give money to the badly strapped Hauptmanns. Hicks sought out Anna Hauptmann, got her approval of the plan, and sent her to see her husband. On February 11, Hauptmann wrote to Mark O. Kimberling that until notified to the contrary, he no longer wanted to see Lloyd Fisher or his other attorneys. "For your information," he continued, "I am desirous of seeing Mr. Samuel Leibowitz. It is my definite understanding that arrangements have been made by my wife to such an interview."[20] Learning of his dismissal, a dismayed and livid Lloyd Fisher told reporters he saw little that Leibowitz could accomplish.

Leibowitz's initial meeting with Hauptmann was on February 13, the first anniversary of the condemned man's conviction—and four days before the reprieve was to run out. Anna looked on as the famed attorney shook hands with the prisoner through the bars of death row cell 9, saying that he only wanted to get at the truth and that whatever Bruno told him would be reported back to the governor and Mrs. McLean. The encounter was brief, with Hauptmann's professing his innocence. Before leaving, Leibowitz asked him to think over how the child was taken and express his opinions at the next meeting.

The governor was back from the hospital, and Leibowitz contacted him the next day with assurances that he could crack Hauptmann, despite the fact that so far everyone else had failed. But the celebrated lawyer needed help in getting the confession and asked the governor to assist. In Leibowitz's opinion Lloyd Fisher was the reason Hauptmann had never cracked. He wanted Harold Hoffman to get Fisher to come with him to see Hauptmann, to tell Hauptmann that he knew he was guilty. Fisher couldn't believe what he was hearing when two days later the governor relayed the Leibowitz proposal. He refused to be part of it.[21]

Leibowitz's second visit with Hauptmann was on February 17, the day the reprieve expired. As requested at the previous meeting, Bruno provided his theory on how he would have perpetrated the crime: by having accomplices, including one on the Lindbergh staff, and using the inside staircase rather than the ladder. Leibowitz began pounding away at him to tell the truth—"Tell the truth, Hauptmann, or you're sure to die!" By day's end Justice Trenchard had rescheduled Hauptmann's execution for the week of March 30.[22]

Faced by reporters on leaving the meeting with Hauptmann, Leibowitz refused to say whether his client had confessed. Asked if he thought Bruno was innocent, the barrister replied, "No, I said all along he was guilty." Reading the accusation in the next day's papers, a highly agitated Anna Hauptmann called Hicks, who suggested she get hold of Fisher. At a meeting with Anna and Hicks, Fisher rejected the idea that Leibowitz be immediately replaced by him. It might give the erroneous appearance that Leibowitz was being dismissed because he was about to get Richard to break and confess. No, let Leibowitz play out his hand his own way.[23]

That night Fisher heatedly confronted Leibowitz, with Harold Hoffman looking on. The Great Defender, as Leibowitz was known, held to his guns, insisting that the only way to get Hauptmann to confess was for Fisher to shift his position and accuse the condemned man of having taken part in the crime. Fisher consented with one proviso: If Hauptmann did not admit his guilt, Leibowitz would publicly announce that he had changed his mind and now believed Bruno was innocent. Leibowitz agreed. On February 19, he and Fisher met with Hauptmann. For three and a half hours Leibowitz cajoled, reasoned, provided vivid descriptions of electrocution, pleaded with the prisoner—and with Fisher's tacit consent, bluntly accused Bruno of being implicated. Hauptmann maintained his innocence and did not crack. Fisher had won. Leibowitz reneged on his deal to proclaim Hauptmann's innocence, telling waiting reporters he was withdrawing from the case and that Bruno was guilty.

In New York on Valentine's Day, Paul Wendel was kidnapped by Harry Weiss, Martin Schlossman, and Murray Bleefeld, who had been sworn in by Governor Hoffman to assist the Burlington County detective, Ellis Parker, Sr. Wendel was driven to the Brooklyn home of Bleefeld's father, told he was the captive of an Italian mob that was holding him accountable for activities that damaged them, taken to the basement, chained to a chair, and for six days systematically beaten, starved, and interrogated. One of those asking the questions was Ellis Parker, Jr., who remained in constant contact with his father by telephone. The calls were all charged to Ellis Sr.'s office in Burlington County. On February 20, Paul Wendel confessed to kidnapping Charles Lindbergh, Jr. Several revisions of his confession were made. In the early versions he insisted on signing his name as Doc. He was forced to write his own name, and the final confession was sent on to Ellis Parker, Sr. Wendel was patched up and made presentable. When his clothes came back from the dry cleaners, his captors neglected to remove the laundry tag.[24]

On February 24, he was bundled up and driven through the Holland Tunnel into New Jersey, his captors thereby violating the newly enacted federal statute against kidnapping, being called the Lindbergh law. Weiss intermittently prodded Wendel with a pistol, warning him to stick by his confession. At Mount Holly they shoved Wendel out of the car in front of Parker's house. Not suspecting Parker of complicity, Paul banged on the Old Chief's door. Once inside he became aware that Parker was more interested in his forced confession than in his insistence on innocence. Parker met with a fellow member of the New Jersey Crime Commission, William J. Ellis, who was also the commissioner of a mental institution at New Lisbon, New Jersey. Ellis not only accepted Wendel as a mental patient, but he had him housed in his own quarters. Wendel's questioning at the institution was conducted by Ellis Sr. with assists from Anna Bading, Ellis Jr., and Gus Lockwood. An even more detailed confession was soon extracted. On February 28, Ellis Jr. informed Wendel's son that his father had confessed to kidnapping the Lindbergh baby. According to Bleefeld, the son said, "I always knew they'd get my father for this."[25]

A leak was detected among the governor's investigators and traced to Hicks, who by now had been cut off by Mrs. McLean and the *American Astrology* editor, Paul G. Clancy. Zoe Hobbs was also proving to be a liability.

Zoe Hobbs had written to the governor, "It is my opinion that the person who committed the crime is too well protected by persons, or a person, high up, who knows that the solving of the crime would reveal a skeleton in the closet of either the Morrow or Lindbergh families. The easiest way out is to kill Hauptmann and to forget it."[26] Zoe, in her quest to discover this skeleton, cut an eclectic path. She had begun her investigation of the families with the 1929 kidnapping threat against Constance Morrow, attempted to tie it to the 1932 disappearance of the Eaglet, and ended up somewhere between Indian symbols that members of the Morrow family might have seen when Dwight was ambassador to Mexico and the symbol on the ransom note, not to mention the symbols Jafsie referred to in a Massachusetts speech. By the beginning of February, Hobbs was pursuing the nervous breakdown of Dwight Morrow, Jr., in January of 1928 and Elisabeth Morrow's rumored engagement to Rev. Roddy in the spring of 1931. Zoe became progressively more scattered, if not delusional. In a March 27 letter to the governor, she said, "I am personally known to Adolph Hitler" and then went on to suggest that she ask Hitler to help Bruno Richard Hauptmann. The governor's telegrammed reply, two days later, was "ABSOLUTELY SEND NO WIRE OVERSEAS!"[27]

- - -

The latest investigation news the governor's people were providing journalists focused on Millard Whited and Amandus Hochmuth, two pivotal prosecution witnesses who had placed Hauptmann near Hopewell at the time of the kidnapping. Records showed that Hochmuth was nearly blind from cataracts—when later interviewed by Hoffman, he could not see an object two feet away on the desk. Public accusations that Whited had perjured himself at the Hauptmann trial and that the governor might present this and other findings before the court of pardons brought David Wilentz back prematurely from his Florida vacation—and reintroduced Charles Lindbergh into the fray. Wilentz contacted the exiled Lone Eagle, who confirmed long distance that Whited was telling the truth regarding his postkidnapping statements to the Lone Eagle.

On leap year day—four years since the fateful 1932 weekend before leap year day when the baby disappeared—the *New York Herald Tribune* headlined a state-police accusation that the governor's men were trying to tempt certain troopers into admitting the case against Hauptmann had been framed. Hoffman responded with a scolding letter to the paper, in which he upbraided Schwarzkopf, proclaimed that the Lindbergh case had been bungled, hinted that the state police had quit on the job vis-à-vis his reinvestigation, challenged the current charges as to the bribed troopers, and demanded the names of his men accused of perpetrating the temptation.[28]

One bit of Lindbergh-Morrow data presented to the governor by Leo Mead, head of the Mead Detective Agency, was the rumor that the Morrow family suffered from epilepsy and that this may have contributed to the death of Elisabeth and the troubles of Dwight Jr. The report also speculated that when Anne and Charles Lindbergh learned the Eaglet had inherited epilepsy, "they arrived at the conclusion it was better to lose the child than to have it grow up and become an imbecile or a degenerate of some type."[29]

On March 1, Dwight Morrow, Jr., a student at Harvard University, returned to his Cambridge, Massachusetts, living quarters and discovered that some of his papers were missing. He called the police and reported his suspicion that they had been stolen.

Schwarzkopf's allies announced they would try to pass a bill in the state legislature that would prevent H. Norman from being ousted as superintendent of the state police when his five-year term expired in June.

Within the week the governor promised his old friend the Democratic boss Frank Hague additional patronage jobs. The price for these desperately needed positions, according to Schwarzkopf's supporters, was Schwarzkopf's departure from the state-police organization he had founded.

— — —

Lloyd Fisher planned a new appeal.[30] Jafsie Condon returned from Panama and announced no plans to visit New Jersey. Gaston B. Means, from Leavenworth prison, confessed that a mentally unbalanced relative of Anne Morrow Lindbergh's hired him to steal and kill the baby, which he did with an unnamed female accomplice and two male accomplices who were now dead.

— — —

On March 20, a new execution date was set by Mark O. Kimberling: 8:00 P.M. March 31.

— — —

Robert Hicks reported on Nosovitsky's activities in New Jersey but did not know his current whereabouts. Jafsie agreed to be interviewed by the governor at his Bronx home, then ensured that this would not occur by demanding that Wilentz be present and that the questions he was to be asked be submitted to him in writing beforehand. Hunterdon County's prosecutor, Anthony Hauck, was outraged to learn that Hoffman and a U.S. agent had visited Hauptmann's attic and studied the controversial floorboard.

— — —

Paul Wendel, who had signed a confession that the public had not seen, was being held at the mental facility, where his baby-sitters included Gus Lockwood, Ellis Parker, Jr., and Anna Bading. Wally Stroh was in place at the Tombs and ready to testify against Nosovitsky. He was in the care of Bill Pelletreau, who, like Stroh, would gain financially if Nosovitsky could be found and proved to be involved with the crime.

Gus Lockwood took a breather from guarding Paul Wendel, drove over to his favorite watering hole near the statehouse in Trenton, got drunk, and during a boastful lapse let it slip that Parker had the Lindbergh kidnapper. Whether the reporter from the *Trenton Labor News* actually overheard Lockwood or was told what Gus said is debatable. The next day the *Labor News* ran the story that Parker had a suspect. His secret out, the Old Chief straightaway mailed copies of Wendel's confession to all eight members of the New Jersey Court of Pardons, which on the coming Monday would hear Hauptmann's zero hour bid for clemency. The confession reached the jurors Friday, March 27. It was a compelling twenty-five-page typewritten statement, signed by Wendel, that meticulously detailed how he alone had entered the Lindbergh house, taken the baby, and disposed of him. There was no note or covering letter to tell the jurors who had sent them the confession. Since Wendel had confessed to Parker, it wasn't all that hard to figure out.

After going over the confession, Attorney General Wilentz had Schwarzkopf order Parker to turn Wendel over to the state police, which the trooper superintendent did in a Saturday, March 28, telegram addressed to the Old Chief at his county courthouse office. On receipt of the wire, Parker made arrangements for his Mercer County counterpart, James Kirkham, to take possession of Wendel. The transfer occurred that night near the county line. Assuming Wendel had been picked up for old embezzlement charges, the Mercer County detective was nonplussed when Paul presented him with a copy of the confession. Wendel was taken before a justice of the peace, where he was arraigned for murder and remanded to the Mercer County jail in Trenton.

By the time Wilentz and Schwarzkopf reached the county jail, word of the arrest had got out, and a small crowd of spectators and media people had gathered. Wendel renounced his confession, displayed bruises and welts to confirm that he had been tortured, and recounted his abduction and how he was coerced into saying he had taken the Eaglet. It was 3:00 A.M. when he signed a statement disavowing guilt in the Lindbergh crime and accusing the Parkers, Murray Bleefeld and his father, Harry Weiss, and Martin Schlossman of kidnapping him. The New York PD and the Brooklyn DA prepared to open investigations. So did J. Edgar Hoover, since transporting a kidnapping victim across state lines was now a federal offense.

Governor Hoffman was still denying to reporters any connection with the kidnapping when on Monday morning, March 30, he entered the court of pardons and, in his official capacity as head of that body, joined the other seven members to hear Hauptmann's final plea for clemency and evaluate the Wendel confession and disavowal. The session began at 11:00 A.M. and ended at 4:00 P.M. After deliberating another hour, all the judges, including Harold Hoffman, voted to deny the prisoner's petition. The governor also announced that he was not granting Hauptmann another reprieve. The execution would proceed as scheduled at 8:00 P.M. the following evening.

Two last hopes for postponement remained. One was the Mercer County grand jury, to whom Lloyd Fisher had also presented Wendel's confession and who were meeting on the matter and hearing the testimony of witnesses. The second was Justice Trenchard.

The next morning Hauptmann was issued his death garb, which had been slit along the trouser legs to allow for the attachment of the electrodes. The back of his head was shaved as well. After reading Wendel's confession, Justice Trenchard refused Lloyd Fisher's request for a delay. Death preparations continued on through the day. Six P.M. arrived, and then 7:00 P.M. At 7:50 P.M. the Mercer County grand jury foreman telephoned Colonel Mark O. Kimberling, principal keeper of the state prisons, asking for a stay of execution. It was Justice Trenchard who had established the week of March 30 for the death. Mark Kimberling had set the day and hour. Granting the doomed prisoner one last gift of time, Kimberling, already cited to be the next superintendent of the state police, exercised his prerogative of changing the day and hour and put off the lethal event until 8:00 P.M., Friday, April 3, pending the grand jury's decision.

– – –

The day of April 2, in a zero hour effort to garner new information, Harold Hoffman sent four investigators to the Lindbergh estate: Leo Mead of the Mead Detective Agency, former state trooper William Lewis, private detective William Saunders, and Frank Holmes, a friend of the governor's. The quartet was stopped on the grounds by the caretaker, Joe Lyons, and turned back. They subsequently insisted they had gone to survey the Lindbergh house and take certain measurements.

– – –

At 11:50 P.M., April 2, after a fifteen-hour session, the Mercer County grand jury simply quit its examination of the Wendel confession and went home without having voted on whether to indict or not indict the disbarred attorney. It was a highly unusual action, particularly in light of the fact that the jury wasn't to meet again until the coming Monday, April 6, three days after Hauptmann's scheduled execution.

— — —

The Trenton State Prison death house measured eleven feet by twenty-three feet. It was the evening of April 3, and fifty-seven people were present to witness the killing. Bruno Richard Hauptmann appeared at the door at 8:41 P.M. and was hurried to the electric chair by two guards. Straps were adjusted and electrodes fastened in place, leaving only Hauptmann's nose and mouth visible. One of the guards held a clock up so the prisoner could watch the time. The clock was half a minute fast. Mark O. Kimberling lifted his hand. Robert G. Elliot, the sixty-seven-year-old executioner, grasped the rheostat. Kimberling's hand came down. The switch was pulled, unleashing two thousand volts of electricity. After three minutes the current was shut off. Richard Hauptmann's body sat slumped in the chair. At 8:47.5 P.M. he was pronounced dead.[31]

Book Five

AUTHOR'S VIEW

Prelude

FOUR YEARS LESS ONE MONTH AND TWO DAYS OF ANGUISH, TURMOIL, AND controversy was legally ended at 8:47.5 P.M. Friday, April 3, 1936—but the matter was not to rest. The Lindbergh-Hauptmann affair has developed a life of its own, due in part to the disturbing, unanswered questions that continue to fascinate laymen and legal scholars alike. Books and untold articles have been written on the subject. Moot courts continue to try the merits of the case.

If Lindbergh had played a hoax by masking the death of his son under the veil of a kidnapping, he had done so masterly and with apparent impenitence had let the wrong person die for the crime. The extent to which Lindbergh wanted the death behind him and forgotten becomes vividly evident with the admission by one of his later children that not until he was twelve did he learn, from outsiders, he once had an older brother, Charles Jr., who had been kidnapped and killed.

The New Jersey State Police, working under the severe limitations Lindbergh had imposed and contending with a relentless and often ruthless press, solved nothing deductively, lasted out the money chase, and managed to be in on the arrest of Bruno Richard Hauptmann. For Hauptmann's trial the state police provided prosecuting attorney David Wilentz with some highly dubious evidence and witnesses. As for Wilentz, he had prosecuted the accused with effective and dramatic intensity. Edward J. Reilly's defense was tangled, his communication with his client a disgrace.

Harold Hoffman's involvement in behalf of Hauptmann tends to befuddle and confound those who find time to examine his actions. Why would a governor with as bright a political future as his have maneuvered himself into such a hopeless position, putting his career at risk?

- - -

After nearly eight years with the material, this author has come to believe, like Harold Hoffman, that Richard Hauptmann did not kidnap and murder Charles Lindbergh, Jr. If Hauptmann had been involved, it was with the extorting of the ransom money. It is just as likely that he and Fisch had occasionally bought hot, or stolen, money as a speculation—the going rate had been as little as ten cents on the dollar in parts of New York during the depression—and that one of their purchases had included at least fourteen thousand dollars of the Lindbergh loot. Equally possible was that Fisch had bought the ransom money on his own and left it with Hauptmann, not saying what it was. Who, then, was the seller?

Based on thousands of pages of recently uncovered information and prolonged probing, this author strongly suspects that J. J. Nosovitsky forged the last twelve ransom messages and extorted the fifty thousand dollars. Nosovitsky's previous involvement in the case may well have been dismissed or negated under the protective wings of certain police officials or due to the personal motives of J. Edgar Hoover. Fingers had been pointed at Nosovitsky, whose more nefarious dealings made headlines, but nothing ever came of it. He had even volunteered to appear and discuss his part in the case, and then he vanished. Had Harold Hoffman been able to produce Nosovitsky at the court of pardons hearings, Hauptmann's execution might never have taken place.

If Nosovitsky was the forger-extortionist who had obtained the fifty thousand dollars after writing twelve ransom messages, what of the original letter he copied, the one found in the Lindbergh nursery March 1, 1932? Who wrote that communication? The letter, or a facsimile, had been taken to New York City and displayed to underworld types, which is where Nosovitsky might have seen it and copied the style—but who was the author?

In 1986, I flew to Los Angeles to meet with ninety-three-year-old Harry Green, who had been Harold Hoffman's friend and lawyer. According to Green, he and the governor had always adhered to the two-person theory: one killer, someone different receiving the money.

"What was more," Green said, "the governor knew who killed the child. People never understood why the governor risked his career for Bruno Hauptmann. It was because he always knew there wasn't a kidnapping."

27

AN INTERNATIONAL SPY

ON DECEMBER 15, 1927, A DAY AFTER CHARLES LINDBERGH, ON A GOODWILL mission to Mexico, landed his *Spirit of St. Louis* before a cheering crowd of 150,000 at Mexico City's Valbuena Airport, William Randolph Hearst, the brazen press baron of San Simeon, was called before a U.S. Senate subcommittee to account for what may have been efforts by his empire of twenty-four daily newspapers to undermine the purpose of Lindy's flight.

Dwight Morrow, newly installed as ambassador to Mexico, had arranged for Lindbergh's visit in the hope of gaining favor with the Mexican president Plutarco Elías Calles. Morrow's long-term objective was to normalize relations between Mexico City and Washington, a near-Herculean task since the pro-Communist policies of Calles and his predecessor, Álvaro Obregón, had resulted in their country's defaulting on its foreign debt, confiscating American-owned property without compensation, and threatening the wholesale cancellation of oil leases held by U.S. companies.

Catholicism had also suffered in Mexico, and William Randolph Hearst was Catholic. Obregón and Calles had nationalized Mexico's churches, closed Catholic schools, and forced nuns and priests to wear mufti. Like the newspaper czar, other influential U.S. Catholics had viewed Morrow's ambassadorial appointment as a warning that President Calvin Coolidge not only might be placing the needs of America's oil industry, in which the J. P. Morgan group had a vested interest, ahead of their church's plight in Mexico but that he might be planning to abandon efforts to help.

In the weeks prior to Lindbergh's December 14 landing at Valbuena Airport, the Hearst papers had launched an exposé campaign in which four U.S. senators, whom William Randolph did not particularly admire, were accused of having secretly received money from the Calles government for backing legislation favorable to Mexico: William E. Borah of Idaho, George W. Norris of Nebraska, Thomas J. Heflin of Alabama, and Robert M. La Follette, Jr., of Wisconsin. The allegations, according to Hearst officials, were based on documents that had come from the personal files of President Calles in the National Palace, the secret archives of the Mexican consul general in New York City, and the comptroller general's office in Mexico City. The material had been purchased by the Hearst organization for $20,150 and showed that Mexico paid Borah $500,000 for his support, Norris and Heflin $350,000 each, and La Follette $15,000.[1] Denials were immediate and vehement.

President Calvin Coolidge ignored the Mexican document controversy, but not the U.S. Senate, which convened a subcommittee inquiry for the first of its seven sessions on the day after Lindbergh was scheduled to arrive in Mexico.[2] William Randolph Hearst, the first witness called, retreated a step or so from his chain's hawkish stance by testifying that though he was sure the Mexican documents were genuine, he doubted that the accused senators had received any money. As more was heard from his staff and others, including the four imputed senators, it became evident that Hearst had mistakenly placed confidence in the authenticity of the material he had permitted to be purchased and published. He and his associates had been hoodwinked by the elaborate and ingenious scam of a master con artist–forger. Adding to William Randolph's embarrassment was that this man, who went into the *Congressional Record* as the only suspect in the perpetration of the fraud, had previously been promoted and genially apotheosized in Hearst newspapers as an "international spy and super-forger." His name was Jacob J. Nosovitsky.[3]

In the early days of the Lindbergh kidnapping, complaints were received by both the New York Police Department and the New Jersey State Police naming Nosovitsky as the perpetrator. Nosovitsky did fit Jafsie Condon's physical description of Cemetery John, right down to the accent and cough. Nosovitsky was also well-known in New York City's underworld, the type of criminal to whom Morris Rosner might well have shown the original Lindbergh ransom message. Soon after a New York Police Department official assured inquiring New Jersey trooper investigators that the NYPD had checked out Nosovitsky and he was not implicated in the Lindbergh case, the matter was dropped.

Three years later, on the eve of Hauptmann's execution, interest in J. J. Nosovitsky's participation in the crime, perhaps only as an extortionist, was revived with a fury by the New Jersey governor's investigators. The state police also swung into action, trying to find out what Hoffman's detectives were learning. It was too late for everyone, including Hauptmann. Nosovitsky had dropped from sight. The electrocution took place.

Half a dozen years of collecting bits and pieces on Nosovitsky's background add up to an enormous, often comical mosaic of daring escapes and espionage high jinks, pure bunk and later bunco, forged documents by the ream, blatant extortion, and paltry bigamy. He was, in fact, a fallen Reilly, Ace of Spies, mixed with an amateur production of *Peer Gynt*. His main commodity was information, and he learned its value early and well, working for both the U.S. and British secret services, then taking his dark crafts into the private sector.

Fiction may well have bested fact regarding the origins of Jacob Nosovitsky. Born during May of either 1889 or 1890 in Chenassy, province of Kiev, Russia, Nosovitsky claimed that at the age of fifteen he joined the Socialist Revolutionary party, an extremist group that killed the czar's father and made several attempts on the life of the czar himself.[4] Wounded in a 1907 gunfight in which four policemen died, he was packed off to Archangel, where he remained in a prison camp until 1911. The year 1912 found him attending the University of Kiev. Two years later he was back in Archangel for his most specious revolutionary activities. He escaped the camp, survived a swampland chase, and eventually reached a safe haven in Norway.

February 10, 1916, marked Jacob Nosovitsky's arrival in the United States, where he remained a Communist.[5] News that his parents had died of starvation in Russia and that his two brothers had been killed, most likely by the Bolsheviks, converted him to a die-hard anti-Red. At least that's the motive he gave when he appeared at the U.S. State Department's New York City office and volunteered to fight bolshevism. The State Department sent him to the Justice Department, where he was taken on as a nonsalaried undercover operative who would receive minimal expenses. Still active with the Communist party, he reported its activities to the Justice Department throughout 1917 and 1918.[6]

Nosovitsky's connection to powerful men started with Sir Robert Nathan, head of the British secret service in the United States, who offered the Russian undercover agent seventeen hundred dollars a month to do the same thing for Scotland Yard as he was doing for the Americans. The State Department approved. Nosovitsky devised a plan whereby he could travel regularly from New York without arousing suspicion: become a surgeon on a passenger ship between the two places. Sir Robert Nathan introduced him to a wealthy American capitalist residing in a rented castle in England: Henry W. Marsh. Marsh, who was to become Nosovitsky's biggest fan, got him a position as surgeon with the Cunard Line's *Mauritania* as well as obtaining needed medical credentials. From then on the Russian forged his own documents.

Nosovitsky by now had acquired many of the skills valuable to the dark art of espionage, such as the use of aliases and cover stories. He was fluent in many languages, including French and German. He had also mastered both the reading and writing of English, but he spoke with a decided guttural accent. His greatest knack seemed to have been in counterfeiting important documents and forging signatures. A pair of suspicious State Department officials, L. Lanier Wilson and W. L. Hurley, had put him under surveillance and conducted a background check without immediately discovering that he was working as an undercover agent for both the British and the U.S. Justice Department—as is reflected in the December 6 and 8, 1920, correspondence between Hurley and a special assistant to the U.S. attorney general, J. Edgar Hoover.

A major Nosovitsky coup was tracking down the secret paymaster for the English Communist party. He would later write that on returning to New York City, he was met in the outer harbor by Hoover, who had come to retrieve the information. According to Nosovitsky, J. Edgar was pleased with the intelligence regarding the paymaster. Cunard and the *Mauritania*'s doctor, however, were unhappy over his portraying a surgeon. Henry Marsh arranged for Nosovitsky to become the ship's doctor on the steamer *Melita* out of Canada, which also sailed between the United States and England. On both the *Mauritania* and the *Melita* he went under the name of Dr. Jacob Nosovitsky, to whom his fraudulent credentials were made out—including a certificate of medical registration from the state of Michigan. His favorite alias for the period was Dr. Jacob Anderson. His favorite middle initial was to become J.

Nosovitsky's link to the New York Police Department, which would be long running, initially began on September 16, 1920. After pulling to a stop halfway between the J. P. Morgan and Company office building and the U.S. Assay Building, a horse-drawn wagon loaded with iron sash weights exploded. The destruction was catastrophic. Thirty people were dead and three hundred injured. Not content that the U.S. Secret Service, the New York Police Department, and the Burns International Detective Agency were all assigned to catch the culprit, Henry Marsh tried to convince a reluctant Nosovitsky to undertake an independent investigation of radical elements that might have been responsible. The crime didn't strike the Doctor, as Nosovitsky was known, as a Communist-type operation. Marsh explained that there was a large sum of money available for such an undertaking and brought Nosovitsky to Colonel Arthur Woods, a former chief of the New York Police Department and a nephew by marriage of J. P. Morgan, Jr. After the Doctor expressed his views, Woods had him go to Washington and talk with J. Edgar Hoover, still a special assistant to the U.S. attorney general.

According to Nosovitsky, Hoover conceded that the bombing had probably not been done on orders from the Communist party, but since he strongly suspected that a criminally inclined individual Red probably set off the explosion, he wanted what Woods wanted: for the Doctor to penetrate Communist circles, seeking the mad bomber. Back in New York, Woods paid Nosovitsky five thousand dollars to undertake the assignment.

The crime was never solved, but Marsh was pleased with the Doctor's input. So much so that he activated his dream: an International Investigation Bureau to combat worldwide communism—run by Nosovitsky. The estimated operational cost, several hundred thousand a year, was to be raised by Marsh and his friends. Nosovitsky took what would prove a permanent leave of absence from the British secret service and made himself available to the grand scheme. His first assignment for Marsh took place in Europe. When he reported finding no great Red conspiracy, funds for the International Investigation Bureau dried up.

- - -

Henry Marsh came up with another cash partner in his war on communism: Colonel Arthur Woods. Woods and Marsh commissioned Nosovitsky to go to Mexico and assess the extent to which the Communist movement had taken control of the government of President Obregón. The contracted price for the assignment was twenty-five thousand dollars, which Nosovitsky dearly needed.

Nosovitsky arrived in Mexico well aware that Marsh and Woods, bona fide Red-phobics, wanted validation of a pervasive Bolshevik conspiracy, which he quickly found did not exist. On gingerly suggesting that the peril might not be as grave as suspected, Nosovitsky was warned by Marsh that he was expected to deliver the incriminating facts. The Doctor set about creating a Red menace for Marsh's palate. He enlisted the aid of Linn A. E. Gale, an expatriate U.S. Communist who had fled to Mexico to avoid the American draft, in composing a report to Zinovyev, an official of the Third International in Moscow, which supposedly outlined Communist activities in Mexico. To further authenticate the fabricated report, he managed to have it signed by both the national and international secretaries of the Mexican Communist party.

The second step in Nosovitsky's strategy was to introduce a motion at the Mexican Labor party convention held in Pachuca that asked that the organization embrace the principles of the Communist party. The proposal was rejected, but the resourceful Nosovitsky now wrote up another report, again with the help of Gale, in which the offer to the convention was detailed—and, without Gale's awareness, was altered to feed on Marsh's fears.

Returning to New York, Nosovitsky presented Marsh and Woods with copies of the two spurious reports allegedly sent to Zinovyev in Moscow. They were gratified, and Nosovitsky received fifteen thousand dollars from Woods's paymaster. Marsh, on reflection, wanted more conclusive documentation to prove the existence of a die-hard body of Communists capable of overthrowing Mexico's current regime and establishing a Soviet form of government.

Nosovitsky sat down and composed a totally fictitious constitution for the nonexistent Red Army of Mexico, the official title for which was The Constitution of the Red Army of Mexico. Marsh and Woods seemed to be pleased. Nosovitsky accompanied them to Washington, where the two superpatriots gave the documents to high government officials in hopes of delaying U.S. recognition of the Obregón government. It was the end of March 1921, and Nosovitsky would later claim that among those who saw the material were J. Edgar Hoover and the secretary of state. Questions began to arise over the authenticity of the Red Army papers, particularly at the State Department. Nosovitsky's final payment of ten thousand dollars was refused him on the charges that he had boondoggled.

— — —

The relationship between J. Edgar Hoover and Jacob Nosovitsky is intriguing. The immaculate Russian stated that they first met when he was returning to America with information concerning the Soviet paymaster for England, information Hoover took from him and examined in New York Harbor. Hoover contradicted this, maintaining that they had been introduced socially and never had professional dealings. How and where could such a social encounter have occurred? Through Woods and Marsh? Nosovitsky claimed that at Woods's request he went to see Hoover in Washington regarding the Wall Street bombing. Woods and Marsh were the types of people Hoover would cotton to later in his career. Had Hoover met with Nosovitsky as a result of the bombing, and wouldn't that constitute official business? Or was it that they never met on the matter?

If Hoover had no professional ties to Nosovitsky, who had not been with the Justice Department since 1918, what was J. Edgar doing shielding him from State Department personnel in 1920 and 1921? W. L. Hurley of State had alluded to this in his December 6, 1920, letter to Hoover by suggesting he wasn't being given the facts regarding Nosovitsky. Hoover acknowledged the oversight but seemed to have done little else to fill Hurley in on Nosovitsky, with whom he still claimed to have no official connection.

On March 27, 1921, Nosovitsky, under the alias of Dr. Joseph Anderson, was refused reentry into the United States at the Nuevo Laredo, Mexico, border crossing. On the twenty-seventh, and again on the twenty-eighth, Nosovitsky wired J. Edgar Hoover to please contact the local U.S. consul and get him out of the country. He was let in on the twenty-ninth, but the American consul officials seized documents he was carrying, along with two photographs. Once in Laredo, Texas, Nosovitsky asked a local Bureau of Investigation agent to pick up the Colt automatic pistol he had left at the customs office before entering Mexico and to send it to J. Edgar Hoover in Washington.

A series of communications between Hoover and Nosovitsky indicates that the two may have met on the Russian's return to America. The strongest evidence that their relationship was also professional is seen in an April 12, 1921, letter J. Edgar wrote to W. L. Hurley. In it Hoover asked that the State Department return to Joseph Anderson—Nosovitsky's alias during the Mexican trip—the documents and photographs they had taken "in order that the same may be placed in our confidential files."

Hoover, like most everyone else who crossed Jacob Nosovitsky's path, was to pay handsomely for the privilege. J. Edgar's turn came eleven months later, in a March 6, 1922, letter from the Firestone Tire and Rubber Company, informing Hoover that the company was negotiating with Dr. Nosovitsky, who wished to handle their tires and who had already given them a first order of $1,786.95. Nosovitsky had also assured the company that Hoover would provide them a personal reference, which was why Firestone enclosed an envelope. The company also wondered if Hoover would comment on the doctor's integrity and, if possible, Nosovitsky's ability to handle the financial end of the transaction.

A handwritten letter from Nosovitsky to J. Edgar Hoover, received five days later, on March 11, shed more light on the matter:

> Dear Mr. Hoover,
> In order to provide a living for my family and remain in New York I opened a Automobile Supply Store and I am making very good. I have invested all the cash I could get in my store, but it is very difficult to conduct a business without having credit from the Rubber Manufacturers, therefore I have applied to the Firestone and United Rubber companies for a little credit. The above mentioned companies require some references about my character. Not having any influential friends who could help me, I have taken the liberty to refer to you as the person who will testify as to my honesty.

I shall never forget the favor you are doing me and shall always do my best to serve you when the time comes.

I Remain Your Faithful
Jacob Nosovitsky

P.S. I am coming to Washington about March 15th. Can I see you and talk over certain matters?

Nosovitsky had written the letter to Hoover on stationery that bore the printed letterhead of the

National Tire Company
High Grade Tire
wholesale—retail
3166 Broadway
126th Street
New York City

That same day Hoover responded to Nosovitsky:

Dr. Jacob Nosovitsky,
Apartment A,
520 West 188th Street
New York City

Dear Doctor,

I received your letter, and was indeed glad to hear from you. I had hoped to see you in New York upon my last visit, but it seems that I missed you, and you missed me, which was most unfortunate.

I am very much interested in your contemplated enterprise of engaging in opening an automobile supply concern, and needless to say I wish you the very best success in this matter.

I received a communication from the Firestone Tire & Rubber Company requesting information concerning your reliability and integrity. I hesitated answering that communication until I received word from you, for I did not want anything in writing of the character, not knowing what our radical friends might be up to. I am, however, today writing to the Firestone Tire & Rubber Company advising them of my knowledge of you.

I anticipate being in New York at a very early date, and I
shall then, of course, make another effort to see you.
With the very best regards, I remain,
Sincerely Yours

Hoover's letter to the Firestone Tire and Rubber Company in behalf
of Nosovitsky, also written on March 11, reads in part, "While I have no
knowledge of his financial standing, I have known him personally, and I
have always found his integrity above suspicion, and have considered
him thoroughly honest. It's impossible, as I have stated, to advise as to
his financial standing, and whether he is able to handle an amount of the
size indicated by you, as our relations have never involved any pecuniary
element."

Hoover seems not to have been concerned that Nosovitsky might
show his letter to a third person—a letter that contained a reference to a
possible official and secret operation. In a letter to Republic Rubber
dated March 22, 1922, Hoover provided the same endorsement of Dr.
Nosovitsky he had given Firestone. The Goodyear Tire and Rubber
Company wrote J. Edgar on March 28. In addition to the polite request
for an endorsement, Goodyear let drop that "Dr. Nosovitsky in the
course of conversation mentioned that his wife is a very wealthy woman,
worth about one quarter of a million. Will you please advise if you know
this is the case."

Hoover responded to Goodyear on March 31, 1922. He again said he
had no information regarding the good doctor's financial standing, made
no mention of a wealthy wife, and went on to say he had always found
"his integrity above suspicion, and have considered him thoroughly honest." On April 10, he told essentially the same thing to a representative of
R. G. Dun and Company, which had been hired by several of the tire
companies to obtain a broader assessment of Dr. Nosovitsky's financial
standing. By now the other shoe had dropped.

In the first week of April, Nosovitsky began to sell off, in bulk, his
stock of tires and accessories. On April 10, he confronted his creditors
with news that he had disposed of all the goods that had come from them
and was unable to account for any of the proceeds, other than to say he
gambled some of them away.

It was May 1, 1922, when J. Edgar Hoover's boss, William J. Burns,
director of the Bureau of Investigation, received a letter from an attorney, John Warren Hill, who accused Nosovitsky of obtaining credit
under false colors and selling off the merchandise he did not own. Hill

asserted creditors had been warned by Nosovitsky not to charge him with a crime because he was currently investigating the Wall Street bomb explosion for Arthur Woods and further claimed he had once worked for the Justice Department. Another pertinent question was whether Nosovitsky actually knew J. Edgar Hoover, or had he forged letters of commendation that bore Hoover's name?

Burns answered Hill the following day, confirming that Nosovitsky worked at Justice back in 1917 and 1918 and had once been employed by Colonel Woods regarding the Wall Street bombing but that the relationship had terminated in the spring of 1921. Mr. Hoover was talked to and explained that Nosovitsky had been introduced to him through a mutual friend in 1919, and though they had visited one another from time to time in New York, their relationship was strictly personal, and at no time was there any official Justice Department business transacted between them. Hoover confirmed having written commendations as to Nosovitsky's character but not to his financial status. Characterwise, Hoover had found nothing derogatory concerning the Doctor and said that until this occurrence, "Nosovitsky had always given indications of being thoroughly reliable."

An apparently cordial correspondence continued between Hoover and Nosovitsky at least until September 1, 1922,[7] at which time Hoover wrote to the Doctor, who was in Ward K of New York City's Bellevue Hospital with an unspecified malady, saying in part, "I expect to be in New York at a very early date, and will, of course, make an effort to get in touch with you."

Dr. Jacob Nosovitsky cut an imposing figure. Tall, slender, and suave, he had a penchant for well-tailored three-piece suits, in the upper left pocket of which he kept a miniature German-type pistol.[8] His keen eyes were greenish gray and seemed to change color with his moods, his nose was long, his shoulders broad, his hands powerful. He tended to boast, but his manner in the main was deferential. He was known to frequent racetracks, horse rooms, as well as an occasional burlesque house, and was believed to have a wife in Canada whom he visited on occasion.

Nosovitsky's list of aliases now included, or soon would include, Jack Nosovitsky, Jacob J. Nosovitsky, J. J. Nosovitsky, L. Lanier Winslow, Esq., L.L., N-100, Jake, Jack, Doc, the Doc, J. J. Nosow, J. J. Nossow, John Jacob Naso, Jake Naso, Harry Sanders, J. J. Nasan, Dr. J. J. Brinkman, Dr. J. J. Saunders, Dr. Jacob Anderson, Dr. James Anderson, J. J. Anderson, Nosan Anderson, Nasan Anderson, Mr. Williams, George Merrill, McDonald or McConnel, J. J. Shanely, and Mr. Greenbergh.

Testifying during his 1932 trial for extortion, Gaston Means swore that he had paid the one hundred thousand dollars given him by Mrs. Evalyn Walsh McLean to a man named Jorgenson. Another alias for Nosovitsky, who acknowledged knowing Means, was John Jacob Jorgenson.

— — —

Max Sherwood, né Schlansky,[9] head of the Eagle Detective Agency in New York City, was also the guiding light behind the Eagle Industrial Association, an organization to promote private detective agencies whose prime customers were companies that wanted strikes thwarted and unions kept from organizing their work forces. Nosovitsky's skills were just what Sherwood needed. In the fall of 1924, the Eagle Association printed up copies of Nosovitsky's fraudulent Mexican documents, including his Red Army manifesto, and under the new title, "Red Rule Hangs over Mexico," sent it out as an industry come-on to businessmen across America.

— — —

Sometime between 1916 and 1932, Nosovitsky married Rebecca Colinian at Cornwall, Ontario. No information could be found concerning the divorce, but on January 8, 1924, at Montreal, in a traditional Jewish ceremony he took a second wife, Esther Levine. Later in the year, under the aliases of Jacob and Estelle Nosow, Nosovitsky and Esther were employed by Max Sherwood's Eagle Detective Agency.[10]

— — —

Whether William Randolph Hearst himself heard of the "Red Rule Hangs over Mexico" piece and asked Nosovitsky to undertake certain investigations regarding Communist activities in the United States and other countries—as Nosovitsky would claim and could be the case—or whether Nosovitsky sought out Hearst reporter Victor Watts in an attempt to wreak revenge on Colonel Woods for refusing to pay the balance of his Mexican-operation fee is debatable. But after contact was

367

made with the Hearst chain, Watts most likely tried to persuade Nosovitsky to write a far broader account of his activities than a simple recounting of the dealings with Woods.

— — —

On July 30, 1925, Nosovitsky called on Hoover again—at the Bureau of Investigation in Washington, D.C.—to get a recommendation attesting that he was qualified to take on an assignment Hearst was offering. It appeared that J. Edgar had finally had his fill of the Doctor. His handwritten notation on the report carrying the request reads, "We will under no condition recommend him, first because it is contrary to policy and second he is not worth it."[11] Because of this initial connection with the Hearst operation, Nosovitsky agreed to write a series of stories for its papers, a fact that would soon become obvious to J. Edgar Hoover.[12]

On Sunday, September 20, 1925, the first of eleven autobiographical articles, entitled "Confessions of an International Spy," appeared in Hearst's *New York American* and other of the chain's publications. Dr. Nosovitsky described at great length his relationship with high-ranking Communists as well as with Marsh and Woods. Hoover was mentioned, but sparingly, and the matter of J. Edgar's letters to the rubber companies was excluded. Nosovitsky detailed many of his forgeries, including the so-called Constitution of the Red Army, and generally had a good time in print. Hearst personnel verified most everything he said, where it could be verified. The primary players in the drama, including J. Edgar Hoover, seemed not to have been available for comment. The series constituted the highest public praise Dr. Nosovitsky was ever to receive— and, apparently, the zenith of his financial status.

— — —

Assistant attorney general of the United States William J. Donovan's turn to get acquainted with Dr. Nosovitsky came nearly a year later. Among those making the introduction was J. Edgar Hoover, now the director of the Justice Department's Bureau of Investigation.[13]

A complaint had been registered with Donovan regarding Julius J. Kron, Edward Chaims, and Dr. Jack Anderson, also known as Nosovitsky, who were trying to negotiate a deal with Count Széchenyi, the Hungarian minister to Washington, for information that allegedly would verify a Communist-inspired uprising in Hungary. Hoover wrote to

Donovan, counseling against any further negotiations with Nosovitsky and associates.

― ― ―

In August of 1926, during an interview at the Mexican consulate general in New York City, Edward Chaims whispered to an assistant of Arturo M. Elías, the consul general, that he possessed proof that some very well known Americans were involved in a gun-running plot on behalf of the revolutionaries in Mexico: pro-Catholic plotters. The cautious Elías wanted proof. Negotiations went on for three months, during which time false documents were readily produced by Nosovitsky to validate the Red-scare shakedown tactic. In the end Elías and his adviser on public relations, Charles W. Ervin, claimed they had laughed Nosovitsky right out of the consulate—but made no mention of the incident to the press or authorities for another two years.

― ― ―

Nosovitsky, in the early months of 1927, began a long and intricate scam—involving a mass of forged documents—that would eventually lead to Hearst's unwittingly printing the notorious Mexican papers that accused four innocent senators of being on President Calles's payroll. On August 24, Dr. Cuthberto Hidalgo (most likely Chaims) went to the Mexican consul general in Los Angeles and offered to sell the same documents Hearst had purchased for twenty-five hundred dollars. When later told of this, Hearst asked how they could be offered to the Mexicans when he had them.[14]

The fall and winter of 1927 were particularly bad periods for Nosovitsky, who despite all the activity, was in dire need of funds. He and his wife, Esther, resided at 1206 Forty-eighth Street, Brooklyn, under the name of E. Nossow—Estelle Nossow—and, presumably, J. J. Nossow. But on September 15, he arranged to rent a room at Mrs. Schneiderman's apartment, at 4608 Tenth Avenue, Brooklyn, within easy walking distance of 1206 Forty-eighth Street. For Mrs. Schneiderman's consumption he was Dr. Jacob Anderson, a physician who owned a chemical plant in Canada—and he produced fake medical certification from Michigan to prove his claim. Dr. Anderson also professed to being single. Mrs. Schneiderman, as it turned out, had a twenty-year-old daughter who was also single: Mollie.

On September 19, four days after taking a room at Mrs. Schneiderman's, Mollie and Dr. Anderson eloped to Poughkeepsie, New York. Before the week was out, the good doctor borrowed eighteen hundred dollars from Mollie, saying he was going to Montreal to get a house and furniture and send for her. Mollie waited at her mother's apartment. When her husband hadn't returned by December 8, she went through his papers and spotted one that read, "In case of accident; notify E. Nosso, 1206 48th. Street, Brooklyn." Mollie Schneiderman traveled the short distance to the Forty-eighth Street address and found E. Nosso all right, Estelle Nosso. She found something else, hiding in the back room: her husband, Dr. Anderson. Mollie didn't realize Jacob was also married to Estelle. He was fooling around; that was bad enough. And he had her eighteen hundred dollars to boot. She had the good doctor arrested the next day on a charge of grand larceny. He was sent to the Raymond Street jail, still under the name of Dr. Jacob Anderson.

— — —

Arturo M. Elías, Mexico's consul general in New York City, also had problems in preparing just what to say at the U.S. Senate's hearing on the validity and purchase of the Mexican papers by the Hearst news empire, at which he and other officials had been requested to testify. Among the expert witnesses slated to be heard by the Senate subcommittee was the renowned international spy, Dr. Jacob Nosovitsky. The invitation was rendered, in no small part, because Nosovitsky had let it be known that he knew something about the hoax.

Nosovitsky had been unexpectedly indisposed. On December 14, 1927, the day before the hearings were to begin in Washington, D.C., he was arraigned at the Fifth Avenue court, Brooklyn, and held without bail pending an appearance before the grand jury on Mollie Schneiderman's complaint of grand larceny. At the same time Senate clerks were wondering what had become of Nosovitsky, New York newspaper reporters were taking notes on the marital troubles of Dr. Jacob Nosovitsky, the so-called international spy. Mollie swore under oath that she was Dr. Jacob's wife—Dr. Jacob Anderson, the only name she knew him by.

On Monday, January 9, 1928, the *World* added insult to Nosovitsky's injury by giving front-page coverage to Arturo Elías's detailed disclosure of the international spy's attempt to sell him forged documents on an alleged Catholic gun-running conspiracy.

Less than a month later, on February 1, 1928, Nosovitsky's grand larceny trial got under way at the Brooklyn Supreme Court. The doctor refuted his having run out on Mollie and, to prove she was in touch with him while he was away, claimed that he had love letters she wrote him while he was staying at the Breslin Hotel in New York as well as in Montreal. Dr. Nosovitsky claimed he didn't steal because he had a receipt to prove that he paid the Schneiderman family thirty-six hundred dollars. On February 24, he was acquitted of grand larceny. Four months later, on June 6, he was confined to the New York County Penitentiary on Hart's Island, to serve an indeterminate term of between three months and three years for bigamy.

Inmate J. J. Nosovitsky was made assistant to the resident physician at Hart's Island, where he was known as the Doc. Subsequent to producing medical papers from Michigan that showed he was a medical doctor, he was put in charge of the TB ward. Nosovitsky got on well with his fellow inmates, to whom he spoke of a close association with Gaston B. Means. The Doc also told them almost everything that had appeared in "Confessions of an International Spy."

Following his release from Hart's Island, Nosovitsky continued to run scams in both New York and New Jersey, often with a woman partner. He spent time in Chicago, Detroit, and Montreal, but his home remained New York, and at least one address shows he resided in the Bronx during a period when Jafsie Condon's letters were being published in the *Bronx Home News*. Nosovitsky maintained his connection with the Eagle Detective Agency and affiliated himself with at least one strong-arm gang in New York that was known to perpetrate murders. He gained a reputation among New York police officials of being a bad hombre, which was another, but tacit, way of saying he was considered capable of murder. In the fervid period of rampant kidnapping-extortions during 1930 and 1931, it was likely that his skills at forgery came into play. Two of the cities he most favored, Chicago and Detroit, were hotbeds of this sort of extortion.

Jacob Nosovitsky's most-publicized skills were forgery and scams. William Randolph Hearst had learned about this the hard way. So had J. Edgar Hoover, William J. Donovan, and a good portion of the New

York City underworld, where getting your name in the paper made you something of a legend. It would seem plausible that the Doctor would have been among the first criminals Morris Rosner sought out to view the first ransom note the night of March 2, 1932, ostensibly to identify the author.

Clandestinely Nosovitsky was, his entire life, a purveyor of information who showed little remorse at selling out an associate. This had made him valuable to American and British intelligence. Whether this was the original basis of his association with J. Edgar Hoover is moot. Nosovitsky said it was. Hoover insisted the relationship was social, not business.

When in June of 1932 Anne B. Sloane had written the New Jersey State Police, complaining that Nosovitsky had kidnapped and killed the Lindbergh baby, trooper investigators had to rely on the New York Police Department, which assured them Nosovitsky wasn't involved.[15] At approximately the same time at the *New York American,* a Breckinridge representative met with two ex-convicts who had served time with Nosovitsky at Hart's Island: Wally Stroh and Arthur Graham. Both believed the Doc had stolen the baby, and Stroh offered a motive, confessed to him by Nosovitsky: The Morgan bank interests (Woods was Morgan's nephew by marriage, and Dwight Morrow had been a company partner) not only refused to pay him the fifty thousand dollars owed for a Mexican assignment, but they tried to frame him with a Mann Act charge, which prompted him to commit bigamy by marrying Mollie Schneiderman. While at Hart's Island, according to Stroh, the Doc had often talked about getting revenge. He had also been obsessed with perpetrating a foolproof kidnapping—snatching a child, because children couldn't identify you—and claimed to have contacts to do so in New Jersey.[16]

There was reason to discount the credibility of Stroh and Graham: They hadn't come forward until a reward was posted well after the perpetration. As for Mrs. Sloane's complaint, the New Jersey investigators were told by the New York City police that the woman was a chronic pest who sought revenge for the murder of her criminal son by a gang including Nosovitsky. The NYPD admitted Nosovitsky was a rough criminal but assured the NJSP he was not involved with the kidnapping. That pretty much ended official interest in J. J. Nosovitsky—until Governor Hoffman's investigation reached its final days in 1936.

What is there to say Nosovitsky was involved or wasn't involved with the crime? Handwriting experts commissioned by the New Jersey State Police continue to insist that all the ransom messages had been written by one person: Bruno Richard Hauptmann. Experts brought in by the endless army of authors, scholars, and lawyers who are fascinated with the case firmly believe that two different people were responsible for the messages: that one person wrote the original letter found in the nursery and a second person wrote the remaining twelve in a style closely resembling the initial communication.

Jesse William Pelletreau was certain Nosovitsky had written all thirteen notes. Examining an extensive collection of Nosovitsky's writing, the Jersey City private detective looked for a match for what he considered to be the unique *k* in the ransom messages. Nosovitsky's *k* seemed almost identical to the prototype ransom-letter *k;* so did other key letters gleaned from the samples. Nowhere, in Pelletreau's estimation, was Nosovitsky's *k* more like the prototype *k* than in the bank-slip signature of J. J. Faulkner and in the subsequent letter Faulkner wrote Governor Hoffman to proclaim Hauptmann's innocence.

Pelletreau's belief that Nosovitsky had also kidnapped and murdered the child was negated by the findings of his fellow investigators and what information the state police and the NYPD had on hand. The preponderance of data established that Nosovitsky was far away from New Jersey the night the alleged kidnapping-murder occurred. The role he could have played in the crime was as an extortionist: writing ransom messages in the style of the first note and receiving the payment carried by Condon.

Assuming that Nosovitsky was Cemetery John, the man who was given fifty thousand dollars at St. Raymond's back in April of 1932, was it in Breckinridge's interest to confirm this when his aides purportedly showed a picture of the Doc to Jafsie Condon two months later? Condon allegedly said Nosovitsky was not John. If, indeed, Lindbergh had concocted the kidnapping scenario, had gone to extremes to protect the nonexistent abductors from being caught after receiving the ransom, the capture of the actual extortionist would be a most unwelcome and untimely event. The kidnapping hoax could not afford to have a suspect. This author could find nothing to confirm or disprove that Condon had been shown a photograph of J. J. Nosovitsky.

The New York Police Department appeared to be the root source for both the New Jersey State Police and the BI information regarding Nosovitsky's lack of complicity—and the NYPD may have had a reason to protect him. The international spy was a professional, if not compulsive, informer. Due to the Freedom of Information Act, thousands of pages of material regarding him have confirmed this fact. So have Justice Department and Bureau of Investigation documents found in Harold Hoffman's collection. His relationship with the Eagle Detective Agency and other private-eye organizations reveals that he had good connections with the New York police. Documents found in the governor's file tend to confirm this.

The only thing Jacob Nosovitsky had to offer the NYPD was information. What he may have received in return was immunity from prosecution for many of the scams he pulled. But would this provide him protection in a case as notorious as the Lindbergh kidnapping? That would have depended on how important he was to his source at the police department. There were indications that at one time he made himself very important by providing the police with the most valuable of all information—the name of a fellow gang member who perpetrated a murder.

Was J. J. Nosovitsky the kind of man who could not only have perpetrated the extortion but might also have displayed the sort of remorse that would move him to write the J. J. Faulkner letter to Hoffman that exonerated Hauptmann? Unfortunately for the governor and Hauptmann, Nosovitsky was not located, the question never answered.

In a series of 1935 and 1936 letters, J. Edgar Hoover admitted that Jacob Nosovitsky was J. J. Faulkner. At the same time he categorically rejected the idea that the international spy had anything to do with the Lindbergh case.

The New York Police Department has never turned its files regarding the Lindbergh kidnapping over to the New Jersey State Police archives or to the FBI. After a protracted series of communications, this author was taken to the NYPD's legal-section library at 1 Police Plaza in New York City, where he was given access to the three cardboard banker's boxes that contain what remains of the department's files on the Lindbergh-Hauptmann case. Nothing was found in them to indicate that Noso-vitsky had been the man who received the ransom money in St. Raymond's Cemetery back in 1932. However, there was something else that did. The author was shown a copy of his criminal record, which included his aliases. Jacob Nosovitsky was J. J. Faulkner.

28

FAMILY AFFAIRS

"THE KILLER WAS RIGHT IN THE LINDBERGH HOUSEHOLD," HARRY GREEN told this author during their California talks in 1986. "It was Elisabeth, Anne's older sister, who died before the trial began. She did it out of jealousy. The governor was told this after Hauptmann was convicted. It was explosive. We had statements, but we needed more to make it stick. That's what the governor was trying to do at the end: prove it. That's why he gave the stay of execution—and ruined his life."[1]

For an incipient racial supremacist such as Charles Lindbergh, the daughters of Dwight and Elizabeth Morrow were prime Presbyterian breeding stock. Constance, the youngest of the three sisters, was still in prep school. That left twenty-three-year-old Elisabeth and Anne, twenty-one, a Smith College senior whom at first the Flying Colonel hardly noticed. It was Christmas vacation of 1927, and Lindy had flown to Mexico on a goodwill junket initiated by the U.S. ambassador to that country—Dwight Morrow.

Morrow, who was fifty-four, had met the twenty-five-year-old Lindbergh earlier that year, when both men were staying at the temporary White House on Dupont Circle in Washington, D.C.[2] Lindy, there for only the night, was being welcomed home to America after his historic flight across the Atlantic. Morrow had come at the behest of a schoolmate from Amherst College, President Calvin Coolidge, who wanted Dwight to accept the Mexican ambassadorship. In the world of law and finance, the rags-to-riches saga of Morrow, a partner of J. P. Morgan's, was the American dream incarnate. Though his celebrity was modest compared with that of Lindbergh, many who knew him considered Dwight a saint—an honor the ages would deny the handsome aviator. No one knew at the time that the two men were fated to become integral parts of each other's lives. Not only would the financier be responsible for the Lone Eagle's finding a wife, but Morrow, who was a trustee of the Guggenheim Foundation for the Promotion of Aeronautics and had urged that the organization give Lindbergh a fifty-thousand-dollar grant, would help make him a wealthy man.[3]

— — —

Small, slight, mussed, and "diffidently aggressive," Dwight Whitney Morrow, as a young man, had a habit of standing with the fingers of his hands held tightly together until he gathered his confidence or became amused.[4] Self-made and with a phobia about poverty, he performed at Morgan and Company in a manner that was nothing less than spectacular. "Morrow," in the words of one biographer,

> mastered every subject through sheer diligence. He mutualized the Equitable Life Assurance Society and oversaw Morgan lending to Cuba. He also masterminded Kennecott Copper, a public company formed around the Morgan-Guggenheim syndicate in Alaska and other properties. Daniel Guggenheim was awed by Morrow's retentive brain and said that "six months after Morrow had started upon his investigation, he knew more about copper than I or any of my six brothers." In his absentminded way, however, Dwight neglected one detail of the Kennecott

operation: "You have forgotten to provide for our commission," Davison gently chided him.[5]

Morrow's absentmindedness, rooted in his nearly trancelike powers of concentration, was legend among the Morgan partners. On one occasion he spent a dinner at Thomas Lamont's gesturing with a well-gnawed olive pit before the butler offered a plate. Another tale recounted Morrow riding a train and frantically searching for his ticket to give to the waiting conductor, only to discover that he had it between his teeth.[6]

Dwight Morrow and Thomas Lamont were the principal Morgan and Company statesmen and theoreticians. Along with Russell Leffingwell, they "gave the House of Morgan its patina of culture, its reputation as a home to bankers who wrote essays, gave speeches, joined foreign policy councils, and served on foundation boards." Dwight seems to have had a very specific and private vision. "As a student of ancient civilization, Morrow wanted to clothe the mundane, often sordid world of the twenties in some larger classical dimension."[7] Politics was one way of achieving this. Political life, which had always held a fascination for him, loomed even larger as his interest in banking diminished, but when an opportunity arose to assume public office, Morrow was as indecisive as he was about assuming the presidency of Yale. However, part of the classical dimension he so dearly coveted had already been achieved—by his wife, Betty.

Diminutive Elizabeth Morrow was the ideal consort for a rumpled, obsessive, absentminded poet–philosopher–business genius trapped between materialism and idealism. Born in Cleveland, Elizabeth Reeve Cutter graduated from Smith College in 1896, then studied at the Sorbonne in Paris and in Florence, Italy. She had a passion for education and taught school prior to her marriage to Dwight on June 16, 1903. Betty, as Morrow called her, was thirty at the time of their marriage, as was he. Their courtship, which was sparked at an Amherst dance when both were students, had lasted ten years. By 1927, they were rich, had maids, valets, cooks, and one chauffeur and limousine to drive Dwight from Englewood to the Hudson River ferry and another to pick him up on the Manhattan side and deliver him to the Morgan office. Betty ran the household with a benevolent but no-nonsense efficiency. She pandered to the social obligations requisite for their station but, like her husband, did not feel all that comfortable at functions given by the wealthy and powerful, who were their peers and friends.

It was with their children that the family idyll and privacy was attained by Dwight and Betty. They were a gay and loving clan bonded by "common factors of intelligence, curiosity, wit, independence, energy, and youthfulness."[8] Holidays were jubilant sacrosanct events. During the working week breakfast was usually the only meal at which the children saw their father, and it was often a raucous encounter. Dwight, who could not keep a tune, always whistled the same ditty on his descent from upstairs into the kitchen, where there was a scramble for his attention. The girls, sometimes all three at once, would rush to kiss him. There was a good deal of competition and many complaints, particularly over kissing. The girls much preferred the gentle Cutter kisses of their mother compared with their father's loud Morrow smacks. Even so, it was a festive and loving time.

Literature was a common denominator among the Morrows, some of whom read more voraciously than others. Reading aloud was also a popular family entertainment—listening to accounts of the leper colony in *Ben-Hur* was so real to the children that they feared catching the disease.[9] Writing letters to one another became an activity that Anne made into an art form. Betty excelled at composing poems and passed the passion for this on to the youngsters. Travel was requisite, and Dwight reveled in taking the family on tours of America and Europe, particularly to the historic sights of the ancient world.

Like their parents, the three Morrow girls were short. Elisabeth was the closest to Dwight in temperament and humor,[10] then came Constance. The circle they moved in was wealthy but generally removed from that of the New York City socialites: Uncle Jack was J. P. Morgan, Jr., himself; Tom Lamont was another unofficial uncle. In public the sisters' deportment was impeccable. Alone and tittering, the three daughters could create quite a racket. By December of 1927, Elisabeth was the great beauty of the family. Constance came second. But Anne was strikingly pretty, and her distinctive looks grew on those who knew her. Anne was more reserved but highly competitive with Elisabeth when it came to boys.

Dwight, in his usual deliberate fashion, agonized over whether to accept the Mexican ambassadorship. Associates at J. P. Morgan, who had always expected that the president would name his former college chum secretary of the treasury or at least make Morrow ambassador to the Court of St. James's, viewed the assignment in Mexico as a shortcut to political suicide. It had been so in the past, and now relations between the two countries were at a new low. American Catholics and powerful oil interests wanted to cut off ties with the government of Plutarco Elías Calles, who had continued with the left-wing policies of his predecessor, Álvaro Obregón.

Feeling that it was an unrewarding appointment, Betty Morrow was among those who didn't want her husband to take the ambassadorship. Given her druthers, she would have preferred to remain in the United States and oversee the construction of the new estate they were having built in Englewood as well as a summer mansion in Maine. After protracted consideration Dwight finally told the president that yes, he would accept the position. Before leaving America, he had Charles Lindbergh come to his Manhattan apartment, where, acting on a suggestion from Walter Lippmann, Morrow proposed that the Lone Eagle fly *The Spirit of St. Louis* to Mexico on a goodwill mission.[11]

Lindbergh, who wanted to demonstrate the feasibility of night and winter flights before remanding the craft to a museum, accepted Morrow's invitation. No one had expected Lucky Lindy to attempt a nonstop flight, which is exactly what occurred on December 13, 1927, when he took off from Washington, D.C., at 12:26 P.M. and, thanks in part to stormy skies, got lost.[12] Morrow, President Calles, Mrs. Morrow, and Constance had come to Valbuena Airport in Mexico City at 8:30 A.M., the scheduled time of landing. They and 150,000 other bystanders spent the balance of the morning and early afternoon sweltering in the sun. According to Mrs. Morrow's calculations, Lindbergh set down at exactly eighteen minutes before 3:00 P.M.[13] Like the rest of the crowd, she had been thrilled by his arrival.

A three-day train trip brought Elisabeth and Anne Morrow from Texas to Mexico City. It was now December 21, and Constance was jumping up and down on the station platform to get a glimpse of them. Daddy Dwight was there as well, and the reunion was huggy-kissy. En route to the embassy, the arriving sisters were told that Colonel Lindbergh was there—a very nice boy, very nice, but he and Daddy were going out tonight. Elisabeth and Anne were somewhat agitated by all this public-hero stuff breaking into the family party. Who was this boy? Anne projected him to be a stereotypical media hero, a baseball-player type—a nice man, perhaps, but not at all intellectual, not of their world at all. She certainly wasn't going to worship Lindy, a name she considered to be odious.[14]

The gates to the embassy opened. Their car entered and stopped beside a wall of geraniums that rose at their right. To the left was a red velvet carpet descending a stone staircase, on which officers were standing at attention. At the head of the stairs was a great movie-scene door. How ridiculous, was all Anne could think of. An exhausted Elisabeth plunked herself down on the steps. The Morrow girls finally ascended and joined a reception line of celebrities waiting to meet the Lone Eagle, who was in evening dress and standing against a great stone pillar. Mrs. Morrow hurried up and made the introduction. "Colonel Lindbergh, this is my oldest daughter, Elisabeth." Anne found him to be much slimmer and taller than she anticipated and more refined than in the newspaper's grinning Lindy pictures, more poised. When it was her turn to be introduced, he looked down at her with clear, straight blue eyes. His firm mouth did not smile as he bowed and shook Anne's hand.[15]

They were opposites in so many ways, the elfin Morrow family and the tall, gangling Charles Lindbergh. Dwight and Elizabeth were happily married and devoted to their loving, demonstrative offspring. Lindbergh's parents had separated when he was five, and he had desperately sought affection from each. Displays of warmth were a hard commodity to come by from a doting, overprotective but distant mother who, throughout his life, shook hands with him goodnight. His father, a pacifist-isolationist U.S. congressman from Minnesota, distrusted the East Coast international establishment, of which the J. P. Morgan interests were a leading devil, and was hung in effigy for his opposition to America's entry into World War I. A stoic, the elder Lindbergh had once endured an operation without taking an anesthetic. When young Charles, who did not know how to swim, fell into a river inlet, his father refused to go to his rescue, reasoning that this was a perfect opportunity for the boy to save his own life by learning how to swim.[16]

Charles Lindbergh grew up a diffident, often sullen, monosyllabic young man who was decidedly shy around women. He was invested with the regional bigotries of his day, which were myriad. His sense of humor seems to have evolved in the rough-and-tumble world of open-cockpit pilots, which rendered him something of a locker room flying jock with a propensity for coarse, barracks-type practical jokes. What he knew best was airplanes. What he did best was fly. Even so, there was a decided ability to write. He was patently self-assured, if not vain, and enjoyed being in the company of great people, even though he protested he did not. He had an immediate and lasting affection for Dwight Morrow and made no secret of this.

When his mother, Evangeline, arrived in Mexico City for the holidays, she immediately befriended Dwight's sister Alice, who like herself was a teacher. Mrs. Lindbergh also seemed to get on well with the Morrow girls. Her son was more reserved with them.

Beautiful and bubbly Elisabeth was his table partner the first night that she and Anne attended a dinner with him in Mexico City. Lindy seemed to take to her and even more to Constance, who was on his other side. Anne, quiet and mousey, sat across the table. She had always been envious of her older sister, even though much of the attention Elisabeth received was the result of her frail, often sickly constitution. The sibling rivalry for boys was a more direct contest and one in which Elisabeth had a decided edge, to the consternation of Anne. Elisabeth was forever falling in and out of love, and it came as no surprise when she developed a crush on Lindbergh. So had Anne and, for that matter, Constance.

As the holiday vacation in Mexico progressed, Elisabeth's ability to communicate with Lindbergh, who seemed to pay no attention to Anne or to her opinions, roused old anxieties in the middle sister. Of one particular dinner at which Lindbergh seemed transfixed by what Elisabeth was saying, Anne wrote of being sick of heartbreak and of her odious envy of Elisabeth, her confidence, her forceful charm, the fact that people seemed to notice her more, her quick wit. She felt achoke with misery, that she was of no use, no value, had nothing to offer Lindbergh or anyone.[17] Others seemed to think Lindbergh fancied Elisabeth, and rumors to this effect were to persist long after the holidays.

Sickness was a subject the family, and especially Mrs. Morrow, tended to downplay and possibly could not fully come to grips with. Dwight often worked to the point of exhaustion, which may have contributed to his contracting pneumonia just before Christmas of 1912. There were hints of congenital illness on his side of the family, and coworkers at both Simpson, Thacher, and Bartlett (the law firm at which he was a partner prior to joining Morgan and Company), and the house of Morgan tried to obscure the fact that he suffered from prolonged spells of "diffidence" (which is to say, depression and nervous fatigue). Fragile Elisabeth was afflicted with a wide variety of ailments, many of which were not specified even in the family diaries and correspondence. What no one seemed to have wanted to admit was the possibility that both Dwight and his daughter Elisabeth, the child closest to him in temperament, had chronic neurological disorders.[18]

What could not be obscured was Dwight Jr.'s nervous breakdown. It occurred in January of 1928 at Amherst College. Elisabeth rushed to his side and stayed with him for much of the winter. When the family went back to Mexico, Elisabeth stayed behind to tend to Dwight Jr., who had requested she be with him.

In 1928, Charles Lindbergh came to visit the Morrows in the United States, and little attention was paid when he took Anne flying. It was Elisabeth in the plane with him, or anywhere else, that set tongues talking. Even sprightly Anne believed the Flying Colonel was taken by her sister, and she was not happy. Anne was madly in love with the handsome twenty-six-year-old world idol, whom she referred to as a "shy, cool boy" and agonized over. By midsummer, word of a Lindy-Elisabeth wedding was building. By October, Elisabeth was in Europe, recuperating from a bout of bronchial pneumonia. In Manhattan on November 21, newsmen and photographers boarded the ocean liner S.S. *Olympic,* which was returning from Cherbourg, France, and besieged Elisabeth with questions regarding her betrothal to Lindbergh. She would neither confirm nor deny the rumors nor discuss her plans. Elisabeth did agree to pose for pictures in her stateroom, and the news photographers managed to get shots of her before J. P. Morgan, Jr., in whose party she was traveling, barged in and ordered the media out. United Press and the International Newsreel Photo Service issued stories and photographs of Elisabeth that appeared across the country, saying that she was reported engaged to marry Colonel Lindbergh.[19] But by now Anne was quietly seeing Lindbergh, so quietly that in an October 21 letter to Constance she asked her baby sister not to tell their mother of the budding romance.[20]

Perhaps due in part to Elisabeth, unquestionably because of the ubiquitous media that hounded him, Charles Lindbergh's wooing of Anne Morrow began as much of their early married life would be led: surreptitiously. At the onset he taught her, in the name of privacy, how to elude crowds and mislead people, particularly reporters, unless, of course, you needed them. Dwight's embassy spokesman in Mexico had wasted no time in denying published reports that there was any romance between Lindbergh and "a member of the Morrow family."[21] When Dwight Morrow finally learned that it was Anne, not Elisabeth, who intended to wed the Flying Colonel, his first response, in true patriarchal fashion, was to object.

Following her return to America and the public denial of her engagement to Lindbergh, Elisabeth once again fell ill and was under a doctor's care. Whether the affliction continued to be bronchial pneumonia appeared unclear, but its severity was greatly understated to her mother, a woman who had a difficult time comprehending and coping with family maladies. In a late-November letter from Mexico, where she and her parents were spending Thanksgiving, Anne urged that sickly Elisabeth not even undertake the relatively short journey from the Leffingwells' Long Island estate, where she was convalescing, to the Morrow home in Englewood. Anne's previous letter had intimated a budding romance with Lindbergh—he was referred to in the text by the code name Boyd. The November letter again alluded to the relationship, almost unmindful that delicate Elisabeth was also infatuated with the young aviator.[22]

The printed correspondence from Anne to Elisabeth changed drastically. The letters, which for so long had contained the breathless and often rambling intimacies of two close sisters, became quite impersonal, if not formal. Also, there were fewer of them, at least in the published collections of Anne's correspondence and diaries, which from late 1928 until July 2, 1929, showed no communication at all.

- - -

For Harry Green, Harold Hoffman, or any of the investigators trying to home in on Elisabeth's background and potentially violent reaction to Lindbergh's not marrying her, the diaries would be of little value. The volume covering 1922 to 1928 wouldn't be published until 1971; the volume covering 1929 to 1932 would reach print in 1973. They never were to know that when Lindbergh and Anne had their first child, Elisabeth suffered a mild heart attack.[23]

Harry Green contended that Elisabeth had been described to them as an emotionally troubled young woman whose mental problems were exacerbated when Lindbergh proposed to Anne. "The papers said Lindbergh was going to marry Elisabeth," Green told the author. "He chose Anne instead, and Elisabeth never recovered from the shock. She couldn't contain her humiliation and hatred." The governor was told that odd events had occurred at the Morrow mansion, in which the staff was sure Elisabeth had a hand. Anne's dog had been killed mysteriously. Elisabeth loved animals, but the servants suspected it was she. There was also the matter of the baby's being found in the trash closet of the Morrow home. "Someone had thrown him out with the trash. One of the servants found him in there," said Green. "There was a problem with sending the baby to school, too."[24]

Enrolling Charles Jr. at the Montessori-type school Elisabeth had founded in Englewood allegedly created a controversy in the Morrow household. Anne objected on the pretext that the infant was too young. Her mother insisted that he go, for the sake of family harmony, and as usual Mother got her way. Older children at the school picked on baby Charles, kicked him, pulled his hair. Mrs. Morrow refused to let him quit. Elisabeth often accompanied the infant back and forth from the Morrow estate. Then one day the servants were told that Elisabeth was never to be left alone with the Eaglet. It happened anyway.

— — —

The first two volumes of Anne Morrow Lindbergh's diaries and letters, *Bring Me a Unicorn* and *Hour of Gold, Hour of Lead,* were published in 1971 and 1973, respectively, and covered the years from 1922 to 1932. That the author would display prudence in her choice of material is understandable, even more so since she quotes an early bit of advice received from her husband to be regarding the press, which says in effect that you should never say anything you wouldn't want shouted from housetops, nor write anything you wouldn't mind seeing on the front pages of a newspaper.[25] Still and all, the reprinted letters and diary entries provide interesting insights into her relationship with Elisabeth. The earlier volume details their competitiveness with boys and their mutual infatuation with Charles Lindbergh when he came to visit their father in Mexico City over the Christmas holiday of 1927. Anne's letters to Elisabeth, which had exuded the confidences that only two close sisters can exchange, became cool and diffident in the wake of Lindbergh's entering their lives.

As the fiancée and then bride of Charles Lindbergh, Anne, the shy middle daughter of the Morrow clan, was coming into her own, and it seems reasonable that she had less time or concern for sisterly matters, which could account for the drop-off in correspondence with Elisabeth. But there is no diminution in the letters Anne wrote to Constance. *Bring Me a Unicorn,* which covers the essentially non-Lindbergh period from 1922 to 1928, includes twenty-five letters Anne sent to Elisabeth and twenty-four she wrote to Constance. *Hour of Gold, Hour of Lead* comprises the 1929–32 time frame, during which Anne became engaged to, and married, Lindbergh, gave birth, flew north to the Orient, and suffered the death of her child. Here there are slightly more letters to Constance than in the previous book, twenty-seven, whereas the number of letters to Elisabeth drops to eleven, less than half the number found in the first volume. By the same token, the number of letters Anne wrote to her mother falls from thirty-four in the first book to nineteen in the second.

Only six letters from Anne to Elisabeth are reprinted for the period between June of 1929 and the end of 1931.[26] By then Dwight Morrow's sudden death had brought the Lindberghs back to America, where the construction of the Hopewell estate was nearing completion. Their child disappeared from the new home on March 1, 1932. The first letter for 1932 from Anne to her older sister that appears in *Hour of Gold, Hour of Lead* was written seventeen days later, on March 18. It is the book's first communication with Elisabeth since October of 1931 and possibly the first message from Anne since the death of her son.

March 18 was the day after Elisabeth's twenty-eighth birthday, and in light of the tragedy that had just befallen the family, Anne's letter is remarkably contained and often trivial. She describes little flowers in the room and their mother hanging a hand mirror on the wall. Elisabeth is told that life at the house has become regular once more. As for the missing child, Anne admits to not realizing anything emotional except when some small annoyance sets her off. She says it is possible to live there and think nothing about the baby. She wonders if she sounds crass and indifferent but admits she would do anything to maintain her self-control because it is necessary—something like sitting in church and fighting back the memories of her father on those Sundays of yore, not giving in to the tears.

Was Anne talking about a child who was missing or one who had already passed away? And was she writing to a sister who was implicated in the death or one who knew nothing of it? Nowhere in the text does Anne speculate on getting the baby back from his abductors or discuss the efforts to do so. She mentions that Lindbergh and Breckinridge are working with great zeal and with infinite patience, caution, and cheerfulness, but she fails to say what they are working at. Recovering a kidnapped child? Or pretending that the expired boy has been kidnapped?

Anne writes on, admitting that it did not feel like Elisabeth's birthday the previous day. She speaks eloquently of her mood shifts, of there being no sense of continuity, of their minds being too weak to grasp joy or sorrow. She returns again to the great sorrow caused by their father's death. Then she apologizes for the length of the letter, lets Elisabeth know she is relieved to have written it, and hopes that her sister doesn't mind.[27]

If Harold Hoffman had ever seen or heard of this letter, which he hadn't, he might have interpreted the text as saying that the child had already died, something that supposedly would not be discovered for another eight weeks. Holding to the supposition that Elisabeth was connected to the baby's demise and that Lindbergh had created the kidnapping ruse to save her from incarceration and shame, then Anne's letter could also be construed as an attempt to make her older sister feel that she was still part of the family circle.

There is no letter to Elisabeth regarding the discovery of a child's body in the woods on May 12, 1932, but Anne wrote to their mother about it, and again she appears remarkably unruffled in recounting the facts. Once more the wording could be interpreted as referring to a child who had been known to be dead prior to his reported disappearance.

In the first section of the June 10, 1932, letter to Elisabeth, who is now abroad, Anne writes chitchat. In the second section of the same letter, she reports that Violet Sharpe has just killed herself and refers to the misery and sorrow the crime has evoked. She questions whether the consequences will ever end.[28] Her next day's diary entry talks about how they have once more found themselves smeared all over the paper's front pages (because of Violet Sharpe's suicide). She goes on to say that the avalanche of the crime is burying the memory of her dead son.[29]

Anne's last mention of her older sister in *Hour of Gold, Hour of Lead* is a diary entry for December 28, 1932. She recounts Elisabeth Reeve Morrow's marriage that day to Aubrey Neil Morgan of Wales, how there were rose petals, and how Elisabeth, in a brown suit, raised her hands and waved as she ran through the crowd.[30]

Hour of Gold, Hour of Lead is divided into two sections, each with its own introduction. The first is "Hour of Gold," the 1929–32 golden years, during which she and Charles Lindbergh were married, had a child, and built a dream estate near Hopewell. "Hour of Lead" deals with the tragic year of 1932. In its introduction, most likely written in 1972, Anne addresses the subject of her behavior back in March of 1932, forty years earlier—behavior Laura Vitray and Charles Williamson had witnessed in part and pondered. Anne wonders how she could have written those letters she only recently recovered, correspondence she hasn't seen since the day it was composed.

Why even bother to publish the letters and diary extracts regarding the event? She presents her reasons, some of which deal with the grief and pain at losing a child—but none that specifically says, or strongly suggests, when and how that child was killed and by whom.[31] Some forty years after the fact, could it be conceivable that Anne has gone back to keep the fib intact, to make sure the record supports her husband's scenario and there are no slipups that could point to her sister? Harry Green thought yes.[32] The author tends to agree.

29

ENDGAME

THERE IS NO SINGLE, IRREFUTABLE ITEM OF EVIDENCE THAT LINKS ELISABETH
Morrow to the death of her nephew, Charles Lindbergh, Jr. Even the
affidavits Harry Green swore to have had in his possession were at best
hearsay and, if true, related to an incident to which there were no witnesses other than Elisabeth herself. In the sixty years since her death, new
channels of information have provided access to previously unavailable
documents. In addition, this author has been the recipient of unique
data, and has conducted, with researchers, an exhaustive search of local
New Jersey newspapers. As I examined the material, old and new, a pattern emerged, an overview in which the accusation regarding Miss Morrow gained a curious credulity—and provided tentative answers to many
previously unanswerable questions.

Radio had brought Harry Green and Harold Hoffman together. Green, a New Jersey attorney with a night-school law diploma, was a one-fourth owner of a local radio station whose beam had been blocking the signal of a far more powerful New York City transmitter. The conflicting parties agreed to abide by the decision of an arbitrator, in this instance Harold Hoffman, who was then a member of the U.S. House of Representatives. Green and the congressman were to remain lifelong friends. When Hoffman moved on to the New Jersey Department of Motor Vehicles and introduced a method of vehicle registration intended to cut down on the epidemic of auto thefts, Green was appointed to supervise the operation. Though he had campaigned rigorously for Hoffman's election in 1934, Green had no official position in the governor's administration. Monitoring the Hauptmann trial was one of the first assignments given him by the state's newly installed chief executive. "Governor Hoffman asked me to do it and I did," Green stated. "I was there every day. I reported back to him every few days. He was interested, but he was involved with his tax program. He was trying to save the legislation whatever it took when he heard about Elisabeth."[1]

Harry Green believed that he was one of the few Harold Hoffman associates who knew the allegations regarding Elisabeth Morrow Morgan—allegations made in mid- or late August of 1935.

— — —

According to him, the child's death had indeed occurred at the Lindbergh estate. "He was lying on the ground with his head bashed open, and she [Elisabeth] was upstairs ranting. After Hauptmann was convicted is when the chauffeur came to see Governor Hoffman with the information. He was the first to say what happened. There were more."

Green was not clear as to the name, but the chauffeur seems to have been Henry Ellerson of the Morrow household staff, who claimed that other servants at the Englewood estate knew the truth about the child's demise. Had anyone witnessed Elisabeth kill the child? Green said no but pointed out that there was nobody at the house except the two of them. Had the child's head been "bashed in" inside or outside the house? Harry Green couldn't say. Had the child been thrown out the window or carried out to the spot where he was found? Green didn't know. Had the bashing in resulted from the fall from the window or from an instrument, and if it was due to an instrument, was the instrument recovered? Harry Green had no answers, nor could he say what constituted Elisabeth's ranting or just how out of control she was.

The chauffeur had not only come to Governor Hoffman with the tale, but he had also signed an affidavit detailing the information. It was an act of conscience on the chauffeur's part, in Green's opinion. Elisabeth was already dead, and Hauptmann was appealing his sentence. The chauffeur didn't want to see Hauptmann die for a crime of which he was innocent.

Had Green seen this affidavit?

Yes. The governor had entrusted it to him for safekeeping. And there was an affidavit from one of the Morrow maids, but he couldn't recall which one.

Could Green produce these affidavits?

No. "I had them in my storeroom, and there was a flood," he explained. "The janitor, without consulting me, just dumped them. Threw them out on the dump because all the papers were ruined."

Had Ellis Parker seen the affidavits?

Green wouldn't say, but he doubted if many people had. "The governor needed absolute proof before mentioning her. What he found out made him sure she was the answer. I believe it, too. But it took a while before he began looking. Maybe he should have acted faster.

"When you put it all together, you can see Lindbergh's thinking. It wasn't mean. He did it all to save her."

- - -

The earliest conspiracy scenario evolved by Harry Green and Harold Hoffman had the crime begin on Saturday, February 27, 1932, and proceeded somewhat as follows:

The Whateleys, Elisabeth, and the baby had been at Sorrel Hill. Disobeying the order never to leave Elisabeth alone with the Eaglet, the Whateleys drove in to Hopewell to do some quick shopping. The Whateleys returned from Hopewell to the Lindbergh estate and found the baby on the ground, dead from a head injury. Elisabeth was out of control. No one else was at the house. Lindbergh was contacted and told by Ollie Whateley what had occurred. Whether Anne knew at this juncture is moot. Lindbergh went to the estate and was joined by Henry Breckinridge. The publicity-phobic pair contemplated what to do. Notifying the police was synonymous with calling the media. Word that the child had died, even of natural causes, would be page-one news around the world. Revealing that he had been killed by his aunt guaranteed headlines and a scandal. It would be the end of Elisabeth. Even if she avoided criminal charges and received medical treatment at a private facility, the fragile beauty would be stigmatized for the rest of her life. So would the Morrow and Lindbergh famlies. Was there a way to avoid this? A way of distancing her from the death?

The child's injuries were too specific and severe for them to say that the damage had been incurred accidentally, by his falling out of his crib or from the nursery window. Could they claim an intruder had entered the nursery and killed him? For what motive? Hatred of Lindbergh? Other grievances? Fabricating an alibi along these lines would require cooperation from the Whateleys. Could they be counted on? Trusted? What of Elisabeth's whereabouts that fateful Saturday?

But was it even necessary to mention Elisabeth to the authorities? Suppose they behaved as if she had never been there? What of the Morrow employees who knew she had gone to the Lindbergh estate that Saturday morning? The chauffeur who had driven her, the household maids, others? What of the school employees, if any, who were aware of her trip? How many actually had known she was there?

Lindbergh and Breckinridge—the team that had astutely hoodwinked the media on numerous occasions, including Charles's marriage to Anne—had no practical knowledge of crime. To formulate one would require expert advice, such as that possessed by William J. Donovan, who had been assistant attorney general of the United States. Was this Donovan's connection with the case, to act as adviser? Or had they conferred with someone else? Anyone with Donovan's knowledge could have described the type of police interrogation the staff and family members would have to endure as the result of a murder investigation, even for accidental homicide.

Another category of bogus crime had come under discussion, one with advantages for the predicament at hand: kidnapping. To claim the child had been kidnapped meant that no corpse need be produced at the present time. It also afforded a degree of latitude in their saying when the baby disappeared, which not only gave the planners more time to prepare their conspiracy but took Elisabeth off the spot. They could now claim that the child had been stolen well after Elisabeth left the estate— with no staff members other than the Whateleys knowing this wasn't so. Of equal importance, the police and press would concentrate on tracking down the kidnapper, and this might greatly minimize the investigatory attention paid to the family and, particularly, to Elisabeth.

The delay in reporting the child's demise was not by itself a crime. To delay for the purpose of falsifying the facts concerning the death constitutes, at the very least, a conspiracy to obstruct justice. Sometime over the weekend of February 27, the decision was reached to conspire and say the Eaglet had been kidnapped.

Harry Green and the governor had no idea when and by whom Elisabeth was taken from the Lindbergh estate that weekend. Green had no idea what became of the child's body. Neither did the governor, who paid a degree of attention to Ellis Parker's insistence that the baby in the woods was not the Eaglet. When Anne Lindbergh was told also remains a mystery.

Preparations to stage the bogus kidnapping covered at least two days. Lindbergh, the compulsive and exquisite planner, saw to almost every detail. Someone other than Breckinridge had filled him in on the fine points of ransom-kidnapping. A ransom note was written, and the Whateleys rehearsed their alibis. The plan required one more participant, and she reached the estate around noon, March 1: Betty Gow. She, too, was rehearsed. The nursery was wiped clean of incriminating fingerprints. The baby's crib was arranged with the blankets pinned in place and an indentation made on the pillow. A two-section ladder was positioned under the nursery window, then taken some seventy-five feet away and left on the ground near its third section. Untraceable footprints were carefully made in the mud. At 10:20 P.M. Ollie Whateley picked up the phone and asked the operator to put him through to the police. When Constable Williamson answered, Ollie calmly said, "Colonel Lindbergh's son has been stolen. Will you please come at once."

Lindbergh and Breckinridge managed to take charge of the investigation, which allowed them to further isolate Elisabeth and the family from the tragedy. This control was partially achieved because of Schwarzkopf. His adulation of Lindbergh and natural xenophobia resulted in all law-enforcement agencies other than the troopers and certain local police investigators being kept out of the initial inquiry. Because of Schwarzkopf's acquiescence, Lindbergh managed to prevent his wife and members of the household staff from being interviewed in the immediate wake of the so-called crime. Only when one trooper overtly disobeyed his orders and chatted up Betty Gow did Red Johnsen become a suspect and the object of headlines. Despite the seemingly severe news controls invoked by the troopers, Henry Breckinridge saw to it that the crime stayed in the headlines as long as possible.

Green and Hoffman didn't speculate about whether Lindbergh and Breckinridge were sophisticated enough in matters of crime to have known that the families of kidnapping victims were a prime target for extortionists. But as the author has shown, William J. Donovan may have been aware of this. So may have the young lawyer in Donovan's office with underworld connections, Robert Thayer. It was Thayer who brought Morris Rosner to Lindbergh one day after the child was reported missing. That same night it was Rosner who took the original ransom note, or a copy, to New York City, a major kidnapping and extortion center, and displayed it to underworld characters proficient in the art of the snatch, as well as forgeries on the pretext that they might recognize who the author was. One of the city's most publicized forgers was also a celebrated extortionist, J. J. Nosovitsky, a man with whom Donovan once had truck.

Harold Hoffman, in his series of articles for *Liberty* magazine published during the early months of 1938, mentions Elisabeth, but only in passing and not as a suspect. The name of Jacob Nosovitsky does not appear, nor is reference made to the mysterious Russian Pole whose discovery Harold Hoffman had depicted as holding "dramatic possibilities which may overshadow anything that has thus far occurred in the case."[2] At the same time the ex-governor did not shut the door on either Elisabeth's or Nosovitsky's involvement with the case. "I do have a theory," he wrote in the January 29, 1938, issue of *Liberty,* "but it is only a theory, unsupported by convincing evidence and made up of irregular little pieces of fact, testimony and conjecture fitted into sort of an incomplete mental jigsaw puzzle. I would not dare to display that incomplete picture to the public."[3]

Signs that the governor had been pursuing a secret suspect, or suspects, can be found in his investigatory files at the tiny East Brunswick Museum in East Brunswick, New Jersey, which has been collecting the governor's artifacts and personal papers. Going through both the state police and the East Brunswick collections, the author was left with a distinct impression that the governor had been pursuing objectives not found in the reports—which lent credence to Harry Green's subsequent assertion that Harold Hoffman had kept Elisabeth-related intelligence out of the general file.

The cornerstone of the conspirators' plot was time and magic: The world had been tricked into believing that the child had disappeared on Tuesday, March 1, rather than dying on Saturday, February 27, back in 1932.

So where were the major players of the conspiracy that Saturday, Sunday, and Monday?

According to the sworn affidavits eventually given the police by the Lindberghs and their household staff in the wake of the child's disappearance, Henry and Aida Breckinridge had come from New York to spend the weekend at Sorrel Hill with Anne, Charles, and the baby. The Whateleys were there, of course, but Betty Gow, as usual, had the weekend off. A Morrow maid by the name of Miss Root had escorted the baby from Mrs. Morrow's estate in Englewood and remained at Sorrel Hill until Sunday evening, when the Lindberghs drove her and the Breckinridges to the railroad station at nearby Princeton Junction for their respective journeys home.[4]

The author believes that more than likely, Henry Breckinridge came to Sorrel Hill on Saturday, February 27, but not as a casual weekend guest. He had been called because of the baby's death, summoned to advise Lindbergh on how to save Elisabeth and the family. At long last, and possibly with the assistance of William J. Donovan, the idea of turning the death into a kidnapping was arrived at and a plan worked out.

The author was unable to find records that indicate the whereabouts of William J. Donovan over the February 27 weekend of 1932. He was no more successful developing information of this sort regarding Miss Root, the nursemaid who accompanied the baby and supposedly went home Sunday evening. Aida Breckinridge's movements also remain a mystery. But there was one pronounced snafu that several members of the conspiracy inadvertently participated in, thanks to the man who prided himself on never forgetting an appointment: Charles Lindbergh.

According to the writer Joyce Milton in her recently published biography of the Lindberghs, *Loss of Eden,* Henry Breckinridge was actually at the NYU All Alumni Centennial Dinner and had telephoned Lindbergh, who was scheduled to speak at the gala, but failed to appear.[5] The source of Milton's material seems to be the FBI's 407-page Summary Report of the crime, in which it is inferred that Henry was in attendance.[6] There are reasons to question the summary's information. First off, the bureau had been effectively cut off from the investigation. While special agents eventually gained access to many peripheral characters, like Condon and Thayer, they never officially interviewed the Lindberghs or Breckinridge and very often went on rumor and hearsay. A second reason is that the Summary Report is reputedly gleaned from individual agent's reports, but a search of the entire bureau documentation on the case, an estimated 140 individual volumes consisting of an average of three hundred pages each plus various appendixes, which was conducted by this author's representative, lawyer Joel Starr, during the month of February 1993, uncovered no mention of the NYU banquet, Breckinridge being there, or Lindbergh not attending. New York University's seating list of the centennial's eighteen hundred guests does not include Breckinridge's name, but it places Lindbergh on the nineteen-man dais, not as a speaker but as one of two guests of honor.[7] The FBI Summary Report is dated February 16, 1934, a year and eleven months after the fact, and goes into exquisite detail, backing up the proposition that Lindy got the date of the Waldorf banquet wrong because he was misinformed.

Daniel J. Guggenheim had been Lindbergh's benefactor and friend. It was Guggenheim's Foundation for the Promotion of Aeronautics that had sponsored the Lone Eagle's post-France flights across America in *The Spirit of St. Louis* and helped make him a wealthy man. At the alumni dinner Guggenheim was to receive a special tribute for the good work he had done on behalf of American University from the Chancellor of NYU, Elmer Ellsworth Brown.[8] Lindbergh accepted an invitation to be one of two special guests. The fete was to take place at New York City's Waldorf-Astoria Hotel on March 1, 1932, and thanks in part to Lindbergh's announced appearance, it had received advance publicity in the local newspapers. On the Friday before the big event, an NYU secretary called to remind Lindbergh's office, possibly speaking to Elizabeth Sheet, Lindy's secretary, of his commitment that coming Tuesday. Festivities were to get under way between 6:00 and 6:30 that evening, and the caller was assured that he would be prompt.

One of the first things Lindbergh did after discovering his child was gone was call Henry Breckinridge. Did he call him at the Waldorf-Astoria? Most likely not. But if he did, why wasn't Henry, who claimed to have rushed straight to Sorrel Hill, in dinner clothes? The Waldorf event was formal—and no newspaper account of Henry's arrival at the estate says he wore formal garb.

The FBI Summary Report states that once at home, Lindbergh called the Waldorf and apologized for his absence. The author could find no corroboration for this.

Anne Morrow Lindbergh, in her published correspondence and diaries for the evening of March 1, 1932, makes no mention of the missed

NYU alumni celebration or of anyone's attempting to reach her husband regarding the waiting dinner guests at the Waldorf-Astoria. If, as the evening's sponsors had believed, Henry Breckinridge was trying to reach Lindbergh regarding his absence, would Anne, forty years later, have bothered to include it with the other events of that critical night? The answer is most likely no. But why not incorporate it into her 1932 sworn statements of March 11 and 13 to the state-police investigation team that was trying to ascertain everything that occurred at the house March 1, including that evening's incoming phone calls. The signed transcripts for Anne, Charles, and the staff contain no reference to such a call from Breckinridge or to Lindy's phoning the Waldorf. But they mention a call from Betty Gow's boyfriend, Red Johnsen, at around 9:00 P.M.—and another that came in earlier, from Charles Lindbergh, who told Anne he would be late for dinner.

Lindbergh's call to Anne, saying he would be late, had been received at approximately 7:00 P.M., an hour after the NYU sponsors, who didn't have his unlisted number in Hopewell, were so desperately attempting to locate him.[9] Where had he been calling from? The first assumption would have to be New York City, the place he usually went to work each day. He had claimed to have remained overnight in Manhattan the previous evening, February 29, and there had been no indication he left the city prior to his 7:00 P.M., March 1, call to Hopewell. Charles Lindbergh was not a frivolous fellow and certainly not one who displayed a high profile. The two most likely New York locations at which to find him would have been the office he maintained at Henry Breckinridge's law firm and the East Side Morrow apartment, where he and Anne stayed when in the city.

If Lindbergh had been in New York City until 7:00 P.M., March 1, why couldn't Henry Breckinridge find him when the panicked sponsors of the NYU centennial dinner contacted Henry about their missing guest of honor? The call from NYU came in at around 6:00 P.M., which would have given Breckinridge a full hour to get to Lindbergh. It was reported in the newspapers that the dinner's sponsors had talked directly to Henry—by phone. Would they have phoned him when he was right there attending the function? Could the phone conversation not have happened? Had they only left a message for him? If they had left such a message—say at his office—wouldn't whoever answered the phone have known that Lindbergh was there, assuming he was, or that he was over at the Morrow apartment? Wouldn't it seem reasonable that Breckinridge, having gotten direct or indirect word of his client's failure to appear at the Waldorf-Astoria, could have reached Lindbergh, if Lindbergh was still in the city? Obviously Henry had not. But had he even tried? Or had he known that Lindbergh was somewhere else, tending to more serious business? Could Henry have been with him? There was a saying among cold war espionage operatives that a lie stays in place, and the truth shifts. Could 7:00 P.M., Tuesday, March 1, have been a lie? Could it have been part of a rehearsed cover story meant to mislead investigators and the media—a fib that backfired by staying in place when the truth began to emerge? In later press accounts even the NYU sponsors tried to push back the time the event began.

Green inferred a simpler and more predictable explanation of the NYU matter. In the rush to prepare their grand conspiracy, Lindbergh and Breckinridge had completely overlooked the alumni dinner until Henry received the sponsors' phone call. With the curtain about to go up on their grand conspiracy, the Waldorf-Astoria gala was ignored. At 7:00 P.M., Lindbergh could very well have been at Hopewell, or he may have driven back into the city so he could turn around and motor home again, making it appear as if he had just come from work. Henry Breckinridge may have driven back to New Jersey with him or stayed on in Manhattan, waiting to be called back out to Sorrel Hill after the feigned discovery of a bogus kidnapping.

During the deluge of early media coverage of the child's disappearance, Breckinridge had done what he could to quash the NYU snafu by having the dinner's sponsors agree that they had given Lindbergh the wrong date. The explanation turned out to be vintage Lone Eagle–Colonel Henry sleight of hand. Reporters, rushing off in all directions after nonexistent kidnappers, paid little heed to a missed dinner at the Waldorf-Astoria. The Lindbergh-Breckinridge news blackout was once more firmly in place, with friendly publications being fed what the conspirators wanted them to write and with hostile journalists reduced to secondhand sources and wanton rumor. It was left for reporters far less sophisticated than the Lone Eagle and Colonel Henry had anticipated to discover another weak link at the very root motive of the conspiracy's master plan: Elisabeth.

If it was to protect Elisabeth and the Lindbergh-Morrow family names that a conspiracy was conceived and carried out, the deception had been amazingly successful. Elisabeth was not mentioned in any sworn statements given to official investigators by Charles and Anne Lindbergh, Ollie and Elsie Whateley, Betty Gow, Henry Breckinridge, or even Henry Ellerson, the Morrow chauffeur who allegedly drove her to the estate on

Saturday, February 27. In the files of the official state-police investigation as well as in the records of the attendant inquiries, such as those conducted by the Bureau of Investigation and the New York Police Department, there is nothing to indicate that Elisabeth had been at Sorrel Hill that weekend.

Henry Breckinridge controlled the flow of the crime and manhunt information emanating from investigation headquarters at the Lindbergh estate and in Trenton. Aida Breckinridge was the unofficial press secretary for Anne Morrow. Family spokesmen, such as Arthur Springer, secretary of the Morrow estate, made sure Mrs. Dwight Morrow, Constance Morrow, Dwight Jr., Lindbergh's mother, and other relatives were protected from the media. The spokespeople also issued press releases concerning each of their wards, often with direct quotes, and allowed an occasional interview and photograph. Mrs. Morrow had been the most quoted, then came Lindy's mother, and for a time, Elisabeth.

Confusion about Elisabeth's whereabouts occurred from the outset. Many publications reported that she had gone to Sorrel Hill in the wake of the kidnapping; others said she hadn't or made no mention of her. Arthur Springer confirmed for the *Evening News of Newark* that on the morning of March 2, Elisabeth had accompanied her mother, Mrs. Dwight Morrow, to the Lindbergh estate, where they planned to stay. The story appeared in the paper's early edition for the second. In a later edition that day, Springer was quoted as saying Elisabeth had remained in Englewood while her mother and her mother's sister had gone to Hopewell. On March 3, the *Bergen Evening Record*, a local New Jersey publication with excellent area sources, forced Arthur Springer to admit that he didn't know where Elisabeth was.

The story in the *Bergen Evening Record* that prompted Springer's admission was datelined March 3. It ran on page two and was captioned ELISABETH MORROW NOT IN ENGLEWOOD, FAMILY REFUSES TO DIVULGE HER WHEREABOUTS. The text went on to say that

> the whereabouts of Miss Elisabeth Morrow, sister of Anne Morrow Lindbergh, and an aunt of Charles Augustus Lindbergh Jr., is carefully guarded from the public by her family.
> Members refuse to divulge where Miss Morrow is

staying, though admitting that she has not attended her Little School on the Englewood Hill for the last few days. At the nursery school at the Memorial House, which Miss Morrow volunteered to supervise this year, it was said that Miss Morrow has not been seen there for the last week.

Rumors that she is ill began to circulate last Tuesday, when she became indisposed following the extraction of an infected tooth.

Arthur Springer, secretary of the late Senator Morrow, today said that he did not know her whereabouts, and refused to try to find out.

Miss Morrow's absence was first discovered this morning when teachers at the Little School on the Englewood Hill told reporters that she had not appeared at the institution yesterday and that she was not expected today. The Englewood Memorial Building nursery school reported that she has been absent for the last week.

When approached shortly before noon today, Springer said that he does "not know where she is," and swept the matter aside by stating that if "Miss Morrow were any place where the family would feel apprehensive for her safety, I would know."

Mr. Springer was called to the telephone as a last resort, when two other secretaries were unwilling to satisfy inquiries. It was at first said that Miss Morrow had not been seen at the Morrow estate during the last few days.

The page-two March 3 exposé in the relatively obscure *Bergen Evening News* divulging that Elisabeth was missing and that her current whereabouts were being kept a secret was ignored by a media intent on deluging the public with every iota of information, verified or rumored, that directly related to the manhunt and kidnapping and to whom Anne Lindbergh's older sister appeared to be only a peripheral character in the tragedy. Nonetheless, what appeared to be a minor media blitz to establish that Elisabeth was not in the least missing also began on March 3 with the *New York Mirror,* which claimed that she had remained at the Morrow Englewood estate and had forgone teaching her kindergarten class the previous day. The *New York World-Telegram,* an afternoon publication, ran a page-nine article, again on March 3, entitled CHILD'S AUNT TELLS CUTE THINGS HE DOES, which quoted Elisabeth as reputedly saying about her nephew, "He used to come to the school a great part of the time to play with other little children, although he wasn't enrolled. He would play in the swings and slides and he was always very cute and lively." On the following day, the *New York Telegraph* ran essentially the same story on its front page. A March 5 release from the Associated Press placed Elisabeth at Hopewell, doing what she could "to aid" and reporting that she had gone to her private school in Englewood only long enough to transact necessary business.[10] A March 10 newspaper release included a 1929 photograph of Elisabeth along with the news that she had remained behind at Englewood and had taken "the reins from Anne" in regard to a critical function at Sorrel Hill: supervising the Morrow household staff, which prepared the meals for personnel manning the investigation headquarters set up at the Lindbergh estate.[11]

The post–March 3 newspaper accounts that claimed Elisabeth was at Englewood—and, ergo, not missing—appeared to be general press-release material and contained nothing to indicate that a reporter had actually talked to her. Nowhere in the text of these releases was there anything to effectively counter the *Bergen Evening News* claim that Elisabeth was not at Englewood when the child was reported stolen.

"They had taken her away somewhere," contended Harry Green, who was certain that the Morrow household staff had been sworn to secrecy in the matter. Green further believed that Elisabeth had been brought back to Englewood after a week or so, in an attempt to establish that everything was normal, and that later she was again sent away. This jibed with the first actual sighting of Elisabeth, reported March 9 in the *Bergen Evening News,* which stated she had been seen walking rapidly from the Morrow house shortly after 11:00 that morning.

An indication that the Green-Hoffman scenario had taken into account the information in the March 3 *Bergen Evening News* article surfaced in Los Angeles on June 25, 1986. Green, who was lunching with the author, said, "Look at the *Evening News.* They printed the story. We already knew it."

Green later indicated that photographs of Elisabeth taken before and after the child's demise would provide further proof of her implication. The earliest postdeath picture the author could locate was an Associated Press photo taken June 13, 1932, showing Elisabeth disembarking from the ocean liner S.S. *Mauritania* at Plymouth, England. She was wearing a black armband in memory of her nephew—and she had changed dramatically, aged and transformed to the point where she was almost unrecognizable. The eternal smile was gone, and her face was gaunt and masklike.

"People who knew her said she was never the same after her nephew's death," Green contended. "She never forgave Anne for marrying Lindbergh. She got even and paid the price."

On March 1, 1932, the whereabouts of an object, not a person, was to cast its own shadow on the Lindbergh plot. The ransom message, sealed in an unmarked envelope, was the instrument intended to establish that a kidnapping had been perpetrated and to steer investigators away from truth regarding the Eaglet's death. At first, Lindbergh and Breckinridge officially denied that a letter had been found. Later they claimed a ransom envelope was discovered when Lindbergh, Anne, and Betty Gow first rushed into the childless nursery.[12] By March 21, 1932, an announcement revealed that the ransom message was found some hours after the baby's disappearance.[13]

Lindbergh, Anne, Gow, and the Whateleys, who were in and out of the nursery until constable Charles Williamson and Chief Wolfe arrived at 10:55 P.M., made no mention of seeing the ransom letter in their sworn statements. However, a short time later Lindbergh pointed to an unopened, unmarked envelope on a sill in the nursery and told the two Hopewell policemen it contained word from the kidnappers. How did he know? And who left it there? Apparently not Anne and the staff, who still weren't aware that a message existed. Was it placed there by the nonexistent kidnappers? When opened, the envelope did contain a ransom message. So Lindbergh was right again, just as he had been earlier when viewing the empty crib and telling Anne, "They've stolen our baby."[14]

Charles Lindbergh was a creature of discipline, so it was understandable that he calmly waited out the hour or so it took for fingerprint experts to arrive, dust the envelope and letter, and then have the message read. In this instance, Lindy certainly gave the impression that fingerprints were important to the police's case. But seldom again. Lindy and Breckinridge treated the next twelve messages with near reckless abandon vis-à-vis fingerprints.

In their 1993 book *Crime of the Century: The Lindbergh Kidnapping Hoax,* Gregory Ahlgren and Stephen Monier are also troubled by the appearance of the first ransom message. Ahlgren, a criminal defense lawyer and Monier, a veteran chief of police, ask why, if the note had been left by the kidnappers, wasn't it seen earlier?[15] They postulate that perhaps it wasn't seen earlier because it wasn't there. What the two crime experts find atypical is that the message was left on a windowsill. In their experience, a professional criminal would have been more likely to leave the note in the empty crib.

Monier and Ahlgren are further fascinated by Lindbergh's behavior after "finding" the ransom letter: he has Betty Gow come upstairs and points out the envelope for her, thereby establishing that it is there. He then has her go downstairs and fetch a knife, ostensibly so he can use it to open the letter. With the knife in hand, he leaves the message sealed. Monier and Ahlgren find that Lindbergh's restraint in not opening the letter until fingerprints were taken was admirable. But was it believable? The instinctive action of any parent whose child had been taken would be to rip open an envelope left behind and to learn what the contents said. In the opinion of Ahlgren and Monier, Lindbergh didn't need to open the letter. He knew what it said because he wrote it.[16] According to them, he knew something else: there was no kidnapping and the baby was already dead. Monier's and Ahlgren's conclusion, with which the author disagrees, is that Lindbergh knew of the death because he was responsible for the child's demise.

On December 28, nearly ten months after the death of her nephew, Elisabeth married Aubrey Neil Morgan of Brynderwem, Llandaff, Wales, at the Morrow home in Englewood. The bride had as her maid of honor and only attendant her youngest sister, Constance. She was given in marriage by her brother, Dwight Jr. Her best man was her uncle, Brigadier General Jay J. Morrow. A description of the wedding and who attended the ceremony was not made public.

Relatively few pictures of the once-photo-prone Elisabeth appeared in the wake of her marriage. Those that did showed a decidedly different woman from that of the days before her nephew's death. During the spring of 1933, due to continued bad health, she and her husband went to live in Pasadena, California. In mid-September of 1934, Bruno Richard Hauptmann was arrested and a month later transferred to New Jersey to stand trial for the kidnapping and murder of the baby. Less than a month later Elisabeth was reported to be acutely ill after undergoing an emergency operation for appendicitis at Pasadena Hospital. She remained hospitalized as reports appeared in the papers that her condition had been complicated by a throat infection that led to pneumonia as well as by a heart problem for which she had initially entered the hospital. By November 25, her mother was by her side, and on the twenty-seventh she was reported to be "sinking." At 2:50 A.M. December 3, 1934, Elisabeth Reeve Morrow Morgan died at the Pasadena Hospital. She was thirty years old.[17] Many of the obituaries claimed she had never fully recovered from the death of her nephew.[18]

"We heard rumors that it may have been a suicide," Harry Green related. "Colonel Lindbergh had identified the German's voice, and that was really that. It was over for Hauptmann. That could have been too much for her. We believed it was possible but couldn't find proof."

Governor Harold Hoffman, according to Green, never doubted that Elisabeth was implicated in the child's death but couldn't come up with the corroboration he considered necessary to convince a court of law—or even to delay Hauptmann's execution one more time.

Green provided no answer as to who moved the dead child away from the Lindbergh estate prior to March 1, 1932, and what was done with the body. No suggestions were offered on who had written the first ransom message, which was placed in the nursery. Green, when interviewed by the author in 1986, professed to have no idea who copied the original note, forged the next twelve messages, and extorted the fifty-thousand-dollar ransom. Green had a habit of pleading senility when, in the author's opinion, it suited his purposes. Asked directly about J. J. Nosovitsky, the old lawyer remained expressionless a moment, flashed a puckish smile, and muttered, "Oh, that fellow." Then he nodded to himself.

30

DESTINIES

- - -

WALTER LYLE, THE GAS STATION ATTENDANT WHO WROTE BRUNO RICHARD Hauptmann's license-plate number on a ten-dollar gold certificate from the ransom loot, received seventy-five hundred dollars from the reward of twenty-five thousand dollars posted by the state of New Jersey back in 1932. He was the largest recipient.[1] The second biggest payment went to William Allen, the trucker's assistant who entered the woods on Mount Rose Hill to relieve himself and came across the decomposed remains of a child. Allen had been attempting to get his share of the reward since 1932 and prompted a degree of official consternation when he appeared in a Coney Island freak show as the man who found the Lindbergh baby. The two bank tellers who spotted the bill on which Walter Lyle wrote Hauptmann's license-plate number each received two thousand dollars. Cecile Barr, the unflappable cashier at the Greenwich Village movie house who identified Hauptmann as giving her a folded bill from the ransom loot the night of his birthday, was rewarded with one thousand dollars. One thousand dollars went to Joseph Perrone, the taxi driver who identified Hauptmann as the man who paid him to deliver a ransom message to Condon. Another one thousand dollars went to Lyle's assistant at the gas station the night Hauptmann passed the ransom bill. Two men responsible for placing Hauptmann near the scene of the alleged kidnapping-murder, Amandus Hochmuth and Millard Whited, were each given one thousand dollars. Charles Rossiter, a surprise witness at the trial who testified to having seen Hauptmann changing a tire on his car near the Princeton airport three days before the kidnapping, got five hundred dollars. The last three thousand dollars in reward money was divided among bank employees who had spotted ransom currency.

Arthur Koehler, the wood expert, put in a claim for a share of the reward and was turned down. Jafsie Condon made no request for any of the reward money.

Rewards were paid on the recommendation of H. Norman Schwarzkopf and with the approval of Governor Harold Hoffman. At his reward interview with the governor, Amandus Hochmuth reasserted his sworn testimony that at the time of the child's disappearance, he had seen Hauptmann drive past with a ladder in his car and head for the nearby Lindbergh estate. During the course of the meeting, Hoffman asked Hochmuth to identify an object resting on top of a cabinet several feet away. The object was a vase of flowers. Amandus, who was seventy-seven years old and suffered from cataracts in both eyes, said it was a woman's hat.[2] As late as 1988, a state policeman who was present when Hochmuth identified Hauptmann as the driver of the car with the ladder inside insisted that the old man's eyesight was perfectly all right in 1932.[3] The governor's investigators found documentation that Hochmuth had been determined legally blind.

Millard Whited initially told state-police investigators that he had seen no one around the Lindbergh house at the time of the child's disappearance. He later admitted that he had repeated everything the troopers rehearsed him to say in identifying Hauptmann as being near the scene of the crime. At the Flemington trial Whited denied receiving money for his testimony before the Bronx extradition hearing on Hauptmann back in 1934. Talking to Harold Hoffman in 1936, he confessed to having been paid a $150 fee by the state police, plus $35 dollars a day for expenses and a promise of reward money.[4]

The U.S. Justice Department, under the so-called Lindbergh law, which was enacted in 1932 as a result of the Eaglet's abduction and death, obtained a federal grand jury indictment against Ellis Parker, Sr., and Ellis Parker, Jr. The case was tried in the federal district court at Newark in the spring of 1937. Both men were found guilty of kidnapping Paul Wendel. The Old Chief received a sentence of six years in prison; Ellis Jr., a term of three years. On February 4, 1940, Ellis Parker, Sr., died of "an organic cerebral condition" at the Lewisburg Federal Penitentiary in Pennsylvania.[5] He was reported to be sixty-eight years old, but there were claims that he was much older.

Murray Bleefeld, Harry Weiss, and Martin Schlossman, the abductors of Paul Wendel, were tried in Brooklyn in February of 1937 for violating the New York State kidnapping law. Found guilty, each man received a twenty-year term at Sing Sing prison in Ossining, New York. Attempts to link Harold Hoffman to the Wendel kidnapping failed, but rumors persisted that the governor knew of Parker's scheme and did nothing about it.

— — —

In 1977, the New Jersey State Police, incessantly criticized for their handling of the Lindbergh-Hauptmann case, "reviewed" their initial investigation with new and scientific means and found that their original conclusion was perfectly correct: Bruno Richard Hauptmann had acted alone in kidnapping and killing the Lindbergh baby. Critics were not silenced. In 1981, by executive order of New Jersey's governor, Brendan Byrne, the case files were opened to the public with the establishment of the Lindbergh Archives at the New Jersey State Police Museum in West Trenton. Today these archives offer one of the most comprehensive sources of documentation of a crime ever assembled.[6]

The Federal Bureau of Investigation's documentation on the Lindbergh-Hauptmann case is composed of some forty-five thousand pages, which are available to the public, by appointment, at the FBI's Washington, D.C., headquarters. More sensitive data can be accessed via a Freedom of Information Act application. The 407-page FBI Summary Report and promotional material regarding the Lindbergh crime give a clear impression that the bureau played a major role in successfully concluding the case.

— — —

Signs that Governor Harold Hoffman had been pursuing a secret suspect can be found in his investigatory files, much of which were garnered from the state-police records on the case. Hoffman did not return the material to trooper headquarters, and it was all but forgotten until 1985, when an estimated twenty-one thousand pages of reports and related documents were discovered in his widow's garage and turned over to the tiny East Brunswick Museum, in East Brunswick, New Jersey, which had been assembling the governor's artifacts and personal papers. Learning of the find, the New Jersey State Police made no immediate effort to claim the material. By the time they demanded return of the data, the museum had already begun to sort through and classify the individual items. An arrangement was worked out in which the state police copied all the material and allowed the Hoffman Collection in East Brunswick to retain the originals. As of this writing, the accommodation has deteriorated, and the state police have legally moved to recover all crime-related documents from the museum.

In 1986, based in part on material found in the newly discovered Harold Hoffman Collection, Bruno Richard Hauptmann's eighty-seven-year-old widow, Anna, brought a ten-million-dollar civil-action suit against New Jersey officials she alleged had framed her husband. Named in the court papers were David T. Wilentz and four former state troopers who played a prominent role in the investigation of the crime: Lewis J. Bornmann, William F. Horn, John B. Wallace, and Joseph A. Wolf. Among other accusations, the defendants were said to have individually and as part of a conspiracy "suborned perjury, manufactured fraudulent evidence, concealed true facts of an exculpatory nature, and participated in bribery."[7]

Anna had previously sued the state of New Jersey in 1981, accusing the state of the wrongful, corrupt, and unjust execution of her husband. The case was dismissed, and she appealed to a higher court, which upheld the dismissal. Her 1986 complaint-and-demand action in the U.S. district court was destined not to help her cause any more than the 1981 litigation. The state of New Jersey asked the court to dismiss the determined widow's latest suit, saying that Anna Hauptmann's quest to clear her husband's name should be left to historians. The court agreed. Anna's appeal to the U.S. Supreme Court was rejected. She and her lawyer Robert Bryan continue on their odyssey to establish the dead man's innocence.

A year after the Hauptmann trial, Edward J. ("Death House") Reilly, the chief defense attorney, entered a mental institution. He suffered from paresis brought on by syphilis. Fourteen months later he was released on application from his attorney, Samuel Leibowitz. Plagued by the incurable disease, Death House returned to practice of law as best he could. In 1940, at the age of fifty-six, he died of a stroke.

Judge Thomas W. Trenchard retired in 1941 after serving thirty-five years in the New Jersey State Supreme Court. Though highly respected, the venerable Trenchard was still nagged by what critics, including legal scholars and fellow judges, claimed was his bias against Hauptmann during the Flemington trial. He died of a cerebral hemorrhage the following year.

In 1937, Lloyd Fisher, an assistant defense counsel during the trial and Hauptmann's prime attorney until his electrocution, was appointed by Governor Hoffman to succeed Anthony Hauck as prosecutor of Hunterdon County. Fisher practiced law in Flemington until, at the age of sixty, he died of cancer.

— — —

On June 22, 1937, three and a half years after the death of Elisabeth Reeve Morrow, Elisabeth's widowed husband, Aubrey Neil Morgan, took as his second wife her youngest sister, Constance. The nuptials were held at Mrs. Morrow's summer estate in North Haven, Maine.

— — —

In 1936, Mark O. Kimberling was appointed by Governor Hoffman to replace H. Norman Schwarzkopf as superintendent of the New Jersey State Police.

— — —

When Harold Hoffman failed to reappoint him as superintendent of the New Jersey State Police, H. Norman Schwarzkopf, who had founded the trooper organization, became president of a New Jersey bus line and attained new notoriety as the narrator of one of the golden age of radio's most popular weekly half-hour adventure broadcasts, *Gang Busters*. He was back in his beloved army for World War II, where his experience with police matters resulted in his heading a nine-man U.S. military mission to Iran in 1942. He spent five years in the country.[8] His primary task was the reorganization and training of the Imperial Iranian Gendarmerie, whose strength he increased from some seven thousand to twenty-one thousand men while molding them into a highly efficient national police force. Their new uniforms closely resembled those worn by the New Jersey State Police, whose outfits he had personally designed back in the 1920s. Schwarzkopf was awarded the Distinguished Service Medal for his work in Iran, but it seems that he was never without a detractor. The same Iranian accomplishments for which H. Norman was honored by the U.S. military came under severe criticism, this time from the Soviet Union, who called him a CIA operative.

Schwarzkopf continued on in the postwar army and gained the rank of brigadier general. He organized the constabulary and the civil-intelligence unit in the American zone of occupied Germany and later, during February of 1950, headed the U.S. military mission to Italy. He was back in Iran in June of 1953, briefly and successfully, to help in a British-, and CIA-, engineered coup that ousted the regime of Mohammed Mosaddeq and reinstalled the shah.

Following his separation from the army in June of 1951, Schwarzkopf accepted several positions in New Jersey's government, one of which was heading an investigation into the financial dealings of his old antagonist, ex-governor Harold Hoffman. H. Norman Schwarzkopf died in 1958 at the age of sixty-three.

Thirty-three years later, during 1991, his son, General H. Norman Schwarzkopf, evened the score in his father's misadventures with the media in as dazzling a public relations gambit as has been seen in modern history. General Schwarzkopf commanded the joint UN-coalition military forces aligned against Iraq in the operation known as Desert Shield, later known as Desert Storm. His father had often appeared awkward in containing a manipulative press corps that throughout the Lindbergh affair tended to beleaguer and belittle him. During the Desert Shield campaign it was General Schwarzkopf who manipulated the media, brilliantly, into believing and reporting that part of the coalition's strategy was to invade Kuwait by sea. Iraq believed it as well, and while a goodly number of its troops dug in and waited for the amphibious onslaught, General Schwarzkopf's columns swept inland, entrapping the entire enemy army and giving the United States one of its most decisive, spectacular, and needed victories since World War II.

Hailed by the media, the public, and politicos as the ultimate victor in the Hauptmann trial, Attorney General David Theodore Wilentz used this new-found acclaim to gain influence within New Jersey's Democratic party. By 1940, his Middlesex Democratic organization was second only to Mayor Hague's Hudson County Democratic machine.[9] When Boss Hague was vanquished as Jersey City's Mayor, Wilentz and several more county leaders made their move by founding the National Democratic Club of New Jersey, which wrested power from the old party commit-tees. The 1950s saw Wilentz and a few other leaders become so powerful that they could choose gubernatorial and senatorial candidates. During the 1960s the former New Jersey attorney general became a force on the Democratic National Committee and had a say in the selection of presi-dential and vice-presidential nominees.

Dave Wilentz grew affluent from a prestigious law practice. Among his firm's many significant clients were Atlantic City casinos. Wilentz's two sons joined him in his law practice, and in 1979, one son, Robert, left to become chief justice of the New Jersey Supreme Court. His daugh-ter, Norma, married Leon Hess, the billionaire founder and chairman of Amerada Hess Corporation and the owner of the New York Jets football team.

When his old friend and adversary Harold Hoffman fell on financially hard times, Dave Wilentz quietly came to his rescue with money, a fact the ex-governor's daughter Hope revealed to the author in 1990.

David Wilentz died at his home in Long Branch, New Jersey, in 1988. He was ninety-three years old.

– – –

The much-maligned Harry W. Walsh of the Jersey City Police Depart-ment, the man who never wrote reports, recited to a co-author his inside account of the Lindbergh case for the *Jersey City Journal,* which pub-lished it in eight installments back in 1932. Lieutenant Jimmy Finn of the New York Police Department favored *Liberty* magazine with late-1935 exploits entitled "How I Captured Hauptmann." Harold Hoffman wrote of his involvement in fourteen 1938 episodes for *Liberty.* They were preceded by C. Lloyd Fisher's version of events, which *Liberty* ran in August and September of 1936. Mrs. Evalyn Walsh McLean was an-other *Liberty* magazine autobiographer. Her ten installments appeared in 1938, but not all of them dealt with the case. Paul Wendel related his experiences in *Liberty* with a 1938 series of articles entitled "Wendel

Tells All—My 44 Days of Kidnapping, Torture and Hell in the Lindbergh Case."

John F. Condon's account came out in a 1936 book, *Jafsie Tells All,* which was serialized by *Liberty* under the same title, beginning on January 18, 1936. In *Questioned Document Problems,* published in 1940, handwriting expert Albert D. Osborn detailed his part in the case. Special Agent Frank J. Wilson provided a personal version of events in his 1965 book, *Special Agent.* Anne Morrow Lindbergh mentioned the period in two of the books containing extracts from her diaries and journals: *Hour Of Gold, Hour Of Lead,* published in 1973 and *Locked Rooms and Open Doors,* which reached print in 1974.

Secrecy had become a durable thread in the weave of Charles Lindbergh. He had conducted his early courtship of Anne in a clandestine fashion, had been downright covert regarding their wedding, was furtive as ever while taking charge of the investigation of his missing son, and, assuming there was a plot to make the child's death appear to be a kidnapping-murder, implemented it with exquisite deceit. The secrecy was to persist long after Hauptmann's execution. In addition to Jon, who was born in 1932, Charles and Anne were to have four more children: two sons, Land and Scott, and two daughters, Reeve and Anne Spencer. In certain respects the family was close. But there were "forbidden subjects."[10] According to the writer Joyce Milton, a primary taboo was the kidnapping of baby Charles, which Lindbergh never discussed even with Anne, let alone with his children and their spouses. Their daughter Anne found out she once had an older brother as a result of a confrontation with a man who claimed he was Charles Lindbergh, Jr. Milton writes that Scott was ten years old before he learned about the crime and, ergo, about Charles Jr., from a book.[11]

That there were limits on his purposes and powers never occurred to thirty-year-old Charles Lindbergh. What he thought was right, what he did was best, and that was that to the most famous young man on the planet Earth. By now he was also a very prosperous one as well, allowing him even more self-assurance. When he disagreed with a president, as in the case of Franklin Delano Roosevelt's assignment of airmail routes to the U.S. Army Air Force, he attacked publicly. There was one matter over which Lindy admitted being indecisive: whether to continue on in the advancement and promotion of aviation or go into politics—that was to say, run for the presidency himself. Events in New Jersey led to a different decision. Governor Harold Hoffman unexpectedly reopened the investigation into the kidnapping-murder of the Eaglet—and Charles Lindbergh fled America, fled, as was often the case when he traveled, in secrecy. His fall from grace had begun, but the world didn't know it yet. He never would.

The Lone Eagle chose self-imposed exile in England, where he arrived with Anne and their second son, Jon, on December 31, 1935. Jon's safety was another reason given by the family for the rejection of their homeland. Lindbergh's highest self-proclaimed priority was no longer aviation or politics but anonymity, to live life unnoticed. He went about it in a curious fashion.

After two months in a London hotel, Lindbergh installed his family in a rented house in Kent and soon, by word as well as action, half-convinced the rapacious English press to respect his privacy. When it appeared that the London media had lost interest in him, Lindbergh and Anne burst from seclusion to take tea with England's new king, Edward VIII. It was early May of 1936. Later in the month they were among the illustrious guests attending the bachelor monarch's first dinner party.[12] Solitude behind them, the Lindberghs toured the Continent and beyond, hobnobbing with royalty and the likes of Italo Balbo. In India it was dinner with the viceroy. Germany was a different matter.

A U.S. military attaché in Berlin felt that Charles Lindbergh, whom the Germans admired, might be just the man to determine the actual strength and power of the Nazi Third Reich's vaunted Luftwaffe. The attaché managed to have the German air minister, Hermann Göring, the second most powerful man in Adolf Hitler's regime, invite Lindbergh to visit Germany. Lindbergh flew there with Anne on July 22, 1936, for a nine-day stay.

The Nazis rolled out the welcome mat and knew exactly how to stroke, coddle, and impress the American Eagle. He was not shown concentration camps or anything else that dealt with repressive measures against groups and organizations considered undesirable or enemies of national socialism. Not only did the Germans seduce the Lone Eagle into thinking their existing air strength and production of new war planes was far greater than actually was the case, but they inspired the usually taciturn Lindbergh to make a speech that both lauded Nazi air power and cautioned against bombing defenseless civilians. The following day he gave another talk. Hitler's propaganda mill, whose scare tactics had been frightening neighbors into believing the government's war machine was invincible, never did a more effective job than in exploiting what Lindbergh said. Lindy seemed not to mind. He had become an unabashed fan of Germany's air force.

Charles Lindbergh, long disenchanted with the promise of his native America, also became an unabashed fan of Germany per se. His admiration for its energy, virility, spirit, organization, planning, and accomplishments convinced the Lone Eagle that the future belonged to the Teutons. He also expressed a partiality toward Herr Hitler, as he referred to the Führer. Anne Lindbergh perceived certain troubling aspects about the totalitarian Third Reich; her husband did not. Always the pragmatist, he tended to view those who were anti-Nazi as disliking Germans.

The Lindberghs returned to Germany on October 10, 1938, where Charles was to be the guest of honor at the Lilienthal Aeronautical Congress in Munich. Lindbergh's host was Germany's World War I ace Ernst Udet, who Anne believed was an anti-Nazi. Udet arranged for the Lone Eagle to fly a new Messerschmitt 109. He also boasted of technical and numerical superiority in the construction of aircraft and cited inflated production figures. To back up his claims, he took Lindbergh around the country, showing off new planes, airfields, and factories. Udet and other German officials who talked with Lindbergh were part of a detailed strategy worked out by Hermann Göring intended to convince Lindbergh that the Luftwaffe's fleet of bombers had the capability of destroying whatever nations went to war with Germany.

Possibly because he believed that his oversolicitous hosts would not dare lie to him, Charles Lindbergh took what they said as dictum. So did the U.S. military attaché in Berlin, who reported back to General H. H. ("Hap") Arnold, the chief of the U.S. Army Air Corps, that the Nazi Luftwaffe had ten thousand planes, an armada that could wipe out the combined air forces of England, France, and Russia. In truth, the Germans had half that number of planes, many of which were flawed or simply not airworthy, but Lindbergh's exaggerated estimates were more often believed than not. He had become the crier of German invincibility.

Exactly when Anne and Charles Lindbergh's dalliance with Lady Astor and the infamously pro-Hitler Cliveden set began is debatable, but America's golden couple was to become a familiar decoration for the table of the outspoken peeress, who had been born Nancy Langhorne in

Virginia. Added to Lindbergh's Germanophile views, his Cliveden association began to draw criticism. So did his friendship with Dr. Alexis Carrel, a French doctor who had been awarded a Nobel Prize for his contribution to surgery.

Carrel had written a best-selling book that championed racial superiority and suggested that the superior genetic types—there was none higher than the Scandinavian—be protected from inferior and defective strains via euthanasia, specifically by gassing. Though more a pro-German than an anti-Semite—he counted Albert Einstein among his closest friends—Carrell was perceived as pro-Nazi. Lindbergh considered the doctor a genius and a confidant. Before abandoning America, Lindbergh had worked with Carrel at New York City's Rockefeller Institute in developing a mechanical heart. During the summer of 1938, the Lindberghs gave up their country home in England and moved to an isle off the Brittany coast of France called Illiec, on which there were three houses and a chapel. Illiec had been bought for the Lindberghs by Dr. Carrel, who lived on a neighboring isle.

On October 18, 1938, Lindbergh was back in Berlin, attending a stag dinner at the American embassy. Hermann Göring was the last to arrive and, to the surprise of the U.S. ambassador and Lindbergh, presented the Lone Eagle with the Service Cross of the German Eagle, the highest decoration the Third Reich could award a civilian. The medal was ostensibly given for Lindbergh's previous contribution to aviation. Anne, who viewed it as an albatross that would forever haunt her husband, urged him to give it back. He saw no harm in keeping the decoration, and did. Anne's prescience would prove correct.

Ten days after receiving the medal, Lindbergh decided to move his family—he and Anne now had two children, Jon and Land—to a house near Wannsee, on the outskirts of Berlin, pending the terms of the lease. An even better offer was made: Albert Speer, the city planner for Berlin, would build the Lindberghs a house anywhere they wished. Anne and Charles returned to Illiec to consider their options. On November 9–10 in Germany, an eighteen-hour anti-Semitic reign of terror erupted—the Night of Glass, or Kristallnacht. Anne was shocked. Lindbergh was "surprised and skeptical" of the reports on Jewish persecution by the Nazis.[13] Even so, he canceled plans to move to Germany.

Charles Lindbergh never perceived the struggle between the Allies and Nazi Germany for what it was: a primal conflict between good and evil. Back on his native soil in the spring of 1939, the man who had made the world a smaller place by flying the Atlantic Ocean now proclaimed that

that same body of water would protect the United States from the very Nazi air might he had so greatly admired and dynamically championed. He was still a national hero and quickly became the leading spokesman for the country's isolationist movement. He proclaimed that these foreign wars were of no consequence or peril to America. Lindy told the listening nation that the Führer himself had assured him of this. Though he continued to condemn the effeteness of France and England and to speak glowingly of Nazi air might, the Lone Eagle stubbornly maintained he was not pro-German, merely anti-war. Asked which side he wanted to win after France and England finally tried to stop Hitler, he answered simply, "Neither." With France conquered and London being reduced to rubble under the massive Luftwaffe bombing raids known as the Battle of Britain, Lindbergh proclaimed that England was lost and demanded the United States cut off whatever aid it was providing.

Charles Lindbergh knowingly took on the main proponent of aiding England and stopping Hitler, President Franklin Delano Roosevelt, who was certain Lindy was a Nazi. The Lone Eagle, with his typically sublime tunnel vision, did not cotton to FDR's style of oratory and therefore did not consider him much of a speaker. He termed the president in no uncertain terms a warmonger. When FDR accused the Lone Eagle of being a "defeatist," Lindbergh, in a huff, resigned his commission in the Army Air Force Reserve. Lindbergh's popularity was gaining among the right wing and isolationist segments of the population. But more and more of his former friends were dropping him. His and Anne's had been an enlightened circle. Now he was aligning himself with some of the foremost bigots and hate merchants in the nation. The criticism caused by his views reached into the Morrow household itself where Anne's mother and sister both publicly disavowed him. His own mother, who was pro-Ally, stopped talking to him.

The isolationist view was extremely popular among average Americans, who were more against war than against the Nazis. Lindbergh fared worse with the literary establishment, which was overwhelmingly anti-Hitler and had never cared all that much about Lindy to begin with. In 1940, James Thurber wrote a scathing spoof on Lindbergh entitled THE GREATEST MAN IN THE WORLD. One of the Lone Eagle's most fervent detractors was the acerbic columnist Dorothy Thompson. At the time of the kidnapping, she and her then husband, Sinclair Lewis, voiced the opinion that Lindbergh himself had killed the child. Her comments about his pro-Nazi stand were far more fervent and widely quoted.

Lindbergh was piously racist in an America that itself was blatantly racist. The peril for him and for tens of millions of his fellow citizens were the blacks, yellows, and browns, not to mention the Communists. The only hope for civilization, in Lindbergh's view, was the propagation of the white race. This was not at issue in the pending European conflict, and he cited it as another reason for the United States to stay out of the conflict.

Though stung by accusations of anti-Semitism, Lindbergh could not bring himself to see, let alone admit, that the Germans had mounted a massive Final Solution to eliminate the Jews. In a war civilians often get killed, and that was that regarding the Jewish question in Europe as far as Lindy was concerned. He also had opinions regarding America's Jews, which he intended to express in Des Moines, Iowa, on September 11, 1941, at a gathering sponsored by the powerful America First Committee, of which he was a ranking member and a premier spokesman. The undertaking proved star-crossed. By chance FDR was to speak on the radio earlier that same evening. In the spirit of fairness, the America First organizers, much to Lindbergh's distress, allowed the speech to be broadcast in the Des Moines auditorium. FDR made an all-out attack on the Nazis—and was applauded eleven times by the supposedly hostile gathering. A minute after his talk ended, Lindbergh entered the auditorium, took the podium and, for the first time since his arrival from Europe, was booed more than he was cheered, and this from a supposedly partisan crowd.

Three groups were pressing for this country's entry into the war, he told an audience of seventy-five hundred: the British, the Roosevelt administration—and the Jews. He did not deny that Jews had some reason to be unhappy with Hitler, but then he warned, if not threatened, the Jews not to use the media they controlled—movies, radio, newspapers— to drag this country into war. Aiding them in this effort were the Jews in government. There was more on how the Jews in this country should behave.

The accusation against the Jews was an unwelcome surprise for those members of the American First hierarchy. The condemnation and protest against what Lindbergh said was deafening and came from conservatives as well as liberals, Republicans as well as Democrats, even from American Firsters. The nation's press unanimously joined in. Cartoonists portrayed the Lone Eagle in Nazi uniform as well as kissing Hitler's boot. America's national hero had become a national disgrace, a Nazi lackey. A street that had been named after him was renamed. In Little Falls, Minnesota, the sign on the water tower which proclaimed that this was the home town of Charles A. Lindbergh was painted over. He was dropped from the board of directors of Pan Am, which stopped calling itself the Lindbergh Line and got rid of its logo, a drawing of the *Spirit of St. Louis*. Through it all, Charles Lindbergh never doubted that his cause was just, never stopped hating Franklin Roosevelt, never desisted from urging America to stay out of the war. Then came Pearl Harbor.

With the country at war, Lindbergh decided to fight for America. His ego and taste for deceptive ploys affected the way he went about it. Rather than simply go to a recruiting office the day after Pearl Harbor and enlist—a move that would have regained him the admiration and respect of his countrymen—Lindbergh waited nearly two weeks before contacting the head of the Air Force, General Hap Arnold. After a series of delays and excuses, he ended up in the office of the Secretary of War, Henry L. Stimson, who politely denied Lindbergh's request to join the armed forces by saying that a defeatist was not a capable leader of soldiers. It was a stinging rebuke, one Lindbergh was sure had been orchestrated by the man he continued to perceive as an arch devil: President Roosevelt.

Lindbergh's efforts to help the war by working in various sectors of the aircraft industry were thwarted by the unfriendly administration. Only Henry Ford, a scurrilous anti-Semite, had the power and inclination to hire Lindbergh. By 1945, with the connivance of military officers who held him in high esteem, Lindbergh, without the administration's knowledge, became a civilian adviser to the air force in the Pacific and flew combat missions against the Japanese—downing at least one enemy plane in a dogfight. But the old leanings persisted. Visiting Germany immediately after the war, he was appalled by the callousness he felt the Allies displayed in their treatment of the defeated civilians. He assiduously avoided visiting concentration camps, which he refused to call concentration camps. To him they were German prison camps, and he seemed unimpressed by the one installation he inadvertently visited. Charles Lindbergh saw no difference between American-run prison camps for captured Japanese soldiers he had heard about and what the Nazis did to the Jews.

FDR had died in office. Germany and Japan surrendered unconditionally. And the Gyntian travels of Charles Lindbergh continued. Estranged from everyone who had been close to them, he and Anne entered the postwar world virtually alone, save for their children. Lindy was no longer the relaxed, boyish grinner of yesterday. He looked far older than his forty-three years. His political ambitions had ended, at least for the time being. He and Anne and the children settled in Darien, Connecticut.

Fences slowly began to be mended. He was reinstated on the board of Pan Am, became the U.S. Air Force's roving troubleshooter as well as advising them on rocketry and space matters. Charles and Anne reconciled themselves with their respective mothers and families. He remained ardently anti-Communist. When the Russians blockaded Berlin, Lindy took an active roll in the U.S. airlift into that city.

Lindbergh was mellowing. More and more he involved himself in good works. Even so, many could never forgive him for his stand on the Nazis, and he would never admit that perhaps he had been wrong regarding them. He still had the ability to rile antagonists, but many of his deeds were amazingly just and productive, drawing the applause of former detractors. According to his biographer Leonard Mosely, "Sometime in this period of his life, Charles Lindbergh seemed like an actor in a small-town repertory theater who has to play most of the male parts in the script, one moment twirling his mustache as the villain of the piece, a few minutes later reappearing as the blue-eyed hero."[14] With the advent of the McCarthy era in the early fifties, he was back to mustache twirling. Though not an advocate of McCarthy's methods, he was not particularly bothered by the Wisconsin senator's efforts to root out communism. Happier scenarios were on the way.

During 1953, an autobiography Lindbergh had been working on for a dozen years was published under the title *The Spirit of St. Louis*. The book became a best-seller, received a Pulitzer Prize, was made into a movie, which starred James Stewart as Lindbergh, and earned the author a substantial amount of money.

On April 7, 1954, by order of President Dwight D. Eisenhower, not only was Lindy's commission restored, but Lindbergh was upgraded and sworn in as a brigadier general in the U.S. Air Force Reserve. At the same time he was appointed to the Air Force Scientific Advisory Board, which put an official certification on the work he had been doing for his country since the war's end. That year was also a time of loss. Lindbergh's mother, Evangeline, died, a passing he did not take well. The following year, 1955, Elizabeth Morrow, Anne's mother, died. The fortune she left added to the Lindberghs' already substantial wealth.

Anne broke away from the rigors of raising a family and coping with a famous husband to write *A Gift from the Sea*—a book dealing with the many problems confronting a contemporary woman, mother, and wife—which became a best-seller and made her into one of the most popular authors of the decade. In 1970 Charles published his wartime diaries.

Lindbergh's priorities had changed dramatically. He saw other dangers beyond communism, and far graver jeopardy. The Lone Eagle had begun to oppose the very science and technology for which he had been the symbol and spokesman most of his adult life. Nature, not progress, was the answer. He was against the building of the SST, which he saw as an environmental hazard. For a man who remained inveterately skeptical of people and manipulative and devious in many of his dealings with them, he at long last found a species he could trust: animals. Always an insatiable traveler, he visited every corner of the earth and became actively involved with the World Wildlife Fund as well as the International Union for the Conservation of Nature and its Survival Service Commission, the Nature Conservancy, and the Oceanic Foundation. He was in the forefront of those protecting the whales, the Alaskan polar bears, the one-horned rhinoceros of Java, marine life in Hawaii, and countless other endangered species. He found peace and solitude on the Hawaiian island of Maui, where he and Anne built their final home.

In 1974, Charles Lindbergh was hospitalized in New York City. Told he was suffering from an advanced form of lymphatic cancer and didn't have long to live, Lindy insisted on flying back to Maui. He spent his final days getting his affairs in order and preparing for his death and funeral. He lapsed into a coma on the evening of August 25, 1974. The next morning at 7:15, with Anne by his side, he expired.

— — —

Badgered by an unrelenting hostile press and fervid antagonists within the New Jersey Republican party, Harold Hoffman did what he could in the wake of Bruno Richard Hauptmann's execution to shore up his political career. Rather than backing off from the Hauptmann matter as advisers urged—he was desperately short of funds as well—the governor doggedly tried to continue with the investigation that had played such havoc with his life. It didn't matter that no one cared or was listening; Harold Hoffman insisted on proving he was right about the case and that everyone else was wrong. It was exactly what his enemies wanted.

Despite the bipartisan setbacks he had encountered, Hoffman still entertained national political ambitions. With the 1936 elections coming up, his supporters thought it feasible for the governor to maneuver himself into being a presidential or vice-presidential nominee. In a way he had no other choice—and nothing to lose. A New Jersey governor by law could not succeed himself in office. This was providential, since there was a strong likelihood that if allowed to run, Hoffman would not have received his party's nomination.

Harold Hoffman later blamed his humiliating reversals of fortune not on the policies of his administration, such as the ill-fated tax legislation, but solely on the stand he took regarding Bruno Richard Hauptmann and the kidnapping. In a series of articles for *Liberty* published during the early months of 1938 and entitled "What Went Wrong with the Lindbergh Case: The Crime, the Case, the Challenge," the by then ex-governor defended his actions in an often rambling, often detailed account of what brought him into the fray and why he'd done what he'd done. His written belief in Hauptmann's complicity ranged from none at all to that of a mild coconspirator, but the general tenor of the articles was clearly on the side of the German carpenter not having been involved.

One thing Harold Hoffman was able to maneuver was a $12,000-a-year job for himself as executive director of New Jersey's Unemployment Compensation Commission, the UCC, from which he mounted a nonstop campaign to be elected the GOP's gubernatorial candidate in the 1940 primary elections. His effort was vigorous but fell short when he lost, just barely, to the candidate of his perennial enemy, the Clean Government Group. In June of 1942, with World War II in full sway, he received a commission in the U.S. Army's transport command. In June of 1946, he separated from the army with the temporary rank of colonel and returned to his post at the Unemployment Compensation Commission. When the administration of Governor Alfred E. Driscoll formed the Division of Employment Security within the state's Labor and Industry Department, Harold Hoffman left the UCC and became the DES's first administrator, a post that paid $13,500 per annum. He implemented his income as a dinner speaker, thanks in part to his own popularity and in part to the Thomas Brady Agency, which booked most of the engagements. His gratis performances were usually in New York City, as the ringmaster of bashes sponsored by the Circus, Saints and Sinners, an organization that had made him its honorary life president.

Robert B. Meyner, a Democrat, was installed as governor of New Jersey on March 18, 1954. Rumors of improprieties in Hoffman's handling of state funds had been wafting for some time, and during his first month in office, Governor Meyner asked two respected businessmen to make a survey of the accusations. Their findings left little doubt that state money had been intentionally mismanaged, if not stolen. Presented with the preliminary findings at a meeting with Meyner and the state's attorney general, H. Norman Schwarzkopf, who was now head of the Department of Law and Safety, was asked if he could objectively investigate the case, in light of his well-publicized conflicts with Hoffman over the Lindbergh crime. Asked by Meyner if he thought he could carry on an unbiased inquiry, Schwarzkopf answered in the affirmative. He was assigned to delve further into the charges, two of which asserted that Hoffman had improperly transferred some $2.5 million of state funds to a bank run by a friend of his—and that he had deposited $300,000 from New Jersey's disability fund into his own bank in South Amboy, where it had lain in a dormant account, drawing no interest for the state.

That same afternoon Governor Meyner suspended Harold Hoffman from his state job pending a full investigation into his financial affairs. Hoffman loyalists went on the attack, assailing Meyner for a political witch-hunt even before the details were made public. The Democrats knew only part of the story. When all the facts came to light, the picture painted was unnerving. Harold Hoffman, plagued by debt, had, among other things, sold political favors and fallen victim to blackmail.

The crisis began during Hoffman's successful bid for a congressional seat in 1926. A running mate reneged on a promise to pay Hoffman's campaign expenses, which came to $17,000. Life in Washington, D.C., and "the expensive naïveté of a newcomer congressman" saw the initial $17,000 debt sharply increase.[15] Costs incurred by his private investigation of the Lindbergh-Hauptmann case aggravated the matter. Dunned by creditors who could imperil his political reputation, Harold Hoffman began to draw on inactive accounts at the bank of which he was still president. When he stepped down as governor in 1938, his borrowing had reached $300,000. To avoid disclosure, he was forced to pay another $150,000 to a state official who was blackmailing him.

On May 1, 1954, less than two months after his suspension by Governor Meyner—with the investigation into his affairs continuing and most of the truth not yet known—Harold Hoffman gave his eldest daughter, Ada, a letter to be opened only after his death. A month and three days following that, on June 4, he was found dead in the New York City apartment of the Circus, Saints and Sinner's organization, which he often used. Most reports assert that he died of a heart attack while bending over to tie or untie his shoe. Rumors floated to the effect that he committed suicide. Ten thousand people are said to have attended his funeral. Intense pressure was put on Governor Meyner to clear the name of Harold Giles Hoffman.

"The governor had personal problems that interfered with the investigation," Harry Green revealed. "There was only so much he could do to prove she was the one. Time ran out before this happened. But we were close."[16]

In the letter to his daughter Ada, opened posthumously, Harold Hoffman admitted to the embezzlement and apologized for the sad heritage bequeathed his family. "Morality, in its ultimate determination," the fallen ex-governor wrote, "is a funny thing."[17]

NOTES

Chapter 1 MOTH TO FLAME

1. Conflicting figures exist regarding the distances between the Lindbergh estate and other locations. This is partially due to the changes in road construction, routing, and cartography since 1932. The FBI Summary Report of the crime (62-3057, February 16, 1934, New York) states that the Lindbergh house is located ten miles northwest of Princeton, New Jersey, twenty miles north of Trenton, New Jersey, and about fifty miles south of New York City. Traveling two different routes, the author found the current distances between the estate and New York City to be fifty-eight miles and sixty-one miles. The average driving time back in 1932 between the estate and Manhattan seems to have been approximately two hours.

2. Whipple, *The Lindbergh Crime*, 233.

3. This version of Wally Stroh's story comes from Jesse William Pelletreau's own writings (collection of the author), not from the accounts in the *New York American*.

4. Ibid.

Chapter 2 WHAT THE POLICE WERE TOLD

1. Kennedy, *The Airman and the Carpenter*, 82.

2. There are minor contradictions concerning this call. In a statement made ten days later, Lindbergh claimed that he waited upstairs in the nursery while Whateley telephoned the Hopewell sheriff, and after finding out the phone lines were not cut, he personally called Colonel Henry Breckinridge (his lawyer) in New York City and after that made the call to the New Jersey State Police at Trenton (statement to Lieutenant John J. Sweeney, Newark Police Department, March 11, 1932, Lindbergh Archives). In his January 1935 testimony Lindbergh stated that after he found the telephone wires weren't cut, he called the state police and then Colonel Breckinridge (transcripts of the State v. Bruno Richard Hauptmann, 1935, Lindbergh Archives). In the FBI Summary Report the claim is made that on arriving at the scene, Chief Harry H. Wolfe suggested to Lindbergh that he contact the state police, and this was done at 10:40. The facts seem to bear out the FBI, which in those days was still the BI, the Bureau of Investigation.

3. Corporal Joseph A. Wolf's Major Initial Report, 371, March 1, 1932, Lindbergh Archives.

4. Ibid.

5. Lindbergh Archives.

Chapter 3 CROWDED IDOLS

1. Charles A. Lindbergh, *Autobiography of Values*, 75.

2. Charles A. Lindbergh, quoted in Time, *Time Capsule 1927*, 37.

3. *Time*, January 7, 1928.

4. McElvaine, *The Great Depression*, 55.

5. In his *Autobiography of Values*, printed three years after his death, Lindbergh says the plane was flown to Rochester, New York, and serviced there (p. 126). According to a May 28, 1929, front-page box in the *New York Times*, the plane was at Roosevelt Field, where, on Lindbergh's orders the day before, it was prepared for the trip.

6. In his *Autobiography of Values*, Lindbergh contends that after the wedding he and Anne slipped out of the Morrow house and "into the back of a big car and out of the gate without being recognized" (p. 127). Newspaper accounts of the event say the couple was seen driving out of the estate, and give some detail as to what they were wearing.

Chapter 4 THE EAGLET

1. Donald E. Keyhole, *Saturday Evening Post*, May 30, 1931.

2. Anne Morrow Lindbergh, *North to the Orient*, 255; Kennedy, *The Airman and the Carpenter*, 48.

3. Kennedy, *The Airman and the Carpenter*, 49.

4. Anne Morrow Lindbergh's statement to Lieutenant John J. Sweeney of the Newark Police Department, March 11, 1932, Lindbergh Archives.

5. Anne Morrow Lindbergh's signed statement to Lieutenant John J. Sweeney and Detective Hugh Strong of the Newark Police Department, March 13, 1932, Lindbergh Archives and Harold Hoffman Collection.

6. The nursery's bathroom was adjacent to the side of the nursery.

7. Anne Morrow Lindbergh, *Hour of Gold, Hour of Lead*, 225.

8. Bessie Mowat Gow quoted by Charles A. Lindbergh in his statement to the New Jersey State Police, March 11, 1932, Lindbergh Archives.

9. Charles A. Lindbergh quoted by Bessie Mowat Gow in her statement to the New Jersey State Police, March 3, 1932; Whipple, *The Trial of Bruno Richard Hauptmann, 164.*

10. Ibid.

11. Ibid., 115.

12. The FBI Summary Report's title page alone misspells Whateley as Whately and refers to the Lindbergh family dog, Wahgoosh, as Trixie. Pages 49 and 50 refer to Lindbergh as forgetting "a speaking engagement" at New York University that was "given by the board of Regents." Lindbergh was not to be a speaker but a guest of honor, and the dinner was held under the auspices of the Alumni Federation in cooperation with the alumni associations of several schools of NYU. The search through the forty-two-hundred-plus pages of material on the Lindbergh case at the Federal Bureau of Investigation's headquarters in Washington, D.C., was conducted by Joel Starr in March 1993.

Chapter 5 OLD ENEMIES AND FRIENDS

1. Charles A. Lindbergh quoted in the *New York Times*, March 2, 1932.

2. The encounter between Charles A. Lindbergh and the Hearst journalists recounted in Vitray, *The Great Lindbergh Hullabaloo*, 22.

3. Ibid., 53.

4. Anne Morrow Lindbergh, *Hour of Gold, Hour of Lead*, 227.

5. Vitray, *The Great Lindbergh Hullabaloo*, 85.

6. *New York Times*, March 3, 1932.

7. Ibid.

8. Ibid.

Chapter 6 COLONELS

1. Kennedy, *The Airman and the Carpenter*, 93.

2. In 1907, the FBI was known as the Special Agent Force. In 1908, it became the Bureau of Investigation. On July 1, 1932, its name was changed to the U.S. Bureau of Investigation. It became the Division of Investigation on August 1, 1933. On July 1, 1935, it was given the title Federal Bureau of Investigation.

3. Coakley, *Jersey Troopers*, 30.

4. Harry Green, interview with author, June 25, 1986, Los Angeles, California.

5. Coakley, *Jersey Troopers*, 57.

6. Ibid., 50.

7. Whipple, *The Trial of Bruno Richard Hauptmann*, 7.

Chapter 7 SLEIGHT OF HAND

1. Bessie Mowat Gow, signed statement to Lieutenant John J. Sweeney and Detective Hugh Strong of the Newark Police Department, March 10, 1932, Harold Hoffman Collection.

2. Vitray, *The Great Lindbergh Hullabaloo*, 54.

3. *New York Herald Tribune*, March 3, 1932; Paul T. Gebhart quoted ibid.

4. Vitray, *The Great Lindbergh Hullabaloo*, 84–85.

Chapter 8 NOBLE GANGSTERS

1. A movie costing under one hundred thousand dollars was designated a B by the Hollywood studios of the day. An A movie cost over one hundred thousand dollars. The B was usually the second attraction in the popular double features of the day.

2. He was registered under the name of Kelly because he wasn't allowed in the city.

3. William Kennedy, telephone conversation with author, March 1989.

4. The chief argument against adoption of the Cochran bill focused on objections to the death penalty, lack of federal funds with which to enforce the legislation, encroachment on states' rights, the creation of an overdependence of the states on the federal government, and the centralization of too much power in the federal government.

5. FBI Summary Report, 144.

6. Ruth Pratt quoted ibid., 142.

7. Ibid., 144.

8. Ibid., 141–44.

9. Ibid., 144–54.

10. Ibid., 141–56.

Chapter 9 GO-BETWEENS

1. FBI Summary Report, 141–56.

2. Ibid.

3. Lindbergh Archives.

4. Robert Thayer quoted in the FBI Summary Report, 147.

5. Anne Morrow Lindbergh, *Hour of Gold, Hour of Lead,* 230.

6. An objector frequently cited by historians was Rev. Charles E. Coughlin, pastor of the Shrine of the Little Flower church in Royal Oak, Michigan. A notorious demagogue, Father Coughlin hosted one of the most popular radio shows in the Midwest and was already speaking favorably of Adolf Hitler.

7. FBI Summary Report, 141–56.

8. Lindbergh Archives.

9. FBI Summary Report, 141–56.

10. Waller, *Kidnap,* 40–41.

11. FBI Summary Report, 18.

Chapter 10 JAFSIE

1. Lindbergh Archives.

2. Ibid.

3. Condon, *Jafsie Tells All,* 27.

4. Reports over a period of weeks in four different newspapers (the *New York Herald Tribune,* the *New York Times,* the *New York American,* and the *New York Daily News*) gave the author the impression Jafsie looked younger than his age.

5. Condon, *Jafsie Tells All,* 30–35. In his early written accounts of these events, Condon referred to the unknown perpetrators in the plural: *kidnappers.* Subsequent to a suspect being brought to trial in 1935, he generally treated the same references in the singular: *kidnapper.*

6. Ibid.

7. Anne Morrow Lindbergh, *Hour of Gold, Hour of Lead,* 232.

8. Condon, *Jafsie Tells All,* 35.

9. Ibid.

10. Ibid., 48.

11. In one set of Division of Investigation reports, Condon is introduced to Rosner under the alias of Dr. Stico; in another set of reports, he is referred to as Dr. Stacey.

12. Condon, *Jafsie Tells All*.

13. Kennedy, *The Airman and the Carpenter*, 95–96.

14. John F. Condon, "Jafsie Tells All," *Liberty*, January 18, 1936, 7.

15. Ibid., 6–7.

16. Condon, *Jafsie Tells All*, 52.

17. Man on the phone quoted ibid., 56.

Chapter 11 JUGGLING

1. Charles A. Lindbergh quoted in Fisher, *The Lindbergh Case*, 38.

2. Charles A. Lindbergh quoted ibid., 38–39.

3. FBI Summary Report, 14.

4. Anne Morrow Lindbergh, *Hour of Gold, Hour of Lead*, 227

5. According to Fisher, Irey's initial contact with Lindbergh and Breckinridge was to convince them that Al Capone and his associates had nothing to do with the kidnapping, and Capone was trying to use Lindbergh to get himself out of jail (*The Lindbergh Case*, 31).

6. FBI Summary Report, 127.

7. Vitray, *The Great Lindbergh Hullabaloo*, 119.

8. Henry Breckinridge quoted ibid., 130.

9. Ibid.

10. The first note had been left on the windowsill; a second was sent to the Lindbergh estate; the third had been mailed to Henry Breckinridge at his New York City office; the fourth had been sent to John F. Condon.

11. FBI Summary Report, 141–56.

12. The dialogue between John F. Condon and the man on the telephone quoted in Condon, *Jafsie Tells All*, 57–58.

13. The *Bronx Home News* was an afternoon paper; the *New York American* was a morning paper that hit the newsstands the night before.

14. The exchange between Condon and the cab driver quoted in Condon, "Jafsie Tells All," *Liberty*, February 1, 1936, 33.

15. Lindbergh Archives.

16. Ibid.

17. Al Reich quoted in Fisher, *The Lindbergh Case*, 56.

18. The dialogue between Condon and John quoted in Condon, "Jafsie Tells All," *Liberty,* February 1, 1936, 34.

19. FBI Summary Report, 152.

20. Ibid., 153–54.

21. Morris Rosner quoted ibid.

22. Ibid., 154.

23. McLean, "Why I'm Still Investigating the Lindbergh Case," pt. 4, *Liberty,* 1938, 38.

24. Condon, "Jafsie Tells All," *Liberty,* February 8, 1936, 33.

25. Lindbergh Archives.

26. The exchange among Charles A. Lindbergh, Henry Breckinridge, and Condon quoted in Condon, "Jafsie Tells All," *Liberty,* February 15, 1936, 44.

Chapter 12 OPEN SECRETS

1. Lindbergh Archives.

2. Fisher, *The Lindbergh Case*, 72.

3. Ibid., 71.

4. Charles A. Lindbergh quoted ibid., 72.

5. H. Norman Schwarzkopf quoted in Waller, *Kidnap,* 68.

6. H. Dobson-Peacock quoted in Fisher, *The Lindbergh Case*, 73.

7. Ibid.

8. Lindbergh Archives.

9. Fisher, *The Lindbergh Case*, 74.

10. Lindbergh Archives.

11. Ibid.

12. Fisher, *The Lindbergh Case*, 74.

13. Waller, *Kidnap,* 70.

14. Ibid., 71.

15. Fisher, *The Lindbergh Case*, 79.

16. Kennedy, *The Airman and the Carpenter*, 110–11.

17. Ibid., 111.

Chapter 13 PAYOFF

1. Lindbergh Archives.

2. Ibid.

3. Condon, *Jafsie Tells All*, 149.

4. Man in the cemetery quoted ibid.

5. Ibid., 156.

6. Ibid.

7. Ibid.

8. Lindbergh Archives.

9. Kennedy, *The Airman and the Carpenter*, 112; Waller, *Kidnap*, 79.

10. Waller, *Kidnap*, 80.

11. Ibid.

12. Fisher, *The Lindbergh Case*, 86.

13. Condon, *Jafsie Tells All*, 173.

14. Charles A. Lindbergh quoted ibid.

15. A Division of Investigation summary report and printed accounts from different sources say the footprint was on top of a grave. Other reports, including one from a DI operative, claim the prints were on the ground between the graves.

16. Fisher, *The Lindbergh Case*, 88.

17. Vitray, *The Great Lindbergh Hullabaloo*, 189–90.

Chapter 14 A STAR IS BORN

1. Kennedy, *The Airman and the Carpenter*, 109.

2. Fisher, *The Lindbergh Case*, 84.

3. FBI Summary Report, 186.

4. *New York Herald Tribune*, April 12, 1932; *New York Times*, April 12, 1932.

5. Woman at the bazaar quoted in the FBI Summary Report, 179.

6. Ibid., 180–81.

Chapter 15 A MATTER OF JOHNS

1. Fisher, *The Lindbergh Case*, 97; "The Case New Jersey Would Like to Forget," *Liberty*, August 8, 1936.

2. John Hughes Curtis's John quoted in Fisher, *The Lindbergh Case*, 97–98.

3. Lindbergh was at Condon's making final preparations for paying the ransom later that night.

4. Curtis's John quoted in Fisher, *The Lindbergh Case*, 99.

5. After receiving one hundred thousand dollars on March 6, Gaston B. Means extracted another four thousand dollars from Mrs. McLean.

6. The *New York Herald Tribune*'s summations for May 10 and 11, 1932, state that May 9 and 10 are the sixty-ninth and seventy-first days, respectively, since the child was kidnapped. What happened to the seventieth day?

Chapter 16 EAGLES DEPART

1. *New York Herald Tribune*, March 11, 1932, 1.

2. *New York Times*, May 13, 1932, 1; *New York Herald Tribune*, May 13, 1932, 3.

3. Waller, *Kidnap*, 102.

4. *New York Times*, May 13, 1932, 2; *New York Herald Tribune*, May 13, 1932, 3.

5. Fisher, *The Lindbergh Case*, 112–13.

6. *New York Times*, May 13, 1932, 3.

7. Schwarzkopf quoted ibid.

8. Ibid.

9. *New York Herald Tribune*, May 13, 1932, 2.

10. Fisher, in *The Lindbergh Case* (p. 437), reveals that Detective Sergeant Cornel D. Plebani, the first curator of the Lindbergh Archives, stated that the coroner Walter H. Swayze did not perform the autopsy.

11. Autopsy report, Lindbergh Archives.

12. Ibid.; *New York Herald Tribune*, May 13, 1932, 2.

13. *New York Times*, May 13, 1932; *New York Herald Tribune*, May 13, 1932. Harry Walsh claimed he did tell Schwarzkopf. State-police spokesmen claimed that there were actually two small holes, the second of which was made by Walsh's stick, and that the autopsy never included the Walsh hole because it was so small. All other evidence indicates there was only one hole.

14. The words of Charles A. Lindbergh and Erwin E. Marshall quoted in the *New York Times*, May 13, 1932, 2.

15. Autopsy report, Lindbergh Archives.

16. Ibid.

Prelude to Book Three

1. The Lindberghs later donated their estate at Sorrel Hill to the state of New Jersey, which used it as a children's home.

Chapter 17 MONEY TRAILS AND OLD DOUBTS

1. Kennedy, *The Airman and the Carpenter,* 110.

2. FBI Summary Report, 216.

3. Fisher, *The Lindbergh Case,* 89; the FBI Summary Report gives the date as April 10.

4. According to the FBI's Summary Report, the NYPD took action on May 1, 1933, regarding outstanding ransom money. Rather than embrace the trooper's practical single-page list, Finn and the head of the Fed Bank's money division in New York City produced their own modified inventory of outstanding currency a year later. The NYPD distributed 30,000 copies to banks, brokerage houses, and selected retail businesses. An accompanying "private and confidential" circular, which made no mention of the state police or Bureau of Investigation phone numbers, said the men to contact in case a listed bill was discovered were Finn or his immediate superior, Inspector John Lyons. The number at which Finn could be reached—and the one that most of the money found in New York City would be reported to—was CAnal 6-2051.

5. Finn and Curtin, "How I Captured Hauptmann," *Liberty,* November 16, 1935, 56. According to the Museum of the City of New York, Greenwich Street, which runs many blocks south of what today is considered Greenwich Village, was then considered to be in the Village.

6. Condon quoted by Wally Stroh in his statement and autobiography, from the papers of Jesse William Pelletreau, collection of the author. Other statements by Stroh can be found in the Harold Hoffman Collection, and in the Lindbergh Archives.

7. Fisher, *The Lindbergh Case,* 163.

8. Ibid.

9. FBI Summary Report, 162.

10. Letter from H. Norman Schwarzkopf to Ellis Parker, Sr., August 24, 1932, Harold Hoffman Collection.

11. Letter from Parker to A. Harry Moore, August 26, 1932, ibid.

12. Fisher, *The Lindbergh Case,* 147.

13. Ibid., 150.

14. Kennedy, *The Airman and the Carpenter*, 121.

15. Anne Morrow Lindbergh, *Hour of Gold, Hour of Lead*, 273.

Chapter 18 MONEY CHASE

1. Time, *Time Capsule 1933*, 9.

2. Albert D. Osborn was the son of Albert S. Osborn, who was also an expert in "the field of questioned documents," as the craft of handwriting analysis was known.

3. Kennedy, *The Airman and the Carpenter*, 157.

4. Ibid.

5. Ibid., 158.

6. Fisher, *The Lindbergh Case*, 17.

7. Arthur T. Keaten quoted in Kennedy, *The Airman and the Carpenter*, 158.

8. John Lamb quoted ibid.

9. Ibid., 176.

10. Fisher, *The Lindbergh Case*, 178; according to the *New York Herald Tribune*, September 22, 1934, the DI used black pins for five-dollar bills, red pins for tens, and green for twenties.

11. Waller, *Kidnap*, 204.

12. Finn and Curtin, "How I Captured Hauptmann," *Liberty*, November 2, 1934, 44.

13. Kennedy, *The Airman and the Carpenter*, 159.

14. Waller, *Kidnap*, 215; Kennedy, *The Airman and the Carpenter*, 160, has 4U13.14.

15. The dialogue between Walter Lyle and his customer quoted in Waller, *Kidnap*, 213.

16. There were twenty-five New York City policemen, sixteen federal agents, and nineteen New Jersey State Troopers, according to the *New York Herald Tribune*, September 21, 1934, 3.

17. Ibid., September 24, 1934, 1.

18. Waller, *Kidnap*, 220.

19. John B. Wallace quoted in Kennedy, *The Airman and the Carpenter*, 168.

20. Fisher, *The Lindbergh Case*, 187; Waller, *Kidnap*, 221.

21. Albert D. Osborn quoted in Kennedy, *The Airman and the Carpenter*, 180.

22. Ibid., 176.

23. Ibid.

24. Schwarzkopf quoted in Fisher, *The Lindbergh Case,* 202.

25. The exchange between the New Jersey state troopers and Anna Hauptmann is taken from ibid., 203.

Chapter 19 THE MOST HATED MAN IN THE WORLD

1. The total amount recovered was $14,600. A breakdown of ransom loot is given in an undated joint memo from Jimmy Finn of the NYPD, William F. Horn of the NJSP, and Special Agent William F. Seery of the DI to Mr. Breslin re "Ransom Money Recovered to Date," Lindbergh Archives. The one-page document states that 390 ten-dollar gold certificates and 493 twenty-dollar gold certificates (amounting to $13,760) were retrieved from the Hauptmann garage on September 20, 1932. On September 25, another 84 ten-dollar gold certificates ($840) were discovered in the garage. Even though the total came to $14,600, the media and law-enforcement agencies tended to round off the figure to an even $14,000 when referring to the find in Hauptmann's possession. The memo further stated that to date $19,685 in ransom loot had been recovered from all sources, including Hauptmann's garage.

2. Questions asked by Inspector John Lyons quoted in the official transcript of Bruno Richard Hauptmann's interrogation, Lindbergh Archives; Hauptmann's responses ibid.

3. Exchanges between Lyons and Condon and between Condon and the men in the lineup are quoted in material in the Harold Hoffman Collection.

4. *New York Times,* September 25, 1934; *New York Herald Tribune,* September 25, 1934; *New York Daily News,* September 25, 1934.

5. Anthony Scaduto quoted in *Kidnapped: Reliving the Lindbergh Case,* New Jersey Network Production, 1989.

6. Kennedy, *The Airman and the Carpenter,* 204.

7. Frank Fitzpatrick's, Russell Hopstatter's, and Russell M. Stoddard's remarks about Tom Cassidy quoted ibid., 204, 205.

8. Fisher, *The Lindbergh Case,* 250.

9. Kennedy, *The Airman and the Carpenter,* 204.

10. Daniele Tomasetti in *Kidnapped: Reliving the Lindbergh Case.*

11. Kennedy, *The Airman and the Carpenter,* 216.

12. Millard Whited in *Kidnapped: Reliving the Lindbergh Case.*

13. Fisher, *The Lindbergh Case,* 253.

14. Bruno Richard Hauptmann quoted in the *New York Times,* October 7, 1934, 28.

15. The October 15, 1934, Bronx County Courthouse proceedings are described in the *New York Times,* October 16, 1934, 1, and in the *New York Herald Tribune,* October 16, 1934, 1; the questioning of Hauptmann by David Wilentz is quoted in the *New York Herald Tribune,* October 16, 1934, 1.

16. Wilentz quoted in the *New York Post,* October 16, 1934, 1.

17. *New York Herald Tribune,* October 17, 1934, 1.

18. Kennedy, *The Airman and the Carpenter,* 222.

19. Howard Knapp quoted in the *New York Times,* October 16, 1934, 1, and in the *New York Herald Tribune,* October 16, 1934, 1.

20. The exchange between Wilentz and Joseph Furcht is quoted in the *New York Daily News,* October 20, 1934, 1.

21. Ibid.

22. *New York Daily News,* October 19, 1934, 3.

23. Kennedy, *The Airman and the Carpenter,* 222.

24. Hoffman, "What Went Wrong with the Lindbergh Case," *Liberty,* February 5, 1938, 17.

Chapter 20 HULLABALOO

1. Alan Hynd cited in Scaduto, *Scapegoat,* 118.

2. John H. Curtiss quoted in *Time,* January 7, 1935, 16.

3. Descriptions of the Flemington scene come in part from Kennedy, *The Airman and the Carpenter,* 254–59; *New York Times,* January 3, 1935; *New York Herald Tribune,* January 3, 1935; and *New York Daily News,* January 3, 1935.

4. *David Brinkley's Journal,* "Trial of the Century: Press Coverage of the Hauptmann Trial . . . 'It Was a Sickness,' " WNBC-TV, January 3, 1961.

5. Whipple, *The Trial of Bruno Richard Hauptmann,* 48.

6. Edward J. Reilly's remark cited by Thomas H. Sisk and quoted in Kennedy, *The Airman and the Carpenter,* 240.

Chapter 21 TRIAL OF THE CENTURY

1. Reilly quoted in the transcripts of The State v. Bruno Richard Hauptmann, 1935, Lindbergh Archives.

2. Fisher, *The Lindbergh Case,* 280.

3. *Time,* January 14, 1935.

4. *New York Herald Tribune,* January 4, 1935, 1.

5. Charles A. Lindbergh quoted in the transcripts of The State v. Bruno Richard Hauptmann, 1935, Lindbergh Archives.

6. The exchange among Reilly, Wilentz, and Justice Thomas W. Trenchard was reported in the *New York Times,* January 5, 1935, 1, and in the *New York Herald Tribune,* January 5, 1935, 1.

7. The exchange between Joseph Perrone and Bruno Richard Hauptmann quoted in the transcripts of The State v. Bruno Richard Hauptmann, 1935, Lindbergh Archives.

8. The exchange between Wilentz and Condon quoted in Whipple, *The Trial of Bruno Richard Hauptmann,* 228.

9. Reilly and C. Lloyd Fisher quoted in Whipple, *The Trial of Bruno Richard Hauptmann,* 292.

10. Arthur Koehler quoted in the *New York Herald Tribune,* January 24, 1935, 1.

11. Fisher quoted in Whipple, *The Trial of Bruno Richard Hauptmann,* 365.

12. Ibid., 63.

13. The exchange between Wilentz and Bruno Richard Hauptmann quoted in Whipple, *The Trial of Bruno Richard Hauptmann,* 436.

14. *New York Herald Tribune,* January 26, 1935, 6.

15. The exchange between Wilentz and Bruno Richard Hauptmann regarding the spelling of *boat* quoted in Whipple, *The Trial of Bruno Richard Hauptmann,* 404–5; the observation by the newspaper reporter from the *New York Herald Tribune,* January 26, 1935, 9.

16. The exchange between Wilentz and Bruno Richard Hauptmann regarding Cemetery John quoted in Whipple, *The Trial of Bruno Richard Hauptmann,* 406; Whipple renders the alias as "Perlmeyer."

17. Bruno Richard Hauptmann quoted in the *New York Herald Tribune,* January 26, 1935, 9, and in the *New York Times,* February 1, 1935, 13.

18. Fisher, *The Lindbergh Case,* 345.

19. Waller, *Kidnap,* 460.

20. Wilentz quoted in Lamoyne A. Jones, *New York Herald Tribune,* February 14, 1935, 1–8.

21. Reilly quoted ibid.

22. The reporters' song from Kennedy, *The Airman and the Carpenter,* 258.

23. Wilentz quoted in Whipple, *The Trial of Bruno Richard Hauptmann,* 337.

24. Jones, *New York Herald Tribune,* February 14, 1935, 8.

25. Whipple, *The Trial of Bruno Richard Hauptmann,* 399.

26. The exchange between the county clerk and the jurors quoted in Whipple, *The Trial of Bruno Richard Hauptmann,* 340, 341, and in Waller, *Kidnap,* 492.

27. Waller, *Kidnap,* 492.

28. Trenchard quoted in the transcripts of The State v. Bruno Richard Hauptmann, 1935, Lindbergh Archives.

Chapter 22 HAROLD GILES HOFFMAN

1. Letters from George M. Hillman to A. Harry Moore's secretary, from Moore to Ellis Parker, Sr., and from Parker to Moore in box 5, the Harold Hoffman Collection.

2. *New York American,* March 20, 1932, 1.

Chapter 23 BOLD STROKES AND BRUNO

1. All quotations and description in this section, on Hoffman's October 16, 1935, visit to Bruno Richard Hauptmann on death row, are from Hoffman, "What Went Wrong with the Lindbergh Case," *Liberty,* January 29, 1938–April 30, 1938. Bracketed emendations are Hoffman's.

2. Ibid.

3. The exchange between Hoffman and the juror, in which the juror quotes Condon, quoted ibid.

4. Ibid., February 5, 1938, 17–18.

5. Evalyn Walsh McLean, "My Say," *Washington Times,* January 12, 1938.

6. Hoffman, "What Went Wrong with the Lindbergh Case," *Liberty,* February 19, 1938, 51.

Chapter 24 THE BUBBLE BURSTS

1. Hoffman, "What Went Wrong with the Lindbergh Case," *Liberty,* February 19, 1938, 47.

2. Scaduto, *Scapegoat,* 73.

3. Bradway Brown, a wealthy young Philadelphia manufacturer, was found shot dead in his Palmyra, New Jersey, home on January 16, 1933, in what some thought was a suicide. After a year of deduction and tracking, Ellis Parker, Sr., brought the killer to justice, thus proving it was murder.

4. Exchange between Jesse William Pelletreau and Hoffman quoted in the papers of Jesse William Pelletreau, collection of the author.

5. Scaduto, *Scapegoat,* 236–37.

6. Kennedy, *The Airman and the Carpenter*, 433.

7. Hoffman quoted in the *Trenton Evening Times*, December 5, 1935, 1, 23.

8. Hoffman, "What Went Wrong with the Lindbergh Case," *Liberty*, February 19, 1938, 48.

9. Ibid.

10. The exchange between Hoffman and Pat Grady quoted ibid.

11. Ibid., 50.

12. Letter from Bruno Richard Hauptmann to Hoffman, December 16, 1935, box 5, folder 1, Harold Hoffman Collection.

13. The *Trenton Evening Times* ended its Tuesday, December 24, editorial on the Lindbergh's self-imposed exile saying, "That the Lindberghs may find peace and quiet, free from cheap politics and moronic claptrap, will be the hope of their shamed and embarrassed countrymen."

Chapter 25 THE ROCKY ROAD TO REPRIEVE

1. Twenty-page summary, n.d., 12, the papers of Jesse William Pelletreau, collection of the author.

2. Ibid.

3. Harold Hoffman quoted ibid., 13.

4. Letter from J. J. Faulkner to Hoffman, January 1, 1936, quoted in the *New York Daily News,* final edition, January 10, 1936, 3–6.

5. Letter from Hoffman to Schwarzkopf, January 3, 1936, Harold Hoffman Collection. Included on the list were objects such as the ladder and the chisel found at the Lindbergh estate the night of the crime, all reports on Violet Sharpe and the Morrow household staff, all statements by and reports on Betty Gow and all information on Red Johnsen, everything said by Jafsie Condon, including a phonograph record made by him in the presence of the state police, any statements or reports concerning Robert Thayer and Morris Rosner, a complete set of photos of the ladder, showing all fingerprints on the ladder, the set of fingerprints that Dr. Hudson believed were those of the baby, statements by a Morrow-household butler named Septimus Banks, Dr. Van Ingen's measurement of the child taken prior to the kidnapping, statements and reports on Amandus Hochmuth, evidence regarding the footprint found outside the nursery window, the cast of the footprint taken at St. Raymond's Cemetery subsequent to the payment of ransom by Jafsie Condon, all statements used in radio broadcasts by Superintendent H. Norman Schwarzkopf, and all reports or statements made by Inspector Harry Walsh of the Jersey City P.D.

6. Mark O. Kimberling, invitation to the electrocution of Bruno Richard Hauptmann, January 6, 1936, Harold Hoffman Collection.

7. Sanford E. Stanton, *New York American,* January 17, 1936.

8. Dennis Doyle's letter to Ellis Parker, Sr., is described in Doyle's statement to Detective Ralph Lewis of the New York Police Department and Detective William F. Horn of the New Jersey State Police, June 28, 1936. The statement is on file in the Lindbergh Collection at the New Jersey State Police Museum.

9. Hoffman quoted in Robert Conway, *New York Daily News,* January 12, 1936, 3.

10. Wilentz quoted in the *Trenton Evening Times,* January 11, 1936, 1.

11. The architect of the jail had been profoundly influenced by ancient Egyptian tombs, which the building resembled.

12. The papers of Jesse William Pelletreau, collection of the author.

13. Stroh's comments are taken from his statements in May 1936 and his writings of September 1936 as well as his later encounters with Pelletreau (the papers of Jesse William Pelletreau, ibid.). Since Stroh used various spellings for the Doc's last name, the author has settled on one for this particular segment: Nosovitsky.

14. Six letters from Max Sherwood to Hoffman, 1936, Lindbergh Archives.

15. Wally Stroh's and Dennis Doyle's sworn statements to Captain J. J. Appel and Detective Ralph Lewis of the New York Police Department and Detective William F. Horn of the New Jersey State Police, May 28, 1936, Lindbergh Archives. It is in this affidavit that reference is made to Stroh's and Doyle's prior meetings with Gus Lockwood and the *New York American* journalist.

16. Fisher, *The Lindbergh Case,* 393.

17. Damon Runyon, *New York American,* January 12, 1936, 3.

18. Harold Hoffman, "What Went Wrong with the Lindbergh Case," *Liberty,* February 19, 1938, 52.

19. *Trenton Evening Times,* January 12, 1936, 1.

20. Runyon, *New York American,* January 12, 1936, 2.

21. *Trenton Evening Times,* January 12, 1936, 2.

22. Pauline Hauptmann quoted in the *New York American,* January 13, 1936, 5.

23. Anna Hauptmann's cable quoted in the *New York Times,* January 13, 1936, 3.

24. Ralph Hacker quoted in Runyon, *New York American,* January 12, 1936, 3.

25. Wilentz quoted ibid.

26. Conway, *New York Daily News,* January 13, 1936, 3.

27. *New York American,* January 13, 1936, 1.

28. Ibid.

29. Hoffman quoted ibid.

30. Representative Blanton quoted ibid., January 14, 1936, 6.

31. Charles A. Lindbergh's statement in *Paris Soir* quoted ibid.

32. Crawford Jamieson quoted ibid.

33. Hoffman, "What Went Wrong with the Lindbergh Case," *Liberty*, February 19, 1938, 52.

34. Ibid.

35. Ibid., 53.

36. The exchange between Wilentz and Hoffman quoted ibid.

37. Ibid.

38. Note on New Yorker Hotel stationery, Harold Hoffman Collection.

39. The exchanges between Anna Hauptmann and Hoffman quoted in Hoffman, "What Went Wrong with the Lindbergh Case," *Liberty*, February 26, 1938, 24.

40. Wilentz quoted ibid., 26.

41. Hoffman quoted in Conway, *New York Daily News*, January 16, 1936, 3.

Chapter 26 COUNTDOWN

1. Mary McGill, Dr. Erastus Mead Hudson's secretary, was erroneously called Mary Maxwell in the Stanton article.

2. Hoffman quoted in Richard L. Tobin, *New York Herald Tribune*, January 18, 1936, 1.

3. Fisher, *The Lindbergh Case*, 399.

4. *New York Herald Tribune*, January 19, 1936, 4.

5. Box 16, folder 604, Harold Hoffman Collection. The information focused on a story that the actress Rosalind Russell, the second woman lead in the touring play *Second Man*, told her producer.

6. Letter from Hoffman to Schwarzkopf quoted in the *New York American*, January 31, 1936, 1.

7. Included among the questions were the following:

> Who was the person to whom John had said, during a telephone conversation with Dr. Condon, that the latter wrote articles for the newspapers?
>
> Who was the Italian who had spoken curtly to John, apparently directing him?
>
> Was he the same person or someone else?
>
> Who was the woman, also apparently Italian, who had spoken so mysteriously to Dr. Condon, telling him to meet her at the Tuckahoe station?

Why hadn't the state police questioned Dr. Condon about a reputed $250,000 bribe he claimed to have been offered?

Since Hauptmann was in prison and could not have made the bribe offer, who was his accomplice?

Was not Dr. Condon, whose words were so greatly relied upon by the prosecution, believed when he said he was still convinced that more than one person was involved with the crime?

If Lindbergh believed that Condon was in contact with the actual gang of kidnappers, then why had he entered into negotiations with John Hughes Curtis?

What did Curtis say or show to him that persuaded Lindbergh that Curtis was dealing with the kidnappers?

Was the deciding factor Curtis's description of John, which exactly tallied with Jafsie's description of his John?

Wasn't it true that just before the Hauptmann trial, the state had brought Curtis to Philadelphia where he refused to say that his John wasn't the member of a gang, and that consequently that the affidavits he gave to the Assistant Attorney General, Robert Peacock, weren't used as part of the state's case?

And how did all this fit in with state's accusation against Curtis, who had been charged with having known the whereabouts of the abductors and willfully withholding this information from the authorities?

Was the state right in obtaining a conviction of Curtis based on obstruction of justice after having had contact with a gang of kidnappers, or was the state right in prosecuting Hauptmann as a lone wolf?

Since it is evident that the prosecution was wrong in either one case or the other, is it not obvious that the state and the courts are not infallible, and that every possible inquiry is warranted before final action is taken in this important case?

Did it seem possible that one of the baby's thumb guards could lay in the driveway to the Lindbergh house for a whole month without being found?

Wasn't it easier to believe that it was put there just before its alleged discovery by accomplices inside or outside the household?

Since everyone agreed the bank-receipt slip for $2,980, signed J. J. Faulkner, was not in Hauptmann's writing, why had the search for Faulkner been abandoned?

8. Exchange between Schwarzkopf and Wilentz quoted in Fisher, *The Lindbergh Case*, 402. Schwarzkopf's statement the following day is from the Lindbergh Collection, New Jersey State Police Museum.

9. Five letters from Hoffman to Hoover, January 18, 1936, box 5, Hoover file, Harold Hoffman Collection. In the first letter Hoffman asked for data regarding Jafsie's phone number, which was found written on a wooden beam in Hauptmann's closet shortly after his arrest in 1934; the governor also revealed that the New Jersey State Police case files provided no information on the DI search of the closet. The second letter requested intelligence on the bureau's not being allowed into the Hauptmann apartment at the time it was discovered that a board in the attic was missing. The third letter wanted information on the articles found at the Hauptmann home. The fourth asked if Hoover's men had examined the kidnapping ladder and if the ladder had been sent to the bureau's Washington, D.C., laboratory. The final communication inquired as to whether photos of the prints found on the ladder were sent to the DI's identification center.

10. Letter regarding Mike Sololiski, box 5, Hoover file, Harold Hoffman Collection.

11. Hudson quoted in Fisher, *The Lindbergh Case*, 398.

12. Letter from Zoe Hobbs to Hoffman, January 17, 1936, box 5, file 3, Harold Hoffman Collection.

13. Box 21, legal file, ibid.

14. Letter from Harold Keyes to Hoffman, January 20, 1936, box 12, ibid.

15. Telegrams from Hobbs to Hoffman, box 5, file 3, ibid.

16. Tobin, *New York Herald Tribune*, January 20, 1936, 3; *New York American*, January 22, 1936, 3.

17. Henry W. Jeffers quoted in the *New York American*, February 2, 1936, 3.

18. *New York Times*, February 7, 1936, 1; *New York Herald Tribune*, February 7, 1936. Another powerful foe that Harold Hoffman seemed never to acknowledge as a threat or favor with political patronage was a GOP faction called the Clean Government Group. Headed by Arthur T. Vanderbilt, an Essex County lawyer, the CGG was fundamentally conservative but, realizing that change was in the political air, gave lip service to liberal and reform ideals. It particularly didn't like Boss Hague and had been outraged when newly elected Governor Hoffman conspired with him to get the tax bill passed, an issue it used to gain strength within the New Jersey GOP during the September 1935 state primary. The CGG, as much as any force, was responsible for Hoffman's being stripped of his party's leadership earlier in the week. Whether the Clean Government Group could stop him from becoming a delegate to the GOP national convention remained to be seen. But its members were keeping up the pressure, and a war with Hoffman was fine with them.

19. Editorial, *Trenton Evening Times*, February 7, 1936, 6.

20. Letter from Bruno Richard Hauptmann to Mark O. Kimberling quoted in Fisher, *The Lindbergh Case*, 404.

21. Hoffman, "What Went Wrong with the Lindbergh Case," *Liberty*, March 5, 1938, 49.

22. Samuel Leibowitz quoted in the *New York American*, February 20, 1936, 1.

23. Hoffman, "What Went Wrong with the Lindbergh Case," *Liberty*, March 5, 1938, 49.

24. Waller, *Kidnap*, 564.

25. Murray Bleefeld's account of Paul Wendel's son's remark quoted in Scaduto, *Scapegoat*, 250.

26. Letter from Hobbs to Hoffman, box 5, file 3, Harold Hoffman Collection.

27. Letter from Hobbs to Hoffman, March 27, 1936, and telegram from Hoffman to Hobbs, March 29, 1936, ibid.

28. *Trenton Evening News*, February 29, 1936, 1.

29. Letter from William Lewis of the Mead Detective Agency, box 21, Harold Hoffman Collection.

30. Tobin, *New York Herald Tribune*, March 15, 1936, 29. Fisher's appeal was based on the claim of six points: (1) Millard Whited had perjured himself at the trial; (2) Hochmuth was partly blind at the time he saw Hauptmann near the Lindbergh estate; (3) Condon's stories in print and at the trial were contradictory; (4) a new witness could testify that Isador Fisch had driven to the Lindbergh's estate prior to the crime; (5) a German resident of Cuba received a letter from Fisch, asking him to get rid of some hot money; (6) Hauptmann had received an unfair trial and should have a new hearing. Fisher claimed the Fisch data were new.

31. *New York Herald Tribune*, April 4, 1936, 1.

Chapter 27 AN INTERNATIONAL SPY

1. *New York Times*, December 16, 1927, 1.

2. Senate Special Committee to Investigate U.S. Propaganda or Money Alleged to Have Been Used by Foreign Governments to Influence U.S. Senators, 70th Cong., 1st sess., December 15, 16, 17, 20, and 27, 1927; January 4 and 7, 1928.

3. Ibid., 290–91.

4. The Socialist Revolutionary party, subsequent to the revolution, would split with the Bolsheviks. It would be an SRP woman who shot and wounded Lenin.

5. On February 18, 1916, at the U.S. District Court in Detroit, Michigan, Jacob Nosovitsky filed a declaration of intention to become a citizen, in which he stated that he had emigrated from Windsor, Ontario, Canada, and gave his last place of foreign residence as Montreal and his current address as 73 Elizabeth Street West, Detroit.

6. FBI, Freedom of Information Act, report on Jacob Nosovitsky, May 1922.

7. This is the last date on which the Justice Department Freedom of Information Act file shows communication between Nosovitsky and Hoover.

8. FBI, Freedom of Information Act, report on Jacob Nosovitsky, May 1922.

9. Max Schlansky's name was changed to Sherwood on May 14, 1917, according to information in the Lindbergh Archives.

10. *New York World*, July 3, 1926.

11. Bureau of Investigation, annotation at the bottom of a memorandum for the director, July 30, 1925.

12. FBI, Freedom of Information Act, letter from J. Edgar Hoover, September 24, 1925.

13. FBI, Freedom of Information Act, memorandums from J. Edgar Hoover to Colonel Donovan, January 30, 1926, and February 15, 1926.

14. Senate Special Committee to Investigate U.S. Propaganda, testimony reported in the *New York Times*, December 16, 1927, 1.

15. Letter from Anne B. Sloane to the New Jersey State Police, June 1932, Lindbergh Archives.

16. Stroh's sworn statement to Captain J. J. Appel and Detective Ralph Lewis of the New York Police Department and Detective William F. Horn of the New Jersey State Police, June 28, 1936, Lindbergh Archives.

Chapter 28 FAMILY AFFAIRS

1. Harry Green, meeting with author, June 1986, Los Angeles, California.

2. Nicolson, *Dwight Morrow*, 311.

3. Captain Harry F. Guggenheim, the millionaire philanthropist who controlled the fund, had already met Lindbergh and would become a close friend and something of a mentor.

4. Nicolson, *Dwight Morrow*, 25.

5. Chernow, *The House of Morgan*, 289; Daniel Guggenheim quoted in Nicolson, *Dwight Morrow*, 140. Davison was Henry Pomeroy Davison, a senior partner at Morgan and Company and an Englewood, New Jersey, neighbor of Morrow's. Davison and Thomas W. Lamont, another partner and Englewood neighbor, were responsible for bringing Morrow into the Morgan organization.

6. Chernow, *The House of Morgan*, 288.

7. Ibid., 287, 288.

8. Nicolson, *Dwight Morrow*, 158.

9. Ibid.

10. Ibid.

11. Chernow, *The House of Morgan*, 294.

12. Nicolson, *Dwight Morrow,* 312. Chernow, in *The House of Morgan* (p. 294), says it was December 14.

13. Nicholson, *Dwight Morrow,* 312–18.

14. Anne Morrow Lindbergh, *Bring Me a Unicorn,* 89.

15. Ibid.

16. David McCullough, *The American Experience,* WGBH Boston and WNET New York.

17. Anne Morrow Lindbergh, *Bring Me a Unicorn,* 103.

18. Nicolson, *Dwight Morrow,* 137–40.

19. A Hearst-chain newspaper photo shows Elisabeth returning aboard the S.S. *Olympic* with the caption saying she "is reported to marry Colonel Charles A. Lindbergh, hero of the first nonstop flight across the Atlantic." Associated Press reported, "Numerous newspapers have intimated that it won't be long before Col. Charles A. Lindbergh, now visiting the Morrow ranch in Mexico, and Elisabeth will announce their engagement."

20. Anne Morrow Lindbergh, *Bring Me a Unicorn,* 215.

21. U.S. Embassy spokesman, Mexico City, quoted in Mosley, *Lindbergh,* 138.

22. Anne Morrow Lindbergh, *Bring Me a Unicorn,* 215, 237.

23. Anne Morrow Lindbergh, *Hour of Gold, Hour of Lead,* 136.

24. Harry Green, meeting with author, June 1986, Los Angeles, California.

25. Anne Morrow Lindbergh, *Hour of Gold, Hour of Lead,* 4.

26. Ibid., 49–202. On July 2, 1929, Anne, now Mrs. Charles Lindbergh, wrote a chitchat letter to Elisabeth from Kansas city, Missouri. On August 13 of the same year, she wrote Elisabeth from the White House, amused by the fact that President Herbert Hoover's wife referred to them as the Lingrins. The next letter to Elisabeth, also chitchat, was sent from Trinidad on September 23, 1929. The following correspondence, in November of 1929, found a pregnant Anne back at Englewood and expressing enthusiasm over Elisabeth's impending school project but feeling it might be slightly indiscreet to submit an application for the yet unborn baby. The only letter printed in the book for 1930 is a July 30 get-well message following Elisabeth's mild heart attack—suffered shortly after the June 22 birth of Charles Lindbergh, Jr. The next reprinted letter was sent a year and two months later, in October of 1931, from the British "airplane carrier" H.M.S. *Hermes,* which was en route to Shanghai. The Lindberghs' trip over the top of the world to the Orient had been completed, and Anne related to Elisabeth how their airplane had capsized and nearly sunk in the "treacherous" Yangtze.

27. Ibid., 234.

28. Ibid., 269.

29. Ibid.

30. Ibid.

31. Ibid., 4

32. Harry Green, meeting with author, June 1986, Los Angeles, California.

Chapter 29 ENDGAME

1. All statements in this chapter by Harry Green were made during his meeting with the author, June 1986, Los Angeles, California.

2. Stanton, *New York American,* January 17, 1936, 1.

3. Hoffman, "What Went Wrong with the Lindbergh Case," *Liberty,* January 29, 1938, 8. The *Liberty* articles provide other indications that the governor had his own secret suspect and cache of information. After visiting Mrs. Evalyn Walsh McLean in Washington, he recounted, "She told many interesting things in a spirit of confidence that I may not violate. These things may some day be part of Mrs. McLean's story."

4. Charles A. Lindbergh, signed statement to the New Jersey State Police, March 11, 1932; Anne Morrow Lindbergh, statement to Lieutenant John J. Sweeney of the Newark Police Department, March 11, 1932, and her signed statement to Lieutenant John J. Sweeney and Detective Hugh Strong of the Newark Police Department, March 13, 1932; Aloysius Whateley, signed statement, March 3, 1932; Elsie Mary Whateley, signed statement, March 10, 1932, Lindbergh Archives.

5. Milton, *Loss of Eden,* 213.

6. FBI Summary Report, 49.

7. Seating list for the All Alumni Centennial Dinner, March 1, 1932, Alumni Collection, New York University Library, New York.

8. *New York Times,* March 2, 1932.

9. Elsie Whateley gave the time in her March 10 statement. Anne, in her statement of March 13, bracketed the time between 6:15 P.M. and 7:30 P.M. Since in that time bracket Anne and Gow fabricated the child's nightshirt subsequent to Lindbergh's call, the author places the estimated time of the call closer to 7:00 P.M.

10. *Bergen Evening Record,* March 5, 1932, 5.

11. *Los Angeles Herald Examiner,* March 10, 1932.

12. Time, *Time Capsule 1932,* 69.

13. Ibid.

14. Ahlgren and Monier, *Crime of the Century,* 227.

15. Ibid., 229

16. Ibid., 230

17. *New York Post,* December 3, 1934; *New York Times,* December 4, 1934.

18. For example, the *New York American,* December 4, 1934.

Chapter 30 DESTINIES

1. Kennedy, *The Airman and the Carpenter,* 407–8.

2. The incident concerning Amandus Hochmuth's mistaking a vase for a hat was recounted in *Kidnapped: Reliving the Lindbergh Case,* New Jersey Network Production, 1989, and in Harold Hoffman, "What Went Wrong with the Lindbergh Case," *Liberty.*

3. *Kidnapped: Reliving the Lindbergh Case,* New Jersey Network Production, 1989.

4. Kennedy, *The Airman and the Carpenter,* 407.

5. Joseph McNamara, "The Detective's Downfall," *New York Sunday Daily News,* May 5, 1985.

6. It houses some two hundred thousand pages of material plus most books, articles, newsreels, television programs, and movies dealing with the subject. Also on display are the exhibits introduced at the trial and additional physical evidence recovered by the police.

7. The complaint was filed June 20, 1986 at the U.S. district court in New Jersey by Anna's lawyer, San Francisco–based Robert Bryan, who also demanded a jury trial.

8. For most of this tour of duty, H. Norman Schwarzkopf was accompanied by his wife, Ruth, and his three children: Norman Jr., Anne, and Sally.

9. *New York Times,* July 7, 1988.

10. Scott Lindbergh quoted in *Parade,* July 5, 1992, 2.

11. Milton, *Loss of Eden,* 435. Scott Lindbergh is quoted in *Parade,* July 5, 1992, as saying he read about the crime in a newspaper story.

12. The dinner included an American as infamous as Charles and Anne were celebrated, the king's current paramour: Mrs. Wallis Warfield Simpson, who showed up with her husband.

13. Mosley, *Lindbergh,* 237.

14. Ibid., 346

15. *Life,* June 28, 1954.

16. Harry Green, meeting with author, June 1986, Los Angeles, California.

17. Stelhorn, *The Governors of New Jersey, 1964–74,* New Jersey State Document.

BIBLIOGRAPHY

Books

Ahlgren, Gregory, and Stephen Monier. *Crime of the Century: The Lindbergh Kidnapping Hoax*. Boston: Branden Books, 1993.

Allen, Frederick Lewis. *Only Yesterday*. New York: Harper & Row, 1931.

———. *Since Yesterday*. New York: Harper & Row, 1939.

Chernow, Ron. *The House of Morgan: An American Banking Dynasty and the Rise of Modern Finance*. New York: Atlantic Monthly Press, 1990.

Cline, Howard F. *The United States and Mexico*. New York: Atheneum, 1963.

Coakley, Leo J. *Jersey Troopers*. New Brunswick, N.J.: Rutgers University Press, 1971.

Collins, Max Allen. *Stolen Away: A Novel of the Lindbergh Kidnapping*. New York: Bantam Books, 1991.

Condon, John F. *Jafsie Tells All*. New York: Jonathan Lee, 1936.

Crystal, George. *The Life Story of Harold G. Hoffman: A Modern Fighter*. Hoboken, N.J.: Terminal Printing and Publishing, 1934.

Davis, John H. *The Guggenheims, 1948–1988, and the American Epic*. New York: Shapolsky, 1988.

Dunlop, Richard. *Donovan: America's Master Spy*. New York: Rand McNally, 1982.

Fife, George Buchanan. *Lindbergh: His Life and Achievements*. New York: World Syndicate, 1927.

Fisher, Jim. *The Lindbergh Case*. New Brunswick, N.J.: Rutgers University Press, 1987.

Galbraith, John Kenneth. *The Great Crash 1929*. Boston: Houghton Mifflin, 1988.

Goldstone, Robert. *The Great Depression*. Greenwich, Conn.: Fawcett, 1968.

Hermann, Dorothy. *Anne Morrow Lindbergh: A Gift for Life*. New York: Ticknor & Fields, 1992.

Kennedy, Ludovic. *The Airman and the Carpenter*. New York: Viking Penguin, 1985.

Klingaman, William K. *1929: The Year of the Great Crash*. New York: Harper & Row, 1989.

Lindbergh, Anne Morrow. *Bring Me a Unicorn: Diaries and Letters 1922–1928*. New York: Harcourt Brace Jovanovich, 1971.

———. *The Flower and the Nettle: Diaries and Letters 1936–1939*. New York: Harcourt Brace Jovanovich, 1976.

———. *Hour of Gold, Hour of Lead: Diaries and Letters 1929–1932*. New York: Harcourt Brace Jovanovich, 1973.

———. *Listen! The Wind*. New York: Harcourt, Brace, 1938.

———. *North to the Orient*. New York: Harcourt, Brace, 1935.

Lindbergh, Charles A. *Autobiography of Values*. New York and London: Harcourt Brace Jovanovich, 1977.

———. *Of Flight and Life*. New York: Charles Scribner's Sons, 1948.

———. *The Spirit of St. Louis*. New York: Charles Scribner's Sons, 1953.

———. *The Wartime Journals of Charles A. Lindbergh*. New York: Harcourt Brace Jovanovich, 1970.

Luckett, Perry D. *Charles A. Lindbergh*. Greenwich, Conn.: Greenwood Press, 1986.

McElvaine, Robert S. *The Great Depression*. New York: Times Books, 1984.

Manchester, William. *The Glory and the Dream*. Boston: Little, Brown, 1973.

Milton, Joyce. *Loss of Eden*. New York: HarperCollins, 1993.

Mosley, Leonard. *Lindbergh: A Biography*. Garden City, N.Y.: Doubleday, 1976.

Nicolson, Sir Harold. *Dwight Morrow*. New York: Harper & Row, 1935.

O'Brien, P. J. *The Lindberghs*. N.P.: International Press, 1935.

Scaduto, Anthony. *Scapegoat: The Lonesome Death of Bruno Richard Hauptmann*. New York: G. P. Putnam's Sons, 1976.

Sloat, Warren. *1929: America before the Crash*. New York: Macmillan, 1979.

Thomas, Gordon, and Max Morgan. *The Day the Bubble Burst*. Garden City, N.Y.: Doubleday, 1979.

Time. *Time Capsule 1927: A History of the Year Condensed from the Pages of Time*. New York: Time-Life Books, 1968.

———. *Time Capsule 1932: A History of the Year Condensed from the Pages of Time*. New York: Time-Life Books, 1968.

———. *Time Capsule 1933: A History of the Year Condensed from the Pages of Time*. New York: Time-Life Books, 1967.

Ungar, Sanford J. *FBI*. Boston: Little, Brown, 1975.

Urdang, Laurence, editor. *The Timetable of American History*. New York: Simon & Schuster, 1981.

Vitray, Laura. *The Great Lindbergh Hullabaloo: An Unorthodox Account.* New York: William Faro, 1932.

Waller, George. *Kidnap: The Story of the Lindbergh Case.* New York: Dial Press, 1961.

Whipple, Sidney, B. *The Lindbergh Crime.* New York: Blue Ribbon Books, 1935.

———. *The Trial of Bruno Richard Hauptmann,* edited with a history of the case. Garden City, N.Y.: Doubleday, Doran, 1937.

Wright, Theon. *In Search of the Lindbergh Baby.* New York: Tower Books, 1981.

Articles

Condon, John F. "Jafsie Tells All." *Liberty,* January 18, 1936–March 21, 1936 (10 installments).

Finn, James, and D. Thomas Curtin, "How I Captured Hauptmann." *Liberty,* October 12, 1934–November 7, 1934 (7 installments).

Fisher, C. Lloyd. "The Case New Jersey Would Like to Forget." *Liberty,* August 1, 1936–September 12, 1936 (7 installments).

Hoffman, Harold G. "What Went Wrong with the Lindbergh Case: The Crime, the Case, the Challenge." *Liberty,* January 29, 1938–April 30, 1938; July 2, 1938–July 9, 1938 (16 installments).

Hynd, Alan. "Everyone Wanted to Get into the Act." *True,* March 1949.

McLean, Evalyn Walsh. "Why I'm Still Investigating the Lindbergh Case." *Liberty,* 1938 (10 installments).

Wendel, Paul. "Wendel Tells All: My Forty-four Days of Kidnapping, Torture and Hell in the Lindbergh Case." *Liberty,* 1936.

Archives and Files

Bronx County District Attorney's Office, Bronx, New York.
Harold Hoffman Collection, East Brunswick Museum, East Brunswick, New Jersey.
Lindbergh Archives, New Jersey State Police Museum, West Trenton, New Jersey.
New York City Municipal Archives, New York, New York.
New-York Historical Society, New York, New York.
New York Police Department Files, New York, New York.

Author's Collection

Dengrove, Edward, and Ida Libby Dengrove. Notes and transcripts of conversations.
Green, Harry. Notes of conversations.
Nelson, Hope Hoffman. Papers.
Pelletreau, Jesse William. Papers.

Depositories of Material Obtained through the Freedom of Information Act

Federal Bureau of Investigation, Washington, D.C.
National Archives, Washington, D.C.
U.S. Department of Justice, Washington, D.C.
U.S. Department of State, Washington, D.C.

INDEX